# Studying the event film

*The Lord of the Rings*

edited by Harriet Margolis, Sean Cubitt,
Barry King and Thierry Jutel

Manchester University Press

Manchester and New York

*distributed exclusively in the USA by Palgrave Macmillan*

Published by Manchester University Press
Oxford Road, Manchester M13 9NR, UK
and Room 400, 175 Fifth Avenue, New York, NY 10010, USA
www.manchesteruniversitypress.co.uk

Distributed in the United States exclusively by
Palgrave Macmillan, 175 Fifth Avenue,
New York, NY 10010, USA

Distributed in Canada exclusively by
UBC Press, University of British Columbia, 2029 West Mall,
Vancouver, BC, Canada V6T 1Z2

British Library Cataloguing-in-Publication Data is available

Library of Congress Cataloging-in-Publication Data is available

ISBN 978 0 7190 7199 7 paperback

First published by Manchester University Press in hardback 2008

This paperback edition first published 2012

Printed by Lightning Source

# Contents

# List of illustrations

# Acknowledgements

The editors gratefully acknowledge assistance with research and access to information provided by a grant from the UK Economic and Social Research Council (ESRC Grant No. 000-22-0323) as well as by research grants from the Faculty of Arts and Social Sciences, University of Waikato. We also appreciate and acknowledge the co-operation and assistance of the British Film Institute and of Scoop (scoop.co.nz) with some of our illustrations that have been previously made public, and to the various photographers who have allowed us to use their previously unpublished photos. We also thank IMDb, The Internet Movie Database, Inc., for allowing us to reproduce their credit listings for the *Lord of the Rings* trilogy.

On behalf of all the contributors, we acknowledge the particular assistance of our university libraries and librarians, as well as the librarians elsewhere in the world who have made our research possible.

Sean Cubitt thanks Alison Ripley Cubitt, and Barry King dedicates this book to the memory of his parents, Jack and Betty King.

# Notes on contributors

**Judith Bernanke** lectures in the Department of Communication and Journalism at Massey University, Wellington, New Zealand. Her interdisciplinary graduate degree is in music, art history, and English literature. Her research interests include visual rhetoric, comparative arts, cultural representations and identity formation, and the interrelationship of cultural values and expressive practices. She has written and performed the music for the short film *Hammond's Arcana or the Paradise of Birds* (New Zealand, 2007). Her current research project is a study of arts journalism within the New Zealand context.

**Henry Bial**, Assistant Professor of theatre and film at the University of Kansas, is the author of *Acting Jewish: Negotiating Ethnicity on the American Stage and Screen* (University of Michigan Press, 2005), editor of *The Performance Studies Reader* (Routledge, 2004), and co-editor (with Carol Martin) of *Brecht Sourcebook* (Routledge, 2000). At the invitation of the University of Canterbury theatre faculty, he initiated the Lord of the Rings Field Station to investigate *Rings* tourism in conjunction with the 2003 Performance Studies conference in Christchurch.

**Danny Butt**, www.dannybutt.net, is an independent consultant and researcher in new media, having previously been Director of the Creative Industries Research Centre at the Waikato Institute of Technology, Hamilton, New Zealand. He is on the Working Editorial Committee for the *Digital Review of Asia Pacific* and has published widely on new media, the creative industries, and cross-cultural relations. Before working in the academy, Danny held a range of positions in the music, publishing, new media, contemporary arts, and advertising industries.

**Sean Cubitt** is Director, Media and Communications Program, University of Melbourne, Australia. He is the author of *Timeshift: On Video Culture* (Routledge, 1991), *Videography, Digital Aesthetics, Simulation and Social Theory* (Macmillan, 1993), *The Cinema Effect* (MIT University Press,

2004), and *EcoMedia* (Rodopi, 2005), and co-editor with Ziauddin Sardar of *Aliens R Us* (Pluto, 2002) and with Rasheed Araeen and Ziauddin Sardar of *Against the Grain: The Third Text Reader* (Continuum/ Athlone 2002).

**Kevin Fisher** lectures on film and media studies in the Department of Media, Film, and Communication Studies at the University of Otago, Dunedin, New Zealand. He has published on film spectatorship and digital special effects, including 'Tracing the tesseract: a conceptual pre-history of the digital morph' in *Meta-morphing: Visual Transformations in the Culture of Quick Change* (University of Minnesota, 2000). His Ph.D. from the UCLA Department of Film, TV, and Digital Media researched representations of altered states of consciousness in post-Second World War Hollywood cinema.

**Ann Hardy** lectures in the Screen and Media Studies Department at the University of Waikato, Hamilton, New Zealand. Her work combines a long-time interest in New Zealand cinema and a more recent focus on researching the intersections of media, religion, and culture in local audio-visual production.

**Craig Hight** lectures in the Screen and Media Studies Department at the University of Waikato, Hamilton, New Zealand. With Jane Roscoe, he co-authored *Faking It: Mock-Documentary and the Subversion of Factuality* (Manchester University Press, 2001) and he is currently writing a follow-up volume on television mock-documentary series. His other recent research explores the implications of digital technologies for documentary aesthetics and practice, and theoretical issues related to documentary hybrids.

**Deborah Jones** is a Senior Lecturer in the School of Management at Victoria University of Wellington, New Zealand. She has degrees in English and Management Studies and teaches communication and organisational studies with a focus on difference and power. She is lately interested in nationalism as well as gender, ethnicity, and age, and has initiated an ongoing study of the New Zealand film industry from an organisational perspective.

**Stan Jones**, Senior Lecturer in the Screen and Media Studies Department at the University of Waikato, Hamilton, New Zealand, co-founded the first film studies programme in Aotearoa New Zealand in 1987. He has written on German Expressionism (*Der Sturm: A Focus of Expressionism* (Camden House, 1984)), modern German literature, Wim Wenders,

Marcel Ophüls, and New Zealand film on the German market. His current research interest is in cross-cultural appropriation in the context of national/global identity in cinema.

**Thierry Jutel** is a lecturer in the Media Studies Programme at Victoria University of Wellington, New Zealand. Recent publications include essays on *The Lord of the Rings* and the geography of the virtual in *Cultural Studies in Aotearoa New Zealand* (Oxford University Press, 2004) and 'Studying media texts' in *Media Studies in Aotearoa / New Zealand* (Pearson, 2004). He has also produced several short films, including *Being Santa* (dir. Chris Gable, 2005) and *Why I Ate Myself* (co-written with and directed by Kelly Pendergrast, 2005). His current research involves a film studies textbook and several film projects in development.

**Misha Kavka** teaches film, television, and media at the University of Auckland, New Zealand. She is the co-editor, with Elisabeth Bronfen, of *Feminist Consequences: Theory for the New Century* (Columbia University Press, 2001), and has published articles on feminist and psychoanalytic theory, Gothic cinema, New Zealand film, and reality television in New Zealand. Her current project is a cross-cultural study of the affective basis of reality television programming.

**Kimon Keramidas** is a Ph.D. student in the theatre program at the Graduate School and University Center of the City University of New York. His graduate work there focuses on theatre and performance as components in cross-media and multimedia cultural objects. He has published in the *Journal of Slavic and Eastern European Performance*, and is involved in projects dealing with interactive technology and pedagogy. At the invitation of the University of Canterbury theatre faculty, he participated in the Lord of the Rings Field Station to investigate *Rings* tourism in conjunction with the 2003 Performance Studies conference in Christchurch.

**Barry King**, Professor of Communications, Associate Dean International, and Director of the Centre for Performance Research at Auckland University of Technology, New Zealand, has published in *Afterimage*, *Cultural Studies*, *Semiotica*, and the *American Journal of Semiotics*. He was a lead writer and Associate Director of the Television Violence Study (2003) commissioned by the Ministry of Culture and Heritage (New Zealand). His research interests include the sociology of acting and performance, visual sign analysis, and the cultural impact of television, stardom, and celebrity. He is working on a comparative study of the acting profession in New Zealand and the United Kingdom, as well as the impact of synthespians on the discourse of contemporary stardom.

**Geoff Lealand** is an Associate Professor in Screen and Media Studies at the University of Waikato, Hamilton, New Zealand. He specialises in researching and teaching in the areas of children and media, television studies, and media education. With Helen Martin, he has coauthored *It's All Done With Mirrors: About Television* (Dunmore Press, 2001). Forthcoming publications cover foreign film and television production in New Zealand, the format television trade in New Zealand, and a study of children's and youth television.

**Suzette Major** lectures in the Screen and Media Studies Department at the University of Waikato, Hamilton, New Zealand. With a Ph.D. on the marketing of ideas, she specialises in marketing the arts and the creative industries. Her previous research has explored the role of marketing in New Zealand films, and she is currently working with the Creative Industries Research Centre in examining the significance of the creative industries in New Zealand.

**Harriet Margolis**, the editor of *Jane Campion's 'The Piano'* (Cambridge University Press, 2000) and author of *The Cinema Ideal: An Introduction to Psychoanalytic Studies of the Film Spectator* (Garland, 1988), has published internationally on Sherlock Holmes, women's romance novels, feminism and film, adaptations and cultural value, and self-directed stereotypes as a rhetorical strategy.

**Allen Meek** lectures in Media Studies and Visual Culture in the School of English and Media Studies at Massey University, Palmerston North, New Zealand. His recent publications include 'A century of exile: national cinemas and transnational mediascapes' in *Moving Pictures, Migrating Identities* (University Press of Mississippi, 2003), 'Mourning, media and the "virtual space of spectrality"' in *Space and Culture*, 8 (2000), and 'Exile and the electronic frontier: critical intellectuals and cyberspace', *New Media and Society*, 2.1 (2000).

**Brett Nicholls** teaches film and media studies at the University of Otago, Dunedin, New Zealand. In addition to games, he has published work on postcolonial theory, and television. Current obsessions include *Metal Gear Solid*, the Matrix universe, and chutney.

**Roy Parkhurst** lectures in visual and material culture and digital media in the Massey University College of Creative Arts, Wellington, New Zealand. His research interests lie in media studies and critical theory. He is currently working on a study of Gilles Deleuze, non-linear dynamics, and complexity theory and its applications to cinema history and theory. With Struan Ashby, he has made the short film *Hammond's Arcana or the Paradise of Birds* (New Zealand, 2007).

**Ryan Reynolds** lectures in theatre and film at the University of Canterbury, Christchurch, New Zealand. He and his co-authors participated in the 9th Performance Studies International Conference, touring and analysing *Lord of the Rings* tourist destinations. He is an actor with the experimental Christchurch Free Theatre.

**Jo Smith** lectures in the Media Studies Programme at Victoria University of Wellington, New Zealand. She received her Ph.D. from the University of Otago in 2002. In addition to work in *Deep South* (a University of Otago e-journal), she has a chapter, 'Situating cinema: in / from Aotearoa / New Zealand', in *Doing Media Studies in Aotearoa, New Zealand* (Longman Pearson Education, 2004).

**Alice Te Punga Somerville (Te Atiawa)** lectures in English at Victoria University of Wellington, New Zealand, specialising in Maori, Pacific, and Indigenous writing in English. Born and raised in Aotearoa New Zealand, she received her Ph.D. from Cornell University, and spent time at the University of Hawaii at Manoa during her doctoral studies. She has published in the areas of 'mixed-race' Maori/Pakeha writers, and diasporic Maori writing, and her research interests bring literary texts together with comparative, Indigenous, Pacific, Maori, postcolonial, and cultural studies.

**Stephen Turner** teaches literary and cultural studies in the Department of English at the University of Auckland, New Zealand. He has published articles on the cultural politics of settlement in Aotearoa / New Zealand; other articles appear in *Programming the Nation: New Zealand Television* (Oxford University Press, 2004) and *Cultural Studies in Aotearoa New Zealand* (Oxford University Press, 2004). His current research project is a book of essays provisionally entitled *Broken History*.

# Timeline

1892: John Ronald Reuel Tolkien born, Bloemfontein, South Africa.

1914–1918: First World War. Tolkien fights at the Battle of the Somme; contracts trench fever in October 1914, and returns to England.

1937: *The Hobbit* published by George Allen and Unwin.

1954: *The Fellowship of the Ring* and *The Two Towers* published by George Allen and Unwin.

1955: *The Return of the King* published by George Allen and Unwin.

1961: Peter Jackson born in Pukerua Bay, Wellington, Aotearoa New Zealand.

1978: Animated film version of *The Lord of the Rings* produced by Saul Zaentz and directed by Ralph Bakshi.

1981: BBC Radio adaptation of *The Lord of the Rings*; adapted by Brian Sibley; features Ian Holm as Frodo.

1992: HarperCollins publishes *The Lord of the Rings* illustrated with Alan Lee's drawings.

1995 November: Peter Jackson mentions his interest in filming Tolkien to Harvey Weinstein of Miramax.

1997 April: Miramax acquires option on *The Lord of the Rings* from Saul Zaentz. Script development commences.

1998: Philippa Boyens joins Jackson and Fran Walsh as co-scriptwriter.

1998 July: Weinstein decides *The Lord of the Rings* must be made as one film. Jackson given four weeks to find a company that will accept a two-film adaptation.

1998 August: New Line announces that three pictures will be made, the shoot to commence in May 1999, and the films to be released within one year. Script development and pre-production move into high gear.

1998 October: Pre-visualisation team begins work.

1999 July 10: New Line announces Elijah Wood will star as Frodo.

1999 October 11: Filming commences in Wellington. The first scene to be shot has the Hobbits cowering under a bank to avoid the Black Riders. Miniatures shoot begins.

2000: Co-producer Tim Sanders leaves the project.

2000 September 26: New Zealand Film Commission certifies to local
   tax authorities that the first film is complete 'to double-head fine cut'
   ('double-head' indicates that there is no print with the soundtrack
   attached: instead it is played on a separate but synchronised mag-
   netic head at projection; 'fine cut' indicates that, though synchronised
   sound and special effects may be missing, the basic edit is complete
   and the film's running time established).
2000 December 22: Main shooting wraps. During its last weeks, effects
   supervisor Mark Stetson and Weta Digital's Charlie McClellan and
   John Sheils depart. Jim Rygell replaces Stetson.
2001 January: Time-Warner instructs Shaye to cut back on staff at New
   Line.
2001 January 12: Reintroduction of www.lordoftherings.net, the official
   website for the film trilogy *The Lord of the Rings*, and release of a
   two-minute preview trailer with *Thirteen Days*, New Line's latest release.
2001 January 19: Trailer and library of video available on website.
2001 February: Website offers download of a five-minute film about
   the making of the trilogy.
2001 May: 25-minute rough-cut of footage shown at Cannes Film
   Festival.
2001 June: Joe Nimizki, head of marketing, quits New Line.
2001 September 21: NZ Film Commission certifies double-head fine cut
   of *The Two Towers*.
2001 Autumn: American Film Institute-supported Tolkien-related study
   materials and on-line assistance available to schools.
2001 October: Weta Digital completes post-production of *The Fellowship of the Ring*.
2001 December 10: world premiere of *The Fellowship of the Ring* in
   London.
2001 December 19: *The Fellowship of the Ring* opens in theaters in
   North America.
2002 February/March: *The Fellowship of the Ring* nominated for thirteen Academy Awards, winning four; also receives five BAFTAs,
   including best film.
2002 August: *The Fellowship of the Ring* (theatrical version) released
   on video and DVD.
2002 November: *The Fellowship of the Ring* (extended version)
   released on DVD.
2002 December: world premiere of *The Two Towers* in New York.
2003 November: *The Two Towers* released on DVD.
2003 December: world premiere of *The Return of the King* in
   Wellington.
2004 November: *The Return of the King* released on DVD.

# Introduction: how to study
# an event film

*Harriet Margolis*

This book sets out to introduce students and general readers to a relatively recent phenomenon, the event film, in order to outline the phenomenon's size, shape, and complexity. A single book is unlikely to encompass all one might say about the results of studying a particular event film precisely because event films are such large phenomena. In addition to traditional approaches derived from film studies and textual analysis that one might apply to a film, the event film's nature as a media and marketing event requires understanding it in global and economic terms. When one takes a specific example of the event film for consideration, the details of that film's production as well as its text are usually enough to fill not just one but possibly several books. As a term, 'the event film' emphasises the interrelatedness of the phenomenon's components, and so the interrelatedness itself becomes another topic to be considered.

*Studying the Event Film* takes a particular trilogy of films as a case study for how one might understand the sort of phenomenon that event films tend to be. Various aspects of *The Lord of the Rings (LOTR)*[1] are unique, and it has become a benchmark for understanding what future event films might look like. In this book we hope to lay out parameters for understanding and studying event films at the same time that we offer what we think is a unique perspective on one specific example.

We, the editors and contributors to *Studying the Event Film*, have all had strong attachments to Aotearoa New Zealand during the time *LOTR* has been an active event. Many contributors are native to Aotearoa New Zealand; most of us have lived in the country during the films' production and release. A successful marketing effort has made Middle-earth and New Zealand almost synonymous in the minds of an international audience exposed to the merchandising and advertising associated with the trilogy. Most of us contributing to this volume can still remember that, before Middle-earth, there existed an Aotearoa New Zealand, and we can still tell the difference.

Event films are a relatively new category within the history of cinema. They tend to be global phenomena, and while certain genres (romantic comedies, documentaries, for example) are unlikely ever to produce an event film, the event film is not a genre itself. None the less, like genres, the event film does have origins and a history, and it can be considered in aesthetic terms. These things will be discussed below, but to begin, we must understand that the event film transcends the (any) individual film.

In its own time, the event film can never be just a film. It is a conglomeration of activities, including film production, film marketing, merchandising,[2] tourism, entertainment journalism, and scholarly endeavours. The event film, by definition, involves large sums of money: money for salaries, for equipment, for technicians, for facilities, for stars, for marketing that engages international media involved in promoting international entertainment. The event film is associated particularly with what remains of the Hollywood studio system of filmmaking, and with the marketing strategies associated with large-budget films that need to recoup costs before they go into profit, with huge pressure on opening weekend box-office performance.

The event film, however, is not attached to a particular place, in that it might be filmed somewhere other than Hollywood, California. Somewhere like Aotearoa New Zealand, for example, 'half-way around the world' from California, and really an example of 'same-same, but different', perched geographically as it is amid American and Asian influences, with its own Indigenous culture to provide the backbone of a particular national identity. Why not? Blessed with beautiful scenery, Aotearoa New Zealand is a country whose currency fluctuates, and whose recent governments, though formed by politicians with opposing views, have been enamoured of something called 'creative industries'.

In Danny Butt's contribution to *Studying the Event Film*, 'Creative industries in Hobbit economies: wealth creation, intellectual property regimes, and transnational production' (Chapter 8), he examines the relation between creative industries and 'Hobbit economies', questioning whether that relation is necessarily positive. These creative industries, including the screen industries, promise possibilities of great wealth not dependent on extracting natural resources the land might or might not hold. They can attract and keep well-educated, highly paid residents in the country, attracting other industries to work in partnership alongside them or to service them and their employees. Recent governments have been keen to support the development of the screen industries in Aotearoa New Zealand, and at the time *LOTR* was in production the NZ dollar was very low relative to the US dollar.

Hollywood sometimes, as now, feels threatened when it sees large-budget films going offshore from California, or even the entire United States. During the 1960s, some Hollywood blockbusters, such as *El Cid*,[3] were shot in Spain because it was cheap. In later decades, *Star Wars* was filmed in Tunisia for the same reason. Australia has more than one relatively new studio developed primarily to support big-budget offshore productions such as *The Matrix* and its sequels. In other words, what are now known as 'runaway' productions (see Miller *et al.* 2001) have appeared earlier in film history.

The filming of *LOTR* in Aotearoa New Zealand didn't occur just because it was cheap to do so. It also didn't occur just because a basically unknown young New Zealander named Peter Jackson decided that he wanted to make those particular films in his home town, never mind the fact that the producers offering money were affiliated with Hollywood studios that had their own film production set-up, while his home town and country were not equipped in general with the accoutrements of a film industry. *LOTR* happened because a number of factors came together at the same time, with some being more important than others but no single factor being the determining one.

Certainly, though, technology is a major factor in the story, along with money. Digital technology for special effects is, of course, at the heart of *LOTR*, and there is no denying the trilogy's technological achievements. In fact, the story of the technological developments that enabled the production of *LOTR* sometimes overwhelms the films themselves as a narrative of interest. Groundbreaking developments in software and telecommunications with applications beyond Middle-earth have attracted international attention from businesspeople and scientists. For example, the FastSCAN technology developed for motion-capture in *LOTR* has also turned out to be useful for medical purposes (Patterson 2004). The best known among the many software programs developed are probably Massive (Multiple Agent Simulation System in Virtual Environment) and Virtual Katy, both of which make it easier and faster to produce movies on the scale of *LOTR*.

From the 1990s, 'standard studio fare . . . based their appeal primarily on their stories or their stars, [whereas] the studios' event films . . . based their appeal on action, special effects, superstars, and simple marketing hooks' (Perrin 2001: 36). From this point of view, these films' narratives often offer no more interest than as a plausible frame for the special effects – which are the film's real point. That is not, however, true of *LOTR*, based as it is on one of the twentieth century's most popular books. (The dossier section 'Adapting a script' below (Chapter 17) presents some of the scriptwriters' concerns to capture philosophical and ethical dilemmas raised by Tolkien's characters and their experiences.)

*LOTR* is also unusual among event films in that few of its actors could be called stars before their association with *LOTR*. Nor, as Barry King's 'Dispersing Elijah: stardom and the event film' (Chapter 12) argues, could Elijah Wood, despite featuring as Frodo, be called the trilogy's star. King notes that both the technology and Jackson's directorial style militated against any one actor's surfacing as the films' star. (The difference between 'stars' and 'actors' is one of the topics that the dossier section on acting covers.)

It is also not true that Peter Jackson makes only special-effects-based action films. *Heavenly Creatures* was Jackson's first film to involve digital special effects (especially computer-generated imagery, or CGI), and its sensitive depiction of a sensational historical event came unexpectedly from a director whose first three feature films exemplify 'splatstick', a comic genre almost invented by Jackson. *Heavenly Creatures* indicated a surprising maturity that seemed unlikely given, for example, Jackson's *Meet the Feebles*, a puppet film so gross that, despite supporting it financially, the New Zealand Film Commission (NZFC) didn't want its name attached to it (Pryor 2003: 69).

*LOTR* was something else entirely – 'one out of the box', as New Zealanders say – not just for Jackson but for the entire world of filmmaking. When J. R. R. Tolkien originally approached publishers with *The Lord of the Rings*, he was disappointed that they insisted on breaking up his one novel into three parts, for ease of publishing and to hedge their bets financially. Unsurprisingly, producers interested in a film version have also not wanted to risk committing to the entire novel on the scale that it would require. The timeline at the front of this volume provides a capsule summary of events culminating in the decision to film *The Lord of the Rings* as three separate films, roughly paralleling the novel's three volumes. With this decision, *LOTR* became a unique project: three films filmed simultaneously, but finished and released separately.

New Line's carefully planned, innovative marketing campaign (which Suzette Major's chapter, 'Cultivating a classic: marketing strategies for the *Lord of the Rings* films' (Chapter 4), discusses) touched on all aspects of the films' promotion, maximising and extending their interest as an event, and in the process setting up the desirability of products associated with it that could outlive the films' immediate moment. Public events like the Wellington world premiere of the third movie and the 'advertorial' value of the major awards ceremonies increased the sense of the film as a media event, parallel to a major sporting competition or celebrity wedding. The design work was promoted as toys; the computer-generated images became elements in computer games released to synchronise with the film and DVD releases; the carefully cultivated fan sites became recipients of significant advertising dollars in exchange for publicising memorabilia. An extraordinary exhibition – '*The Lord of the Rings* Motion Picture Trilogy: The Exhibition' – went on a global tour and broke box-office records both at Te Papa, Aotearoa New Zealand's national museum, and at London's highly popular Science Museum.[4] Toys, clothes, board games, and books about the making of the films as well as the repackaged novels have generated major revenue. In 2006 the exhibition returned to Aotearoa New Zealand, and the books, games, and other such items tend still to be available in bookshops and game stores around the world.

So it is that, although not necessarily fixed in a place, the event film is to some extent fixed in time in its efforts to generate an audience large enough and sustained enough for investors to make their profit. The publicity machine kicks in before a project begins filming in order to develop hype in the lead-up to a film's release. The initial event of the theatrical release, though, is only the culmination of a preparatory publicity campaign that becomes the basis for further events. Spin-offs, in the possible form of sequels or merchandising or games or other related cultural activities, have helped in the past to sustain the event film's prominence in the public mind, along with the film's re-release via other media – on television, or video, or DVD – but again, *LOTR* represents a new wrinkle in its efforts to address the largest possible audience.

New Line's and Jackson's cutting-edge approach to the release of the DVD versions, and particularly to the different DVD formats, is a story of its own, which Craig Hight – 'One (special extended edition) disc to rule them all' (Chapter 2) – and Jo Smith – '*The Lord of the Rings* in the living room: changing technologies of cinematic display and reception' (Chapter 3) – separately study in this book. There have been the usual sales to airlines, broadcast and subscription television, and video and DVD sell-through. What is unusual is that *LOTR* has significantly extended the attraction of buying DVDs. Releasing the theatrical versions and the extended versions of the DVDs separately kept raising the films' profile well beyond the end of their commercial release. By providing nearly an hour of extra footage for each film, and up to nine hours of additional materials on bonus discs, the DVD releases reached a scale of audience anticipation nearly equaling that of the initial theatrical release.

On top of this and to some extent simultaneously, the *LOTR*-based games discussed below by Brett Nicholls ('The ludic integration of the game and film industries: *The Lord of the Rings* computer games as entertainment meritocracies', Chapter 25) have appealed to and maintained interest in the films on the part of the demographic increasingly caught up in commercially marketed digital games and their equipment. Here again there are innovations. Nicholls's examination of *LOTR*'s game offshoots finds that they reward successful players with material from the films that has been embedded in the game environment, which represents new interrelations between the two media.

In contrast with the audiences considered by Nicholls, Major, or Stan Jones, Geoff Lealand looks at a strangely neglected audience for *LOTR* in '*The Return of the King* and the child audience' (Chapter 6). He considers the general public perception of violence on screen in order to understand why Kiwi parents have not been concerned about exposing their children to *LOTR* even though its level of violence might be equal to or higher than that of other screen narratives they find objectionable. While event films are not necessarily made for either children or adults, as a fantasy *LOTR* would seem to appeal first and foremost to children, the traditional audience for fantasy films. Yet *LOTR* has not especially been marketed as a children's film, in contrast with either the Harry Potter series or the first Narnia film – the other event films with which *LOTR* has inevitably been compared.

In the case of *LOTR*, some aspects of the event film were relatively limited (the appearance in Wellington, for example, of sculptures of figures from the film on the façades of public buildings) or even specific in time (the parties held on the occasion of the premieres or Oscar night), while others have lingered on and are likely to do so for the foreseeable future (the engraved gold rings and other memorabilia such as swords and scabbards intended for an adult market). 'The Lord of the Rings *Location Guidebook* written by Kiwi and *The Lord of the Rings* fanatic Ian Brodie, is only available in New Zealand (due to rights issues) and became the nation's greatest domestic bestseller in 2002' (Donald 2003: 722), with many copies bought for gifts to send to overseas families and friends, and many sold to tourists riding the promotion of Aotearoa New Zealand as Middle-earth. One estimate (reported at a conference in Aberystwyth) is that over three hundred websites devoted to the fan cultures of Tolkien and the trilogy were online in various languages. The same conference is one stage in the development of the largest qualitative audience research project ever undertaken, with twenty-five teams in as many countries analysing twenty-five thousand World-Wide Web questionnaire responses gathered during the release period of *Return* (see Stan Jones's contribution, 'The international reception of *The Lord of the Rings*; case study, Germany', Chapter 5, for further details). In addition to the Allen and Unwin official guidebooks to the films (several written by Brian Sibley, renowned not only for popular publications on cinema but for the much-praised BBC Radio adaptation of Tolkien's books), there is Sibley's own authorised biography of Peter Jackson, *Peter Jackson: A Film-Maker's Journey*. Several scholarly anthologies, in addition to the current volume, have also appeared, with more sure to follow. The event film's very existence depends on good media coverage and never-ending marketing – once again, pointing to the vital connection between event films and big budgets – but its success depends on generating this level of interest.

As Stan Jones puts it later in this book, *LOTR*'s 'effectiveness as a transnational product – "blockbuster made in New Zealand" – is manifest statistically'. *LOTR* has been phenomenally successful in less quantifiable ways as well. On theatrical release the films immediately became part of the cinematic canon, as well as films that people watch repeatedly (encouraged in this practice by the timed release of the different DVD editions and their contents). Not all event films become part of the canon, though; this is another way in which *LOTR* has altered the benchmark by which future event films will be judged.

A 'blockbuster made in New Zealand'. That is part of *LOTR*'s fascination. For Aotearoa New Zealand, the production of *LOTR* here is something like a liminal moment, after which nothing will ever be the same. Our perspective from Aotearoa New Zealand enables us, for example, to comprehend some of the production's economic aspects in relative isolation, since nothing like this has ever before been seen here (in contrast with, say, Los Angeles). As a result of *LOTR*, Wellington boasts state-of-the-art post-production film facilities equal to any in the world; it has also seen housing costs in its suburbs near those facilities increase dramatically.

'Tourist encounters', by Ryan Reynolds, Henry Bial, and Kimon Keramidas (Chapter 22), describes another example of unanticipated changes. Tourism has been a fact of life in this country since the nineteenth century, but tourists' desires associated with *LOTR* have altered the way in which natives describe and present the country to outsiders. *LOTR* tourism, based on concepts of authenticity and the natural environment, has not required the building of a theme park, as in the case of tourism associated with the products of studios such as Disney or Universal. Instead, Aotearoa New Zealand itself has been branded as a theme park, another innovation in the expanded domain of the event movie, but also surely an unusual experience for a country as a whole.

This introduction is a collective effort, written by me on behalf of the editorial team, representing a summation of our contributors' work as well as our editorial debates. Credit even for the words must be shared among us (with any mistakes, of course, being mine alone). Although this introduction is a collective effort, I would like to personalise it, to write as someone who has lived at the base of Wellington's Mount Victoria since the time that *Heavenly Creatures* was about to be released in 1994, and Peter Jackson's status in the world was about to change.

In my travels to and from Mount Victoria to Victoria University and around and about Wellington over the ensuing decade or so, I have seen many film crews at work, including Jackson's and Costa Botes's crew for *Forgotten Silver*, which turned a war memorial into a Biblical set, and Jackson's crew for *King Kong*, which quietly used the opera house in downtown Wellington to stand in for a New York theatre. While *LOTR* was shooting, even on the days and nights that it was shooting just up the hill behind my house, it was a remarkably discreet presence. All its personnel were sworn to secrecy, yet many of my friends and students had jobs on the project, while the government and the NZFC were constantly talking up the project's positive value for Aotearoa New Zealand generally and its screen industries particularly.

During the long years of producing *LOTR*, Wellington became Welly-wood and Aotearoa New Zealand became Middle-earth. The Department of Conservation developed protocols for film shoots on national conservancy lands, and Wellington, along with other regional centres, developed local liaison offices to help offshore filmmakers have an enjoyable experience in exchange for their contribution to the local economy. These local liaison offices even united to work together as Film New Zealand, encouraged to do so by the national government. Enrolment in film courses of all sorts skyrocketed, and most people in the screen industries were at work on some project or another. Digital technology became increasingly available, and many filmmakers who had been turned down for public funding made a digital feature.

Along with Jane Campion, Jackson became *the* role model for budding young filmmakers in this and other countries. As Deborah Jones notes in ' "Ring leader": Peter Jackson as "creative industries" hero' (Chapter 9), Jackson became a creative industries hero for 'his entrepreneurial *and* creative skills, his authentic New Zealandness, and his patriotism . . . His typicality as a New Zealander connects traditional themes of national identity – technical ingenuity, humility, teamwork – with the "new economy" themes of creativity, technological innovation, and entrepreneurial skills in the global arena'. He became someone who could periodically give politicians the benefit of his advice, and talkback radio hosts switched from admiration to disenchantment as Jackson's success soared and realisation grew of what this meant for his personal fortune. Jackson had done the unforgivable in a country that values egalitarian conformity. He had become a tall poppy,[5] and by standing out he attracted unfriendly attention. In his own country, Jackson is much admired, but not unquestioningly.

While New Zealanders, individually and collectively, bask in the pride they feel for *LOTR*'s success, some with memories of the tax-shelter years in the 1980s,[6] or with a knowledge of past examples of national cinemas that have relied too heavily on runaway productions, have expressed concern about some government policies that enabled *LOTR* to benefit from public largesse (see Part VI, 'There, back again, and beyond: production infrastructures and extended exploitation'). Having benefited from 'the Frodo economy', the government has been keen to see such high-profile offshore projects as *The Last Samurai* and *The Chronicles of Narnia: The Lion, the Witch, and the Wardrobe* settle in Aotearoa New Zealand, providing an ongoing, relatively free, and definitely sophisticated source of marketing for 'Brand New Zealand'.

Before *LOTR*, before *Xena* and *Hercules*, Aotearoa New Zealand could hardly be said to have had a film industry. The NZFC, established in 1978, was the primary source of funding, with a legal requirement to support New Zealand filmmakers. Its limited budget meant that only a few feature-length films per year got made – in the good years.

New Zealanders, though, are passionate about the cinema; historically, the country's per capita film attendance has been among the highest in the world (see 'Going to the pictures', the opening chapter of Gordon Miram's *Speaking Candidly*). Films were publicly screened here in 1896 – as early as almost anywhere – and they have been made here since 1898. The earliest wandering cameramen worked for overseas companies, taking images of the country's spectacular scenery for international audiences, but a native interest in cinema's technology and its financial possibilities soon arose. When sound came to cinema, more than one person in the country tried to develop a sound system for moviemaking in order to avoid the high cost of importing one. Although the film is a mockumentary, *Forgotten Silver*'s inventive Colin McKenzie is grounded in reality. People tend to compare Colin McKenzie with Peter Jackson, for reasons Thierry Jutel's 'Peter Jackson's cinema and Colin McKenzie's legacy' (Chapter 10) illuminates. However, there was in fact a New Zealand filmmaker, Rudall Hayward, the son of theatre entrepreneurs, who was always trying to make an historical epic and who did succeed in making a number of feature-length fiction films during the 1920s and 1930s.

Hayward operated very much in the private sphere of filmmaking before the Second World War. Yet the New Zealand government was involved from the beginning in much of the filmmaking here meant for public consumption at home and abroad, usually designed to attract both tourists and immigrants. Much of the history of government involvement in filmmaking has had to do with supporting Aotearoa New Zealand's tourism industry, which has been a thriving concern since the nineteenth century and which currently is one of the country's best sources of foreign exchange (see, for example, Black (2006: 26) for a typical comparison involving 'meat or dairy products'). From this point of view, *LOTR*, for all its uniqueness, also proves there's nothing new under the sun.

Not surprisingly, the New Zealand government, once it got on board the *LOTR* project, determined to lever as much economic benefit as possible from its investment. One way in which this worked was that both state-owned enterprises and private corporations co-operated, along with the government, in exploiting *LOTR* for their own purposes, always, of course, acknowledging New Line whenever images or other material from the films were used. Air New Zealand, for example, had various characters from the films painted on their planes, and their advertising favourably compared their ability to get people to places with the length of time it took the Hobbits to get there. New Zealand Post issued domestic and international stamps picturing places as they appeared

**Figure 1** Auckland Airport 2004, Air New Zealand plane on wet tarmac.

**Figure 2** Two New Zealand Post stamps from 2004, one identified as 'Erewhon (Edoras)' and the other as 'Edoras (Erewhon)'.

in the films (acknowledging New Line's copyright) as well as how they appear in reality. Meanwhile, Pete Hodgson, a member of Parliament, was appointed Minister for The Lord of the Rings to co-ordinate the government's financial involvement with the project ('Hodgson confirmed' 2001). As Prime Minister Helen Clark said, '*Lord of the Rings* has the potential to expose New Zealand to the world on an unprecedented scale' (Griggs 2001). For Aotearoa New Zealand, at least if the government had anything to do with it, *LOTR* would definitely be an event, with a domestic economic impact unlike any Hollywood-based production could ever manage in the United States.

On the eve of *Fellowship*'s premiere, Jackson told the BBC that 'the film for a long time has been a thing of hype and anticipation and it'll be a huge relief for me when it becomes just a movie' (Griggs 2001). Yet *LOTR* could never be just a movie, since it has always been an event film, even the quintessential example of an event film – at the same time that it can be seen as the (inevitable) culmination of earlier practices.

Hollywood studios have a long history of marketing on the basis of how much has been spent on a film. Since the 1940s, especially expensive films have been referred to as 'blockbusters'. The *Oxford English Dictionary*'s definition – 'an aerial bomb capable of destroying a whole block of buildings' – suggests that the term was figuratively used to refer to something capable of delivering a terrific impact. Applied to the movies, it was associated with Hollywood studio productions, especially those of the 1960s, with the idea that a single superfilm could return a huge profit on a large investment relative to what has since been called 'niche marketing'.

The studios developed the blockbuster into a production practice, in which pre-production connected increasingly with post-production. Budget (for items such as casting, costuming, sets, locations, and so forth) and marketing became increasingly interconnected; production values were high; casting (and sometimes producers, writers, and directors) involved big names, and increasingly involved international pools of talent (leading to an offshoot called the Europudding). At the same time, from 1975 and the release of *Jaws*, the studios adopted 'the concept of the blanket release – studios could make a lot of money very fast by opening a hugely publicised film in lots of cinemas' (Schembri 2004–5: 16). This release practice now attempts to protect the studios' investment, since currently available technology for pirating copies threatens studio profits.

Because the blockbuster originates before video, and before the sorts of merchandising tie-ins associated with *Star Wars* (now known as *Star Wars Episode IV – A New Hope*) and its descendants, it stood more discretely as a film. Related profits available to the studios tended to do with music; fashions in clothes or toys spawned by blockbusters were not generally revenue generators for the studios. *Star Wars* marked a watershed, for it made more money off sales of related products (such as lunch boxes) than from the film itself. Its global success was also significant, and it is now common for big-budget Hollywood films to make a profit not from their US theatrical release (where they are more likely only to recoup costs) but from their overseas ticket sales.

So, unlike the earlier blockbusters, an event film is modular in that it is composed of characters, images, music, songs, and ideas that can be removed from the primary film text to serve separately as self-sufficient elements in a range of media environments. This modular quality permits the film to occupy many parts of the moving image economy, maximising its profitability. The event film's ability to generate sales well beyond the theatre sometimes leads to an alternative name, the 'tentpole' film, since so much ancillary exploitation depends on the film's existence. Marketing plays an immense role, aided by the fact that something about the project causes it to make news outside the professional domain even before its release. In the case of *LOTR*, the fact that Tolkien's *The Lord of the Rings* was one of the twentieth century's most popular books and that no one had ever successfully adapted all of it for the screen created a media stir. Add to that the fact that the adaptation would parallel the book in being broken into three parts, that all three films were being made simultaneously, and that this adventurous project would go forward with a relatively unknown director (almost handicapped by what art house and fanboy credibility he had) who insisted on working in his home country far away from Hollywood studios and their executives, and it is easy to see why the media pitched in with pre-release coverage most producers could only dream of.

Because the economic aspect is a critical identifier of the event movie, we need to study *LOTR*'s corporate pedigree. *LOTR* involves two of the world's largest media corporations (for a complete list of production companies involved in making the films, see 'Credits' in Part VII; for more discussion of the corporate interaction involved in producing the films, see also the dossier section entitled 'Corporations, lawyers, small domestic economies, technology, and profits' in Part VI). Founded in 1967, New Line merged with Turner Broadcasting in 1993, and was part of the acquisition of Turner holdings by Time-Warner in 1996. Harper-Collins, Tolkien's publisher, is a wholly owned subsidiary of News Corporation. The synergy between the two players devolved on a brilliant update of the public relations campaign pioneered by *The Blair Witch Project*, which used the electronic equivalent of word-of-mouth to promote a low-budget horror film to cult status. The difference was that *LOTR* used the immense fan base for Tolkien's books to generate rumour, speculation, anticipation, and acclaim for the films long before their release; New Line and Jackson also managed that fan base's perception of its own involvement in the production, as Major describes below (Chapter 4).

Among other accepted terms for the event film phenomenon is 'the dispersible film' (Austin 2002: 29), in recognition of the phenomenon's ambition to exploit fully the range of marketable meaning that can be drawn from a common resource – the film as a copyrighted totality. Further alternative terms include the 'megapic' (Thompson and Bordwell 2003: 683), the 'popcorn film', and the franchise film.[7] This last term refers to films that set up a series of films to come. While *LOTR* has been called a franchise film, it was always limited by Tolkien's story. Once the Hobbits were safely home again, there was pretty much an end to it, at least from Tolkien's own pen. In contrast, the *Harry Potter* films could go on for as long as J. K. Rowling writes successful volumes in that series.

The franchise film takes us back to economics and the legal right to exploit a commodity. None the less, although this discussion of the blockbuster and its descendants has emphasised economic aspects, the event film also has an aesthetic component. However, even here economics can be a determining factor, in that marketing and merchandising plans can be driving forces behind aesthetic decisions. An event film's great scenes and spectacular effects can, as modules, be relocated in a number of satellite texts for the purpose of reaching different niche markets and 'sell-through' windows, so they are sometimes designed and filmed with this purpose in mind.

Calling the event film dispersible does not imply an absence of textual structure but rather the willingness to multiply the range of texts drawn from the film's 'universe'. Each new textual excision or extension is designed to appeal to a particular demographic or create a new trend in the search for mass significance and meaning. By this means, the fullest exploitation of marketable meaning can be squeezed from the film as a copyrighted totality (Austin 2002: 29).

Schembri refers to 'a seismic groundshift in the grammar of the blockbuster [after *Star Wars*' success]. The focus went from story and character to special effects and spectacle. This suited the growing importance of foreign markets. Don't bother so much with words and all those pesky subtitles, speak in the universal language of images – and the flashier the images, the better' (2004–5: 17). Maddox, writing at the same time as Schembri, asserts much the same about the event film's aesthetics.

We have reached an era when major Hollywood movies are events – experiences – that lure us into cinemas.

When they work as movies, they stimulate us at a visceral level and touch our hearts. Much of the stimulation comes from remarkable visual effects – at their best in the epic battles and adventures of *The Lord of the Rings* movies. (2004–5: 10)

Yet over and over in this book's study of *LOTR*, writers comment on Peter Jackson's own aesthetics, particularly his liking for a mobile camera. The dossier material 'Acting, on-set practices, software, and synthespians' at the beginning of Part III notes that much of what we see on screen is determined by technology. Yet we also learn that the on-set atmosphere was warm and human, largely owing, apparently, to how Jackson operates as a director.

This section also looks at the impact of Jackson's aesthetics – along with genre, setting, and CGI – on the actors' performances. Many actors expressed their reactions to working in the conditions necessary for achieving the special effects, commenting on the possibility of losing touch with the other performers because of their isolation from each other. A sort of vicious circle seems to some extent to have arisen: the techniques of CGI, meant to create a world perceived to be real and natural, unfortunately sometimes hamper live performers trying to deliver performances that will be perceived as real and natural. (In contrast with Jackson, Robert Zemeckis has since exploited this effect in *Beowulf*.)

One thing the *LOTR* exhibition makes absolutely clear (as does much of the commentary on the extended DVDs) is that Jackson's entire team was committed to creating a world as real as possible so that as much as possible of the images on screen would simply be taken for granted as part of the natural world. They were using realism – a particular style, and thus an aesthetic choice – but they were motivated by pragmatism more than aesthetics. In the case of *LOTR*'s miniatures, which demanded specific sorts of camerawork – e.g., long takes and deep focus – to be convincing, Jackson's personal inclinations and pragmatic decisions seem to have dovetailed nicely.

In 'Realising Middle-earth: production design and film technology' (Chapter 16), Sean Cubitt situates *LOTR* within film theory's discussion of the relation between cinematic presentation and a reality effect. He notes that 'the techniques of deep focus and the long take have become hallmarks of special effects cinema'; for him this is ironic, because film theory has long associated deep focus and long takes with realism. Although *LOTR* is a fantasy film – among the different genres that can be identified in the trilogy – the filmmakers' concern for the characters' believability led to the attention to detail for which the trilogy is known.

One might say that their goal was historical accuracy, except that Middle-earth and its wars and victories never existed.

In 'Howard Shore's ring cycle: the film score and operatic strategy' (Chapter 15), Judith Bernanke considers the trilogy's soundtrack in relation to Wagner's operas and their influence on the tradition of music for the movies. She considers composer Howard Shore's use of 'leit-motifs' or musical themes associated with specific characters and/or themes, and her focus on one particular musical theme demonstrates through example how to do the sort of analysis she describes.

This combined approach of examining the subject under considera-tion in terms of a general context, with specific attention to one small component in order to demonstrate how a particular perspective can influence our understanding of the subject, characterises one of this book's goals: to exemplify the different sorts of readings contemporary film studies is capable of in the face of a new development to be studied. Common to our authors is the idea that the same object looks different when viewed from different perspectives, that a frame for interpretation changes our experience of the object if not the object itself.

The dossier pieces, with which each section of *Studying the Event Film* begins, aim to provide a factual context within which an individual author's contribution takes on some particular component of *LOTR* that stands out from that perspective. Some of our contributors find themselves applying familiar types of analyses to the newest points of interest that *LOTR*'s uniqueness raises; other contributors apply newer approaches to analysis to familiar aspects of *LOTR*. For example, while Bernanke's analysis of Shore's score is part of a pre-existing strand of film studies, other interpretative approaches are newer. A postcolonial approach, for example, has been developed relatively recently, and at least three reasons urge its application to *LOTR*.

First, as a manifestation of commercial globalisation, any event film seems like an arm of economic colonisation in so far as it mutes the pro-ducts of local cultures. Second, Tolkien himself was born in a colony (South Africa), but he lived his life in the mother country (England) and *LOTR* is very much the product of his English heritage, full as it is of past conquests and (then current) imperialist threats. Finally and most obviously, Aotearoa New Zealand is a postcolonial country, in which even the settlers' descendants have cut their umbilical cord to the mother coun-try while Indigenous culture has had a renascence embraced to some extent by all residents of the country in that various Indigenous words, concepts, and practices have entered the common national domain.

In particular, as has been the case throughout the country's history, attitudes toward the land are a matter of constant and urgent concern. As

Alice Te Punga Somerville notes in 'Asking that mountain: an Indigenous reading of *The Lord of the Rings?*' (Chapter 23), the land looks different to a New Zealander overseas, be she Maori or Pakeha. Back at home, many Maori argue that Maori and Pakeha look differently at the land because of their different spiritual ties to the land. Maori call themselves tangata whenua (literally – as Maori filmmaker Barry Barclay stressed – 'people land' but usually translated as 'people of the land'; either way, the phrase has additional meanings and connotations). The tangata whenua apply the concept of kaitiaki to the land; they are guardians of the land and have a responsibility to respect and protect it.

Unsurprisingly, this view of the relation between humans and land evokes comparisons with environmentalist approaches to nature. For a long time, Aotearoa New Zealand has marketed itself as 'clean and green', despite poor practices in the past and present with regard to the destruction of native forests, the introduction of non-native animals, the use of harmful chemicals for agricultural purposes, and the destructive impact of schemes for generating electricity, etc. That clean, green image is perfect for evoking Middle-earth's shires; meanwhile, Tolkien's own view of the appropriate relation between humans and land seems to fit well with the Maori concept of stewardship over the land. In particular, since Maori consider Papatuanuku, the mother goddess, to be embodied literally in land, images of earth diggers on the land or other representations of attacks on the land have generally been seen as attacks on Papatuanuku herself. Saruman's destruction of Isengard and the surrounding forests in order to build up his imperialist forces has usually been read as Tolkien's criticism of the industrial revolution's ravages on Mother Nature. For Maori, Tolkien's grief for the destruction of nature could be taken as being at one with theirs.

From this point of view, one sees how Allen Meek could come to argue (in 'Fantasising history as trauma', Chapter 19) that *LOTR* is

> a mediation, in the context of transnational modes of production and distribution, of the historical traumas registered in both Tolkien's imaginative fiction and in the public discourses of the postcolonial nation where Jackson lives and works . . . Tolkien invented Middle-earth [as] a mythic alternative to industrial modernity . . . Jackson's special-effects blockbuster presents a vehicle by which a globally dispersed audience can negotiate a 'memory' of trauma that is not located geographically or historically.

Even Kevin Fisher, while discussing the apparently unconnected relation between sound and realism in *LOTR* (in 'Sonic resonances of nature and supernature in the *Lord of the Rings* trilogy', Chapter 14), takes the development of Isengard into an industrial eyesore as an example of how synchresis ('the phenomenon whereby any simultaneous audio and visual events produce the illusion of a spontaneous and irresistible bond') works. Fisher, working from Chion's analysis of sound and image, concludes that 'synch-points and microrhythms synchretically reinforce the materiality and vitality of the natural world throughout the trilogy. They also narratively establish nature as the site of conflict between forces of good and evil.'

We have come a long way from talking about the event film in general to talking about *LOTR* in particular. We have also shifted from discussing economics, technology, or even aesthetics to look at our subject's relation to the world in general.

To talk of Papatuanuku, an earth goddess, is to delve into the realms of belief, of religion and spirituality. 'There and back again: *The Lord of the Rings*, contemporary religiosity, and cinema', Ann Hardy's contribution (Chapter 18) compares the different human environments that produced *The Lord of the Rings* and *LOTR*. Tolkien was a deeply religious man, for whom it was self-evident that *The Lord of the Rings* should be read in terms of its religious components. What effect, Hardy asks, has Aotearoa New Zealand's largely secular society had on *LOTR*, given that the filmmakers involved with its scripting and direction are products of that society? Distinguishing between religiosity and spirituality, Hardy argues that spirituality better explains the sort of experience that many people have sought and obtained through their contact with the *LOTR* phenomenon.

While Maori have a culturally innate spiritual relation to the land, Pakeha often also express a deep, essentially spiritual connection with the country's spectacular landscapes. Identifying what characterises the cinema of Aotearoa New Zealand and distinguishes it from other national cinemas is a challenging goal, but historically most attempts have included two separate elements: Maori and the land. From a postcolonial perspective, though, Maori and land are again inseparable, if only because so much of the country's political and social history is tied up in disputes associated with land ownership. So it is not surprising that Part V, 'Reading for meaning: *The Lord of the Rings*, Middle-earth, and Aotearoa New Zealand', the section of *Studying the Event Film* with the largest number of individual chapters, deals with the relation between *LOTR* and the land in which it was made. For these contributors, the influence of the country on the trilogy and the trilogy's influence on the country represent the most interesting aspects of this particular event film.

So, like Te Punga Somerville, Stephen Turner and Misha Kavka analyse in ' "This is not New Zealand": an exercise in the political economy of identity' (Chapter 21) what it has meant for *LOTR* to be so closely associated with the land of Aotearoa New Zealand. '*LOTR*,' they say, 'has been an exercise in *two-way* branding, where New Zealand is not only branded as Middle-earth, but the epic realisation of Middle-earth is itself branded as New Zealand. The brand sticks even more effectively because the actual landscape of New Zealand has been cinematically denuded of its people and culture, emptied to accommodate the visiting cast of Middle-earth.'

While much of Aotearoa New Zealand's natural beauty undeniably remains, since the advent of human residence here many species of birds have died out, virgin forests have been destroyed, and the water, soil, and air have been polluted to various degrees. Genetic engineering or genetic modification is as painful a subject here as anywhere in the world, but for Maori it is particularly problematic, given the importance of whakapapa (genealogy, which connects Maori with each other across time and generations of both ancestors and descendents) to Maori cosmology. Like many of our contributors, Roy Parkhurst, in 'The persistence of cacogenics in nationalist mythology: the case of *The Lord of the Rings*' (Chapter 20), refers to the literally autochthonous birth of the Uruk-hai in Isengard. They are an example of bad breeding, or cacogenesis, which, Parkhurst notes, 'is still likely to be found in association with stories of mad scientists . . . and as a marker of difference'. Its counterpart, eugenesis, was part of the public discourse operative during Tolkien's life, although it came under disrepute after the Nazis adopted it as a public policy.

For Te Punga Somerville, Parkhurst, and Turner and Kavka, it is significant that the actors who embody the Uruk-hai and other soldiers in Sauron's service are generally Polynesians and particularly Maori, for these authors read the casting in terms of a postcolonial understanding that objects to the use of Indigenous peoples as representatives of evil or the embodiment of negative qualities. Given the close association of Maori and land (tangata whenua) and the importance of (a well-maintained) whakapapa, the casting in particular of Maori actor Lawrence Makoare as Lurtz – a character extraneous to Tolkien's version but given significance in *Fellowship* as leader of the Uruk band who kills Boromir at the end of the first film – seems like a bad exploitation of Maori beliefs and imagery, given Lurtz's origins in Saruman's tinkering with the natural order.

While it may seem that this discussion of the importance for Maori of knowing clear lines of genealogy strays too far from *LOTR* as an international phenomenon that will be read largely by people unfamiliar with the existence of Maori and their beliefs, and that the earlier international reception of both *The Piano* and *Once Were Warriors* largely ignored the presence of Maori as Maori in those films, it is none the less true that, apart from *LOTR*, the most internationally successful films from Aotearoa New Zealand have featured Maori as well as their relation to the land. *Whale Rider*, the most recent of Aotearoa New Zealand's locally produced films to break out of the art house circuit into mainstream cinemas, has been read in terms of a universal struggle between young and old, not least by its New Zealand producer, but his comments provoked a domestic debate over the film's authenticity and the more general point of whether local specificity or the pursuit of 'universals' is the key to international success for New Zealand cinema (see, for example, the letters to the editor in *Onfilm* for the first half of 2003).

Almost alone among international critics, bell hooks (1994) objected to the representation of Maori in *The Piano*, and at least one African American academic I know worried about Lurtz even as she watched *Fellowship* in a Middle-earth costume of her own making. For Turner and Kavka, Lurtz is a stereotrope rather than a stereotype, a neat way of acknowledging local specificity as well as international ignorance of that specificity amid recognition of how that specificity feeds into related international discourses.

Once again, our local point of view has shaped how we read *LOTR*. Whether we were born in this country or not, and whatever our academic training, we find ourselves understanding *LOTR* and the phenomenon that 'Peter Jackson' has become through a local perspective. It is once again an aspect of this particular event film that marks it as different, certainly from other runaway productions, but perhaps also as an indication of how global the event film may eventually become.

'The tyranny of distance' is as omnipresent a phrase among Kiwis as 'she'll be right' and 'we don't know how lucky we are'. While our proximity to the event in question has stood us in good stead, as authors our distance from our publisher has not. Most of the research for this book was completed by early 2005. Since then many books have been published, most notably Lindsay Shelton's *The Selling of New Zealand Movies* (2005), Sibley's authorised biography of Jackson, and Kristin Thompson's *The Frodo Franchise: The Lord of the Rings and Modern Hollywood* (2007). Along with Hester Joyce's unpublished doctoral research, *In Development: Scriptwriting Policies and Practice in the New Zealand Film Commission 1978–1995* (2003), Shelton's book sheds unprecedented light on how the New Zealand Film Commission developed, from its official inception in 1978 through its early support, more or less, for Peter Jackson, and eventually for Fran Walsh, as well, specifically through bringing Robert McKee's scriptwriting workshop

to Wellington in 1988 (Sibley 157). While Ian Pryor's earlier, unauthor-
ised biography of Jackson remains a helpful resource, it was always
hampered by Jackson's decision to pull support for its publication, making it hard for Pryor to write the book he had in mind. Sibley, on the
other hand, has had Jackson's co-operation, and Sibley's biography contains all sorts of previously unreleased information.

The single most important publication on the feat of making *LOTR*
and on the phenomenon's importance is Thompson's *The Frodo Franchise*,
which will surely become the definitive book of record for this material.
The Aberystwyth-based international project on global reception of the
trilogy has led to its own publications (see Stan Jones's chapter below).
While some authors, particularly those whose work is faith-based, have
of course analysed the films themselves in more traditional terms of narrative analysis, it says much about the interest *LOTR* fundamentally
offers that the bulk of publications have not followed this traditional
approach. For us, the editors of this book, this trend in academic responses
to *LOTR* confirms our thesis: How to study this event in film history
is itself worthy as the subject of a book.

In summary, *Studying the Event Film: The Lord of the Rings* sets out
not to study *LOTR* itself so much as to use the trilogy as an example
of a significant development in the history of filmmaking. Yet, although
this study focuses on the phenomenon of the event film, it is shaped by
the nature of the specific event film we take as our example. As is always
the case when one prepares an analysis, we begin with a section on
gathering the materials we need. This is followed by Part II, entitled
'Creative industries / National heroes', in acknowledgement that, while
all event films must be situated within an economic context, the economic
context for *LOTR* is specific to Aotearoa New Zealand at the turn of
the century. Parts III and IV, 'Stardom and the event film' and 'Making
a film trilogy', look more closely at specific aspects of the trilogy's production and post-production phases. Part V, 'Reading for meaning: *The
Lord of the Rings*, Middle-earth, and Aotearoa New Zealand', includes
various approaches to understanding the trilogy's meaning, once again
within the specific context of the country that produced the films. Part VI,
'There, back again, and beyond: production infrastructures and extended
exploitation' returns us to economic considerations, but from a different point of view than in Part II. Finally, Part VII provides detailed information about the films themselves, including the credits and critical
awards, along with a sampling of professional reviews from traditional
sources and web-based responses from 'ordinary' viewers. The biblio-
graphy, of course, represents a starting point for further research.

We also invite you to consider the extensive filmography as yet another context within which to understand *LOTR*. Many of the films listed there are predecessors to *LOTR*, whether they be examples of earlier international blockbusters, components of Aotearoa New Zealand's national cinema, or steps in Peter Jackson's development as a filmmaker.

From this point of view, it is obvious that Jackson and Co. did not produce *LOTR* in a vacuum, and that is largely what this book is about. We have assumed a certain familiarity with *The Lord of the Rings* on your part. If, however, you haven't yet read the books or seen the films, well, the story involves a wizard named Gandalf and some Hobbits who live in the Shire . . .

### Notes

1 Throughout this volume *LOTR* is used in reference to the film trilogy, and *The Lord of the Rings* for Tolkien's trilogy. The individual films are generally referred to as *Fellowship*, *Towers*, and *Return*.

   Further on usage: 'New Zealand' is the official name of the country that produced *LOTR*; in the language of Maori, its Indigenous people, this country is known as Aotearoa (land of the long white cloud). Aotearoa is increasingly used alone or in conjunction with New Zealand, and in our editing we have generally let stand whatever practice each contributor has followed (as we have done with references to Sir Ian McKellen or simply Ian McKellen). 'Pakeha' is the Maori word for non-Maori; in general usage it usually refers to New Zealanders of European descent. Finally, 'Kiwi' is a sort of nickname for New Zealanders, after the kiwi bird, itself a national icon.

2 Merchandising (the sale of designs and trademarks associated with the films) and product placement (the practice of placing commercial brands in shot in return for a fee) have long been used as ways of generating money for a film's production as well as profit after its release. Merchandising in particular gets discussed throughout *Studying the Event Film*, but both strategies are discussed in Major's Chapter 4 as well as the dossier sections entitled 'Materials for a study of *The Lord of the Rings* trilogy' (Part I) and 'Corporations, lawyers, small domestic economies, technology, and profits' (Part VI).

3 Halliwell describes *El Cid* as an 'endless glum epic with splendid action sequences as befits the high budget' (1985: 290), suggesting that action sequences have been an early and integral part of developments leading to the event film.

   Production information on films mentioned in this book can be found in the Filmography at the back. As this book's contents show, we value information about a film's production history, starting with director, producer, year, country of origin, and approximate running time.

4 The Exhibition was 'developed and presented by the Museum of New Zealand Te Papa Tongarewa in partnership with New Line Cinema'; it was also 'made possible through the support of the New Zealand Government' (from the Exhibition's entry ticket).

5 One national characteristic Pakeha and Maori New Zealanders have tended to value in common is humility, just as in the past the national culture valued conformity to the point of imposing it with a vengeance. In this environment, anyone who, intentionally or otherwise, sets himself or herself above others is considered to be a 'tall poppy', and is generally a target for condemnation and disapproval. In the wake of *The Piano*'s success and an ensuing controversy about its origins, there was almost a national debate about celebrating the country's successes rather than attacking the people involved. In Jackson's case – in terms of his public persona, at least – one of his positive attributes is seen to be his ability to retain a common touch despite his immense success.

6 For discussion of the tax shelter's effect on New Zealand filmmakers see Murphy 1992: 147–9.

7 Thompson and Bordwell juxtapose event film, megapic, and 'must-see film' as equals (ibid.). 'Popcorn film' may not have attained critical status as a reference to escapist films except in popular reviews to be found, for example, at the Rotten Tomatoes website (www.rottentomatoes.com), but, if parody confirms something's existence, then popcorn film exists as a legitimate label. The Toque, which describes itself as 'Canada's source for popcorn humour, parody, and satire', provides a thoroughgoing parody that associates the popcorn film with the action film, the sort released in the summer – 'a delicious film that, for two hours, could make you forget about your problems and let you sit back and enjoy' (www.thetoque.com/011211/popcorn.html).

# Part I
# A gathering of materials

# 1

# Dossier: materials for a study of the *Lord of the Rings* trilogy and its audiences

*Sean Cubitt and Barry King*

Studying, analysing, involves more than appreciation, although it helps if you enjoy the thing you study. The theatrical release of a film in the early twenty-first century involves more than it used to throughout most of the twentieth century. As before, there is its existence prior to release, the story of its conception, its writing, its pitch to the studios, its financing, the technologies, arts, and crafts that go into it, the lives, the emotions, the cold, hard cash, the heated arguments, the petty politics, and the big business. After its release to the public, there is more to come. While immensely significant, a film's opening weekend is only part of its life. Thereafter, it will have its DVD release, its pay-per-view and terrestrial television screenings, its sales to airlines, its pirated copies. There will be thousands of reviews in hundreds of languages. There will be spin-offs and merchandising. There will be books like this one. If we want, in addition to enjoying films, to understand them, and especially if we want to make them ourselves, we need to get to grips with the complex dynamics that bring a phenomenon like *LOTR* not only to the screen but to people's lives, their bank balances, their fantasies, and their dreams.

In the world of film production, things happen as they do, rather than according to neat chronological schedules. Distribution rights are bought and release dates planned before a camera rolls. Stars join the cast after the shooting starts. But in the case of *LOTR*, the fifteen-month shooting schedule and the weeks of pick-up shoots overlapped with the release of the first and second films. Some effects pre-dated the film's go-ahead for production; some were still in preparation while the last extended DVD was being devised. To the extent possible, *LOTR*'s producers did what they could to extend the life of what they knew to be a genuinely unique film project bigger than any previous event film.

Where does one start? Of course the cluttered desk of the *LOTR* scholar must have a dog-eared copy of Tolkien's book. Because *Studying the Event Film* offers considerations of both the theatrical and the extended versions of the *LOTR* trilogy, we have presumed that the reader has seen *LOTR* in the versions that were theatrically released, and has or has had the extended DVDs near to hand.

*LOTR*'s use of CGI and special effects has provided condensed spectacles for recycling in ancillary markets along with trailers, cast interviews, 'making of' documentaries, and numerous still images. *LOTR*'s producers had an additional impetus to exploit ancillary markets because the story's fantasy setting limited product placement opportunities. The drive to find new markets covered amongst other things board games, collectibles, clothes, battle wear, jewellery, computer games, and stamps. There was also a strong emphasis on promotional events such as premieres and conventions. All these processes and objects extended the films' field of meanings and multiplied the number of texts and cross-references between texts.

These possibilities complicate what we mean when we casually refer to *LOTR* or the individual films in the trilogy.[1] The point of this section is to consider some of these complications. If we look for the parameters of our text, of the fantasy narrative associated with the title *The Lord of the Rings*, then we can take Tolkien's original book and the release of the last extended DVD version of the film in November of 2004 as marking the outer limits of the text itself. But that is only a start.

The analyst not only needs to know the pertinent details of a film's production; she must also order the mass of information she draws together, eventually bringing all the details into something like a coherent whole. The idea of analysis is of course to break a problem up into manageable parts. Once we have done that, the task remains of putting them back together again: to understand how all these activities, all these ideas, words, and actions combined with all these tools and institutions come together to form a large, complex but none the less reasonably typical cultural phenomenon. The first step is to gather and sort our materials into some interconnected but none the less discrete piles.

It is fair to ask what does not fall under the microscope when we undertake to analyse a film. After all, if we begin with the titles, there is a history not only of type design but of alphabetic writing, of English, of language itself that stitches the film into the whole of human history. The economics of production and distribution tie us to the global economy, and discussions of audiences take us to the nitty gritty of people's lives, their biographies, their psychology, and their innermost fantasies.

Film studies distinguishes itself from many other humanities disciplines by undertaking to understand the whole of a film. Many scholars of literature and music are not concerned with this or that copy of the book, this or that recording of the music. Instead they pursue the essence of the text, its Platonic ideal, something apart from the particular paper and ink, or the particular CD you might have to hand. While film scholars may do the same, they are just as likely to question the industries that produce books and records, or the audiences that read and listen. Film studies analyses the full life history of its objects of study.

Conventionally, film scholars sort texts, as Fiske identifies it, into three levels of textuality: (1) primary texts – the films themselves; (2) secondary texts – promotion and publicity, texts about the making of the films, memoirs; and (3) tertiary texts – reviews, cultural commentary, opinion pieces, and books (1987). However, *LOTR* exemplifies what Genette calls transtextuality: 'everything that brings it into relation (manifest or hidden) with other texts' (1992: 81). *LOTR* is, in Genette's terms, 'intertextual' because it references other texts, especially Tolkien's; 'paratextual' because it blurs the line between text and what is outside the text – the crafts of weapon making, the development of collectibles and so on; 'architextual' because it draws on a body of texts or genres, for example, action, fantasy, and epic genres; and 'transtextual' because it brings all these activities into relation with one another.

When we refer to *The Lord of the Rings*, we implicitly comprehend Tolkien's connection with the text as author. In general, as is usual, people have referred to Jackson as standing in a similar relation to *LOTR*. This sort of auteurism is deeply imbedded in ordinary references to films, even among film scholars, in no small part because it is convenient to refer to one person as responsible for a film's production in a way similar to a book author's role. However, given that filmmaking, especially on the scale of the *LOTR* trilogy, is a collaborative venture, film scholars recognise the work of significant crew that goes into the film. Since many significant crew members produce work designed in fact not to catch our attention, not to distract us from the world of the film we are watching, their work often goes unnoticed except by special-interest groups (fellow cinematographers or musicians, editors and sound designers, for example). Their work is usually not celebrated or even documented in mainstream sources of information for the general film audience. In the case of *LOTR*, however, everything seems to have been documented, not least through the touring exhibition originated at Te Papa, which has presented many of the costumes, props, prosthetics, miniatures, and conceptual artwork that fed into the film. Sibley's official guides to the making of the films and the DVD extras document in some detail the materials and techniques used. Costa Botes's documentary, *The Making of 'The Lord of the Rings'*, provides a further layer of detail to our resources.[2]

How much of the extra material on the DVD versions do we necessarily include in our study? While they may not form an integral part of the experience of the film, they are a valuable resource. If we wanted to pursue an auteur theory of filmmaking, we would include at least the director's commentary. We could also include the various trailers released online, the sneak preview shown at Cannes in 2000, the pre-visualisation video that formed such an important part in raising finance for the trilogy, and even the lipstick-cam pre-visualisations used in blocking out scenes with miniatures. Since in *LOTR*'s case the director was also co-scriptwriter, the various drafts of the script could also form part of the work we examine.

Asked 'what's the definitive version of these films', Jackson answered, 'The theatrical versions are the definitive versions. I regard the extended cuts as being a novelty for the fans that really want to see the extra material' (Otto 2003; but see also Jackson's comments on the DVD versions, found in Hight's Chapter 2). *LOTR* is unusual in that it was projected from early on as having two forms: the theatrical releases and the DVD extended editions. It is not, however, unusual for more than one version of a film to be available on DVD.

Because many films were first released in forms their makers never approved, the Director's Cut has become part of everyday film culture. Whether dealing with restorations of films cut by producers for distribution, or films censored at the time of their first release; with movies remade with an eye to repairing or making use of new technologies, or with films that have been minimally changed to extract the last bit of economic value from the collectors' market, films do not always exist in a single version. A look at the running times listed by the Internet Movie Database shows that even innocuous films are released with slightly differing running times in different territories for a variety of practical, financial, or political reasons. *LOTR* is a peculiar example of this, but far from unique.

These different bits and pieces, along with the different editions of *LOTR*, went out in an attempt to 'sell' the project in various ways to different audiences at different points in the project's history. In the set of chapters that complete this section of *Studying the Event Film*, Craig Hight situates the extended DVDs within the history of the technology, Jo Smith considers how digital technology more generally has affected viewing practices, Suzette Major looks at how marketing strategies accommodated and coped with the pre-existing audience for an adaptation of *The Lord of the Rings*, Stan Jones reports on an international project that has researched *LOTR*'s reception by audiences worldwide, and Geoff Lealand considers the possible impact of violence, particularly in *Return*, on the neglected audience of child viewers.

## Notes

1 See Mathijs (2006), which discusses the 'dispersible' quality of *LOTR*.
2 'Wellington filmmaker Costa Botes, a long-time associate of Peter Jackson . . . , assembled a small team in July 1999, . . . to shoot and compile a behind-the-scenes video record. By the time production of the trilogy finally ended . . . , they had over 800 hours of footage. [This is] the first of the three documentary features to be cut from this material . . . "It was never designed to be part of a marketing effort. It wasn't even meant to be seen for another couple of years, when it and its two companion pieces are provisionally earmarked for release as part of a DVD box set. It is presented here, exclusively to this Festival, as a work in progress"' (Costa Botes, quoted by the festival organisers in the Programme Notes for the Telecom New Zealand International Film Festivals 2004: 123).

# 2

# One (special extended edition) disc to rule them all

*Craig Hight*

When *Fellowship*'s Special Extended DVD Edition was released on 12 November 2002, critics and commentators universally hailed it as setting a new benchmark in DVD releases of mainstream cinema.[1] Since then each film in the trilogy has been released as a two-disc set containing the theatrical version of the film and some extras, and a four-disc set comprised of a new, extended version of the film and extensive supplementary material. Read together, these texts illustrate both the emergence of DVD as a medium, and the general form in which DVD cinematic texts have developed.

This chapter discusses the supplementary material of the four-disc versions, packaged under the title of 'Appendices', especially how they allow us a layered experience of each film. All the extra materials, particularly on the four-disc DVD versions, add detail to our knowledge of the films' production. We hear of decisions that key creative personnel made, see new filmmaking techniques demonstrated, and listen to core members of the cast and crew talk about their experiences. However, we should consider the nature of the information we are and are not given. Collectively, these materials shape or *frame* our understanding of a range of industrial practices employed in the films' production, including the professional and personal relationships between cast and crew. They encourage us to *interpret* or, more accurately, reinterpret these films as products of an approach to filmmaking that combines Hollywood industrial practices and the demands of individual and collective creativity.

## The rise of DVD

As a medium, DVD (Digital Video Disc, or Digital Versatile Disc) has enjoyed a rapid rise from its origins as an alternative to the expensive Laserdiscs niche format. Established as a mainstream medium, it has increasingly marginalised VHS both in domestic rentals and as the standard for home video libraries (Bakalis 2003; 'How is DVD doing?'). The medium dates essentially from December 1995, with agreement of a format between competing manufacturers. However, the beginnings of its mainstream dominance began with the release of the million-selling *Titanic* in August 1999 and *The Matrix* the following month. Each of these discs achieved sales that convinced studios, as well as consumers, of the technology's future.[2]

Besides the DVD image's superior quality in comparison with VHS, producers insist that the medium can fulfil distinctive functions. The DVD set, with its supplementary material, provides viewers with information on the production processes of a specific film as well as on the nature of contemporary filmmaking practices. Furthermore, the increased physical longevity of the DVD discs, compared to VHS tapes, also means that they are archives (Burger 2001). The *LOTR* DVDs fully exploit these functions of the medium.

The *LOTR* discs demonstrate the increasing trend of studios to adhere to a two-tiered marketing strategy for DVD releases. Mainstream audiences can purchase a 'standard' DVD edition – the two-disc versions of *Fellowship*, *Towers*, and *Return*. The release of a 'Special Extended DVD Edition' version only a few months after the two-disc set appeals to a consumer elite, either dedicated fans of the films or film buffs, willing to pay the added expense to complete their *LOTR* collection. New Line also adhered to a policy of not repeating content across the various discs, increasing their appeal to the most dedicated consumers of the *LOTR* franchise.

Filmmakers themselves are also increasingly involved in the design and production of the special editions of their creations – supervising the conversion to digital formats of older films, adding commentaries, and featuring prominently in interviews for the now standard 'making of' documentaries. Jackson's commitment to the medium is obvious from his constant and enthusiastic presence within the supplementary material on the Special Extended DVD Editions. Jackson suggests (on the discs themselves) that the production of the DVD versions of the *LOTR* trilogy was an extension of the production of the theatrically released films. He insists they are alternative (and extended) versions that are closer to the original narratives constructed within Tolkien's books. They offer to film buffs, and particularly to Tolkien fans, more comprehensive home-viewing experiences. Jackson also continually stresses that he and his production team recognise the importance of investing production resources into the DVD releases of the films, because these are for posterity.

Since the production of DVD material is not simply to replicate the theatrical experience but to transform and to add to it, how we actually access and navigate the layers of extra materials on DVDs offers important lessons on the nature of DVD itself as a distinctive medium.

## The DVD as a text

Instead of a single text, viewed in a single sitting, we can access the content of a digital text in a number of ways. We are not so much 'viewers' of a digital text as 'users', navigating our way through menus and following the pathways they provide. These menus collectively make up the 'interface' for a DVD. What we choose to play from the menus, the real content of a disc, are parts of a 'database' of multimedia computer files (Manovich 2001: 215). The terms 'interface' and 'database' are computing terms applicable to a variety of digital texts (including Web sites, CD-ROMs, and even computer games).

For DVD interfaces, at least on the special editions, it is increasingly standard for animated menus to employ the films' production design and a musical motif from the film's score. The animated menus of the four-disc *LOTR* DVDs explicitly refer to Tolkien's original literary trilogy. Just as the cardboard packaging for the DVDs itself is designed to suggest an ancient manuscript, so too each disc's interface uses a montage of the opening of Bilbo Baggins's book. Menus constructed as contents pages allow access to the film's chapters as well as to appendices of extra material, modelled on Tolkien's use of appendices in his original trilogy. The backgrounds to menus throughout the discs are also familiar to Tolkien fans because they use the drawings of the Tolkien artists John Howe and Alan Lee, both of whom served as conceptual designers for the films.

The multimedia content of the DVD special editions, what we select using the interface, includes the films themselves and any number of 'extras' – additional features such as subtitles and/or dubbing in various languages, audio commentaries from members of the cast and key production personnel, the script, an archive of production stills and conceptual drawings, out-takes from the film or alternative endings, interactive files such as multi-frame sequences demonstrating the compositing techniques used in special effects, 'Easter Eggs' (partly hidden additional materials), and so on. These extras can be explored through multiple viewings. The *LOTR* special editions, for example, *require* multiple viewings as a consequence of their sheer size, with extra materials that are more than twice as long as the (extended) films themselves. Despite their collective length, these extras are explicitly segmented and exist almost as self-contained individual texts themselves (Manovich 2001: 218–33). They only indirectly offer an overall narrative of the films' production (more on this below). Both the interface and database features of DVDs reflect the interpretative frames that special editions construct for their cinematic texts.

## Interpretive frames

The most common frame that DVD releases construct is invariably a promotional one, with the bulk of additional materials conforming to the familiar frame created by an Electronic Press Kit (EPK). EPKs involve the selective release of information about an upcoming film release. These texts follow a narrow marketing agenda: to build anticipation for a coming movie event through various means. For example, promotional documentaries – making-of documentaries screened prior to the film's theatrical release – are often little more than extended versions of trailers.

The two-disc versions of *Fellowship*, *Towers*, and *Return* conform to this pattern. Their extras include promotional documentaries, trailers, featurettes from www.lordoftherings.net, and previews of the special extended editions of the films and associated merchandise such as video games. These DVDs are the perfect demonstration of Brookey and Westerfelhaus's contention that 'the DVD is perhaps the ultimate example of media-industry synergy, in which the promotion of the media product is collapsed into the product itself' (2002: 23).

The four-disc versions of the *LOTR* DVDs, however, open up more complex and interesting interpretive frames. The bulk of the extras on the special editions are grouped as appendices on discs 3 and 4 of each of the four-disc versions. Produced by Pellerin Multimedia Inc.,[3] these appendices form a substantial archival supplement to the films. *Fellowship* has 'Part One – From Book to Vision' and 'Part Two – From Vision to Reality', while *Towers* has 'Part Three – The Journey Continues' and 'Part Four – The Battle for Middle-earth Begins', and *Return* contains 'Part Five – The War of the Ring' and 'Part Six – The Passing of an Age'. Each four-disc edition contains sections on pre-production, production, and post-production. And each section then incorporates narrowly defined subject areas providing an exhaustive array of information on topics as diverse as the production of foley sounds, previsualisation, or set dressing.

The majority of *LOTR* DVD extras consist of short documentary segments, ranging from two to fifty minutes in length. The large number of these segments demonstrates how important digital video itself has become to the production of DVD extras. The low expense of digital video compared to film stock opens up the possibility for a production team to document many aspects of production practices. Reflecting their origins as part of EPKs, these segments look to studios like a comparatively cheap means for archiving material related to a film, and they are invariably contracted out to specialists in producing this kind of content.[4] There are remnants of this approach within the *LOTR* special editions, but they coexist with a much more intimate, and exhaustive, approach to documenting the films' production.

The bulk of the behind-the-scenes, hand-held location footage was captured by the long-time Jackson collaborator Costa Botes and by Haley French.[5] Both aesthetically and thematically, a natural tension exists between the spontaneity of this camcorder footage taken during pre-production, filming, and post-production, and how it is packaged within formulaic documentary constructions.

The documentary segments rely heavily on interactive modes of representation (Nichols 1991: 44–56) structured around studio-based interviews filmed specifically for the DVD. These interviews, which include only core members of cast and production personnel, act in many instances as voice-overs for specific thematic sequences. Here they are combined with elements such as the location footage, production drawings, production stills, raw special effects sequences, addresses to camera, and walkthroughs of production settings (particularly by Jackson and Richard Taylor, special effects supervisor at Weta Workshop).

The first and most important point is how self-contained both these documentary segments and audio commentaries are. They invite us into the closed and artificial world of the production in a manner that closely parallels our entry into the fictional realm of the films themselves. With the audio commentaries, for example, it is as if we have been invited into the homes of the core film crew to view the film with them, listening as they tell stories of their production experience with the sound of the film turned down. This emphasis on 'personalised' narratives allows commentaries and documentary segments to achieve a number of different objectives simultaneously. They introduce core cast and crew, and, following the educative function claimed for DVD supplements, they also explain some of the specialised roles within the overall production infrastructure.

What we gain in intimacy, however, we lose in terms of breadth and depth of perspective. There is no production metanarrative, or overarching account, to offer an overview of the development of the production for the trilogy as a whole. Considering that the three films were developed and filmed concurrently, the absence of commentary on this is a significant loss (despite occasional references to general writing, design, and other production issues within some of the audio commentaries).

Similarly, these supplements do not offer a 'debate' over the wider aesthetic, social, political, or historical significance of the film trilogy, such as through a comparison with other film texts. They might have taken any number of critical approaches toward these aspects of the trilogy, approaches that would open a space for exploring and reappraising the nature of the films themselves. The DVD release of more historical films, because of the length of time since production, naturally allows for a greater sense of critical distance.[6] Some commentaries open up a new interpretative frame for a film text, such as Camille Paglia's on the *Basic Instinct* special edition. However, this remains a largely neglected potential within DVD production. The absence of such critical commentary on the *LOTR* discs is hardly surprising as, like almost all extra materials on DVDs, these are provided by the people most implicated in their construction, and in this case were recorded during the production of the trilogy itself. Such commentaries illustrate the narrow corporate interests that these DVDs serve.

A consistent feature of some interviewees is an insistence that (just as did the fictional fellowship) the cast and location crews travelled on their own journey, bonding together through the arduous filming process. The cast and crew also suggest that they adopted a collaborative approach to the production, that there were no real divisions between its personnel. In part, this reinforces a sense of a specifically New Zealand production style – drawing upon an assumed sense of egalitarian mateship. In a wider sense, however, this is part of a virtual denial that the production was actually couched within a capitalist mode of production. Tellingly, there are few references to the production team's relationship with New Line or to the overall economics of the production.

Instead, the DVD extras construct two further, complementary interpretative frames. The first relates to the 'authenticity' of these filmed versions of Tolkien's trilogy. We are constantly told of the level of detail undertaken to create a 'realistic fantasy' world, detail above and beyond what was necessary simply for the films' production design. Much of this detail, in costumes, set design, languages spoken, and so on, does not appear on screen. This level of production design evidences a commitment to representing as accurately as possible Tolkien's original conception of Middle-earth and its peoples. Both the 'journey' undertaken on location by cast and crew and the more detailed extended versions of the theatrical film trilogy also fall into this frame.

Again, these extra materials do not tell the full story of the pressures that Jackson and his production team faced. There is no hint here of the grumbling of Tolkien fans before the theatrical release over liberties taken with the trilogy's complex narratives, their questioning of the appropriateness of Jackson as director, and the range of other criticism from Tolkien's heirs.[7]

The DVDs' other key interpretive frame, the use of computer technology in the construction of fictional worlds, is common to DVD releases for films that incorporate significant amounts of digital special effects. The appendices on the *LOTR* special editions offer extensive materials on the digital technologies used during the filmmaking process. They also provide an overview of the specialised roles performed by individuals and teams within the overlapping practices of pre-production, production, and post-production. These materials adopt the rhetoric of revealing the secrets behind the construction of Middle-earth, and celebrating the technological achievements of the largely New Zealand production team. However, this does not inevitably lead to a destruction of the illusions of the films themselves. In fact, this grounding of a cinematic fantasy in the (exhaustively detailed) 'realities' of film production is consistent with a central paradox within digital cinema. Manovich notes that 'new media objects keep reminding us of their artificiality, incompleteness, and constructedness. They present us with a perfect illusion only next to reveal its underlying machinery' (2001: 205).

DVD is a medium that can open new modes of reading cinematic texts, but these modes are often still implicated within the industrial agenda of contemporary cinema. The layered (re-)experience of the *LOTR* cinematic trilogy offered by their DVD releases allows us a complex perspective on the craft of contemporary filmmaking. The exhaustive documenting of the production processes undertaken in creating the cinematic trilogy, in part, opens new spaces for audiences. Users of these discs can explore the level and nature of creative achievement attained by a production team constructing an 'authentic' visualisation of Tolkien's fantasy narrative. Consistently with most other special edition DVD releases, however, the most crucial interpretive frame ultimately serves the wider corporate interests of the studio that owns the rights to the films themselves. Added to our experience of the cinematic fantasy of the *LOTR* trilogy is New Line's detailed quasi-fantasy of the creative 'fellowship' of Peter Jackson's production team.

### Notes

1 See the online Movie Review Query Engine (http://www.mrqe.com/), which collates both theatrical and DVD reviews.
2 See www.dvdangle.com/resources/timeline/index.html for a timeline of key events within the development of DVD.

3 The overall production of the audio commentaries and Appendices are credited to the writer, producer, and director Michael Pellerin, and the producers Kevin Miller and David Rodriguez.
4 Each documentary segment on the *LOTR* discs, for example, was assigned to a separate editor, with a team of editors working on the Appendices as a whole.
5 Arden Entertainment produced some additional documentary footage.
6 A good example is the two-hour documentary included within the special edition of *Cleopatra*. *Cleopatra: The Film That Changed Hollywood* discusses aspects of both the nature of this film's production and its wider historical context.
7 For some idea of the scope and energy of Tolkien fandom see fan sites such as www.tolkienonline.com/, www.theonering.net/index.shtml, www.xenite. org/faqs/lotr_movie/, and www.ringbearer.org/.

# 3

# *The Lord of the Rings* in the living room: changing technologies of cinematic display and reception

*Jo Smith*

The rise of digital technologies such as DVD, plasma screens, and home entertainment systems increasingly tests our understanding of cinema as an event involving a large screen, a public theatre, a film projector, and celluloid images. *LOTR* in all its multiple forms is not simply a celluloid theatrical release and a discrete text whose ideological underpinnings can be uncovered via textual interpretation. It is a media event that film projectors, television, computer consoles, DVD players, and online servers actively reconstitute, circulate, and distribute in various social contexts.

Developments in digital production, distribution, and exhibition raise the question of what it is that we *do* with cinema and accordingly how technologies of display and exhibition (as discursive and material practices) interact with the more textual and aesthetic aspects of a film to shape the audiovisual experience. This chapter revises the disciplinary understanding of film as a discrete object by arguing that the extended edition of *LOTR* on DVD demonstrates the endlessly extendable technological apparatus of contemporary cinema, a process inevitably enmeshed in the workings of capital.

*LOTR* as filmic text is primarily data that then become the raw material embodied by various modes of delivery and exhibition such as the film projector and large screen, the electronic television screen and the VCR, the widescreen plasma screen, the home data projector, and the DVD. Each mode of data management and display produces a singular and particular type of media event. For example, the theatrical release of *LOTR* differs in scale, duration, and narrative detail when compared to the Special Extended DVD Edition and positions the consumer as an interactive user. The VHS release is more linear in structure than its DVD counterpart, prohibiting user interaction, and when panned, scanned, and played back on low-resolution television screens it becomes a poor cousin in relation to its DVD or celluloid relatives.

The nature of the medium thus affects the aesthetic and textual aspects of the audiovisual experience, suggesting that the site of exhibition, the technologies that constitute the sound- and image-play, as well as the textual features are all interactive and dynamic mechanisms producing the audiovisual event. This relationship can best be described through the spatial and temporal concept of an 'architectonics' that addresses the film event's *context* as a designed and technologically mediated space that produces particular experiences of duration. Ultimately, *LOTR* is data that can be reconstituted in a multiplicity of social settings. The film scholar can trace the multi-mediated relationships between consumers and cinematic product and consider how technologies of display and exhibition contribute to new orders of consumption in capitalist economies.

## An architectonics of audiovisual culture

To examine the architectonics of a media event requires attending to the specific manner in which contemporary film spectatorship takes place, a practice that has a long tradition in film studies. As Kipnis has argued, analogue-based film studies (in particular, apparatus theory) often focused on cinematic specificity (the projected image, the large screen, the darkened theatre) to define the field in opposition to the 'noisy lower orders of video and television' (1998: 598). However, Kipnis suggests that conventional apparatus theory produced an artificial elevation of the medium, an approach that has social and cultural implications. She calls for contemporary film scholars to examine how social value accrues to particular technologies when she contemplates why film editors mourn the loss of a tactile relationship to celluloid with the advent of non-linear editing processes or why film is considered 'human, sensuous and creative' while video is machine-like, and aligned with technocrats and engineers (1998: 600). Kipnis's method is a central aspect of an architectonics of media events since she begins the work of critically examining the discourses that value film technologies over those of video. Yet further work is needed to examine the discursive conventions surrounding digital technologies. For example, discourses surrounding the development of plasma screens, Dolby sound systems, and high-pixel resolution DVDs suggest that digitalisation can augment the lowly television set in ways that parallel the hyper-real elements of theatrical cinema, a modification that challenges the hierarchical distinction between celluloid projection and home-based entertainment.

Where Kipnis argues that we must attend to the discursive nature of technological innovation and the social values accrued to these events, Friedberg identifies the material practices that make up contemporary

cinema as a multimedia event (2000). Friedberg identifies three significant changes in film studies engendered by technological innovation when
she argues that we must add the concept of 'screens' to our critical vocabulary for film, as well as understand film as a 'storage' medium available in various formats (including DVD, online servers, computer disks,
and video), and that spectators should be understood as 'users' rather
than simply spectators of screen culture (2000). Her work emphasises
the spatial and temporal elements of the audiovisual event.

Following Kipnis and Friedberg's suggestions, the study of contemporary cinema is not simply about the content of the image but about
the size and proximity of the screens, projectors, and sound systems that
relay the film as digital data. Such a technological set-up is continually
upgraded, refashioned, and augmented by the industry to produce (and
in response to) changing conditions of consumption. Accordingly, film
scholars must examine these technological transformations and the utopic
promises made by advertisers and producers who promote the technologies as engendering a greater absorption as well as a greater interaction in terms of how one navigates the audiovisual event or stores the
audiovisual material. Increases in DVD rentals, as well as the diver-
sification of display systems offered by laptops, gaming consoles, and
mini-DVD players suggest that the large-scale industrial complex of the
cinema theatre (with its celluloid film and projector) runs parallel to
more micro-cinematic systems. These systems are portable, transform-
able, and easily adopted in private homes, on public transport systems,
and via diverse institutional sites; they also engender the more illicit
culture of DVD ripping, pirating, and online sharing. While technologies of display and reception (and their discursive dimensions) are
central to an architectonics of media, one must also account for the site
of display and reception, that is to say, the exhibitionary conditions
surrounding and producing the media event. To attend to the actual
architecture surrounding and producing the audiovisual experience we
make specific assessments of the nature of these events.

In *Atlas of Emotion* Bruno writes, 'Film is always housed. It needs
more than an apparatus in order to exist as cinema. It needs a space,
a public site – a movie "house." It is by way of architecture that film
turns into cinema' (2002: 44). According to Bruno the public-ness of a
theatrical release (its nature as a collective spectacle, the size of the screen,
etc.) is an integral aspect of transforming film into cinema. For Bruno,
cinema spectatorship is an 'architectural practice' in that different modes
of spectatorship are figured into the architecture of the theatre itself,
so that no film remains the same, but is constantly reconstituted and
brought to life in each singular screening. While Bruno's project is to

connect film spectatorship to other spatio-visual arts (including architecture, painting, and map-making), her emphasis on an architectonics of spectatorship provides a useful model for thinking about the specific differences between each incarnation of *LOTR*. Due to these many manifestations, we must return to the site of spectatorship and consider how different modes of engagement, including the various affects and intensive states available, are generated by the architecture surrounding the screen. Accordingly, an architectonics of the audiovisual event requires mapping how aesthetic, social, and economic forces intersect at the site of sight – so to speak (Bruno 2002: 15). To understand the film event in terms of the relationship between text, site, technologies, and user opens out the critical vocabulary of film studies beyond an interpretive approach dependent upon the discreteness of the film as text. Instead, this method highlights the relationship between the embodied user and the technological and textual set-up with which they form part of an assemblage.

An architectonics of audiovisual culture refers to the space of display (theatre versus home), the technology of display, the nature of the information (digital versus analogue recording), and the navigation through this information, not just the meaning of the film as text. An architectonics of the theatrical version of *Fellowship* includes a description of how the full-scale film screen provides a surface on which the grand sweeping vistas and landscape shots, the detailed sets and costuming, and the colour-graded sequences unfold. It considers how this screen-surface engages the audience who are also enveloped by Dolby surround-soundscapes. This analysis reveals how architectural space generates a double consciousness of absorption *and* distraction where attention constantly oscillates between the large screen and the architecture that houses the screen. This absorbed and distracted mode of engagement is also integral to DVD technologies.

## What a difference a DVD makes

As Cubitt notes in *The Cinema Effect*, since the late 1920s the time of consumption of media product is as central to the workings of capital as the time of production, making a consumer's capacity for absorption and distraction in media events (their attention) a prime commodity (2004: 7–10). One novel aspect of a DVD's architectonics is the way that a consumer is alternately absorbed and distracted by the technological set-up, the space of exhibition, and the textual features of the filmic data itself. At this site of sight we can see the logic of capital at work.

The technological set-up of DVD players often involves home entertainment systems (featuring surround sound speakers and large television screens) that aid the DVD's capacity to induce an absorbing audiovisual environment via high-resolution imagery and high-quality sound reproduction. The user's ability to play the *LOTR* trilogy back-to-back produces an intensive sequence of audiovisual events and transforms the space of consumption (the lounge, the bedroom, the aeroplane) into a cinematic space producing a variety of intensities and experiences of duration. The amount of extended and additional data that is stored on the DVD version contributes to an extension in the time of the trilogy's consumption. This expansion of the trilogy's duration multiplies and opens out the many modes of address the film event is capable of, including an interactive dimension that works against the absorbed mode of engagement produced by the sound and image quality of the digital data.

The material structure of the Special Extended DVD Editions of *LOTR* (their bookish cover design, the complex navigational structure, and the excess information available) accentuates the fact that the user must *do* something with this media package. One must navigate the chapter structure of the DVD menu in order to access the content. One has the option of storing the series on a shelf in a manner resembling a library (the lettering on the spine, the artwork, and the casing encourages this). One must pause or restart viewing in response to changes within the (domestic or otherwise) exhibitionary setting. Users load their disc on a player connected to increasingly hi-tech display and sound systems that accessorise the mise-en-scène of the living room, or the travelling subject (for example, the proliferation of sound speakers in contemporary lounge-room culture or the miniature aeroplane DVD players). These instances of engagement (with the technology itself or the environment in which it is housed) produce a form of interactivity that disrupts and distracts the audiovisual user at the same time as the DVD versions and home entertainment systems promise a more absorbing audiovisual event.

The Special Extended Editions are a form of mobile micro-cinema that combines older media forms (the organising principle of the book chapter, the promise of a theatrical spectacle) with new digital technologies to appeal to a diverse range of consumers and new desiring subjects. When one purchases the series one invests not only in a piece of popular culture but also in a form of high art that provides documental and informational value. This kind of added-value logic is endemic to the consumer impulse that attracts people to the purchase of home entertainment systems. Indeed, promotional materials for DVD and home entertainment systems suggest that the ideals of contemporary audiovision involve a more extended apparatus (which is consistently available

in upgraded formats) of television-set-DVD-player-speakers-special extended version DVD (or other configurations such as Xbox technologies
and computer screens). Consequently, the multi-mediated nature of the
DVD appeals to a vast array of social identities. The computer geek
may be drawn to the technological dimensions of the menu screen (which
invokes the similarly embodied logic of computer gaming), while the
aesthete can admire the artworks on the Platinum Special Extended DVD
Edition as well as the collectible nature of that edition (note the branding
of the collection as platinum) and the taste-formation surrounding Tolkien
the author. The television buff can manufacture a pseudo-televisual flow
by viewing documentary footage, commentaries, and behind-the-scenes
footage back-to-back, while the cinephile can become absorbed by the high
definition rendering and surround-sound of the immersive home entertainment system. This broad-based and yet simultaneously elite appeal
scrambles the received wisdom of consumer identity and suggests more
hybrid and mobile taste formations.

The discursive practices surrounding (and producing) our understanding of DVD technologies articulate the logic of capital characterised
as an endless circuit between production and circulation. As Dyer-
Witheford describes it:

> In production, labor power and means of production (machinery and raw
> materials) are combined to create commodities. In circulation, commodit-
> ies are bought and sold; capital must both sell the goods it has produced,
> realizing the surplus value extracted in production, and purchase the labor
> power and means of production necessary to restart the process over again.
> (1999: 91)

Home entertainment systems demonstrate the centrality of the domestic sphere in the reproduction of capital where audiovisual experience
is a prime site of commodification. The mobile nature of DVD exhibition (via laptop and specialised DVD players) demonstrates how modes
of circulation can be renewed and expanded. In these expanded circuits
of production, consumer attention and time become premium values
and the site where capital kick-starts the cycle of production again. The
Special Extended DVD Edition partakes of this economy of attention
(Crary 1999: 117) in its reconfiguration of older modes of audiovisual
engagement that promise cinematic absorption, fidelity, distraction. At
the same time, this DVD version invites novel responses to new technologies through the click logic of the computer screen and the wealth of
information promised by the database. While Friedberg identifies a 'shift'
from spectator to 'user' due to the proliferation of display and exhibition technologies, I suggest that the Special Extended Editions demonstrate

the productive oscillation that exists between these two possible positions as well as the potential for other modes of engagement along and beyond this arc. This instability is key to the logic of capital that requires diverse and endlessly varying appeals to consumers in order to expand the circuits of consumption. This drive for endless variation suggests a dour prospect perhaps summed up in Kipnis's speculation that 'digital reproduction will most likely simply aid the penetration of new markets by multinational media conglomerates, creating new delivery systems for not-very-new and hardly-very-different images and information' (1998: 597).

However, capital's need for continuous variation also requires that it extend itself in ways that are not totally deterministic. While the Special Extended DVD Editions of *LOTR* illustrate the logic of continuous variation in commodity culture, their status as hybrid media objects (both micro-cinema and database) gestures to the new territories opened up by digital technologies that invite us to rethink questions of spectatorship. By attending to the architectonics of audiovisual culture (the dynamics of exhibitionary space, technology, textuality, and discursive practices) we can map the immanent instabilities of commodity culture that simultaneously produce economies of attention *and* economies of distraction as well as other economies yet to be represented in the field of film study.

# 4

# Cultivating a classic: marketing strategies for the *Lord of the Rings* films

*Suzette Major*

Film marketing is about hype, from the unit publicist who gathers and releases material from the movie, to the movie studio and distributor who design the timing and release strategy and develop an advertising campaign to lure the public to the cinema. Such marketing efforts attempt to build excitement and attract as many people to theatres as possible. Without 'bums on seats', a film cannot recoup its production costs; without a hyped audience, an expensive production cannot achieve a profit. Film marketing is therefore about finding, reaching, and maximising audiences.

What happens, though, to a marketing campaign when a specific audience already exists? Before the unit publicist's pen hits the paper, before a distributor or production company designs the advertising material, before the release date is announced. The *LOTR* film trilogy provides such an example. When *The Fellowship of the Ring* first appeared in 1954 it caused a publishing sensation, soaring to the top of bestseller lists worldwide. It has been voted the Book of the Century in numerous polls, and has sold over a hundred million copies (Braund 2002: 67). *The Lord of the Rings*' devoted fan-base, despite their concerns about the adaptation, meant that the cinematic adaptation was largely pre-sold. Those responsible for marketing *LOTR* had not so much to find this audience as to nurture its appetite and affection.

However, alongside this fan-base existed the broader public. The *Lord of the Rings* devotees were not numerous enough to support a blockbuster hit. The marketers also needed to lure other consumers into the cinema, including those who might not have read the books or even heard of Hobbits. Marketing *LOTR* therefore demanded a two-tiered approach – one for pre-existing fans, another for a larger potential audience. This chapter discusses these parallel marketing strategies, showing how both target audiences were reached and lured into the cinema.

For the existing fan-base target market, the use of the Web was significant, with Jackson and New Line Cinema courting fans of *The Lord of the Rings* largely through their interaction with them online. This online interaction was complemented with more traditional film marketing tactics. These tactics, including film advertising, promotion, and publicity, extended the films' potential audience by appealing to the broader public. *LOTR*'s success rests in part on the careful nurturing of both these target audiences throughout the film marketing process.

Some fans were sceptical about the transfer from print to film and needed convincing that the film trilogy merited their devotion. In fact, in 2000 'the TolkienOnline.com fan site had collected 16,000 virtual signatures petitioning Jackson "not to violate the integrity of Tolkien's work"' (Shefrin 2004: 267). For some 'hobbit-obsessed fans' (Lyman 2001) these books have religious significance. The Internet helped *LOTR*'s promoters to build a bridge to the existing fan base, the size of which was indicated by the '1.7 million downloads the first day' of the *Fellowship* trailer's online release (ibid.). In 2001 the film trilogy's official website, www.lordoftherings.net, was 'simultaneously reinaugurated around the world in ten languages' (ibid.). Features included 'an interactive map of Middle Earth, chat rooms, screen savers, interviews with cast members, [and] links to other' websites dedicated to the trilogy (ibid.). This official website, along with other selected websites, provided a steady diet of images and behind-the-scenes news that attempted to demonstrate that Jackson's interpretation of the classic texts would respect the books' richness and epic scope.

All such material provided teasers to the book fans, who largely became converts to the film version. They were no longer just fans seeking information about their much-loved texts but 'active' fans who could develop a sense of involvement in the filmmaking process and therefore take on a sense of ownership and responsibility for the film's success.

Since the *Lord of the Rings* fans were intimately familiar with the story – typically a key element of a film marketing campaign – *LOTR*'s marketing campaign had to use other elements to generate this potential audience's interest. So the campaign offered up information on casting decisions, the identity of key crew members (such as Lee and Howe, whose close association with the *Lord of the Rings* editions provided some assurance of integrity and 'authenticity'), and Jackson's vision of Middle-earth. The appetite for such inside information was strong for the existing fan base, and also grew for the second target audience – the public at large – as the film marketing campaign developed.

That the two target audiences could not know how all these elements would come together on screen added some piquancy, but the closed-set tactic – keeping some information a surprise – was occasionally troublesome. Throughout filming, locations were kept under wraps. Despite the efforts of many fans to elude security and gain access to filming locations, the visual representation of Middle-earth remained largely secret until the film's release. This exceptionally cautious marketing approach was taken so that, in Jackson's words, 'People [would] really discover the film when it's released, not before' (Harris and Dawtrey 2001: 70).

The closed-set policy extended also to the media. Typically, media professionals are invited on set during filming to capture images and interviews for publicity purposes. For *LOTR*, however, set visits were uncommon (Pryor 2003). While journalists wrote of the unfolding epic that making the film itself became, the look of Middle-earth remained in the imaginative realm until the trilogy's first film had its theatrical release. In this way, there would be an element of surprise, even for the most devoted fan, as the film unreeled on screen.

The marketing efforts' guarded nature also surfaced on the Web. While titbits of information filtered through selected websites, only a few clips appeared prior to the films' release. The challenge was to protect the intrigue, while providing enough material to continually stir fans' interest. As the producer Barrie Osborne explained, 'It's a hard thing because you don't really want too much on the net that takes away from the enjoyment of going to the film for the first time and seeing it revealed before you, so it's always a fight about how much imagery gets let out' (Thompson 2003: 57). Photographs of the shoot exemplify such carefully released marketing material. In 2000, an image of a wizard-like character impaled on a spike was published online. It caused intense debate, with speculation that it could be Gandalf, or the evil-wizard Saruman. Even Sir Ian McKellen added to the discussion, stating on the website that it was not him (NZPA 2001).

Rather than alienate the fans, the film marketers recognised the need to build relationships via the Web – not only to curb rumours but ultimately to create 'Internet evangelists' to help promote the film (Lyman 2001). 'The trilogy's filmmakers decided to be as open as possible with the Tolkien Web sites, going so far as to adopt forty of them' (ibid.). As part of the marketing strategy, 'a strange relationship' was therefore formed 'among the cyber-community of fans, the filmmakers and the studio marketers' (ibid.). Such a strategy is a clear example of 'viral marketing' – an endeavour to get consumers involved in the marketing of the product, giving such fans a sense of privilege while also providing a perceived credence to the marketing efforts (a prospective consumer is more likely to trust another consumer, rather than a production company whose job is to speak highly of the film) (Goldsmith 2002).

The fans' move from passive consumers dieting on select images of the film to active participants who felt connected to the production and marketing process was evident in the two-way communication that emerged online. The Internet offered a unique opportunity for market research in which online discussions 'helped the filmmakers to understand what is most important to Tolkien fans and what sort of departures from the books they would not tolerate' (Lyman 2001). 'Online ferment include[d] nitpicking about casting choices, complaints about script changes and gossip . . . about every nuance of the production' (ibid.). The feedback from such Web-based discussion affected not only the marketing but also the script itself.

The craze that eventuated around Figwit indicates the influence of the two-way Web-based communication associated with *LOTR*. 'Figwit', which stands for 'Frodo is great! Who is that?!', was the name that a fan named Iris Hadad bestowed on the twenty-six-year-old New Zealand musician Bret McKenzie, who featured for all of three seconds in *Fellowship*'s Council of Elrond scene. McKenzie had no lines or close-ups, and could easily have gone unnoticed but for the group of Internet fans who took a liking to his character and eventually established an official Figwit website. Jackson, recognising Figwit's importance to the fans, wrote some lines for him in *Return*. McKenzie even got his own documentary, appropriately titled *Frodo Is Great . . . Who Is That?!!*

This example illustrates the remarkably open and respectful relationship that developed in cyberspace among the fans and the filmmakers. On the one hand, the marketing approach for *LOTR* was cautious and secretive; on the other, it was open and dynamic. In essence, however, while Jackson's discourse with online fans might be seen to illustrate the democratisation of media entertainment by Internet culture, from a marketing standpoint it could be seen as a strategic, carefully manipulated move to win fan approval.

The Web's significance as part of a film marketing strategy is not new; *The Blair Witch Project* led the way in this regard. However, communicating directly with fans via the Web is not customary practice. For example, in contrast with the two-way communicative approach taken by the *LOTR* marketers, Warner Bros attempted to shut down *Harry Potter and the Sorcerer's Stone* fan sites bearing their property's name (Gruner and Lippman nd). For *LOTR*, the choice to work with the Internet fans, rather than against them, converting them from book fans into film fans, seems to have paid off. At the time of the first film's release, there were over four hundred websites devoted to *LOTR*, with several hundred more focusing on other Tolkien-related themes (Lyman 2001).

Traditional film marketing tactics came into play to attract the wider public possibly familiar with the story but unlikely to dress up in Middle-earth costumes. The marketers addressed this larger, non-fan-based public by segmenting them into specific target markets, including a mature audience group who may have read the books years ago, as well as females (particularly under twenty-five) whose interest in the film seemed relatively small (as discussed by Russell Schwartz, president of marketing for New Line: Friedman 2002). Interviews with cast and crew as well as publicity that detailed the story and characters targeted the mature audience group. This strategy helped reacquaint these consumers with the texts. In terms of the female under-twenty-five segment, specific advertising was devised, including, for example, a trailer for *Towers* that omitted the battle scenes and focused on key male cast members. Such trailers and commercials were featured with films and television programmes that were attracting a young female audience, for example, during the television hit *Angel*. As detailed by Thompson (2003), changes to the storyline were also made with this broader audience in mind – at times simplifying the narrative or adding scenes to help explain the story. Thompson's analysis concludes that 'the huge enthusiasm evidenced by millions unfamiliar with the book indicates that the changes the filmmakers made did indeed successfully evoke conventions that appeal to a mass audience' (2003: 53).

For both *The Lord of the Rings* fans and the broader public, a key part of the marketing strategy was to maintain interest over a long period. The marketing push was not for just one film but had a three-film focus, and audiences needed to be peppered with new information throughout the entire trilogy to keep the momentum going. Marketing across the three *LOTR* films required continuity as well as individualised attention to each film. In terms of the design, each film was therefore given a different colour: promotional material for *Fellowship* was in green, *Towers* in burgundy, and *Return* in blue. Images across publicity for the three films were similar, but slightly different. Publicity for *Fellowship* dealt primarily with the actors' experience of primary shooting that went on for over a year in New Zealand, whereas by the third film such stories appeared old-hat. Marketing for *Return* had narrowed to the story itself, rather than the making of the story. *Towers* was particularly interesting, as it could have suffered from middle-child syndrome. The answer to this potential marketing challenge came by way of Gollum – a feat of special effects that kept word-of-mouth interest high. *Towers* was also marketed not as a sequel but as a continuation of the story. Promotional materials for *Towers* did not explain the first film's story. Instead the trailer simply read: 'The fellowship is broken'.

It could have been easier to market one epic film rather than three over a three-year period. Decisions (made as early as 1999) about release dates for the three films rested in part on the shoulders of the film marketers. Implicit to any film marketing is the 'timing and release' strategy: the dates of release and the release pattern. The December release dates, with year-long intervals between each film, were not only crucial from a production standpoint (to allow time for post-production work between each film) but also benefited the marketing campaign. The worldwide day and date release strategy that was negotiated with the twenty-five distributors around the globe added to the hype (Harris and Dawtrey 2001), since this co-ordinated effort meant that fans from New Zealand to Italy saw Jackson's vision of Tolkien's world simultaneously. (The worldwide release date was also driven by the need to prevent piracy of the film.) Fans queued for hours to be part of these momentous screenings. However, while the theatrical release was the first opportunity for the public to see Middle-earth on screen, other privileged individuals got a glimpse of this world during a twenty-five-minute preview at Cannes in May 2001. This preview, consisting of scenes from all three films, provided such excitement that it almost eclipsed the entire film festival. It was a clever and carefully considered moment in the marketing strategy that ensured a series of opinion leaders would help promote the films by spreading positive word of mouth.

As the timing and release strategy is implicit to any film marketing campaign, so are the basics of publicity and promotional material. In common with any film marketing campaign, print media formed a significant part of building the hype for the three films. Publicity timed for each film's release included stories in America's *Entertainment Weekly*, British style magazine *The Face*, London's *Time Out*, and Britain's *Sunday Times*. Some magazines and newspapers devoted entire issues to *LOTR*, with special collectors' editions detailing everything from interviews with the cast and crew to stories on the films' popularity.

As with most blockbusters, tie-in promotions existed for *LOTR*. While opportunities for product placement may be few, fantasy films lend themselves to a broad range of merchandising tie-ins. In particular, tie-ins were negotiated with companies that attract a similar target market, including Burger King, JVC, and Barnes and Noble. The film trilogy has been attached to more than forty licensed products, including toys, games, collectibles, trading cards, and swords (Harris and Dawtrey 2001). Such publicity and promotional strategies are standard for any film marketing campaign. All help build interest in the films, and reap financial benefits for the investors. Returns on the investment can be found also in sell-through opportunities, in particular via the video/DVD market.

**Figure 3** Reverse and front of packaging for the board game *Il Signore degli Anelli*, on sale in the Rome railway station bookshop in October 2004.

Indeed the video/DVD sales for *LOTR* films have broken sales records (Netherby and Larman 2002). As with the release of the cinema version of *Fellowship*, the video/DVD market emphasised timing, creating an event by announcing the 6 August 2002 release date of the videos/DVDs. Many outlets opened at midnight, to be greeted by fans costumed in Middle-earth wear. Echoing the ominous powers of the Ring within the *LOTR* story, the trilogy's power to attract fans to spend copious amounts of money on any memorabilia has been almost unprecedented (Netherby and Larman 2002).

The marketing efforts behind *LOTR* provide us with an opportunity to learn how successfully to market a trilogy of films. For those responsible for marketing the trilogy, it could have been easy to rest on their laurels, aware that without a single word from the marketing team, the film would still attract a large fan audience. Rather than treat these films as undemanding products that required only minimal marketing efforts, though, the marketers addressed every possible marketing angle. Each target market was carefully considered, and then specific campaigns, delivered via appropriate media, set out to make each potential audience member become a definite viewer and possibly a fan. The result was a clever strategic approach that turned fans as well as non-fans of the books into fans of the films – and, in the process, the *LOTR* trilogy has earned a level of devotion and success similar to that which the books have enjoyed for decades.

# 5

# The international reception of *The Lord of the Rings*: case study, Germany

*Stan Jones*

> Generally, then, in light of the continuing global expansion of media and communication companies, as well as the complex issues revolving around the issue of cultural imperialism, especially, there is still a pressing need to study the global reception of media products. (Wasko 2001: 15)

*LOTR*'s success as transnational product – a 'blockbuster made in New Zealand' – is statistically verifiable. While much has been written and spoken about what Jackson and Co. put on screen, one response to *LOTR* is to study what consumers have understood *LOTR* to be. Such a reception study would try to investigate empirically who are the 'viewers', 'audience', 'spectators', 'consumers', and so on of which text under what circumstances and to assess, quantitatively and qualitatively, the ways in which they relate to it.[1] Such a study has been conducted, known simply as The *Lord of the Rings* Research Project (Barker *et al.*).

This chapter looks at the primary level of *LOTR*'s reception. It outlines a methodology, in both macro and micro perspectives, used in a particular research project. Run by teams of academics, as distinct from researchers working for or in any film industry, this project represents a major contribution to reception studies. This team, whose organisational centre has been the University of Wales, Aberystwyth; investigated *Return*'s reception around the world at the moment of its simultaneous global release in December 2003 and continuing to mid-2004. Towards the micro end of the project's spectrum are the conditions in the individual distribution territories, one of which, Germany, forms the case study here.

Such research also has its secondary level, which relates to the public discourse generated by the trilogy: the reviews, interviews, synopses, and background articles published in the media by public intellectuals, critics, reviewers and journalists,[2] and the almost inestimable universe of fan-culture, particularly manifested in websites. This last area is another aspect of the project's 'macro' dimension and requires a prolonged investigation, beyond this chapter's scope. What follows sets out a piece of reception analysis as 'work-in-progress'; although publications authored and edited by members of the international team have appeared in the last two years, most especially *Watching The Lord of the Rings: Tolkien's World Audience* (2008) (edited by Martin Barker and Ernest Mathijs, team leaders of the project as a whole), other data are still being analysed and interpreted.

At the 2003 conference of the New Zealand Studies Association in London, the chief organisers, Martin Barker and Ernest Matthijs, described their project as the largest piece of research into film audiences ever attempted. It has investigated the prefiguration of *Return* for audiences through marketing campaigns that establish discursive frameworks for potential audiences through the media in various territories. It then links these frameworks to the varying reception by a range of audiences, their understanding of the film, and their judgement on it from existing experience as film viewers. It further asks whether this displays patterns that allow us to reach conclusions on the use viewers make of, the gratification they gain from, and what they understand by a piece of cinematic fantasy.

This last function is central to the project, as Barker stresses. 'How do people give meaning to the world via *The Lord of the Rings*? Which elements do viewers from different cultural backgrounds use to connect a 'fantasy' with real world commentary, and how does this process make this 'fantasy' important to their own lives? It is these questions the project wants to test empirically' (Barker 2003: 14). Do the above patterns relate to the film's prefiguration, particularly as audiences seek or reject prior understandings or knowledge; or to viewers' perceived connections between the film and concepts of fantasy, allegory, and myth from other sources, particularly as these might indicate a site of and for imaginings? To this end, the participants consulted on standard questionnaires for assessing prefiguration intended for audiences at the opening and for subsequent follow-up interviews. Individual teams then translated these and adapted them for local territories.

In addition to this 'primary' approach, each team has been collecting and collating 'secondary' material: the promotional publicity from distributors, the press reviews, the trailers on television and the Web, and so on. The project does not, however, set out to identify particular audiences (by implication excluding others), nor does it look for a 'representative sample' from any one audience, nor does it claim any ethnographic significance derived from observing subjects in a defined (and possibly shared) social-historical situation. That is not to say, however, that ethnographical criteria may not be applied to understanding its data.

From nineteen states worldwide,[3] forty-seven researchers have co-operated through a centre at the University of Wales, Aberystwyth. The project's website, www.lordoftheringsresearch.net, offers its most open, public declarations to define the common project. As it explains, 'This is not commercial research. We have met with New Line Cinema and explained what we are doing, but we are completely independent of them'. By implication, the project derives from an interpretive community that is academic and scholarly, at least in so far as it has no precondi-tions, save those that it cares to justify and impose for itself.

One of these is the declared intention to publish results, hence the project's underlying premise – 'this is pure research' – that is, without a declared application or restriction, with the implication that the group producing it understands itself as independently defining its own nature and its own premises. The international project can also be seen, in its broadest perspective, as an exercise that could indicate the relative 'polit-ical economy' of such research globally, particularly as this affirms the fundamental civic freedom to conduct such research and the democratic right to publish it and peruse it through both local and global media.

The convenors consulted the international research team to draw up an initial questionnaire, which was then translated and adapted for local circumstances in the various territories. It was put to cinema audiences simultaneously with the film's global release on 17 December 2003. The final stage saw more detailed data being sought from individuals and conference groups drawn from those sampled. In addition, until June 2004 the website displayed a detailed formal questionnaire in a range of languages. Its questions prompted respondents to identify themselves within a range of possible responses to the film. They could go on to explain what the position they allotted themselves actually meant to them. Multiple-choice categories of response appeared as a quantitative meas-ure, charting how much pleasure the viewer derived from the film and the perceived importance of seeing it, relating these to the perceived nature of the fantasy it constructs.

For this latter response, the interviewees got a series of terms to which they could assent, but also a follow-up question on the terms that they would reject. Structuring the questions in this way also allowed responses to be sorted by their country of origin. Imaginary geographies then figured in the question, 'Where is Middle-earth?' as well as further questions related broadly to influences outside the film that may have raised expec-tations about it and invited open-ended evaluations of it. Apart from its value in itself, this last function served to cross-check on whether the categories of response offered were, arguably, leading respondents. Treating the explanatory responses as a discourse about the film also meant that recurrent ways of talking about the experience showed up and could be traced across the categories initially advanced to see how they specified them and/or how they spread across several.

When the questionnaire was trialled, respondents' expectation of what questions they might get in such an exercise led to the inclusion of a question about a favourite character, thus modifying the researchers' concept by anticipating one of their subjects' possible interests.

The follow-up interviews aimed at expanding on the initial responses gained on the night of viewing by more open-ended, qualitative questions enquiring further into the social situation of the cinema visit; into intertextual associations, particularly for respondents declaring an interest in the book and/or actively seeking supplementary information about the film; into the nature of any cultural capital derived from knowledge of such 'lore'; into any evaluation of the film as an adaptation of literature; and as a stimulus for their imagination, particularly as this related to identification with any given character. The final stage of research invited speculation on the significance of the film over time and of its meaning as a blockbuster, the experience of which the interviewee shared with millions of other viewers in different cultures. In this way the follow-up returned to the initial invitation to assign oneself to a category as member of its audience. The final, formal stage of the project involved a conference in Wales in December 2004 together with publications in various forms and various languages by the participants.

Such a scale and range of investigation combines macro and micro dimensions of reception. The macro has these perspectives: 'The culturally variegated nature of spectatorship derives from the diverse locations in which films are received, from the temporal gaps of seeing films in different historical moments, and from the conflictual subject-positionings and community affiliations of the spectators themselves' (Shohat and Stam 1994: 347). To analyse it will require initially the completed analysis from each territory of its own micro dimension, the data collected locally. The micro, therefore, derives from a particular cinematic version distributed and its reception in particular sites at particular times. The next step would move towards the macro by matching data, given each research group's particular approaches, and then integrating their interpretations cross-culturally. This work remains ongoing.

In Germany, three groups were formed from university staff and students: one at the Hochschule für Film und Fernsehen, Potsdam (HFF); one at the University of Halle-Wittenberg; and one at the Hans-Bredow

**Figure 4** *Herr der Ringe* banner and Unter den Linden street sign (Berlin).

Institut, in the University of Hamburg. Their respondents saw the film almost exclusively in its German-language release, although it was shown in larger centres, such as Berlin, in English.

The Potsdam team, led by Professor Lothar Mikos and Dr Elizabeth Prommer, has based its approach on its 'Babelsberger Modell' for media research. This model aims to investigate any given text as a comprehensive media phenomenon by combining an aesthetic product analysis with reception study and discourse analysis in seeking to interpret current media development (convergence, cross-media) and wider social or cultural significance. It has been applied notably to the television series *Big Brother* (Mikos 2000).

The international *LOTR* project, using the 'Modell', integrates into a wider study that the Potsdam group conducted through a graduate seminar on the entire trilogy and related texts, such as additional material from DVD and video releases, and in games adaptations. Its specific aspects include film analysis, computer game analysis, marketing, reception analysis, fansites, discourse analysis (commentary on the film and the games), and the overall context, which itself breaks down into the literary history of the original text, fan cultures, and blockbuster marketing across media. The team has published its results in *Die 'Herr der*

*Ringe' – Trilogie: Attraktion und Faszination eines populärkulturellen Phänomens* (Mikos *et al.* 2007).

To focus on *Return*, the German team designed modules comparable to the international project to be applied in four steps.

First, a survey was conducted in three waves of marketing and of potential viewers' level of anticipation at ten, six, and two weeks before the film opened on 17 December 2003.[4] The Gesellschaft für Sozialforschung und statistische Analysen GmbH (The Society for Social Research and Statistical Analyses), or 'Forsa' (www.forsa.de/), a professional market-research organisation, conducted this survey through telephone polling of three batches of one thousand respondents (fourteen years plus) across the entire Federal Republic. This survey aimed to test the assumption that viewers were more ready to see the film because of its marketing. It asked four questions that established the frequency of cinema-going and then focused on reasons for anticipating *Return* via anticipation of nominated films due for distribution at the same time in Germany: *The Matrix Revolutions, The Return of the King, Scary Movie 3, Finding Nemo, Kill Bill, Luther, Das Wunder von Bern/The Miracle of Bern*, and *Pirates of the Caribbean*.

Second, with reference to the initial questionnaire, students used a version of the standard form translated and adapted for local circumstances. This locally specific version omits, for instance, any correlation of names and addresses with responses as this may breach local privacy laws and is potentially controversial in German public culture. A first questionnaire interviewed three hundred cinemagoers on the film's first weekend. In addition, it was put to 'total fans', the audience for a full showing of the entire trilogy in the night of 16–17 December 2003 (known as 'Trilogy Tuesday' in the States). In accordance with the 'Modell', it deviated from the purpose of the original questionnaire in attempting to gain a 'representative sample' of the film's audience in its first week in Germany.

Third, in light of the above, the Potsdam team opted for follow-up through focus group sessions from among willing respondents rather than individual interviews.

The fourth step involves responses to the German version of the project's online questionnaire.

Here, the macro implications of cross-cultural comparison contained in the entire project appear in a micro dimension through the mutations attendant on translation. For instance, the relatively open-ended English formulation – What did you think of the film? – becomes a much more leading question in German about how the respondent liked the film. Accordingly, the sequence of responses modifies the English descriptive hierarchy, which suggests it was 'enjoyable' to various degrees (or not), to suggest in German a point on a scale of liking (or not). The English formulation connotes prior understanding of an 'enjoyment factor' that might be expected from any viewer – or not. In contrast, the German connotes the gauging of a much more personal experience with far less implied reference to any norm. Where respondents are then asked to allot *Return* a genre definition, the English limits the choices to three from a list of twelve (with the controlling alternative of choosing not to choose any). The German version has no limitation, and it indicates the German cultural context in some of its terms, such as *Märchen* for 'fairytale' or *Suche* for 'quest'. The former is a specialised literary form in German, so that German commentators tend to prefer using the original English for their understanding of this aspect of the film.[5] The latter has the wider connotations of a 'search' in English, so that German respondents, prompted by the context of the questionnaire, have potentially to shift their response an extra step to the fictional narrative context where 'quest' already belongs. The German categories retain several English expressions, such as 'special effects film' for 'SFX', and 'game-world', indicating the adoption of English terms into German popular discourse about the media. A major shift of reference and emphasis marks a question on 'expectations and hopes' about the film on the basis of any previous experience. The German version shifts its expectations of its respondents to a narrower concern with the film itself and offers among its categories for response the German *Alltag* for the English 'the real world'. The former is a much more limited category and refers to what is meant in English by the 'everyday' (the 'real world' can, of course, be in certain circumstances the direct opposite of the everyday). Similarly, the German version of the English question on the 'most memorable thing' about the film refers to a German *Detail* of it, again guiding the response more closely.

More precise thought is also introduced where an enquiry about the experience of viewing as a 'social event' – *Ereignis* in German – requires respondents to determine a category of event before expressing their evaluation of it. And the very open-ended invitation to add anything indicating respondents' 'feelings' on the film becomes in the German version more restricted to the *Emotionen* and precludes any evaluative statements.

As such a questionnaire inevitably prompts its respondents and reveals much about the assumptions of its compilers, the prompting and assumptions revealed through comparison of the Web versions translated into the different languages from the original English source might well be correlated with other cross-cultural findings from the project as a whole.

It may be necessary to separate the responses from the website from those gained by the teams in Germany when using either set of results for cross-cultural comparisons.

The results of the research commissioned from 'Forsa' on prefiguration imply, in the responses to its first question about frequency of cinemagoing, a pretty parlous state in Germany. Across the three waves of questioning, the largest category (29 per cent) of cinemagoers specified one or two visits per year, and was matched at 25 per cent by people simply declaring that they either never went or had not been in years. *Return*'s success in Germany was immediately clear from the two questions on planned viewing among a selection of mainline releases, as it was consistently twice as popular as its nearest rival, *Finding Nemo*, winding up with 45 per cent of declared intentions two weeks out from the premiere. Yet, once again the result needs to be seen in the perspective of the second highest finding at 29 per cent: those declaring they would not anticipate seeing any of the choices. Finally, the pitch of the question shifted towards a more qualitative implication by proposing a number of reasons for seeing the film: being a *The Lord of the Rings* fan; the adaptation from the novel; the frequency of reporting on it; interesting publicity; none of these. Here the book figured narrowly over the fan identity, while a surprising proportion of respondents (13 per cent) did not admit to any of the categories offered, or, at 10 per cent, just did not know! It may be that some fans prefer the cultural cachet of identifying as a Tolkien reader over a fan, while almost a quarter of the respondents remain a blank on the map, at least as far as the prefiguration exercise went.

The team at the University of Halle-Wittenberg also integrates the international project into a wider graduate seminar on the trilogy. As Totosy de Zepetnek sets it out: 'Course work includes readings in audience studies, scholarship about Tolkien and the Ring books, the design of and fieldwork with an audience questionnaire, and evaluation of the questionnaire data' (2004).[6] In contrast to the Potsdam approach, the seminar emphasises the trilogy's production history and the related questions of the 'Englishness' of the fantasy, the associations with New Zealand attached to the film, and the overarching debates about 'cultural imperialism', the 'americanisation of culture', the 'colonisation of the imagination' (ibid.). These criteria derive from his wide-ranging view of such research, as defined in his 'Toward a Framework of Audience Studies': 'Audience studies is about the what, when, where, who, why, and how of a culture product or products' (Totosy de Zepetnek 2000). Closer definitions for the guiding criteria applied by the Halle-Wittenberg team appear at the same site. The questionnaire used is identical with the German version on the project's website, but the scope of the survey in Halle-Wittenberg is more restricted than that from Potsdam, as the team did not conduct a 'prefiguration' survey or follow-up interviews. Their project illustrates a macro concept of cultural studies developed in US academic culture being applied to a working seminar in a German university and to the micro dimension within it of the specialist reception research generating a contribution to the international project.

From the New Zealand perspective, a preliminary survey of their results so far displays an intriguing, if not entirely unexpected response on the location of 'Mittelerde' (Middle-earth) in time and space. The European viewpoint predominates in the frequent identification of the Middle Ages, combined with one specific reference to Ireland, one to France ('the land of knights and castles'), and one to Wales. A surprising deviation can even specify 'Central Europe in the twentieth century', presumably confusing the potential allegory with its setting, and another the Near East (as seen from Europe, of course). New Zealand figures in one comment on the way the film generates a 'Paralleluniversum' (parallel universe) but then perceptively qualifies it by pointing to the inevitable NZ identity attached to what the viewers know of the 'making of'. Time and place can, however, come together bizarrely in two responses specifying New Zealand and the Middle Ages or the seventeenth century. These indicate the inscription of a European imagination on the New Zealand landscape, an aspect of the film that still awaits overall analysis from this reception project.

The approaches of the German teams and their eventual results may contribute to a wider debate among all the participants about the nature of such research and identity politics involved in the 'interpretive communities' of academics who conduct it. As to the 'text' of the trilogy, the German reception should illustrate a process described by Hedetoft: 'This reframing process – a constant interaction between acknowledging the 'foreignness' . . . of the film and relating to it through reinterpretation – can entail more or less radical reactions to and departures from the 'original' set of meanings and messages embedded in the text. In other words, the hybrid third can be more or less alienated from the original product' (2000: 282). To risk a final, macro speculation: To the extent that the evidence is comparable across the territories covered, the international reception project may allow us eventually to discern the transnational blockbuster in the entire phenomenon as a point of reference for understanding what we mean by 'global media'.

## Notes

1　For a history of such research see Gripsrud 1998.
2　How the trilogy is generating increasingly ramified discourse appears markedly in a recent collection published in Germany (Vossen 2004).
3　New Zealand, the UK, Australia, Austria, Belgium, Canada, China, Columbia, Denmark, France, Germany, Greece, Italy, Netherlands, Russia, Slovenia, Spain, Turkey, and the USA.
4　On 10 December, *Return* had its European premiere in Berlin, presumably as a result of the German interest in its financing. However, the highly selective 'audience' for such an event scarcely merited sampling for the international project.
5　I base this assertion on discussions in Professor Mikos's graduate seminar at the HFF, Potsdam.
6　See his definition of his methodological foundations: 'The theoretical and methodological bases in these studies are developed from the systemic and empirical approach to literature and culture as introduced and applied in various fields in the humanities and social sciences', in Steven Totosy de Zepetnek (1998) *Comparative Literature: Theory, Method, Application.* Rodopi, Amsterdam.

　　See also his concept of 'Comparative Cultural Studies' in 'Constructivism and Comparative Cultural Studies' at http://clcwebjournal.lib.purdue.edu/library/totosy(constructivism).html.

　　I am grateful to Professor Lothar Mikos, Dr Elizabeth Prommer, and their students at the HFF, Potsdam, for their collegial and kind acceptance of me into their *Lord of the Rings* graduate seminar. I also thank Professor Steven de Totosy Zepetnek, University of Halle-Wittenberg and editor of *CLCWeb: Comparative Literature and Culture: A WWWeb Journal*, for his ready co-operation and advice.

# 6

# *The Return of the King* and the child audience

*Geoff Lealand*

How do you turn a dumb kiddie story into an 'epic quest'? Make it big, make it long, and make it three times. (Australian *Mad* magazine 400, 2003)

*New York Times* reviewer Peter Nichols offers the following parental guidance for *Return* in his 'Taking the Children' column:

VIOLENCE Combatants are graphically hacked, clubbed, skewered, burned and otherwise slaughtered and maimed. Now it's all pretty routine.
SEX None
PROFANITY Exclamations but no cusses.
For Which Children?
Ages 8–10 Areas of parental objection might logically include the extreme violence and, to a lesser extent, the movie's length. That said, many kids will be fine throughout an entertainment with many engaging characters to follow or root for.
Ages 11–13 *Unless parents have objections, the film is a natural.*
(26 December 2003: B26; emphasis added)

In the United States, *Return* received a PG-13 rating from the Motion Picture Association of America (MPAA), with the accompanying note, 'Parents strongly cautioned'. An alternative rating of A-III (Adults) was bestowed by the United States Conference of Catholic Bishops, while the Christian on line site www.decentfilms.com provided an A+ Overall Recommendation, four stars for Artistic and Entertainment Value, and a positive 1.5 rating for Moral and Spiritual Value. An accompanying note reads, 'Some depictions of intense and sometimes bloody battle violence; scenes of menace and grotesquerie involving orcs and goblins and other "fell creatures"; a single crude expression' (www.decentfilms. com/reviews/lordoftherings3.html, accessed 20 January 2004). Despite these reservations, the film is lauded as 'the grandest spectacle ever filmed'.

In the United Kingdom, *Return* received a 12A from the British Board of Film Classification (BBFC), a classification meaning that it should not be seen by anyone younger than twelve unless accompanied by an adult. The first two films had received PG (Parental Guidance) certificates. Notes accompanying the 2003 classification indicated that the film contained 'intense battle violence and horror scenes'. The BBFC 'placed this work in the FANTASY genre(s)' and no cuts to the running time were made. In December 2003, multiple prints of the film were distributed across the United Kingdom with this 12A certification, and the only voice of dissent was an inconclusive controversy in Henley-on-Thames, where the South Oxfordshire District Council threatened to raise the entry age to screenings of *Return* at the Regal Cinema to fifteen years. The same council, in its 'role as guardians of public morals', was one of the first to ban Stanley Kubrick's A *Clockwork Orange* in the 1970s ('Under-15s').

In respect of a New Zealand classification, the Chief Censor followed the usual practice of replicating either the UK or Australian rating, in that 'if a film has been rated M or lower in the UK or Australia, then the Labelling Body simply issues the New Zealand equivalent rating. Such a film does not have to be examined here' (Bill Hastings, email to author, 17 November 2003). The Office of Film and Literature Classification (OFLC) placed an M15+ Recommended for Mature Audiences 15 Years and Over rating on *Return*.

These variable ratings suggest that regulators around the world had quite different views on the suitability of the third film for young audiences, as well as expressing different notions of where childhood terminates. Most Western societies generally regard the threshold in the shift from 'child' to 'adolescent' or 'teenager' to be twelve years, even though numerous legal definitions rest on ideas of dependency that often extend the status into the teen years. The United Nations definition of childhood, for example, regards it as the life-stage that extends from birth to eighteen years.

These competing definitions of 'child' and 'childhood' mirror the confusion and ambiguity that characterise children's lives these days, challenging the nineteenth-century invention of the child as inhabiting a pre-adult and dependent state of innocence. New marketing categories arise called 'tweenies', 'aspirational culture', and the like. Across the globe, many hundreds of thousands (and possibly, millions) of children have seen *Return*, and the two earlier films – despite the rulings and cautions provided by various film censors. Those who were twelve years old at the release of *Fellowship* could more legitimately go to *Return*. There are no official records attesting to this (cinema chains do not generally collect information on the demographic characteristics of their audience), but observation of cinema queues and other anecdotal evidence indicates that a substantial slice of the global audience for *Return* has been of hobbit height.

These children appear usually to have been shepherded to the cinema by parents, grandparents, or older siblings. Despite the mountains of publicity and discussion about Jackson and the trilogy, little attention has been paid to this child audience. Are these films – *Return* in particular – suitable for children? Are they for children or adults, or both? Are children going to the films voluntarily, or because their parents want them to? Do children understand the films differently than do adults?

Answers (partial) will be tempered by the usual problems associated with understanding the social, psychological, and symbolic dimensions of filmgoing. The film audience is a group of strangers who gather together at an appointed place and appointed time, for a short-lived communal experience; then they disperse back into their private lives and personal spaces. The child film audience – often noisier and more restless – is even more elusive. In most cases, their attendance at films depends on the favour of their elders.

Adults shape and control the child viewer's experience of *LOTR*. The three films are the result of a grown-up view of the world (fantastic and real worlds), and adult worlds of film financing, production, distribution, marketing, and merchandising. The public discourse about *LOTR* has made only brief incursions into forms of children's culture – most usually as gushy profiles of the younger stars such as Elijah Wood and Liv Tyler.

Children are not prominent in the *LOTR* films; they are occasionally seen clinging to the skirts of mothers, or fleeing from looming danger. On one of the rare occasions when they are acknowledged, in *Towers*, boy soldiers are pressed into service for the defence of Helm's Deep ('old men and boys'), with Aragorn reassuring one particularly frightened boy about the potential strength of his sword arm.

The Hobbits, by default, represent ideas of children and childhood in the films. The first film introduces the Hobbits as bucolic innocents, childlike in their pleasures and daily enjoyment of a Brueghel-inspired utopia. They are more emphatically childlike than the quasi-adult Hobbits of Tolkien's books. As one British fan argues: 'The portrayal of the hobbits in the film is at odds with their description in the three books. They are not youth, nor are they children. Tolkien portrays them as adults, albeit within their own world. The hobbits are, however, naïve, and it is this naivety that gives them their childlike quality' (Chesters 2004). In their adventures, the Hobbits are beholden to those figures that loom above them (Gandalf, Aragorn) and, within the rigid social structure of Middle-earth, the Hobbit-as-child occupies various forms of dependency or servitude. They inhabit an adult world where the presence of children poses a risk, through their mere presence, or mischief-making (letting off fireworks in *Fellowship*), or dangerous curiosity (Pippin stealing a globe and gazing on Sauron's eye).

Despite their extended life-span, the Hobbits' coming to adulthood is less determined by the accumulation of years than by the getting of wisdom, and wisdom, it seems, comes only as a result of experiences beyond the Shire. Life within the Shire, as Jackson portrays it, is a prolonged state of childhood innocence and immediate gratification, perpetually sunny days where evil is unknown and the outside world a mystery to be avoided. In many ways, Frodo and Sam's physically fraught journey from the Shire to Mount Doom is their journey from childhood (and, indeed, childishness) to adulthood. As with many such journeys, something is lost (innocence, purity, community) and something is gained (self-knowledge, courage, fraternity). However, the loss of sexual innocence that is the core theme of similar contemporary coming-of-age tales is absent in *LOTR*.

### Suitable for children?

Internationally, various censorship bodies, through their rulings, have expressed some reservations about the suitability of *LOTR* (*Return* in particular) for the child audience. Nevertheless, there has been little commentary on the legitimacy or justification of these rulings. Most parents seem to have regarded the films' content, spirit, and messages as acceptable for those in their care. There has been, for example, little of the criticism that other media texts have attracted from parents and advocacy groups around the world. Explanations for this may include the following:

#### Film is better than television
Most of such criticism (of violent content, and the potential for imitation; excessive merchandising) has been directed at television programmes, and most particularly at animated programmes. Recent targets of disapproval include *Teenage Mutant Ninja Turtles*, *South Park*, and *Pokemon*, with commonplace complaints about excessive violence and relentless marketing.

In contemporary canons of middle-class taste, film retains a stature rarely bestowed on television and, more recently, videogames. Likewise, 'children's film' has a ring of greater acceptability than 'children's television', and the cultural standing of *film-based* children's animation has been reinforced by the success of *Shrek*, *Toy Story*, and *Finding Nemo*. Live-action films such as the Harry Potter series and *The Pirates of the Caribbean* further cement parental approval of contemporary children's films.

### Because parents like them . . .

Both Tolkien and the *LOTR* trilogy benefit from the 'inheritance' factor: the desire of many parents to pass on their enthusiasm for Tolkien's heady mixture of fantasy and repudiation of modernity to their offspring. It is not just bequeathing beloved books; it is also dreams of a pre-industrial utopia.

The faux-historical and mythological foundations along with Jackson's reworking of Tolkien's worlds provide further attractions for parents. Gould, discussing the intense interest in dinosaurs by many children (boys, in particular), quotes the child psychologist Sheldon White's explanation. Dinosaurs are hugely popular because they are 'big, fierce, and extinct' (www.motherjones.com/mother_jones/JF97/outspoken_jump,html). Parental approval of this interest (which often reaches a fever pitch between the ages of four to ten years) may rest on the aura of science and history that surrounds dinosaurs. The assumption seems to be: This is not fantasy, it is palaeontology. Contemporary culture is filled with fantasies of dinosaurs (from *Jurassic Park* to *Barney*), despite very flimsy evidence about their appearance, their vocal abilities, and their behaviour. Fossils tell us nothing, for example, about the skin colours or exoskeletons of dinosaurs.

### Death by sword, mace, or arrow

Tolkien's orcs and trolls, and Jackson's Oliphaunts and flying dragons are close relatives of the dinosaurs; both inhabit bloody tooth-and-claw worlds of kill or be killed. The website www.kids-in-mind.com chronicles in detail the world *Return* portrays. Among examples of death, dismemberment, and damage,

> Orcs take aim with arrows and let them fly . . . Dismembered heads are catapulted over a stone wall . . . Large bits of a stone structure are launched into crowds of Orcs and we hear crunching when they hit and crush them . . . we see Orcs biting their victims, and we see hyena-like creatures tearing and biting at victims . . . swords clank and slash, some characters are run through, some are slashed, some are hacked. (www.kids-in-mind.com/l/lordoftheringsreturnoftheking.htm)

I am not arguing for a crude effects model that claims that violent content in fictional texts leads to imitative, violent behaviour. I mean instead to point out the inconsistencies and ambiguities in responses to different forms of fictional violence. Images of bloody death by sword thrust, or the mangling of flesh and bone by mace or club is more acceptable, it seems, than representations of death by cluster bombs or handgun. This curious inconsistency allows boys to play with pretend swords and spears in the playground, but bans the use of toy guns. The same attitude prompted *LOTR*'s props designers to expend enormous energy on making their weapons – both large and small – as 'authentic' and potentially lethal as possible. The faux-historical framework of Tolkien and Jackson's worlds softens and romanticises the brutality and suffering of violent conflict. It has all become 'pretty routine' (Nichols 2003).

## A child's eye on *LOTR*

This is not to suggest that child viewers of *LOTR* – and of the bloodiest, third part of the trilogy – will have recoiled from the violent content while their elders wallowed in it. Adults and children cheered in unison in New Zealand cinemas when Aragorn beheads the chief orc following Boromir's death in *Fellowship*. The usual parental concerns and official prohibitions and cautions customarily accompanying representations of violence in contemporary cultural texts have not been invoked for *LOTR*.

Instead, parents have led their children to the films, hoping the films might in turn lead the children to the books. Meanwhile, book publishers hope that the films will lead readers not just to the popular publications (such as film spin-offs and guides) in the films' wake but also to the bulging shelves of new editions, reprints, and semi-scholarly works. Most of this material, though, targets older rather than tyro readers.

The price and marketing of the film-associated merchandise suggests that they target adults who like to collect and acquire. In fact, very little child-related merchandising has accompanied the films, in contrast with the Harry Potter films, which came with an onslaught of promotions for chocolates, stuffed toys, pillowcases, and clothing.

To find out more about child filmgoers, I conducted small-scale field research in October 2003, in advance of the New Zealand release of *Return*. First, I spent a morning with Room 8 at Hamilton East Primary School. Of thirty children, aged nine to ten years, 25 had seen *Fellowship* and 23 had seen *Towers*. Sixteen had a video or DVD copy of one film at home, and ten had copies of both films. Legolas was the favourite character in the films, followed by Aragorn and Gollum. More children (17) regarded the films as being 'made for adults' than 'made for children' (6) or 'both' (9). Most (26) considered *LOTR* to be 'New Zealand films'.

**Figure 5a** Logan's drawing of Gimli.

**Figure 5b** Catherine Rose's drawing of Legolas, with tree.

Following a semi-structured discussion, the children drew characters from the films. Initially, they were asked to draw their 'favourite character' and 'the scariest character' but time constraints and the inordinate care many children lavished on their drawings meant that most of

**Figure 5c** Hayley's drawing of Aragorn.

them did a solitary drawing. Several examples of drawings, provided here, show the attention to detail and proportion – despite the children having nothing to copy from, or guidance from their teacher or me. Drawings by several Korean girls display a particularly interesting blend of characterisation and religiosity.

Following this exercise, which provided evidence that the films were very familiar to these children, I spent two hours with brothers Marc (ten) and Jonathan (twelve), and their cousin Mitchell (ten) as they spent Saturday morning, as they regularly do, re-enacting *LOTR* battles in suburban Hamilton. Thick bush on the approaches to an overpass became Mirkwood, and the road that passes underneath became Mordor. Armed with home-made swords, bow-and-arrows, and favourite sticks, the three boys acted out 'the kind of things where people get their heads cut off'. They drew off repeated playbacks of *LOTR*. 'We have seen both films at least twenty times. We interrupt the tape and fast-forward to the best bits, such as the death of Boromir and the Battle of Helm's Deep. We could probably tell you the entire plot.'

None of the boys had read far into the books. 'Our father read the first book to us and *The Hobbit*. But we really didn't pay attention.

**Figure 6** Two boys playing with sticks, bows, and arrows.

The films are so much realer [*sic*]!' Their interest in role-playing began with *Star Wars* re-enactments until 'medieval dramas took our hearts'. They had little interest in Harry Potter and other fantasy material, which they regarded as being 'for younger kids'.

No hurt nor harm seemed to result from their battles, while their parents looked upon their activities with amused tolerance. Neither do I condemn their imaginative play, but I do wonder whether, if it were replica guns rather than swords they were playing with, there might have been a different response.

For all their methodological limitations, these two research exercises do suggest that many young New Zealanders have invested a great deal in the *LOTR* trilogy. They share a sense of ownership with their elders but it is a claim to ownership that has less to do with appeals to nationalism, nor fandom. Instead, there is an incorporation of such fantasy texts into their private – but also shared – culture of childhood.

# Part II

# Creative industries / national heroes

# 7

# Dossier: economics

*Sean Cubitt and Barry King*

In this section, Danny Butt and Deborah Jones contextualise Peter Jackson and *LOTR* in terms of creative industries and cultural capital, while Thierry Jutel looks more particularly at how similar Jackson is to one of his own creations.

When Ruth Harley became the NZFC's CEO in 1997, she spoke of cultural capital as part of an argument that could persuade the government that it should invest in creative industries for its own benefit.[1] She was responding to years of government policy committed to economic concerns as its alpha and omega. Since then, and with a different political party in control, the government has bought into the value of creative industries for the national economy. Industry New Zealand, Investment New Zealand, New Zealand Trade and Enterprise, New Zealand's ambassadorial and consular offices around the world: these government offices and more have worked ever more co-operatively together in promoting, among others, the screen industries of this country, both at home and abroad.

While Butt warns of the fragile nature of this economic success, Deborah Jones examines 'Peter Jackson' in terms of national identity. 'Jackson figures largely as an entrepreneur in the "Frodo economy", as a promoter of "Brand New Zealand", and as a patriot and exemplary New Zealander', she writes. This image of Jackson received a boost in 1999, when he purchased the post-production facilities established by the defunct National Film Unit from its then owner, TVNZ. At the time, he said that he was doing so in order to keep the facility and its adjuncts in New Zealand hands. Since then he has developed the facility, then called The Film Unit, and moved it to Miramar, the Wellington suburb where his other film-related interests are located. Park Road Post, this facility's latest incarnation, is an internationally successful, state-of-the-art post-production house.

Jutel also looks at Jackson himself, examining his career and situating *LOTR* within it. For Jutel, *Forgotten Silver* – a mockumentary that

**Figure 7** Galadriel's light as a party favour from The Film Unit.

by and large successfully presented itself as the real story of an unknown but pioneering New Zealand filmmaker – reveals as much about Jackson as its reception revealed about its (initial) New Zealand audience. For those of us who watched its original screening during a Sunday prime time slot, it was the sort of experience to discuss in terms of when we 'got it' – and it was a matter of pride to claim that we had indeed gotten it, since so many people so publicly embarrassed themselves by not getting it.[2] *Forgotten Silver* has since become available to international audiences, who have received it well; the NZFC has even incorporated bits of it in some of its material for promoting New Zealand cinema.

One of the most immediate ways in which *LOTR* could benefit the New Zealand economy was to provide employment for an astonishing number of people, as it did, all across the country. However, Jackson's employment record is not untroubled. The Bryson versus Three Foot Six case, as to whether a particular person was legally an employee or a contractor, was settled against Weta in 2005 (Sorrell 2005); its repercussions for labour policy in Aotearoa New Zealand remain to be seen. Stories abound of Wellington-based technicians working non-stop for months on end, trying to keep up with Jackson's own example. At the same time that anyone and everyone seemed to want somehow to join the *LOTR* bandwagon, locals gritted their teeth at a story going the rounds that some of the Californians working on the project referred to Kiwis as 'Mexicans with cellphones'.

'The movie business is a business of extremes. Its participants seem to occupy a third world country where the winners live in palaces and the losers live in slums. Virtually all the statistical measures of the business are dominated by extreme events' (De Vany 2004: 211). The very lack of predictability attracts many individuals to the business; it is also the factor that for the lucky few creates a winner-take-all texture of wealth accumulation (Frank and Cook 1995). In a winner-take-all market, the differences in talent between those who succeed and those who fail are likely to be small but the rewards going to different individuals are likely to show a large variation.

This inequality in reward has a cultural effect that legitimates the very inequality it creates. In a normal field of employment, the compensation that participants receive tends to fall in a common range that creates an average level of earnings. As a result, participants bring complementary and matched talents. In the movie business, upwards of 70 per cent or more of total compensation goes to a small number of participants, a concentration that tempts one to see differences between the few and the many as deriving from the unique personal qualities of those who are highly rewarded. Yet the material reality is that motion picture production is intrinsically a collective endeavour in which one person's contribution, however strategic, relies on others' inputs.

At the height of filming, *LOTR*, with its overall production budget of close to NZ$500 million, was directly responsible for 23,000 film industry jobs – actors, writers, film crew – as well as jobs in the building, accommodation, and catering industries (Hufstutter 2003). Although the exact earnings of key participants is unknown (and unlikely to be revealed), some scattered references suggest that the scale of the disparity between earnings of the leading actors and other above-the-line participants was pronounced – to say nothing of the disparity between these fortunate few and the rank and file production workers. At the epic earnings end of the scale, Jackson was reported as receiving a salary of NZ$10 million and 5 per cent of the gross receipts (Catherall 2002). Jackson also received 7.5 per cent of the gross profits of DVD sales and his share of gross ticket receipts moved to 7.5 per cent for the third film. Worldwide, *LOTR* had generated over US$4 billion by mid-2004. It was reported that Jackson received more than US$125 million from the trilogy and associated merchandising (Pulley 2004).

The New Zealand Rich List, published by the *National Business Review*, estimated Jackson's wealth in 2004 as NZ$148 million, up from an estimated NZ$40 million in 2002 (Masters and Hoby 2002; Gill 2004). Other participants were not so fortunate. Sean Astin reports receiving US$250,000 for the three films and though this would have increased with bonuses it pales besides Jackson's take (Astin 2004: 79). Cate Blanchett, who worked for only three weeks and received sixth billing on the credits for each film in the trilogy, is rumoured to have received a fee of US$1million (Smith and Matthews 2004: 101). The fees for leading actors such as Elijah Wood and Ian McKellen are unknown. It seems unlikely that McKellen, following on his *X-Men* success, would have received less than Blanchett, especially given his greater involvement. McKellen is likely to have had some profit participation but this was by no means a universal provision for leading players. When eighteen leading cast members, unnamed because of confidentiality clauses in their contracts, staged a bonus pay revolt because bonus payments for promotion and premiere work on the second film were smaller than on the first, it became known that some actors did not have profit participation deals (BBC 2005). A further dimension of inequality, as the Cate Blanchett example suggests, was time commitment. Liv Tyler, for example, found her involvement extended finally to four and a half years (Davies 2003).

At the other extreme, *LOTR* extras were paid NZ$200 a day and meal allowances, which one international film consultant said was close to slave labour if compared to Hollywood rates. Three hundred military extras used in the filming were not paid at all, only receiving their Army pay and so in effect providing a state subsidy. Former Army Sergeant Dave Yeoman observed that working on *LOTR* was harder work than military operations in Northern Ireland or the Falklands. Military extras had no choice over being involved and various promised gifts in kind did not materialise (Catherall 2002).

While considering the scale of inequality in earnings, one must recognise that *LOTR* had some exceptional features. First, there was a strongly articulated ethos of working together in pursuit of an epoch-making creative endeavour. 'Our project has come together . . . with everybody involved having a real, burning desire to be working on it . . .

Everyone realises they'll never get to work on something like this for the rest of their lives' (MacDonald 2001–2: 116). This rhetoric of a once-in-a-lifetime creative opportunity asserted a moral duty for all participants from the lowest extra to the leading actors.

Second, *LOTR* departed from normal practices in Hollywood producer-distributor-financed motion pictures. Stars either undertake a producer role or contract their services for profit participation, negotiating a contractually defined percentage share (points) of net or gross revenues. The willingness of producer-distributors to accede to profit participation deals stems from the fact that, given the high scale of investment per film – in 2003, for example, the average studio budget was US$64 million – the psychological investment of their stars becomes essential. Capital investment will be jeopardised if stars decide not to give their greatest efforts to making the production the best it can be. Profit participation contracts reassure investors that the capital advanced for production will be protected (Chisholm 1997). In *LOTR*, although the number of participants with compensation packages linked to box-office performance is unknown, it was small because of the absence of major stars in leading roles. Jackson seems to be the only 'creative' participant who earned a star-level compensation.

The conditions of hiring for relatively unknown actors – Orlando Bloom, most obviously, but also Billy Boyd and Dominic Monaghan – relied on the implied understanding that extra dedication in the present would lead to star status and enhanced compensation in the future. (So far, from among these actors, only Andy Serkis has landed a role in another Peter Jackson film.) Viggo Mortensen, an older, slightly more established if not more recognisable actor, has appeared in both an action film (*Hidalgo*) and an art house film (*A History of Violence*) since *LOTR*. Orlando Bloom featured in the commercially unsuccessful and critically controversial *Kingdom of Heaven*, and has appeared in a number of romantic comedies. How substantially the careers of Elijah Wood or Sean Astin, for example, have benefited from *LOTR* remains to be seen. Wood has yet to parlay Frodo into a starring role, although his asking price has probably increased. Karl Urban's career seems to have benefited most from among the Kiwi actors; he now appears in big-budget action films such as *The Chronicles of Riddick* as well as *Doom*. A number of New Zealand actors have derived secondary employment from appearing in *LOTR* conventions, though how substantial a benefit this has been is not clear. For example, for Craig Parker, who played 'Haldir, the elf who died a noble death at the battle of Helm's Deep', it has meant being able 'to travel very comfortably around the world' (Rae 2006: 13).

Third, the justification for steep inequalities in reward is that those who take the greatest risks should receive the greatest reward. But the concept of risk is complicated when applied to *LOTR*. The actual capital at risk was provided by international distributors who advanced to New Line Cinema 65 per cent of the production costs of US$350 million. As Michael Lynne, the co-head of New Line observed: 'The amount of money that New Line actually had at risk was never as much as anybody thought. It was actually relatively small. In actual dollars' (Grainger 2005).

Fourth, the de-unionised nature of New Zealand's film and television industries meant that the actual costs of production were comparatively low. For example, a recent survey of actors found that nearly 60 per cent of the sample earned less than NZ$20,000 in 2004 and the majority of actors worked fewer than eighty days (King 2005: 24). Precise details on compensation are unavailable for the established New Zealand actors who worked on the trilogy, but the general consensus is that the work was of the order of fewer than twenty days. Overseas actors, enjoying the protection of their unions, were paid more than their New Zealand counterparts. Jackson observed that shooting in New Zealand made the cost of each film cheaper by US$50–60 million (Kirkland 2003).

Fifth, the implicit subsidy provided by New Zealand's creative labour relations context was argued to bring enormous benefits to the local economy. Yet even here, the data are murky – an OECD report estimated that the New Zealand government provided a subsidy of up to NZ$400 million against the production costs of NZ$675 million (Louisson 2003).[3] Since it has been estimated that the production crew spent around $NZ500 million in the local economy, the benefit to the local economy is much less impressive than publicised (Oram 2001–2). One could argue that *LOTR* was important for national morale, or even that there were important intangible benefits that money values do not capture (Campbell 2004). Yet even allowing this, it requires a further argument to establish that New Zealand taxpayers and underpaid actors should pay for it.

Marx observed that, in a fully developed capitalist mode of production, the powers of labour appear as powers that descend from the person of the capitalist, as the one from whose pockets wealth flows and returns (Marx 1990: 254 and 1052–3). The culture of publicity and entrepreneurial celebration attributes the collective endeavour that made *LOTR* to Jackson's genius. Jackson's filmmaking skills are not in doubt, nor is his endearing modesty, but the compensation differential he has enjoyed makes him an absolute winner. Time will tell if his personal good fortune will translate into benefits for the New Zealand film industry.

One claim that does not appear to stand is that New Line Productions and Jackson are heroic paragons of entrepreneurial risk-taking. As pointed out above, foreign distributor capital hedged much of the risk to New Line and risk minimising was extended by tax breaks from the New Zealand Government. In short, for the supposed paragons, others shouldered much of the risk and received little of the profits. The New Zealand Finance Minister Michael Cullen once asked, 'What more does Jackson want?' More than he has received so far. In 2005 Jackson and Walsh (as WingNut Productions) filed a complaint in the US District Court, California, seeking damages of tens of millions of dollars against Katja Motion Picture Corporation – a subsidiary of New Line. The Complaint claims that Katja failed to calculate accurately and pay to WingNut its share of the profits and that the rights to the film were undersold in some markets (Rudell 2005; Fritz 2005: 1).

On the one hand, Jackson and Walsh may appear absurdly greedy, seeking yet more remuneration for their work. On the other, they can be made out to be fighting the good fight for the little people against the vertically integrated industry. At issue in this complex and so far unresolved case is not just the mystery of internal accounting but the alleged sweetheart deals offered by New Line to its affiliates in the Warner conglomerate, notably in the games and publishing wings. Jackson's suit argues that, by trading these rights to close affiliates, New Line failed to secure the best deals, available only by taking the franchises to the open market. While common in the television industry, court actions over accounting are rare in the film business, and this one, because of its scale, may create a landmark in entertainment law. Should Jackson win, he may well have yet more clout in the global entertainment business.

### Notes

1 For more on this point see Margolis 2003, especially 26–31.
2 One influential public figure announced on the radio a week or so after the screening that he would no longer believe anything he saw on television.
3 Accurate financial details about the cost of producing and marketing a film are often difficult to establish; in this case, the figures are complicated by currency conversions between NZ and US dollars.

# 8

# Creative industries in Hobbit economies: wealth creation, intellectual property regimes, and transnational production

*Danny Butt*

The last decade has seen the cultural industries' increasing contribution to national economies. However, analysis of the economics of the creative industries in terms of the transnational production of services yields a less rosy picture. This chapter sketches some of the dynamics emerging in attempts by small national economies to leverage their production resources to attract production work on event films.

In New Zealand *LOTR* has met fanfare about the economic benefits of its production to the country's relatively small economy. While significant potential benefits accrue to New Zealand through its role hosting the *LOTR* production, these lie mostly in the *potential* for future activity. This potential is 'precarious' and relies upon a highly embedded, informal economy that characterises the creative industries (McRobbie 2002; Portes, Castells, and Benton 1989). While further critical research on the processes required to activate that potential is needed, this chapter collects arguments in the literature on the 'information economy' and creative industries relevant to the *LOTR* case.

As de Frantz (2003) notes, urban policy-makers use cultural flagship projects as symbolic strategies promoting economic development in the knowledge economy while simultaneously mobilising political support. Because the pathways of future economic benefits in the creative sector are hard to articulate, the pitch for economic development supporting *LOTR* differs from that underpinning, for example, negotiations on agriculture. Economic development policies in the creative industries are constrained by much the same logic as the event film itself; high marketing expenditure, plenty of hype, and the careful management of critical commentary are essential for their symbolic success (Bordwell, Thompson, and Staiger 1985). Campbell quotes Michael Cullen describing why the National Party, usually free-market ideologues, supported the *LOTR* tax breaks: 'No one wanted to look as if they were taking on the hobbits

**Figure 8** 'Business Wellington/Creative Wellington' proclaims the 2003/04 phone book cover.

in the lead up to an election' (2000: 20). When a country appoints its own minister for *LOTR* and provides tax breaks to the tune of an estimated NZ$225 million (ibid.), it is obviously invested in the film's success as a critical, commercial, and symbolic entity.

One result of that investment is the absence of independent analysis of the economic impact of creative productions such as *LOTR*. The only significant study is *Scoping the Lasting Effects of The Lord of the Rings*, a government-sponsored analysis by the New Zealand Institute for Economic Research (NZIER), which relies heavily on government work for its survival (Yeabsley and Duncan 2002). Critical voices have thus far come primarily from cultural commentators who have framed their critique in terms of the impact of 'Hollywood' on New Zealand culture (Calder 2003). But important questions remain unanswered from an economic and industry development perspective about the value of transnational productions such as *LOTR* to the overall screen production sector in New Zealand, and for other small economies in similar relationships with US-led screen production.

### *LOTR*'s contribution to the New Zealand economy

To understand *LOTR*'s role in a small economy such as New Zealand's, one must understand the policy context that led the New Zealand government to consider the multi-million-dollar subsidy granted to the film's producers, without which the film would likely have been shot elsewhere (Yeabsley and Duncan 2002: 18). After the massive government withdrawal from the New Zealand economy in the early 1990s failed to yield sustainable growth, intensive discussion arose about what constitutes a valid role for the government in a market economy. Many economists see stimulating innovation as central to participation in the knowledge economy, as well as being one of the few government interventions in the economy mandated by international economic organisations such as the OECD (Metcalfe and Miles 2000). Economists see innovation – or creating new and improved products and services – as a way to improve productivity.

However, hard data on newer sectors such as the creative industries are limited, and expectations of their likely returns rest more on the popularity of these sectors in other similar societies than on evidence for their economic returns to New Zealand. The work thus far done mostly aggregates existing statistical data from industry sectors that are notoriously hard to define (Webster 2002). Further, the creative industries have vastly different business models in their various subsectors, and little progress has been made on which ones require focus, although New Zealand Trade and Enterprise has singled out screen production for promotion. Contradictions abound: creative industries definitions use the UK definitions based on generation and exploitation of intellectual property (Department for Culture, Media, and Sport 1998), but some of the largest sectors in New Zealand (e.g., advertising and graphic design) are service industries with little intellectual property export potential. The similarities between the rhetoric associated with the economic development of the creative industries and the hype surrounding the 'Internet economy' in the late 1990s are striking: underdeveloped business models, plenty of optimism, and a fear of being left out are the norm.

Still, the figures for *LOTR* are impressive. It represents the largest investment into a screen production in New Zealand, with approximately 3200 person-years' employment for New Zealanders from 1997 to 2001, using approximately five thousand vendors, most of whom are in New Zealand (Yeabsley and Duncan 2002). Much of the NZIER report emphasises the upskilling of both staff on the film and the vendors who provided services for it. 'An interesting aspect of the Weta Digital growth has been the effects they have had – and continue to have – on their suppliers. Every vendor will have learned a lot from the sheer scale of the installation at Weta Digital. They will have gained skills and experience. Supplies have included air-conditioning, travel bookings, and specialist data processing' (Yeabsley and Duncan 2002: 19).

In one sense these are infrastructural effects whose benefits will be ongoing. The effects include development of 'tacit knowledge' in the industry, which, while difficult to quantify, is nevertheless increasingly recognised for its role in fostering innovation. But questions emerge over the transferability of this knowledge to other domains. That is, have the vendors learnt how to undertake a specific kind of work – that of providing services to film productions that are owned offshore? While a certain amount of dependence is inevitable in the global economy, multi-million-dollar state subsidies for productions such as *LOTR* occasion questions about the 'opportunity cost' of supporting this activity over other ways of stimulating the screen production sector. Such questions become more significant when we consider the emerging structure of the event film economy and related industries.

## The event film and economic development

A disjuncture exists between the screen production sector and national macro-economic development agendas. Figures for assessing the growth of industry sectors such as film generally do not investigate the qualitative relationships that determine the sector's strategic potential. For example, NZIER's scoping report shows a linear scale of film industry development, from an undeveloped stage (occupied by Mexico) to a fully developed stage (occupied by the United States). This ignores the differences in the kinds of film industry that exist in these national economies, many of which are determined by particular relationships with US firms. The national positions cannot just be plotted on a grid of relative development, because they are relational. Like other kinds of service industries, relationships in the film industry are highly socially embedded (Granovetter 1985), and tend to be heterogeneous and customised. In other words, a country that grows an industry around providing production services is not necessarily going to develop into becoming a producer and controller of film distribution in the style of US media conglomerates. Aksoy and Robins argue that this results from the inherent 'industrial dualism' of the feature film industry, where independent production companies act as 'shock absorbers' and research units for the majors 'by attracting risk capital and creative talent which the majors can then exploit through their control of distribution' (1992: 17).

The barriers to switching from a production role to moving higher up the film chain should not be underestimated. As Wasko (1994) describes it, the feature film business no longer exists in its own right, but is embedded in a family of products that constitute 'entertainment software' – a US-dominated industry. In fact, the event film fails to make money from its US box-office takings. Profits come from the film's performance in 'ancillary markets' such as home video or DVD and foreign distribution, then from merchandise and product placement (Ohmann 1996). This requires extensive multinational, tightly diversified relationships with 'independent' distributors, video game developers, television companies, and producers of consumer goods – all of which are more or less inaccessible to independent filmmakers.

The film's performance in ancillary markets, however, depends on its success at the US box office. How does a film perform well at the US box-office? By conforming to the norms set by the studios: through ultra-high budgets, generated by spiralling star salaries and the costs of spectacular special effects, and through simultaneous release on a massive number of screens, an extensive marketing campaign, careful selection of launch dates, and tight control of critical commentary to mitigate the effects of any word-of-mouth disappointment among audiences (Maltby 1998: 37).

How does one raise the ultra-high budget required? By following the example of production company Carolco highlighted by Balio: 'Carolco's strategy was to cover as much of the production costs for a picture as possible by pre-selling the ancillary rights piece-by-piece, country-by-country. In this manner, Carolco was able to cover nearly all the $100 million budget . . . for *Terminator 2*' (1998: 65).

The distributors thus determine the flow of film capital. Sewing up a deal with distributors makes finance available for production, but it also makes the producers much less 'independent' than they might appear. As Schamus puts it, 'More and more, as the studios finance and distribute "independent" films, independent producers find themselves rather dependent employees' (1998: 103).

## Films in the transnational services economy

This 'bimodal' industrial structure (Bartos 1996: 307) is linked to the development of the international trade in services and a growing emphasis on information as a crucial input into transnational production processes. Sassen claims that consensus is emerging around distinguishing two types of information critical to a global economy:

> One is the datum, which may be complex yet is standard knowledge: the level at which a stock market closes, a privatisation of a public utility, the bankruptcy of a bank. But there is a far more difficult type of 'information', akin to an interpretation / evaluation / judgment . . . Access to the first kind of information is now global and immediate from just about any place in the highly developed world . . . But the second type of information requires a mixture of elements, which we could think of as the social infrastructure for global connectivity . . . It is possible, in principle, to reproduce the technical infrastructure anywhere, but the same cannot be asserted for specialised kinds of social connectivity. (2002: 22)

Access to this second kind of information gives Hollywood, with its high concentration of networked industry insiders, a unique competitive advantage in the screen production market. According to Sassen (1991), the distinctive way information facilitates dispersal of routine activities (e.g., production) and centralisation of control activities (e.g., intellectual property rights management, marketing, distribution) explains the increasing dominance of cities in global economic activity. According to this logic, the social infrastructure of Hollywood is not easily reproducible in other centres.

Services, particularly entertainment services such as screen production, are knowledge-intensive, usually based on a range of 'immaterial inputs' including cultural and aesthetic knowledge, know-how, social and organisational knowledge, information-based knowledge, and science and technology knowledge. How to create these inputs in a country like New Zealand is far from clear. Certainly, developing skills through participation in transnational productions such as *LOTR* is important, but what about a sustainable network of insiders? How do we develop those?

This involves more than increasing the industry's overall size. A key aspect of services, particularly in the creative industries, is that investment does not equate with profitability as strongly as in traditional forms of production such as manufacturing (see, e.g., Caves 2000: 36). Instead, what tends to happen in smaller economies is that they become destinations for outsourcing. It makes sense to see *LOTR* as an instance of this larger phenomenon.

Outsourcing, one of the most important tools of contemporary organisational management, can be defined as 'the transfer to a third party of the continuous management responsibility for the provision of a service governed by a service level agreement' (Gay and Essinger 2000: 4). For example, WingNut Films, the production company for *LOTR*, has a particular relationship with New Line Cinema through an agreement for the kind of filmmaking services to be provided.

Being an outsourcing destination can be extremely profitable, but it provides few opportunities for developing intellectual property (IP), which is commonly defined as the source of wealth in the creative industries (Department for Culture, Media, and Sport, 1998). For example, New Line Cinema in the United States holds the intellectual property rights for *LOTR*, meaning that whenever the film is screened, or a person wants to use materials for the film for republication, the licence fee flows back to New Line, rather than to the production company that made the work. Digital effects companies such as Weta Digital provide their knowledge labour, including the development of new software, without necessarily retaining intellectual property (though Weta seeks to profit from resale of some of the tools used in production). These arrangements highlight the qualitatively distinct nature of the roles within the production relationship: IP owners license content and receive ongoing revenue streams over time, while subcontractors live from job to job, with little ability to extract ongoing economic rents for their labour. There are also significant differences in the legal capabilities of multinational corporations and individuals to exploit global networks. In the employment relationship, May notes, 'there is an important distinction between property-owning classes and those who work for them . . . with considerable barriers to individuals profiting from the ideas and knowledge they generate' (2002: 73). Tactics include the capture of subcontractors' creative ideas and labour, and defensive use of the copyright and patent systems to ensure that commercialisation costs remain high (or legal risks prohibitive). Increasingly, legal activity centres on limiting the mobility of technical personnel to competitive firms (which remain defined very broadly to the benefit of large organisations over workers or subcontractors).

Since the World Trade Organisation adopted the Trade Related Intellectual Property Rights agreement, the legal regime governing the protection of intellectual property has radically expanded. Once property rights in knowledge are globalised, the possibilities for expanding the division of 'creative labour' geographically become considerable. What we have now are not so much runaway productions but a radically disaggregated production process increasingly distributed over many locations determined by price and capability.

Much of the New Zealand government's rhetoric stimulating a move toward a 'knowledge economy' or 'creative economy' emphasises the threat of the manufacturing sector's migration to developing economies of cheaper labour power. But May (2000) has found that informational marketplaces are highly competitive and possibly more subject to occupational 'task migration' than non-informational work. In other words, lower-paid jobs in the informational market are much more likely to be relocated to different physical locations when this can reduce costs or improve products. Examples include the locating of call centres in India, or the outsourcing of video game art production to studios in Vietnam. There is a high level of instability in country-specific investments in information-intensive products and services, providing challenges to policy-makers attempting to position their regions to contract for provision of these services to multinationals. On the one hand, *LOTR* gets New Zealand on the map as a production destination, but in an increasingly price-sensitive industry this can quickly pass as other countries learn to provide the same skills more cheaply. The NZIER's own report highlights this mobility of work, quoting one *LOTR* contractor:

> I can work on overseas projects as a departmental head, where I would be able to take a few key people with me. This sort of deal is more common on 'runaway' films in third countries, where it is possible and cheaper to bring in, for instance, New Zealand crews to do things. In a film shot recently in Italy the New Zealand director/producer brought in a New Zealand lighting crew. (Yeabsley and Duncan 2002: 25)

What then would a sustainable screen production sector look like outside the United States? It is far from clear – but it does seem that some kind of stimulation of New Zealand-owned intellectual property will be important. Paradoxically, globalisation also provides a renewed argument for an emphasis on culturally specific funding – we can contrast *LOTR*, which could essentially be made at any one of a number of locations, with *Whale Rider*, which cannot. Undoubtedly, there are dangers in adaptations of local content (particularly Indigenous content) to a Hollywood marketing model that demands 'suspense, laughter, violence, hope, heart, nudity, sex, happy endings – mainly happy endings', as studio exec Griffin Mill puts it in *The Player*. But these culturally embedded stories cannot be relocated elsewhere. They will always be connected to New Zealand's society and culture.

For New Zealand's economic development agencies, the questions have no easy answers. How do we make use of the industry development benefits from hosting foreign-owned production, while also stimulating New Zealand-based initiatives such that ongoing economic activity and employment is not subject to decisions made by multinationals offshore, and sustainable returns can accrue to New Zealand? These are the perils Hobbit economies face in their quest for the creative economy.

# 9

# 'Ring leader': Peter Jackson as 'creative industries' hero

*Deborah Jones*

Through the *LOTR* project, Peter Jackson has become an iconic figure associated with two key themes: the project's international success, and its local importance to a reworked New Zealand national identity. These themes take a new twist in Jackson's case. His success as creative entrepreneur within the emerging discourse of the creative industries tells a new story about national identity. New Zealand's prominent artists

**Figure 9** Peter Jackson's stature truly represented: Premiere Night in Middle-earth: 20 December 2001.

are often 'overburdened' with 'grand narratives' of national identity (Wedde 2003: 61). As a small postcolonial nation, New Zealand has been long concerned with what Wedde describes as the 'nationalist' and the 'internationalist' narratives. Wedde uses Sir Edmund Hillary, conqueror of Mount Everest,[1] as an example because 'he showed us who and where we are' (nationalist) and because 'he showed the world we could too' (internationalist) (ibid.).

Jackson represents the 'new creative', a central figure in the rhetoric of the knowledge economy (OECD 1996). Internationally, the United Kingdom, Australia, Canada, and New Zealand are among countries that have been 'mapping' creative industries, creating economic programmes for their development, and generally talking them up as fundamental to the knowledge economy (Cunningham 2004). The film industry, although not new (Jones and DeFillippi 1996), has been reframed as a centrepiece of the creative industries (Screen Production Industry Taskforce 2003). In this context, the *LOTR* project signifies the cornucopia of social and economic benefits that it is hoped the new creative industries can deliver.

This chapter analyses the print media coverage of Jackson as *LOTR* director. Media sources include local daily newspapers, magazines, and film industry and business press, along with selected international coverage, including some websites. Relevant policy documents include government press releases and reports. The analysis uses critical approaches to the new discourse of creative industries that focus on identifying emerging forms of identity and power relations. This chapter links these new forms to the development of a new narrative of New Zealand national identity, in which Jackson figures largely as an entrepreneur in the 'Frodo economy', as a promoter of 'Brand New Zealand' (Oram 2001–2), and as a patriot and exemplary New Zealander.

Jackson exemplifies the new creative entrepreneur, one of the new hybrid identities generated by the previously split – or even opposed – concepts of creativity and industry. Jeffcut and Pratt describe the creative industries as 'occupying a relatively new interdisciplinary space' (2002: 225), characterised by the traditional 'essentialising dualisms' (2002: 227) between 'creative/cultural/artistic', on the one hand, and 'economic/business/industry', on the other. Government policies attempt to reconfigure these old oppositions by rebranding the cultural industries as the creative industries, signalling 'a contemporary policy focus on a sector that is engaged in producing novel cultural products' (ibid.). Scholarly approaches to creative industries consider the new ways that 'creativity' and 'creatives' are regulated, the new forms of identity that are opened up (e.g., the creative entrepreneur), and the seductions of new forms of 'creative' capitalism (Osborne 2003; Prichard 2002). As a development of the neoliberal 'enterprise culture' of the 1980s and 1990s (du Gay 1991), creative industries discourse extends the duty of the individual to be entrepreneurial to include the creative. The new creative must also be entrepreneurial, and the entrepreneurial must also be creative (Osborne 2003).

The 'Frodo economy' refers to the hoped-for and actual economic spin-offs from the LOTR project to the local economy (Johnson 2004: 5). A government scoping report on the 'lasting effects of *The Lord of the Rings*' claims that '[*LOTR*] will leave a unique "footprint" for New Zealand when its production is over' (Walton and Duncan 2002: v). A business commentator speaking just before the first premiere typifies local expectations of economic benefits: 'From the staid corridors of Trade New Zealand . . . to the wacky workshops of *The Lord of the Rings* special effects company Weta, there is an utter conviction that Peter Jackson is indeed Father Christmas. They believe his films will shower gifts upon our companies over the next three Christmases, as each film is premiered to the world' (Oram 2001–2: 42). Jackson is the poster boy for 'Creative Wellington' where he and Weta Digital are based (Rendle 2003). Wellington has been called 'Wellywood', and for the movie premieres the local paper was renamed *Middle-earth News*.

Prime Minister Helen Clark crystallised the official commitment to the national spin-off possibilities: 'Set against the spectacular and diverse New Zealand landscape, *The Lord of the Rings* trilogy has the potential to be a major tourist promotion and investment tool for years to come, by highlighting the country's natural beauty and the creative talents of its people across a wide range of knowledge-based industries' (Clark 2001a). The government launched funding packages to promote and assess positive spin-offs such as the promotion of New Zealand as a film location, as well as of New Zealand-made films; investment in film industry infrastructure; media technology innovation; tourism promotion; a return home of overseas New Zealand talent; and the profiling of New Zealand globally, particularly New Zealand talent, creativity, and innovation (Clark 2001b).

Although the government has commissioned reports to establish the basic numbers (O'Leary and Frater 2002; Pinflicks Communications and NZIER 2003; Screen Production Industry Taskforce 2003; Walton and Duncan 2002; Yeabsley and Duncan 2002), as sceptical commentators have noted, the 'hoard of the Rings' will be difficult to measure (Calder 2003), partly because the creative industries discourse has only recently made visible the economic activities of the creative industries generally, and of the screen industries particularly.

Creative industries are a central plank in a 'Cultural Recovery Package' (Tizard 2002), a nation-building project intended to have cultural as well as economic effects. A presentation by Ruth Harley exemplifies how the new hybrid creative industries provide a rhetorical space where cultural and economic benefits can be reconciled in a reworking of national identity:

> Cultural industries such as film and television, fashion, multi-media, music and tourism are transforming New Zealand's economy. Our commercial interests are indissolubly linked with our cultural interests. There is no place in the new economy for the type of thinking which sees a disjunction between the business world and the art world. Cultural industries are based on national identity. National identity is key to creating a unique positioning for our goods and services. Take film for example. It creates culture, builds identity and markets that identity to the world . . . It is a central ingredient in constructing our identity for ourselves, as a lever to help New Zealanders get the confidence and boldness to foot it aggressively on the international stages. (Harley 2002)

Many film industry analysts see the *LOTR* story as an exemplary narrative of the new creative entrepreneurship:

> It is a story that needs to be told in detail so others may follow and reinvent it for themselves. The story of Peter Jackson and his colleagues is a reflection of what an individual can generate, whilst becoming an inspiration to young New Zealanders that art and the creative industries offer exciting employment opportunities, creative satisfaction and substantial financial returns to the personnel involved but also to the economy. (O'Leary and Frater, 2001: 7)

Jackson's impact on popular culture is reflected in his recognition in 2004 as 'New Zealand's favourite business leader' (Nick Smith 2004), with a recognition factor of 96 per cent in a national poll.

Jackson is not just an exemplar at home but, as 'the hottest director in the world' (Otto 2003), he 'carr[ies] the mantle' for New Zealand internationally (2003), 'personifying our country as a brand' (Harley 2002). *LOTR* does not present a distinctly 'New Zealand story', so how can it be claimed as a New Zealand product, emblematic of both actual and possible economic and cultural development? This is accomplished by 'the sense of ownership the country feels', which 'has become a phenomenon since the first film was released in 2001' (Dixon 2004), along with the reiterated claim that the skills of Jackson and his crew represent national abilities – 'he showed the world we could too', in Wedde's formulation (2003: 61). 'Kiwi ingenuity' is a long-established theme in the rhetoric of national identity, and accordingly 'we should not be surprised that the person to out-Hollywood Hollywood would be someone from a country which invented the can-do mentality' (Calder 2003). The success of New Zealand filmmakers in producing *LOTR* is seen to exemplify Kiwi ingenuity elevated to a high level of creativity, combined with technological breakthroughs. Writ large, these are requisite skills and passions if New Zealand is to be known for (in the words of the Prime Minister when launching the *LOTR* spin-offs funding) 'the creative talents of its people across a wide range of knowledge-based industries' (Clark 2001b).

As Billy Crystal joked at the 2004 Oscars ceremony, 'It's official, everyone in New Zealand has been thanked' (Pakes 2004). Jackson's willingness to acknowledge other New Zealanders' input has reinforced this rhetorical link. As Helen Clark said, it was 'just amazing the way our people on the Oscars stage remembered the folks back home and gave everyone a plug' (Gardiner 2004).

It is essential to the nationalist narrative of *LOTR* that Jackson is not only typically a New Zealander but a patriot: 'He's the Sir Edmund Hillary of New Zealand filmmaking, forging a humble career move in the foothills of Wellington, then taking it to the highest peaks of Middle Earth' (McDonald 2002: 114). Jackson's love for New Zealand and, specifically, his hometown of Wellington identifies him as a patriot who puts his country first, bringing a potential creative industries gold rush to all his compatriots. Eschewing the traditional path of talented New Zealander filmmakers to Hollywood, Jackson has made it clear that he wants to stay based here, asserting that he will 'bring Hollywood to New Zealand' (Sampson 2002: 105). Over Jackson's face on the cover of the leading local business magazine ran the challenge: 'Ringleader: Peter Jackson's doing his bit for New Zealand. *What can you do?*' ('Ring-leader' 2002). Again, creativity and business skills are seen as intertwined, and the creative entrepreneur is not only successful but patriotic – his success emblematic of a nation-building project in a postcolonial world dominated culturally and economically by the United States.

Despite directing one of the biggest ever Hollywood projects, Jackson is seen as not having 'gone Hollywood'. According to one writer: 'Peter Jackson, although he is now extremely rich and famous internationally, still gets a lot of respect from the New Zealand public because he is still the idealised Kiwi guy. He wears shorts and jandals and doesn't flaunt his wealth' (Kiwi Hobbit 2002). His personality is seen to exemplify a certain Kiwiness – the image of the man who can face all challenges with a 'she'll be right' attitude – and this perception extends to the attitude of the local film crews: 'Pitching in! Getting the job done! That's the New Zealand way!' (Sibley 2002b: 37).

The local film industry has criticised new film subsidies that Jackson lobbied for, and many New Zealanders argue that only films that tell 'New Zealand stories' bring cultural benefits and sustain truly local industry – as opposed to Hollywood films made here (Calder 2003; NZ Film Commission 2003). But even the critics of the new policies encouraging international filmmaking see *LOTR* as 'an enormous catalyst in the way everyone thinks about' the local film industry: 'What Peter's done is create a confidence among people that anything's possible. And he's taken the government along on that ride, because they've clearly said that anything's possible' (Welch 2003: 23).

Jackson's iconic position as creative industries hero rests on many iterations of the key themes: his entrepreneurial *and* creative skills, his authentic New Zealandness, and his patriotism. He is an exceptional achiever but with a local accent. His typicality as a New Zealander connects traditional themes of national identity – technical ingenuity, humility, teamwork – with the 'new economy' themes of creativity, technological innovation, and entrepreneurial skills in the global arena. He occupies the position of the new hybrid creative industries subject who reworks the old division between 'artistic' and 'commercial'.

The glamour of film refigures business in popular culture, as the recognition of Jackson as New Zealand's leading business person shows (Nick Smith 2004). The number one 'burning media question for 2004' (Cohen 2004) in *The National Business Review* asked: 'Did Peter Jackson's triumph at this week's Academy Awards mark the first occasion when the New Zealand media unreservedly cheered a work of big business'? The new image of the film industry is linked to other creative industries in both government policy (NZTE 2003–4) and popular culture. A local women's magazine editor exclaims, 'Suddenly we are no longer apologetic about being Kiwi, and two key reasons for that are how well *Lord of the Rings* did at the Oscars, and the success of New Zealand fashion design overseas' (Moore 2004: 54). Success in the creative industries is related to a developing form of subjectivity, described in the business press as the need to 'believe enough in ourselves' and to make 'the world believe in us and our products' (Oram 2001–2: 42). While the recent global government-led reframing of the creative industries was triggered by the United Kingdom (DCMS 2001), it takes a different place in the national narrative of smaller post-colonial countries such as New Zealand, where the development of creative industries as a serious economic sector is a new possibility. As a creative industries hero, Peter Jackson embodies *both* creativity *and* entrepreneurship, the 'new' New Zealander who is a global player while staying at home.

## Note

1 The New Zealander Edmund Hillary and Sherpa Tenzing Norgay were the first people to climb Mount Everest and return alive.

# 10

# Peter Jackson's cinema and Colin McKenzie's legacy

## Thierry Jutel

I have no interest in a career as such. If I were really career-oriented, I'd be in Hollywood now making Hollywood films and earning lots of money. I choose to stay in New Zealand earning a fraction of what I could make in Los Angeles because I want to do whatever I feel like doing. (Jackson, interviewed at the time of the release of *Heavenly Creatures*, 1994)

Business, career development, and creation are intrinsically connected in Peter Jackson's filmmaking. In fifteen years, he went from amateur filmmaker to director of *LOTR*, the most ambitious project in cinema history. Yet Jackson is neither a Hollywood insider nor an ambitious renegade. He is famous for his 'down-to-earth manners', a euphemism suggesting that he neither looks the part nor plays the celebrity game. Unlike most successful New Zealand directors (Vincent Ward, Jane Campion, Roger Donaldson, Lee Tamahori, Alison McLean, and now Niki Caro), Jackson has stayed in New Zealand to make films – big budget films, even by Hollywood's standards.

Jackson gained prominence in New Zealand for his part in making *Forgotten Silver*. Since then he has criticised the NZFC and its funding policies, as well as the New Zealand government, which does and doesn't provide tax breaks for film production while promoting Aotearoa as a filmmaking destination. Few other members of the arts and media communities would declare on television that 'it is as much use talking to [the finance minister] about tax breaks as it is to try to talk a vegan into eating meat' (*Sunday*, TVOne, March 2003). Meanwhile, Jackson built the equivalent of an independent film studio in a Wellington suburb; established his production company, WingNut Films; and acquired the National Film Unit, historically at the centre of filmmaking in New Zealand, for film processing and sound work.[1] He is also a co-founder of Weta Digital and Weta Workshop.

In the New Zealand context, Jackson's films and business ventures occupy a space between Hollywood runaway productions and projects

**Figure 10** Tony Clark impersonates Peter Jackson during the Wellington premiere of *Towers*, 19 December 2002.

situated within the more precarious local film industry. While Hollywood money has financed *The Frighteners*, *LOTR*, and *King Kong*, he seems to have retained extensive creative control of his films. Although his successes do not follow Hollywood models, he has made some of the biggest-grossing films ever. In New Zealand, his success contrasts sharply with the native film industry's overall fragility.

In fact, the development of Jackson's career as director and entrepreneur thus far allows for only one potential point of comparison: the pioneering New Zealand filmmaker Colin McKenzie. However, McKenzie only ever existed in *Forgotten Silver*, which was produced for a drama slot on New Zealand Television and funded by New Zealand On Air (the public-funding agency for television) and the NZFC.

*Forgotten Silver*'s impact on viewers is hard to overstate. It presented the discovery of McKenzie's remarkable and long-lost work. It mixes personal testimony, interviews with experts (Leonard Maltin, Sam Neill, and Harvey Weinstein, among others), archival footage (actual and fake), and other documents to assert and support increasingly preposterous claims for McKenzie's achievements. Information about celluloid film made from egg yolks, gigantic sets built in remote South Island sites, the first sync sound system, and so forth is all driven by Jackson's convincing onscreen performance as narrator. Portraying McKenzie as one of the greatest filmmakers in world history, the film offers him to the country as a new national hero.

Astonishingly, viewers swallowed the tale (Hight and Roscoe 1996; Conrich and Smith 1998), but, once the public realised it had been suckered, it became disgruntled. Because Jackson had achieved artistic and critical legitimacy with *Heavenly Creatures*, he was expected to participate in the ethos of national self-congratulation, not deceive New Zealanders, especially not with taxpayers' money. Yet Jackson never expected such a response (Jackson, in Simmons 1996: 23), thinking that by the end of the film viewers would recognise in the improbable tale that common form of Kiwi humour, 'spinning a good yarn'.

Beyond Jackson's uncanny ability to tap into his country's insecurities, McKenzie's fictional career path illustrates something remarkably akin to Jackson's own priorities: 'I've always liked the idea of the New Zealand hero. The guy who is down-to-earth and does things before other people, but never quite gets it right. So we came up with this idea about a guy called Colin McKenzie who . . . never had that killer instinct to finally achieve greatness' (Barr and Barr 1996: 150). McKenzie's career starts with his humble beginnings. He was an inventor who used ingenious, inexpensive means to develop new film technology, initially concentrating on recording devices and processes including colour and sound, potentially to the detriment of narrative. A sense of the epic drove him, yet he began his career with films that shocked the moral pillars of the time and insulted political authorities; these films include bare-breasted Tahitian women and proto-candid camera skits. He had a penchant for gory and farcical details, not always intentionally, yet he was a sentimentalist. He adapted for the screen one of the most demanding and perilous works (the Bible) and to realise his life project (*Salome*) he had to convince powerful people with competing agendas – businessmen from the American Bible belt, the KGB, and the mafia – to give him money and let him make his films in distant New Zealand. He built gigantic sets; hired armies of technicians, actors, and extras; and took them to the most unwelcoming places in the New Zealand bush. In the process he risked everything. He was a man of his time and place who lived in a world of fantasy.

Besides the fact that Jackson has been much more successful and possesses a self-deprecating sense of humour, the parallels between the fictitious Colin McKenzie and Peter Jackson are irresistible. This is not to suggest that McKenzie is the unconscious manifestation or mirror image of Jackson, reflecting his interior conflicts and aspirations. Too much of the auteur approach is bathed in the cult of expressivity, a conception in which artistic expression allows for the constitution of a voice through the struggle of creation as self-discovery. 'Peter Jackson' is itself a figure made up of multiple people (Fran Walsh, Richard Taylor, etc.), technologies (mo-cap, CGI generally), and business arrangements (Weta, WingNut). What is clear, however, is that McKenzie's single-minded commitment and ambition constitute both a form of anticipatory self-derision and a programmatic stance. Jackson's 1994 statement quoted at the start of this chapter ('I'm not career-oriented . . .') should be read as both a completely genuine assertion (he knows what he *wants*) and a disingenuous avowal (he knows where he is *going* but does not necessarily want to claim it publicly).

Not simply a comical and fictional figure, McKenzie has become part of New Zealand's heritage as the affirmation of the creative powers of settler anxieties. Jackson's emphasis on McKenzie's heroic status distracts us from the irreducible forces of fictional production or, as the Russian inscriptions on the props of McKenzie's restored *Salome* announce, 'bull'. It may seem facile to draw parallels among the heroic yet fictitious world created in *Forgotten Silver*, Pauline and Juliet's hallucinatory and life-transforming fourth-world in *Heavenly Creatures*, the multi-dimensional universe of Middle-earth, and Jackson's own cinematic enterprises, but these continuities and interconnections define Jackson as filmmaker. His sensibility, which requires the elaborate construction of fictitious worlds, is not expressive but generative, based on the conviction that stories – with their hallucinatory, playful, deceptive, and transformational powers – are the stuff of life. As if Jackson wanted to draw attention to these continuities, Thomas Robin, the actor who plays McKenzie in *Forgotten Silver*, appears in the opening sequence of *Return* as Deagol, whom Smeagol/Gollum strangles in a fight for possession of the ring. Colin McKenzie could also have been Gollum.

In *Cinema 2*, Deleuze argues that the cinema inspired by the powers of the false 'does not just present images, it surrounds them with a world' (1989: 68). That world is not a representation of the real world; rather, the powers of the false produce a vision of a world that cannot be judged according to its ability to stand the test of accuracy. Through the powers of the false,

> narration ceases to be truthful, that is, to claim to be true, and becomes fundamentally falsifying. This is not at all a case of 'each has its own truth', a variability of content. It is a power of the false which replaces and supersedes the form of the true . . . Truthful narration is developed organically according to legal connections in space and chronological relations in time . . . But whether explicit or not, narration always refers to a system of *judgment* . . . Falsifying narration, by contrast, frees itself from this system

. . . [C]ontrary to the form of the true which is unifying . . . the power of
the false cannot be separated from an irreducible multiplicity. (ibid.: 131
and 133)

Although *Forgotten Silver* presents viewers with a series of perspectives
and documents that all stand as evidence, they never become a coherent whole. Emotional and intellectual investments in the possibility of
a unifying principle are superseded by irresolvable multiplicities. Most
of Jackson's cinema derides singular, molar, and absolute entities; mise-
en-scène, characters, bodies, and spaces are malleable and subject to
endless, deceptive, and often disfiguring transformations, such as the
sudden evil rictus on Bilbo Baggins' face in *Fellowship* when he comes
in contact with the ring again, or the landscape in *Heavenly Creatures*.
The powers of the false, the productive energies of falsification, and trans-
lational journeys across multiple dimensions appear in all of Jackson's
films. Colin McKenzie's forged identity is not simply a joke; it is the
materialisation of these principles.

In *Bad Taste*, *Meet the Feebles*, and *Braindead*, Jackson revels in the
playfulness and inventiveness that the splatter movie genre allows.
These films have something of the pedantic and disrespectful sensibility of the dedicated dorky film fan. His fascination with props, special
effects, and miniatures is notable since these tools can construct imaginary worlds where the illusion of control is an end in itself. This desire
for control reveals a masculine sense of fascination for contained worlds,
along with the ability to survive organised chaos and excremental excess.
They generate a deeply felt sense of social alienation and a desire to
construct alternative realities, sometimes precocious or contrived, but
always all-encompassing. He experiments with stop-motion animation
and translates this into the conviction that each element in the filmic
world is malleable and should be manipulated. He elaborates complex
and at times hallucinatory mise-en-scènes. He prefers characters whose
motivations do not rely on the suggestion of interiority as the genesis
of psychological depth, but on the exteriorisation of mindscapes onto
the material substance of the film. From this perspective, *LOTR* is about
the possibility of absolute control through the mediation of a ring that
alters the minds of those who possess it.

In *Heavenly Creatures* (based on a true story of two teenage girls who
murdered one of the girls' mothers in 1950s Christchurch), Jackson
explores the irruption of violence and insanity in a repressed environment. Driven by his long-time collaborator Fran Walsh, the film offers an
unusual perspective on this well-known New Zealand scandal (Jackson
in Simmons 1996: 19; Barr and Barr 1996: 152). New Zealand film

(and fiction) is disproportionately invested in exploring the country's real and imagined legacy of Victorian ethos and moral rectitude, whether it be about nineteenth-century colonial New Zealand or the welfare state in the 1950s and 1960s (see Watson 1994). The politics of cultural *ressentiment*, often expressed as guilt and self-hatred,[2] are part of a common symbolic repertory in a society interestingly but awkwardly negotiating the transition from settler to postcolonial society. *Heavenly Creatures* is unusual in that it provides a perspective that is simultaneously ethnographic (the film begins with documentary footage and is the result of intense research) and subjective, through the points of view, the mental state, and the feverish fantasies of the two enthralled companions. A remarkably non-judgemental film that in no way condones the murderous act of the two friends, it contrasts the expected stifling of 1950s morality with the liberating and radical forces of the altered states of mind of the two young women. The falsifying powers of their imagination enable the barren Canterbury landscape to morph into a formal British garden where they can be free.

Jackson's films are about the powers of transformation and about radical alterations. His sensibility, expressed in repulsion for the body and celebration of the grotesque, may be characteristic of a malaise associated with adolescence but it is also necessary for traversing different layers of reality and for transgressing social and moral barriers. Like previous films, *The Frighteners* speaks of the juxtaposition of different levels of reality and of fluidity between these levels. Embodiment is but one of these layers of experience. In *The Frighteners* the intersection of ghosts and humans is the source of drama and dark humour, but also great alienation.

Their mutual status as outsiders initiates the friendship between Pauline and Juliet in *Heavenly Creatures*. They see themselves as deformed physically and socially as a result of living away from home. Their respective physical ailments, which exclude them from physical education classes, are catalysts for their otherwise unlikely rapprochement. Their deformities, however, give them extraordinary powers. Creative powers and enchantment are only possible for distorted minds and bodies ('we are mad'), which explains why Pauline's mother's banality renders her abject.

As is most obvious in that murder scene, mind-altering gifts and powers of transformation do not necessarily lead to improvement. Those powers may be affirmative in the best possible cases but they are always alienating. Bilbo and Frodo Baggins react to the ring's transformational forces with melancholy or extreme violence whereas Pauline and Juliet find a murderous insanity in the exhilaration of their *amour fou*. In this sense the continuity between Lionel of *Braindead*, Juliet and Pauline of

*Heavenly Creatures*, Colin McKenzie, Frank Bannister from *The Frighteners*, and Frodo of *LOTR* may constitute the most obvious auteurist characteristic of Jackson's films.

The extent to which the casting of the ever-pubescent and asexual Michael J. Fox in *The Frighteners* was a strategic decision is hard to assess, but its inflection is important. Like many other characters in Jackson's cinema, he is caught between stable forms of embodiment. In Jackson's cinema, that adolescent and nerdy sensibility ridden with sexual anxiety is not a sign of authorial immaturity; it constitutes an epistemology. It opposes itself to restrictive notions of masculinity, those of the 'kiwi bloke' (Campbell 1995; Phillips 1987).

However, hatred of the body is not simply self-hatred. It extends to the maternal body because of the latter's privileged locus of transitional passage. Most emblematic in this regard are the mothers in *Braindead* and *Heavenly Creatures*. In *Braindead*, the mother becomes an ever-growing monster whom Lionel (Tim Balme), her son, must first conceal then destroy. Even before she becomes a repulsive zombie, she prevents Lionel from meeting girls and flirting. She is dominating, abject, and narcissistic. She has symbolically castrated Lionel, and his matricidal liberation at the closure of the film is so grotesque that it is not an act of violence as in *Heavenly Creatures*.

The most obvious examples of repulsion towards the body and the mother involve grotesque birthing imagery. A character literally traverses the body of another from top to bottom in *Bad Taste* and exclaims, 'I'm born again'. Zombies give birth to a baby zombie in *Braindead*, and Pauline and Juliet give birth to a fictive son in *Heavenly Creatures* as the abject embodiment of their mutual passion. Procreation can only lead to a more intensely felt sense of negating empowerment.

It would be simplistic to dismiss the shame of, and disgust for, the body in many of Jackson's films because of an immature adolescent sensibility. The emphasis on spectacular gore may be seen as a liberating force in Jackson's cinema, particularly in the specific context of New Zealand: 'Because of his place within New Zealand film culture his work is considerably more significant than most gore comedies and splatter movies' (Grant 1994: 3). Yet Jackson never demonstrates a coherent political engagement or a counter-cultural strategy. His films are not expressive in the sense of giving unambiguous shape to alternative attitudes and beliefs. For instance, *Heavenly Creatures* underplays the possible lesbian relationship between Pauline and Juliet (Knox 1995). Colin McKenzie may be an anti-hero who reveals settler anxieties, but he also belongs to a long tradition of pakeha humour. Similarly, in his adaptation of Tolkien's work, Jackson avoids the counter-cultural reception of the texts in the 1960s and 1970s (Dolan 2003).

At its best, Jackson's cinema is speculative rather than committed. He may be metamorphosing the infamous New Zealand cultural cringe into a scandalous celebration of the margins because of their dissenting and liberating abnormalities, but Jackson's films are much more interested in embracing the powers of fictitious worlds and altered consciousnesses than they ever are about providing metaphorical or allegorical narratives.

Middle-earth has many of the characteristics that fascinate Jackson. It is a parallel and self-contained universe with its own history, mythologies, eschatology, languages, and multiple geographical layers at a moment when that world is about to be overcome by destructive forces. Something that all of Jackson's characters share is that ancestral forces and the survival of their species drive them, not personal whims. Pauline and Juliet's embracing of the fourth-world and the radical consequences of their devotion stand as the point of reference. While in most other Jackson films temporal relations are not materialised in a movement towards singularity and completion but rather towards multiplication, irruption, and destruction, in *LOTR* the plot is guided by an epic and teleological flow and a movement towards the unitary, 'a ring to rule them all' or 'the return of the king'. And this may explain why *LOTR* does not achieve the kind of uncompromising and radical extremes of the other films, especially *Heavenly Creatures*. Colin McKenzie may have been the victim of historical forces, but he never was a tragic figure or the initiator of historical unfolding.

## Notes

1 Several biographical accounts revel in the fact that the NFU wouldn't hire him as an apprentice when he was seventeen; Matthews 2002: 16.
2 Examples include Roger Donaldson's *Smash Palace*, Geoff Murphy's *The Quiet Earth*, and Alison McLean's *Crush*.

# Part III
# Stardom and the event film

# 11

# Dossier: acting, on-set practices, software, and synthespians

*Sean Cubitt and Barry King*

An actor, male or female, is an 'emotional labourer' who incarnates a scripted character (Hochschild 1983: 35–55). The actor's function is to embody a verbal description of a fictional or quasi-fictional character. In undertaking the labour of embodiment, the actor manipulates appearance, demeanour, gesture, and speech in order to manifest before an audience a credible simulation of a character and of the character's reactions to a fictional environment as though it were really happening (Noose 1979: 58). As the actor constructs a character, she does so as a concrete person and is, indeed, cast because she has – or can assume, by alteration of, for example, body weight – certain physical qualities.

In everyday life, the person is assumed to be an individual – a unique expression of a self – and only contingently an example of a type. The actor within the framework of a specific cinematic (or theatrical) production is an individual *designed* to represent categorical or symbolic entities and events. Like any entity appearing on the screen or on stage, the actor when performing is a token that stands for a category that exists or could exist in the external world. Even inanimate objects that are functionally circumscribed, such as a telephone on stage or on screen, become a sign of their category (Eco 1976: 224–7).

Even if the actor is deliberately designed to resemble and, in some respects, actually be the manifestation of a social category, she is simultaneously a narrative agent – a character that is part of the imagined world of the narrative and an 'I' that addresses an audience as a 'you' through a body that is a 'me'. Because of her incarnated conflation of a real, physical presence and a signified abstraction or type, the actor is a signifier of plural and potentially conflicting identities. What she does is inherently ambiguous because it combines elements of the personal and unique, as indexed by the physical presence of *the actor in the character*, with elements of the transpersonal and social symbolic in the presence of *the character in the actor*. A particular performance will therefore always strike some balance between referring to the self and referring to the category or type. The balance struck will in turn affect how the audience relates to the performance and the performer.

Irrespective of the medium of performance, there are three general modes of referring through a performance (States 1995: 23).

First, self-expressive performances – the first person or 'I' mode, in which the actor(s) emphasises the self as it performs the character, playing up his or her personal presence and claiming the role of animator of a thinly defined verbal character. This mode is most often equated with star acting and is the kind of performance an actor should give if she wishes to exhibit star potential.

Second, collaborative performances – second person mode ('you') in which the actor(s) interact with the audience in some way, emphasising the 'ritual' or trans-individual quality of the performance and its dependence on the agreement of the audience to accept or reject its parameters. Collaborative performances are not unknown in film, but mainstream cinema rarely positions the actor so much in a tangent to a character. Even where the actor addresses the camera directly as a narrator or does voice-over, this is usually in character, e.g., Michael Caine in *Alfie* or Bruce Willis in *Last Man Standing*.

Third, representational performances – the third person or 'they' mode, in which the actor 'disappears' into the character in order to sustain the fictional world as an observable reality. This mode, because of the apparent identity between the actor and a character, can seem to be *not* acting – in other words, not pretending to be but actually *being* the character.

Setting aside collaborative performance as unusual in film, especially given the in-built separation between performers and their absent, if imagined, audiences, the range of variation in mainstream cinema is confined to expressive and representational modes. Of these, representational performances provide the basic existential furniture of mainstream Hollywood productions. Yet, although such performances are numerous, they are not dominant; expressive performances and the institution of stardom are.

Actors in commercially successful parts are treated as engaging in a form of self-expression with the character, which comes to be seen as issuing from their essential inner qualities. So powerful is the emphasis on the star that excellent representational performances are always construed, usually after the fact, as expressive performances. This assumption is not entirely naive because the technical norms of mainstream cinema – close-ups, lighting, and framing – encourage actors to instil their performance with an element of individuality that will stay the hand of the editor or, increasingly as compositing becomes a norm, ensure that they look good with whomever or whatever their screen image is combined.

Actors seeking to impose – or persuade the director to engineer – an 'impressive' screen image are not driven solely by vanity. There is the matter of competing with other actors for recognition and public favour. Acting has its own competitive spirit, somewhat like athletics requiring stamina and physical skills; yet this spirit is deeply implicated in the process of self-expression, and thus consequential for the actor's self-esteem. Although film actors are insulated from the audience at the moment of performance, they do perform in front of the crew and fellow actors.

Motion picture and television work is structured around semi-permanent work groups. The production team assembles for the duration of a specific project and then, if lucky, moves on to the next. For actors, the intermittency of production provides compelling reasons to exploit existing roles to make a personal mark. Whether stars or journeymen, all actors are under pressure to sustain a reputation for being reliable and capable of producing high-quality performances in a tight time frame. Indeed, the experience of working together becomes the crucial reference point for networking (Blair 2003: 668). Given this labour market texture, the temptation to use tried and tested techniques of ingratiation – developing a persona that is transfilmic and thereby seemingly the actor's private self – is great. For those explicitly seeking stardom, self-expressive performances are the equivalent of personal branding to ensure highly paid and regular employment.

Being a star is about integrating a first-person address into a third-person representational order. It is also about excluding other actors from this kind of self-expressive behaviour. To some extent the logic of casting ensures this result. Notions of (presumed) sex appeal, age, and type appropriateness ensure that a relatively small number of actors play roles that have room for expressive performance. Whole categories of actors – supporting actors, stunt players, body doubles, stand-ins, and walk-ons – are constrained to serve as narrative furniture. For these members of the acting team, few opportunities arise for gilding their performances with anything approaching an individuated 'personality'.

A passage from Michael Dibdin's novel *Cabal* captures a problem the *LOTR* actors encountered: '[At] St Peter's Basilica tourists and pilgrims continued to promenade . . . dazed by the sheer scale of the sacred and secular claims being made on every side, numbly savouring the bitter taste of their individual insignificance' (1992: 3). This reflection on the dwarfing impact of Vatican architecture indicates how scale plays its role in the perception of significance. *LOTR* posed a similar problem of scale, not simply in terms of space but of what filled the space: intensively detailed, lovingly crafted sets and costumes.

Costuming and make-up can aid the actor in character creation, but their spectacular qualities can detract from the appearance of a living embodiment that the actor strives to create. The extensive use of prostheses and the degree of reliance on such devices, much like immobile masks, affects the actor's ownership of her performance. The view that an actor should 'own' her performance depends on assumptions about what the 'essence' of a performance is.

In certain forms of theatre – Japanese Noh theatre, for example – the actor merely embodies the character as externally defined by traditional masks and movements. *LOTR*, with some variation among the films, deploys a comparably surface-based semantics. Yet certain scenes set in the Shire, such as the opening sequences of *Fellowship*, also develop emotional intensity. This mixture of psychologically 'hot' and 'cool' scenes is atypical in fantasy and action genres, in which sweeping and cataclysmic events are interspersed with moments of emotional bonding.

To their credit, Jackson and his team treated both kinds of scenes with the same level of commitment and depth. But the sheer difference in scale between action pieces – such as Helm's Deep – and intimately scaled scenes – such as the Council of Elrond – tended to project different possible worlds rather than different states of the same possible world. This general feature had consequences for the kinds of acting the films required.

Equally, throughout the cycle, many performances either did not derive, or derived only remotely, from what the actors said and did in real time, that is to say, in the time when actors felt they were exercising their craft. As with the use of prostheses, the decision to use CGI in character creation stemmed from aesthetic considerations: chiefly, the intention to create Middle-earth as a self-sufficient fantasy realm, materially and imaginatively unique. The strong emphasis on staging and visual design (scenography) meant that live performance tended to complement rather than drive filming. Other assumptions re-enforced this emphasis on scenography: first, Jackson's belief that the mobile camera functions as 'another character' contributing substantially to the emotional tone of scenes; and, second, the need to ensure that what emerged was not so nearly unique for general audiences. The filmmakers used set pieces that evoked previous cinematic experiences in order to build cross-generic appeal. For example, 'The introduction of the Balrog didn't quite happen in this way, but we just wanted to make a sort of rollicking Indiana-Jones-type sequence out of it, really, to have some fun with it' (Jackson, quoted in Thompson 2003: 49). The action genre's influence also appears in scenes such as the death of Gollum, which in the book occurs because of a ring-bemused stumble into the abyss, but in the film is staged as a life and death struggle with Frodo.

Third, the power of the New Zealand location, however digitally remodelled, was to be a key part of the trilogy's visual appeal. The spectacular rendition of 'nature' in itself tended to confine acting to re-acting and behaving:

> When Theoden chased Wormtongue off the premises, down the stairs with that waterfall that Tolkien describes so precisely; when his subjects parted to see the traitor stagger into exile with the snowy mountains beyond; when he later prayed at his son's tomb and the wind blew hard in his face – all this authenticity will provide so much information about Theoden (and the rest of us: Aragorn, Legolas, Gimli, Merry and Pippin) that acting was not much required at least for the long shots. (McKellen 21 May 2001)

The diminishing effects of scale and spectacle are particularly marked in the first two films:

> All of our characters have been pushed to a point now where their life or death depends on what happens in the third movie, so it's very emotional. And from an actor's point of view, it was the most enjoyable to work because they could really play a lot more intense drama compared to the opportunities they had in the first two films. (Jackson, *Pavement*, Summer 2003: 140)

Sean Astin put it more directly: 'After the success of the first film I think everyone involved was looking for a way to say something meaningful with *The Two Towers*. Peter repeatedly voiced his concern that the movie didn't have enough heart yet, that perhaps action overwhelmed human emotion' (Astin 2004: 279). Again, scale affects the leading players' performances in unavoidable ways, given the physical attributes Tolkien gave his characters. In certain scenes, the characters' physical size undercuts the emotional force of performance. Scenes including 'small' characters in which size is not marked against the human norm are suddenly diminished when cutaways reveal larger humans or Elves. Sudden miniaturisation leading to a consequent evacuation of affect is particularly apparent in scenes of high emotion amongst Hobbits such as the penultimate scene in the trilogy, the departure of Bilbo, Gandalf, and Frodo to the Havens (the Elves' immortal land).

A range of acting styles is on display in *LOTR*, from the emotionally centred acting of Elijah Wood and Sean Astin as Frodo and Sam through to the more traditional repertory approach of, for example, Bernard Hill as Theoden or Ian McKellen or the commedia dell'arte routines of Gimli, Merry, and Pippin. Leading actors were also required to emote, tumble, and parry before blue screens for motion capture,[1] engaging in the equivalent of mime. Much of the acting is equivalent to doing circus stunts. Orlando Bloom as 'Action Elf' is a leading example, but the numerous stunt players constitute an inarticulate, grunting, and growling mass of bodily performances.

This mixture of performance styles is not tied to a specific character; it can appear in the same character at different times. Certain characters, such as Galadriel and Elrond, were pretty much confined to one kind of behaviour, in their case mugging Elvish seriousness, but that was not a general rule. Variability in the performance of leading characters means that there is no general mimetic key governing the overall performance of character. The absence of a general mimetic keying, intentional or not, communicates that character behaviour is substantially a reaction to setting and events. In this sense, despite its proclaimed humanism, much of what happens on screen is behaviouristic. The presence of non-human actors and action sequences merely deepens this existential keying.

One of the distinctive contributions an actor can make to characterisation is, when well done, improvisation. But the space for the camera to capture spontaneity was limited on *LOTR*. In action scenes involving potentially dangerous stunts, tight co-ordination was necessarily the

**Figure 11** Close-up of Galadriel.

rule. While there is nothing ad-hoc about the behaviour of computer-generated characters, even scenes on an intimate scale seem to have provided few opportunities to engage in interesting by-play. The drinking scene in which Gimli (John Rhys-Davies) challenges Legolas (Orlando Bloom) to a drinking contest would appear to be one of the few exceptions to the rule that all acting was tightly scripted, the fact that the script was subject to nearly constant revisions as filming continued notwithstanding, as Rhys-Davies makes clear in an interview on the extended DVD of *Return*.

These features return us to what might be called Jackson's rule: that matters of scenography should have priority over the individual performances. Although this rule was eventually perceived as a problem to be remedied in the third film, for all that, it provided the dominant aesthetic of production. In its use of a vast army of psychologically undifferentiated types – encouraged all the more by Tolkien's litany of creatures – *LOTR* follows the standard premises of a Hollywood epic: include lots of surface action, and confine in-depth characterisation to a small number of leading players. But it goes further in that its spectacle depletes the space available to protagonists to explore the classical Hollywood values of strongly foregrounded psychological motivation (Bordwell *et al.* 1985).

For actors, the problem of 'owning' a performance as a 'personal' expression of a scripted character was compounded by a number of unique challenges, surpassing the 'normal' of the new digital environment of Hollywood productions. These challenges are most apparent in relation to those actors where performance was more than merely behaving – though even leading actors did an unusual amount of this. Leading actors have the best chance to accomplish 'creative' ownership of the content of their performances and how these performances are used. The challenges were as follows.

### Chronological and spatial disembedding of the production process

After initially planning to film chronologically, Jackson made the bold and unprecedented decision to shoot all three films concurrently, sometimes simultaneously, across the range of locations that Aotearoa New Zealand offers. This decision, conditioned in part by weather, meant that the actor's sense of a specific scene took on a modular quality, as a self-sufficient bit of action that would subsequently be fitted into a multi-phased and hyper-mediated narrative space. This narrative space was more complex than what might be found in a single film, even one with a number of subplots. Consequently, it was difficult for actors to visualise the arc of character development or even the quality of the trilogy as whole. Part-and-whole relationships were vexed and ruptured:

> Faith was required because, for the actors at least, there was no control whatsoever. There was simply an eighteen-month roller coaster ride that we hoped would somehow result in a film worthy of the work that had gone into it. Sometimes it was hard, if not downright impossible, to envision the outcome, or even to imagine anyone, including Peter Jackson, had a clear picture of what the finished product would look like. (Astin 2004: 183)

The feeling of being lost in rhizomatic space was intensified by the fact that much of what was nominally delivered by the cast was actually completed in post-production. Computer-generated performances and settings were either not visible or only partially visible to the actors, making it difficult to calculate their relative impact on acting ongoing in the present. For example, Wood and Astin performed live with Serkis, but the image of Gollum, with all its concretising mannerisms, was digitally remastered in the motion capture studio.

## Jackson as *über*-auteur

The radical modularity of the shooting process had specific consequences. It is a commonplace in filmmaking that directors either favour a participatory approach to performance or treat actors as 'cattle'. Reading or listening to promotional interviews, one is struck by the fact that most of the leading players found Jackson a sympathetic and supportive director. It is tempting to see this as the usual 'luvvies' talk and hyperbole surrounding promotional events. But it also points to Jackson's specific role as a 'filter' of collective creativity, a role that extended to the casting process itself (Shefrin 2004: 268).

Interviews with cast members suggest that a great deal of interpersonal bonding occurred between cast and crew. This bonding could be interpreted as a compensation for the unusually fragmented process of filming. Yet Jackson's managerial style combined consultation (with leading actors and crew) with retaining final say under all circumstances: 'Peter being the control freak that he is, was right in there . . . Everything was bettered by him all the way through, so he was always in control. It was a totalitarian system we worked on. His was the last word' (McDonald 2001–2: 129).

Perhaps the clearest indication of Jackson's endearing leadership style is that he extracted a high level of effort and commitment from his cast and crew. This was especially favoured by the non-unionised context of production – a context that Jackson and Osborne have stated was an absolute precondition for production at all. The trilogy was an epic in two senses – as a story form and as a feat of labour. All members of the cast echo Astin's comments on long days of exhausting work (though see Thompson 2004).

The successful combination of autocrat and democrat should be understood as less a matter of personality than of practical necessity. Jackson's dominating aim of remaining visually true to Tolkien's (often vestigial) descriptions meant that there was unusual scope for differing interpretations, which might easily devolve into 'creative' differences if not held in check. Courtesy of digital editing and compositing, Jackson could be part of the creative team and 'one of the boys' and yet exert very tight and detailed control in editing. This fundamental (and some would say necessary) ambivalence meant that whoever was the direct 'author' of a performance, the definitive 'Author' was Jackson himself.

At the same time, the leading actors undeniably sought to exercise a high degree of control over details. Viggo Mortensen, although he came late to the role of Aragorn, was notable in this regard, as the costume designer Ngila Dickson reports:

**Figure 12** Medium shot of Arwen and Aragorn: attention to detail.

'It was terrifying. I didn't know Viggo . . . The week before shooting, Viggo walked into my covered wardrobe dressing room and neither of us was saying very much . . .

'I was standing there and my heart was in my mouth – I was willing to start the process again because I know how much it matters. You cannot act a role like that without feeling like you were in your second skin as that character. And I was certainly prepared to do it, but there was a part of me that knew we were knee-deep in trouble.

'Viggo paced up and down and said, "Do you think we could just put a few more ties on these boots?" And in that moment – I had known the first time he put that costume on that it was ten times better on him and that was actually to do with . . . Viggo's experience and age and life. He imbued that costume with its own life. The terrifying thing for me was that I might have an actor who simply wanted to get rid of it, but he did not do that. He just wanted to add to it. I was in love with Viggo from the beginning' (laughs). (DVDfile.com 2003)

What is revealing about this quotation and others like it is the suggestion that one by-product, intentional or otherwise, of the tight control exercised over production was that acting business tended to be displaced from matters of conceptualisation (arc of character development) to the details of appearance and execution. This displacement suggests the extent to which performance became a resource available to the director.

Having said that, marketing was also an important factor. With the release on to DVD of special extended versions, much material that was excised from the theatrical release can now be seen. As Saruman's (Christopher Lee) death scene (one of five scenes added to the extended version of *Return*) indicates, excised scenes were neither redundant nor of poor quality. This particular excision, which Lee protested against at the time of the theatrical release, evidences the secondary place of performance relative to marketing.

### Extreme fragmentation of performance

It has long been standard practice to shoot actors' performances out of chronological order for various technical and economic reasons. The fragmentation process was exceptionally intense for the *LOTR* actors, owing to the tight time frame and the scope of what was to be done. It was not unusual for actors to play scenes from all three movies in a single day. In addition to the dispersed production process, leading actors found that the opportunity to exercise some conceptual control over the grain of their performances was further inhibited by a policy of multiple takes. It was estimated that Jackson shot nearly fifteen minutes of footage for every page of the script, compared to the normal practice of a minute of footage for one page of script (Astin 2004: 201–2). Constant revision of the script, either overnight or during shooting, prevented the actors from pre-visualising and rehearsing scenes in sufficient detail, introducing further uncertainty into characterisation (Astin 2004: 199).

The logistics of shooting across a large geographical area also led to a radical temporal dissociation of complementary performances, as indicated on the extended version of *Return*: e.g., reaction shots between Wood and Astin on the stairs of Cirith Ungol were filmed a year apart (Extended DVD *Return*). As much as ninety percent of the dialogue was looped in after the filming was completed – partly because the initial recording of dialogue at the Stone Street studios was flawed (Astin 2004: 220). The dislocation occasioned by these practices seems exceptional even for Hollywood.

### Non-human actors

In *LOTR* we find actors engaged in a diverse range of performances: live performances in which the actor's prepared onscreen appearance and behaviour ground the drama; live performances that animate a mask or prosthesis in which the actor appears as a character unlike his or her normal screen appearance; performances that are internal to computer-generated processes; and performances that, although computer-mediated, derive a general form and grammar from a live performance. *LOTR* seems to question the very concept of performance, not least because the creation of non-human actors to act alongside human actors reaches a contemporary peak.

From a businesslike view of the film industry, the extensive deployment of non-human actors in *LOTR* requires a reconsideration of the actor's place in the cinema. Non-human actors are not automatically ascribed a credible personality and motivation on the basis of their behaviour. This ambiguous status as beings throws into doubt what is routinely accorded to a human actor. This is less a matter of the fantasy context, which routinely combines everyday and otherworldly characters. The drive behind *LOTR* is to render all beings from whatever realm photo-realistically. Thus human actors become fantastic, while fantasy figures become 'realer than real' or hyper-real. The use of non-human actors is by now extensive enough in the media to warrant a name, announcing a category of artificial being – 'a synthespian: a personality-construct, a congeries of software agents, the creation of information designers' (Gibson 1996).

Many of the denizens of Middle-earth are synthespians – be they nameless and faceless 'extras' – such as the animated figures created by Massive software – or important characters such as Gollum, the spider Shelob, or the Mumakils in the battle of Pelennor Field. Dramatically, the relationship between actors and synthespians rests on mutual validation. In many of the battle scenes in the trilogy, the realism of synthespians is grounded by the reactions of live actors, leading or extras, to their appearance. Bernard Hill's reaction to the Mumakils or Miranda Otto's to the Witch King during the battle of Pelennor Field are examples from amongst many actor–synthespian reaction shots. We believe these computer-generated figures are alive because these actors show fear at the sight of them.

The visual effects supervisor Jim Rygiel, commenting on the final battle of Helm's Deep, notes a similar interdependency: 'In these scenes, a conflict is raging between tens of thousands of men and Uruk-hai . . . The armies of men and Uruk-hai are composed primarily of digital actors. Real actors with make-up and prosthetics were only used for tight shots' (Doyle 2003: 28). Actors not only lend miniature synthespians realism in close-up. Synthespians rely on copying real-time performances for the plausibility of their movements and facial expressions. This reliance is most apparent if we consider Andy Serkis.

Originally Serkis was offered three weeks' work to do the voice-over for Gollum when Gollum was to be a digitally created synthespian. This arrangement proved less than satisfactory, running up against the typical limitations of computer-generated actors. As Kleiser and Walczak, the originators of the term 'synthespian', make clear, these limitations relate to the expression of emotion: 'Our goal is to create characters with whom the audience can form empathetic relationships. This is much more important than merely making an actor look indistinguishable from a human, and in many ways much more challenging' (Kleiser-Walczak Studios 2005). Jackson indirectly concurred:

> If you look at close-ups of actors, it is all down to very subtle facial movements and their eyes. In one shot sad and one happy, while there's no visible difference on the actor's face, you can tell what the emotion is in the eyes. The emotion that they're playing basically comes from their soul and computers don't have souls. That, to me, was the real secret that we had to crack with Gollum. We had to analyse physically what we can do to recreate that on an artificial level. We couldn't afford to have it look artificial – it had to look totally real. (Serkis 2003: 85)

To achieve the highest level of photo-realism in CGI, it was the emotional texture of performance – the actor's expressive powers – that was found wanting:

It became apparent as the character of Gollum developed during the production of *The Two Towers*, that the original creature, barely glimpsed in *The Fellowship of the Ring*, would need to be changed. Although everyone loved the first Gollum, he was created before Andy Serkis arrived on the scene and astonished us all with the emotional strength of his performance. (Allan Lee, quoted in Serkis 2003: 6)

As Serkis recalls:

They had decided to make Gollum a totally CG (computer generated) creature from early on in pre-production. They had felt it would be impossible to cast any actor, even with prosthetic make-up, because of the extreme physical appearance, nature and demands of the role. However the job of the actor who got the part would not simply be putting a voice on top of an animated creature. In tune with the levels of authenticity they were trying to achieve, they were adamant that Gollum would have to be able to act alongside Frodo and Sam. (Serkis 2003: 7)

Serkis found that in order to produce the distinctive voice of Gollum, he needed to perform Gollum as a character, twisting his body to match the contorted physique of the character. Using a motion capture suit and virtual reality 'goggles', Serkis became the living medium of Gollum, matching voice, expressions, and movements. Compared to actors whose performances were directly filmed but under a relatively mask-like prosthesis, e.g., Lawrence Makoare as Lurtz the Uruk-hai, Gollum was visually and vocally moulded on to Serkis's real time performance so that the latter was present in a computer-generated surrogate. Even if the computer-generated creature was imprinted with acting traces produced by Serkis, the actor realised 'that, unlike any character I've ever played, one of the major challenges would be that I didn't totally "own" the role' (Serkis 2003: 18).

He continues:

I AM GOLLUM! Well actually, Andy, you're part of Gollum. You're the voice and emotions (and eventually the movements) but the body will be taken care of by many talented people, with their own equally valid opinions. Your body will vanish into thin air and be replaced by digital ones and zeroes, so get your head around that. (Serkis 2003: 19)

This wasn't always that easy:

I hate what I'm doing, I hate the fact that I only get one or two chances to get my performance, and even then it doesn't seem to make any difference 'cause nobody seems to have a clue what I'm doing. Why am I here? I know Gollum's going to be animated but I've still got to be able to give my performance. I hate the fact that my shots are called 'reference passes' and then when I step off camera and it's just Elijah and Sean it's, 'OK, now we're going to do it for real'. So what my shots aren't for real? I'm busting a gut here, for what? I wish I was doing this in prosthetics. (Serkis 2003: 51)

Recalling that creating Gollum involved Serkis in four areas of work – on-set performance for 35 mm, motion capture, ADR (automated dialogue replacement), and animation – the concept of Gollum as a puppet manipulated by the actor seriously understates the degree of effort the actor had to give to achieve a portrayal of character. The case of Gollum points to a general condition that all the leading players faced in varying degrees during production – the morselisation or splitting up of elements of portrayal that are inextricably commingled in a live performance.

From the actors' perspective, what is unique to *LOTR* is the potential depth of the conflict between the intrinsically analogical nature of acting as a continuous process and the digital rendering of those events. Other actors were assigned to one or other side of the live and synthesised divide – a divide the production teams found difficult to bridge precisely because they had created it. Yet the image of Jackson as *über*-auteur, with his fingers in every piece of the action, needs to be qualified. When tied to photo-realism, CGI does not free the director from the established conventions for representing the physical world through cinema. Film images – of scenes and performances – have to be convincingly created before they can be usefully manipulated. So the displacement of the actor is far from absolute. In becoming the substance of virtual effects, an actor like Serkis asserts a carnal authority over the image, but only at the cost of intensifying the pace and depth of emotional and physical labour.

The interface between computer- and human-based performances in *LOTR* poses some larger questions about human agency. Does the trilogy signal a new phase in the uses of the actor? Are traditional notions of performance as an inner expression of a concrete individual trained in a specific craft about to be superseded? Will acting as an embodied expressive activity be surpassed by what can be digitally visualised? In the figure of Gollum, *LOTR* demonstrates that the actor's presence is still required, but for how long once gestures and expressions have been coded and stored? Will the voice, the element of human performance most resistant to digital appropriation, remain the last function for the actor to fulfil? In time, with the perfection of CGI, will film acting be significantly redefined as offscreen vocalising, like John Rhys-Davies as Treebeard (a role he took on in addition to Gimli), for onscreen, photo-realistic synthespians? Will this not affect the star system and the underlying structure of employment and reward that stardom pulls in its train? While lookalikes have never been successfully marketed to film audiences, will soundalikes be more convincing, a Tom Hanks imitator more than adequate to voice *Toy Story*'s Woody? There is some irony in the fact that what Peter Jackson has declared the ultimate human story is extensively rendered by non-human actors.

*LOTR* strides significantly towards the advent of the post-human actor, an agent not linked to consciousness who puts into contestation what it is to be human (Latour 1993: *passim*). Theorising the metaphysics of photography, Vilem Flusser speaks of the increasing hold of technical images over cultural perception. Technical images do not signify phenomena but, although this is not immediately perceived in images that strive to be so photo-realistic, signify instead concepts of phenomena. Not the world as captured through light and movement but through computer-generated renditions of light and movement. These renditions immerse the spectator in a world of 'bloodless and simplistic simulations of human thought processes, which precisely because they are so rigid render human decisions superfluous and non-functional' (Flusser 2000: 74). This statement captures well the conditions of existence of many of the human and non-human actors who populate *LOTR*. It also recalls something of the agonies of Serkis, that digitised St Sebastian, peppered with mo-cap dots, as he submits his mind and body to the codes of Gollum.

### Note

1 Motion capture is a technique for converting the movements of human actors into digital form ready for animation. In *LOTR*, the most prominent example involved dressing Andy Serkis in a blue 'gimp' suit dotted with small reflective dots. The blue suit is invisible to the type of camera used, which records only the motion of the dots at key reference points on the body (elbows, shoulders, knees, etc.) or the face (corners of the eyes and mouth, cheekbones, etc.). The reference points are then used to provide information to 3D modellers for the movements Gollum makes in the composite shots.

# 12

# Dispersing Elijah: stardom and the event film

*Barry King*

In a moment of high drama in *Spy Kids 3D: Game Over*, The Guy (Elijah Wood), the one the kids believe can beat the game, suddenly appears. Stepping out of an incandescent field of white light, like an angel or visiting alien, this character whose silhouette has figured elsewhere in the narrative advances towards the camera, emerging from the enveloping radiance. A short piece of business later, and The Guy is vanquished. Bleeding a visual stream of numbers, he dissolves in a pop of white light. Gone but hardly there anyway and who, indeed, was there? The Guy, Frodo, or Elijah?

This cramped cinematic event, vestigial in the narration of *Spy Kids 3D*, teasingly conflates the fictive and the factual. The unabashed brevity of what it evokes, its flaunting of a slight and inconsequential perform-ance, announces the actor himself, the putatively *real* identity that inheres behind multiple fictional identities. Such is the semiotic eco-nomy of the cameo; so little is capable of so much indexical profundity. In disappearing from narrative space, Wood gains a new status as a signifier, an actor who has surpassed the obligations of character, a narrative agent whose value is given by merely appearing. The message of the cameo is unmistakable: Wood is a star.

## But what is a star?

Stardom is a promissory note advanced by publicity and promotion, which the audience may or may not redeem at the box office. But if they do, the rewards and the acclaim the star receives testify that an 'essential' embodiment has occurred. The essence of stardom – constructed but defining – is the agreement that the central dramatic features of the film devolve from the star's participation. Audiences understand that other participants contribute value to what is on screen, but the trans-lation of such values into a living experience is the star's forte. Yet for all the apparent robustness of the process of attribution, the figure of the star remains ambiguous. First, this is because stars are actors – creatures of plural identity. The star's performance may refer to the real person of the actor, to the assumed professional identity or persona, or the identity implied by the character. Such uncertainty is not simply because stars sometimes play different characters. Performance, live or recorded, rests on a multi-dimensional process of identity reference. In performance, the 'I' who speaks can be the 'I' of the star's private identity, the 'I' of a specific character, or the 'I' of the actor's persona. This last 'I' pertains to the actor's professional identity that extends beyond a particular role yet depends semantically on the kinds of roles the actor essays. The process of referring back and forth between identity states is a process of anaphora (Urban 1989). The 'I' that speaks can be Frodo, Elijah Wood, or a composite persona – say *Woody Baggins* – formed by the semantic interaction of character and person.

The play on these identity positions is part of the mystery or aura of stardom. The star is virtually present photographically, yet practically absent. Some authors see this combination of presence and absence as the essence of stardom and the cause of its allure (Ellis 1992). Yet for the 'tease' of identity to occur, the three ways of referring to the being of the actor – as person, persona, or character – must each attain a level of autonomy in their own right.

## An event film

The widespread use of CGI and special effects in *LOTR* provides a particularly efficacious slate of condensed spectacles for recycling in ancillary markets along with trailers, cast interviews, making-of documentaries, and still images. But this modular quality, so desirable from the point of view of the market, sets up tensions that are felt at the level of acting. Especially given Jackson's self-proclaimed mandate to bring Middle-earth alive on the screen, the actors' main task was not to provide individual interpretations of their characters but merely to animate Tolkien's descriptions. This mandate accords well with the norm of character acting that is to make a character appear to be author of the words, actions, gestures, and expressions as they are found in the script (Counsell 1996: 3). But because Tolkien's characterisation is sometimes thin, the director's interpretation became paramount. Still, it was possible to see this as a great opportunity. As one lead actor opined, 'Potentially what will make these movies work on a higher level than most "event movies" is the complexity of the characters' (Mortensen 2001–2).

While the emphasis on 'rounded character portrayal' sits uneasily with the modular imperative that calls for a plural address to different

audiences, it also conflicts with what is held to be the essence of stardom – the delivery of an expressive performance that draws attention to
the actor's persona. In the classical Hollywood film, the star's personal
appropriation of the 'literary' existence of a character performance is
abetted by direction, camerawork, lighting, makeup, costuming – in short,
by the mise-en-scène. The casting and direction of other actors aim to
ensure that a multiplicity of performances is subordinated to the purpose
of celebrating the stars' presence. Beyond the film text's boundary, subsidiary texts and performances are referred back, anaphorically, to the star's
presence, creating a process of 'vortextuality' (Whannel 2002: 206–7).

But for all its talk of stars, *LOTR*'s ensemble acting worked against
the development of a star-centred vortex of reference. Sean Astin might
modestly observe that 'Wood carries the dramatic weight of the film[;]
the rest of the cast are left in the wings of the ring' (Barrett 2003), but
this conjuration of stardom did not meet with universal approval.

> Lee was one of only two really good acting performances in the series,
> among all the simpering maidens and beefcakes and callow hobbits, the
> other being Ian McKellen's splendid Gandalf. Saruman gone! Could it be
> that Peter Jackson decided that what with all the expensive battle scenes,
> there wasn't time? He could have cut half the shots of Elijah Wood's Frodo
> doing his bug-eyed, smudgy-faced worried expression, and freed up about
> 20 minutes. But there we are. Without Saruman, it's not good versus evil.
> It's good versus . . . a sort of swarming amorphous danger. (Bradshaw
> 2003a)

*Variety*, too, felt that Astin, Mortensen, and McKellen (the sole Oscar
nomination – for supporting actor) provided the trilogy's strongest
performances (McLean 2004). When the Screen Actors Guild conferred
the ensemble acting award on the cast, it seemed clear that Wood's chances
of reducing an ensemble of performances into a personal statement of
charisma were slim.

### A glutting of stars

All actors wish to shine, though they may not wish to be stars. Wood,
left to his own devices, might not seek stardom, but promotional discourse could not forgo the audience interest in stardom. Economically,
it was good to have a cast of relative unknowns, but it was good copy
to talk about how they were competing. At the same time, the discourse
surrounding *LOTR* began the process of dissociating stardom from
acting: 'I mean, could Mel Gibson have been Aragorn? Yeah, sure, that
would not be so bizarre. But we never went down that road because
we wanted the story to be the star' (Ordesky 2003).

As a term, 'star' implies an individual human presence, a function that an actor occupies. But in *LOTR*, this 'anthropomorphic' space was never resolved. For the ensemble of leading players, this meant that the opportunity to 'shine' was not denied by a conscious cultivation of a star's image. The 'name the star' contest that followed was further deepened by the fact that leading players sought to ensure that their roles would be seen as outstanding performances, augmenting their future claims to stardom. Ensemble playing did not end actor rivalry and indeed enhanced it by bringing established players like Ian McKellen into contact with novices such as Orlando Bloom. If anything, leading players found themselves deprived of expressive opportunities.

The general atmosphere of a collective mission to make art under extreme circumstances, requiring more than 100 per cent commitment, meant that the actors accepted the subordination of their performances to an epic corporate purpose. So, for example, Wood's status as star was not borne out by the opening credits, which named New Line Cinema and then WingNut Productions. Such corporate participants, it was implied, supersede in creative importance the cast. Indeed, the actors' names appear only in the end credits, literally underscoring the idea that the film did not need stars (McDonald 2001–2: 116). It was not too fanciful to conclude that the star of *LOTR* was Jackson, with his cameo appearances *à la* Hitchcock.

Historically, as the concept of stardom was stretched to embrace the auteur, it was also drained of special value through being equated with the simple power of spectacle and visibility. Because of his fleeting cameo appearance, Bret McKenzie/Figwit at one point found that 1310 websites had mentioned his name, thereby creating instant celebrity for him. Mackenzie observed: 'It's so hilarious because it's been propelled by so little. I'm famous for doing nothing' ('Websites' 2002). Similarly, the New Zealand press, reporting on the racing interests of Peter McKenzie (Elendil), mobilised a very Kiwi fantasy of leaping from obscurity to fame on the basis of very modest achievements, and muddied the concept of stardom even further:

> Trainer has a chance to star again
>   From starring in two group one events of the big screen to a shot at headlining the final two features at the Wellington Cup carnival.
>   That's the fairytale scenario for Levin thespian-turned trainer Peter McKenzie . . . While horses are his hobby, acting has always been a passion for McKenzie, whose multitalented son Bret also featured in LOTR and has just finished shooting a US-pilot comedy series from the makers of *Friends* and *Seinfeld*. (Graham 2005)

In these manoeuvres the term 'star' has become a tautology.

## Pluralising performance

Performance also militates against stardom. In *LOTR*, performance was folded around different conceptions of the acting subject, mixing human and post-human subjects and displacing the actor from the centre of the performance process.

The term 'performance' can refer to three aspects: an organisational performance in which an individual employee is expected to conform to a managerially defined role; a technological performance in which a given piece of hardware performs to specification; a cultural performance through which a symbolic expression occurs (McKenzie 2001: 3–14). The latter performance is commonly understood as what actors do.

In *LOTR*, the first two kinds of performance predominate over the third. Many participants deliver only organisational or technical performances. This is obvious if one considers the use of behind-the-camera crafts, but it is also true in front of the camera. There were 26,000 live extras who performed without lines. Yet the emphasis on doing rather than saying extended up the cast hierarchy to encompass substantial roles such as Lurtz (Lawrence Makoare), the Uruk-hai leader. Even major speaking parts such as Eomer (Karl Urban) follow a logic that is performative in the linguistic sense, underscoring speech as action. With saying equated with doing in this way, surfaces replace psychological depth.

Organisational performances such as these are redoubled by techno-performances. The live action of *LOTR* was populated – thanks to Massive software – by 200,000 digital characters, many of whom were capable of making unscripted decisions within the microscopic scale of their existence. The displacement of live action by techno-performance even enters into the intimate scale of characterisation. The application of prostheses and makeup work to externalise and ossify the expressive, even gestural aspects of an actor's performance, reducing them to animated props (Simpson *et al.* 2003).

Non-human agents also challenge the importance of human agency. The Ring itself can be considered a character since it has the power to alter the emotional states and actions of various human or quasi-human characters, such as Frodo, Boromir, and Gollum. What is true of the Ring applies not only to CG characters but also to the locations. The intensive remediation of the New Zealand landscape by CGI, modelling, and matte processes turned the setting into a kind of actor in itself, deploying the cast as pretexts for spectacle. Caught in the grand sweep of scenes, even leading characters were equated to marionettes. Computer-generated aerial shots, for example of Gandalf riding through the gates of Isengard in *Fellowship* or Frodo, Sam, and Gollum in the Mount Doom sequence in *Return*, recall the top-down optics of many computer games rendering live actors as the product of code. Even Serkis's distinctive, highly rated performance as Gollum was barred from a Best Supporting Actor nomination because of the suspicion that what is seen owes more to the computer than to the actor. Such a view may have devalued Wood's performance since his incarnation of Frodo is mediated by prosthetics, CG compaction of normal height, and trickery in shot scale (as was John Rhys-Davies's performance as Gimli).

The undeniable distinctiveness of Serkis's voice notwithstanding, Gollum is an uncomfortable hybrid, somewhere between live action and a cartoon. The award of Oscars to makeup, costume, and digital design, rather than acting, merely codified what was incipient in *LOTR*, the dominant role of techno-performance. 'The actors do their job, but they are like music accompanying the wonders' (Thomson 2004).

These features also reveal a pervasive visualisation strategy that undercuts the necessary centring of spectator identification that is intrinsic to stardom. The spectator is most often watching the visual gambits of an autonomous, variable camera eye that is unconstrained by the need to respect the eye of the spectator as the centre of what is shown (Aumont 1997).

## The luck of Elijah

Frodo was Wood's breakout role. But in *LOTR*, performances are drawn *through* rather than *from* actors. Leading actors were required to preserve an existential bond with their character in order to support promotion and marketing – and to reap opportunities from postproduction fan convention appearances. To live a character, like Dave Prouse still appearing as Darth Vader at Star Wars conventions, is to make oneself the brand of a character, stamping commodity value on public appearances at fan conventions and certifying that material objects – memorabilia, autographs, memoirs, collectible figures – are genuine indices of the presence of an imaginary realm. Wood's cameo in *Spy Kids 3D* incarnates that imperative.

Elijah's luck is to have found his breakout role in portraying a fictive character that has acquired, through the books' success, the rigidity of a brand. As a result, he can only fill out Frodo; he cannot make Frodo his own without accepting that his career will become an embodiment of a simulation.

'Are you done with Frodo?'
   'I mean, I've left him behind, but part of me will always be connected to that character. A peace [*sic*] of him will always be with me, but in terms

of being recognized as Frodo for the rest of my life, it's something I'm very proud of'. (*Action Adventure* 2004)

In sum, the event film works to reverse the causal proclivities of stardom: reducing the star's persona to a servant of character, without affirming the actor's craft.

Theorising the metaphysics of photography, Flusser speaks of the increasing hold of technical images over cultural perception. Such images signify concepts of phenomena: the world as captured not through light and movement but through computer-generated renditions of light and movement (2000: 74). Wood, the nominal lead in what Jackson declared the ultimate human story, follows the logic of the event film to a condition of post-humanity.

# Part IV
# Making a film trilogy

# 13

# Dossier: production and post-production

*Sean Cubitt and Barry King*

This, perhaps the most detailed dossier section in *Studying the Event Film*, also contains the most technical information about the trilogy's production. It is therefore appropriate that the section as a whole contains the three chapters that deal most specifically with how the film has been put together. Kevin Fisher ('Sonic resonances of nature and supernature in the *Lord of the Rings* trilogy', Chapter 14) and Judith Bernanke ('Howard Shore's ring cycle: the film score and operatic strategy', Chapter 15) deal with aspects of sound, while Cubitt looks at *LOTR*'s visual effects (Chapter 16). As this dossier attests, though, the technical labour involved in creating the films could easily generate further analysis on the scale of a three-volume book of its own.

## Production

How do we learn details of a film's production? The studio public relations machine developed press kits in the last century to help distributors and exhibitors promote individual films, and press kits today continue to provide similar information about the people involved in a production, the sorts of difficulties a production has had to overcome, and anything else newsworthy about a production that might pique the interest of paying audiences. While press kits, now often available electronically via computers, are valuable tools for the film scholar, it is important to remember their primary purpose: to inform distributors, marketers, critics, and theatre operators of the central pitch of the film's marketing.

None the less, many aspects of the production process will be documented, especially in the case of event films, where the scale and complexity of production is itself a selling point for the finished product. Press kits may contain usefully condensed quotations on key aspects, as for example in this quotation from Jackson in the EPK for *Fellowship*:

'From the beginning I wanted to make something that felt real', comments Jackson. 'Tolkien writes in a way that makes everything come alive, and we wanted to set that realistic feeling of an ancient world-come-to-life right away with the first film, then continue to build it as the story unravels'. (New Line 2001)

The same source gives a brisk overview of the effects department at Weta Workshop. Effects supervisor Richard Taylor, for example, approached the project 'like a general going to war', dividing his forces into six departments: Creatures, Special effects, Make-up and prosthetics, Armour and weapons, Miniatures, and Model effects. (It should be noted that the terms 'special effects' and 'model effects' apply to physical or 'practical' effects, as opposed to digital effects, which are referred to as 'visual' rather than 'special'). Unusually, Weta took control of all the special effects departments barring stunts and pyrotechnics, a decision based on the need for a single controlling vision of Middle-earth. The production notes describe the key role of Lee and Howe in producing hundreds of sketches deriving from their work illustrating the Allen and Unwin editions of *The Lord of the Rings*, and the significance of these sketches in securing the films' overall look.

The trilogy was a massive undertaking:

1,100 pages of novel to adapt, 276 days of principal production, three years of postproduction, 1,600 pairs of hobbit feet, 200 orc masks, 10,000 arrows, 48,000 pieces of armour, 12 million circular links for chain-mail construction, 2,000 stunt weapons, a 3,000 person crew, 500 actors, 26,000 extras, seven camera crews, two studios, three movies. (Feld 2004: 10)

With six hundred scenes and 350 sets, *LOTR* is not just a feat of imagination. Even the most ethereal sets had to be built to the most exacting standards. According to Grant Major, production designer, 'You had thousands of people trampling through these sets, and sometimes people were hacking axes into the floor, so they had to be built to withstand a lot! Our sets had to withstand 60 pounds per square foot' (New Line 2001). Major supervised the planting of 5000 cubic feet of plants by the greens department at the Matamata Hobbiton location a year in advance of the shoot. The physical effects team (Steve Ingram, Richard Cordobes, and Blair Foord) was responsible for producing 'rain, snow, fire and wind storms with spray pipes and giant fans, as well as an enormous volume of mist, steam, fog and smoke through the use of special liquids. The team also created fake rivers and streams running through fake forests on soundstages' (New Line 2001).

Under the lead of head wrangler Steve Old, the production of the first film alone required over 250 horses: 'Among them are the five miniature horses used for the Hobbits, and the two proud white Andalusians used to bring *Shadowfax*, the wizard Gandalf's mysteriously wild and courageous steed, to life' (New Line 2001). The contributions of wranglers and greens departments, of location caterers, production accountants, cleaners, drivers, dressers, pilots, carpenters, electricians, and the hundreds of other skilled and unskilled workers employed on the shoot are clearer from a close reading of the press kits than from many more ostensibly political accounts of the films.

The film was shot on Super35mm film, which gives an aspect ratio of 1:2.35 without special lenses. The decision to use Super35 was made largely because Weta was already set up to work with this format, but partly because of a lack of Panasonic's anamorphic cameras in the New Zealand rental market prior to the *Rings* shoot. Anamorphosis, which uses a distorting lens to squeeze a cinemascope image on to a normal strip of 35mm film, creates problems with parallax – the relation of foreground to background – when the camera moves. Jackson likes mobile camerawork:

> The camera is another character in the scene. Just as an actor can express emotion, I strongly believe that moving the camera around enhances the emotion of a scene. The camera can also convey an attitude to the audience that is independent of the attitude coming from the characters, and sometimes it's interesting to use that perspective to give the audience a point of view that the characters aren't aware of themselves. Also, I believe that if you move the camera sensibly, it draws the audience into the film a bit more. They're not just being asked to interpret a series of static shots all by themselves; the camera is doing some of the interpretation for them. (Magid 2001a: 56)

Shooting with a view to adding digital effects in post-production has in the past meant locking down the camera to ensure that there is no movement, making the task of adding effects easier. In *LOTR*'s case, the production extensively used motion control technology, in which a computer records the camera's movements. This recording can then be used to replicate the move, either with other physical elements (e.g., a location can be matched with actors performing in front of a blue screen) or with virtual camera moves reproduced in the visual effects computers. An innovation here was the use of motion control technology to control the movements of a false-perspective set (nicknamed Slave Mo-Co) that allowed actors to perform against one another in real time to a mobile camera.[1] Similarly, for the shot of Gandalf's collapse on the mountain-top after defeating the Balrog, the stage and its lighting rig were both motorised to turn in sync, while the camera dollied in to emulate the Southern Alps location plate secured by Jackson's helicopter shoot. Locked-down cameras were used for specific scenes, for example in the sequence in *Towers* where we observe Theoden's transformation. Here three phases of the face were shot in greenscreen, morphed together, and composited with Theoden's throne. Lock-down was essential to permit continuity across the three takes separated by lengthy processes of prosthetics and make-up application.

Movement is not the only task the cinematographer must face. The Director of Photography (DoP) is head of a department responsible for lighting as well as recording. Key variables include

- the film stock: different film stocks respond to colour and to grey-scales in subtly different ways; they also have finer or coarser grain according to the conditions they are designed to be used in. Creative DoPs will frequently use a film stock in the 'wrong' conditions to secure specific effects.
- lenses and lens filters: lenses come in different focal lengths, and with numerous other characteristics for specialist functions, some of which alter the camera's responsiveness to colour and light. Filters are used to correct anything from reflections to overly harsh light, or to change the colour values of the shot. Most lenses also have various coatings, which again alter their responsiveness to light and to specific areas of the spectrum.
- lights, gels, and filters: DoPs are responsible for the use of lighting rigs as well as daylight, firelight, and other natural sources. Every light source has a distinctive colour range, and can be affected by being reflected off various surfaces. Gels – translucent coloured sheets – can be mounted in front of lamps to change their colour signature, and filters placed between the illumination and the object being lit to soften or diffuse the light.
- camera speed: changing the speed at which a camera runs to make action seem faster (undercranking) or slower (overcranking) can be used, for example, to make lightweight weapons appear heavier. However, the amount of light reaching the film stock depends on the duration of the exposure, so the lighting, film stocks, and lenses have to be brought into the equation to keep lighting levels and colour values within range.
- aperture, exposure, and focus: as in still photography, the cinematographer must work out the balance between these adjustments to the camera settings in relation to the other key variables.

*LOTR* used twenty-one cameras supplied by Arri Munich, including Arriflex 525Bs and 435s, Moviecam SLs for Steadicam work, three Fries Reflex Mitchell cameras, and later four Arriflex 435-Cs equipped with Praxis snorkel lenses (and a 24-foot extending boom arm), and a Rackover belonging to the special effects cinematographer Alex Funke for miniatures, and Arri 35-3s and 2-Cs as crash cameras. In particular, the engineers at Arriflex agreed to adapt the Arri 435, a camera known for both its excellent viewfinder and its steady pin-registration, and also for its built-in capping shutter which closes the film strip off from the lens when not in motion. The adaptation involved changing the two-motor system employed by Arriflex (one for the film, one for the shutter) to allow for the high levels of over- and under-cranking involved in motion control and special effects work, in this instance providing speeds from 150fps down to a frame every ten minutes. The production team took delivery of the first three of these to be produced, but continued to use the Mitchells and Rackover to handle the number of effects shots required for the trilogy. The cameras were equipped with Zeiss lenses between 10mm and 800mm, and Cooke and Angenieux 25–250mm HR T-3.5 zoom lenses. According to Smith and Matthews (2004: 130), 'Jackson also shot some of the film on Hi-Grade lightweight digital video cameras rented to the production by the camera's inventors at Lucasfilm', but they give no further details. Canon telephoto lenses were used for extreme long shots, and some macro and Revolution lenses were also employed. The films were shot on Kodak EXR 50D 5245 and 200T 5293 (under-exposed at 160 ASA), Vision 500T 5279 (over-exposed at 320 ASA), with SO 214 stock used for special effects work. The film was printed to Fujicolor for release prints, in order to soften the slightly harsher Kodak production film stock.

For *LOTR*, Andrew Lesnie sought distinctive lighting palettes for each of the major areas of Middle-earth: lavender-blues for Lothlorien, magenta-salmons for Rivendell's autumnal appearance in the first film, blue-greens for Weathertop, and yellow-greens for the Prancing Pony. In the first film, where several major scenes take place in darkness (Bree, Weathertop, Moria), Lesnie used rim lighting to accentuate edges without revealing the depths of the shadows, thus providing mystery for the Ring-wraiths and depth for the mines. Rivendell's lighting begins with soft autumn colours. Aragorn's night scene with Boromir was lit using lavender-blue ambient lighting with a supporting 20K lamp supplying a beam of moonlight. (The K refers to the power of the lamp measured in kilowatts.) In the subsequent scene with Aragorn and Arwen, however, Lesnie notes,

I decided to apply a more 'classical' blue, which is a bit kinder on skin tones. When you use lilac and lavenders, the actors' skin tones can sometimes veer too much toward magenta. I lit that scene for beauty, because it's one of the rare moments where Aragorn reveals his true feelings to the woman he loves. I've always equated the blue end of the spectrum with the concept of truth. (Gray 2002: 46)

Unusually for feature films, a significant number of scenes were shot with multi-camera set-ups, providing close-ups and reaction shots as well as cover (extra footage to make up for errors or to provide the director with more options in the editing process). Jackson showed a predilection for extreme close-ups, with some shots taken from as close as ten inches from the actor's face. The difficulties for performers reached epic proportions, for example, during Gandalf's struggle with the Balrog:

'There was a lot of kinetic lighting in that sequence', Lesnie says. 'We did close-ups of Ian McKellen where he was surrounded by so many units I lost count of how many lighting cues there were. We needed to show the growing light of the Balrog as it towered over Gandalf, the sparking interaction between Gandalf and the Balrog's swords, and the lightning strike that occurs when Gandalf drives his staff into the bridge, shattering it. Poor Ian was confronted by a complete armada of modern lighting technology. It must have been like a disco for him'. (Gray 2002: 48)

Though used far less in the second film, Jackson's preference for eyelights (small lamps used to create reflections in actors' eyes) presented another test for actors: 'To create that effect we usually used "wands", which were two 2-foot Kino Flo tubes taped together. In close quarters, these wands are ideal and virtually instantaneous tools; they have four intensity levels, and they're perfect for handholding' (Gray 2002: 48). But because Tolkien's description of Galadriel's eyes is so exceptional, Lesnie opted for another innovative technique, the 'Galadrilight', a frame holding hundreds of Christmas tree lights rigged next to the camera to create otherworldly accents and reflections in Cate Blanchett's eyes. 'Her skin is so luminous', remarks Lesnie, 'that sometimes I didn't have to use any fill, because the Galadrilight was doing the work' (Gray 2002: 50).

Lesnie worked closely with supervising the digital colourist Peter Doyle of Hannover-based post-production facility The PostHouse AG, who built a Wellington facility specifically for the project, to grade the films (adjust the colour palette) using purpose-built digital technology from the Hungarian company ColourFront, subsequently marketed as 5D Colossus. Aotearoa New Zealand's extremely bright sunlight gives deep and distinct shadows, while the ozone hole produces extra ultraviolet light to which film stock is sensitive, giving a harsh, cyan effect in camera, while the production design called for a softer Northern misty light. An example of the detailed craftsmanship required to function at this level comes up in an *American Cinematographer* interview with Doyle. Commenting on

'the subliminal idea that the more anger or fear one feels, the sharper things appear to be'[,] Doyle explains, '[w]e built a new set of sharpening kernels [software elements] for *The Two Towers*. They pick up where the lens drops off, and the frequency is just a little bit higher than the film grain, so [they really provide] a nice zing without making the grain scream – thereby avoiding the 'video look' that some digital intermediates have when they get too sharp'.

. . . Shooting on Kodak emulsions and printing on Fuji print stock was a strategy Lesnie had also applied on *The Fellowship of the Ring*. The cinematographer notes that he and Jackson were after a softer contrast than the Kodak print stocks allow, explaining, 'We felt that the Fuji print stock was more forgiving in the lower gray tones'. Adds Doyle, 'Technically, it isn't softer – it has a more extended MTF [Modulation Transfer Function] response in the blue layer than Kodak. The grain, however, has a different look than Kodak stock, and I think that Fuji blends the colors a bit more. With digital grading, you're interested in the density or the dynamic range, grain and sharpness. The more linear the stock's curve, the better'. (Gray 2002: 39–40, 42)

Such detailed work may also require a degree of invention not only in using existing technologies but in developing new tools: 'Andrew and I also built a filter that acts like a lens with all of its color coating ripped off. It doesn't look old and sepia, but there's a touch of blooming in the highlights, like a silver-metal photographic print from the 1890s' (Gray 2002: 44). On a different scale, three 50-ton cranes for lighting rigs weren't enough to shoot the Helm's Deep night-time battle scene.

'We had an 80-foot crane that was built in New Zealand', Lesnie recalls. 'Because the sets were so big, we built the rails for the crane on top of 20 containers stacked two high. This meant we were able to start a shot in front of the main wall and, while major fighting was going on, crane over the top of those guys and push on another 30 or 40 feet right up to where Théoden was directing the battle'. (Gray 2002: 51)

Even so, Lesnie (whose duties also included liaising with no fewer than eight unit cinematographers) told *Empire* magazine that aspects of *Towers* still bothered him:

Some of the colour matches bother me immensely. But thanks to the way we formatted the film this time – 100% of the film is digitally graded as opposed to *Fellowship* which was only 70% digitally graded – I should be able to correct those by the time the special edition came out. At the end of the day, though, there's always stuff you could change. Films are never really finished – they're either taken away from you or the money runs out. (Lesnie 2002)

Herein lies another reason why the extended edition DVDs deserve special study.

It is a truism of film studies that sound is the least studied area of film production. The available resources on sound production and post-production on *LOTR* are no exception. However, a brief glimpse of the challenges of production sound recording comes in an interview with the Oscar-winning sound crew of *Return* in the *Editor's Guild Magazine*:

One of the most difficult production sound sequences for Hammond Peek was Aragorn riding back and forth through the lines and addressing his troops prior to the final battle outside the black gates of Mordor.

'We shot from a moving dolly, tracking behind three or four ranks of foreground troops, with Aragorn on the other side of them about 30–40 feet away. I didn't want to use a personal radio mike on Aragorn because I would get way too much clothes rustle and off mike-axis dialogue with all the head turns. Instead, I had my boom operator, Corrin Ellingford, run up and down beside the dolly on a full pole extension covering Aragorn with a Sennheiser MKH70. Because Aragorn addressed his dialogue to his troops (matching camera and mic direction), the choice was vindicated, and the results were quite remarkable given the distance between mic and actor'. (Boyes *et al.* 2004)

The filmsound.org website, a remarkable source of information on sound effects, design, recording, and analysis, cites the supervising sound editor Mike Hopkins on another moment of the sound recording, this time not synced with the image:

'It was after a rugby game', Hopkins says. 'We had them do the chant that (the) Rohan Army do and the chanting stuff for the Orcs' advance. We actually did the same thing (the previous) year, but it was a cricket match. Unfortunately, at cricket matches the crowds tend to drink a lot more, so we had quite a few drunks blasting off horns and shouting things that weren't appropriate'. (filmsound.org 2004)

Much of the audio recording for the trilogy was done using location (and studio) recordings as guides only, the final sounds coming from foley artists producing artificial sounds to match the actions in separate sound studios. The sound designer David Farmer, for example, recalled for a careers guidance journal that his favorite sound from the first film is the Balrog . . . I tried to stay away from the usual animal sounds. He looks like he's made out of rock and lava, so I wanted his sound to relate to that. I ended up grinding a cinder block against a wooden floor and mixed a bit of an elephant seal's cry . . . and that seemed to be the right approach for the monster – to create something that wasn't vocal. (audiocareers 2004)

Dialogue tracks were re-recorded in ADR sessions, in which actors re-record their lines to a computer-cued film of their previous performances (the practice was known in analogue filmmaking as 'looping'). The more controllable acoustics of recording studios help the recordists, but challenge performers to rise to the emotional intensity of their physical performance, and require extra work from sound editors to provide ambient noises for the scene, since the 'dead' sound of a studio damps out external sound, so reducing the realism of the recording.

The determination of the production team to 'make it real' influenced greatly the production technologies employed. Jim Rygiel, who took over visual-effects supervision from Mark Stetson after the main shoot, estimated that sixty to seventy per cent of the Hobbit scale-shots were done in camera, either through the Slave Mo-Co set up, or by a novel system of weighted levers and wires to destroy the miniatures in the wreck of Isengard, or using such simple effects as puppeteering giant legs across frames which Hobbits shared with humans.

Even more significant was the decision to go for extensive use of miniatures rather than digital effects. Eventually there were a total of 68 miniature and bigature models at scales varying from 1/12th (Rivendell, among others) to 1/166th (the scale of very small 9mm toy trains). The miniatures used for Sauron's tower at Barad-dur were nearly three storeys high, necessitating the use of poles to hold telephone lines out of the way when the model was wheeled from the design workshops to the shooting studio. Once the miniatures had been constructed,

> Alex Funke, our miniatures director of photography, and I would go over the miniatures with a video camera and plot our camera moves. Once the model is standing there in the room, you see angles and great shots that you never even knew about in the early storyboarding stage. It's like going to a location, and I love the physicality of it. (Magid 2001b: 64)

Miniature photography commenced in October 1999, concurrent with the start of principal photography, and continued until a matter of days before the release of the third film. Again, Jackson's mobile camerawork was a key factor in the decision: 'I thought that if I kept the camera moving, people would be sucked into the drama of what was happening, rather than focused on the tricks we were using' (Duncan 2002: 78).

And the pursuit of a sense of reality once again contributed: 'If you want rolling hills off into the distance, or jagged cliffs, or any other kind of natural landscape, matte paintings are believable. But I've always been more miniatures based, given the choice of one or the other' (Duncan 2002: 71).

Similarly, when mattes were used, the tendency was to derive them as much as possible from the local landscapes of Aotearoa New Zealand: 'On location, if we ever saw clouds or a sky or a sunset that looked dramatic, we always put cameras on it; so that over a period of time, we compiled a library of dramatic skies that we could patchwork in with painted elements' (Duncan 2002: 78). The Weta Digital environments department collated location stills and tiled them into a virtual sphere, adding geometry to allow for parallax effects in camera movements, and digitally painting in additional elements. Occasionally, elements had to be removed from shot, as in the case of the sacred volcano Ruapehu, digitally replaced with Mount Doom. The resulting spherical 3D mattes would normally be made to 2K (two thousand pixel) resolution: typically in the trilogy, resolutions were set between 4K and 12K to allow for camera movement, and in at least one instance – the digital cyclorama for the Dead Marshes sequence in *Towers* – a 16K matte had to be built to accommodate Jackson's fluid camerawork and reverse angles in an open landscape.

In addition to the newly adapted Arriflex camera, the visual effects team's electronics engineer Chris Davidson developed an infra-red smoke controller that stabilised the amount of smoke in miniature sets by determining the precise amount of smoke in a room with the aid of low-level red light reflected into a sensor attached to the smoke-making device. Also required for the Isengard miniature, where hundreds of miniature fires were burning, was a 120-channel automated dimmer board allowing the two randomly flickering lights providing the fire effect for each bonfire to be multiplied up to sixty times in a single composition. A key reason for choosing to develop the Arriflex 435 was its exceptional video tap, a line out permitting the cinematographer a live feed of what the camera sees without having to wait for dailies to be printed. Brian Van't Hul designed a real-time workstation running on Macintosh G4 computers that allowed effects cinematographers to matte in other plates, roll shots backwards and at different speeds, or reverse left to right. This innovation was rapidly taken up not only in effects but also by the live-action units. A further example of the 'number eight wire' philosophy of the production (the term refers to fencing wire used to repair anything and everything in Aotearoa New Zealand) was the building of two motion-control rigs, one using a Kuper control system salvaged from a second-hand theme-park ride, because they were cheaper to build than to rent from the United States. Mo-Co grip Harry Harrison and Moritz Wassman's in-house machine shop built several more rigs, which, with a high-speed, long-boom rig rented from Joe Lewis in Los Angeles, brought the number of Mo-Co rigs in use up to six at a time.

The animation director Randy Cook's first job was to take charge of pre-visualisation for the Bridge at Khazad-dum. The first version ran to 140 shots staged with computer-generated characters and sets prepared in Puppetoon.

> Peter cut that down to 80 shots, and then the second-unit director, who shot the live action elements, followed it. The final sequence is extraordinarily close to the pre-vis as far as composition, pace and cutting, even down to the rudimentary gestures I gave the little figurines. (Magid 2001b: 66–7)

Magid, conducting this interview, reflects that the stairway sequence and subsequent fight took almost a year to shoot, involving as it did the difficulties of combining live action with miniature environments. The miniatures cinematography crew had to replicate with extreme precision the exact moves made by Lesnie with the live actors on set. They also had to match the complex lighting, which at several points was restricted to the light emitted by Gandalf's staff. The staff itself existed in several cabled and battery-powered versions, supported by a Chinese lantern on a boom.

Miniature lighting solutions included much use of ultraviolet light, the same wavelength that was so challenging in the natural daylight of Aotearoa New Zealand. For the Minas Morgul models in *Return*, a night-time beauty pass was combined in post with a second pass shot under ultraviolet lamps that brought out the fluorescent paints applied to the model's walls to emulate the effects of algae eating away the fortress. In the sequence in which the lava flows from Mount Doom at the end of the third film, Scott Harens's crew filled 50-gallon containers with a mix of methocellulose and Polysorb tinted with ultraviolet-sensitive Wildfire pigments and released them on to a tilting 10-26-foot light-box lit again with ultraviolet and fluorescent tubes, adding black lacquer swirls, and cork and sawdust debris to the flow.

> Director of miniature photography Chuck Schuman filmed innumerable miniature lava passes at speeds of five to six frames per second, layering each shot. 'We shot a key-light pass, a fill-light pass with no smoke and then another in smoke', explained Scott Harens. 'We used the ultraviolet to shoot mattes, but we found it was more effective to shoot matte passes before we dressed crust onto the lava. Then, after we shot a pass

without the crust, we used orange light coming up through the lava to shoot an interactive glow on the rocks'. (Fordham 2004b: 134)

The shot was matched with an ultraviolet backlit set of the rock that Sam and Frodo cling to, and enlivened with lava bombs made from methocellulose balls rolled in black lacquer, and chickenwire 'rocks' filled with hot barbecue coals dropped from a cherry-picker filmed smashing open at 120 frames per second and shrunk to provide detail in the composite. The practice of taking multiple motion-control passes of a single model in different lighting conditions was also deployed on the Minas Tirith miniature, shot with keylight, extra key to emphasise shadows, various fills, and in conditions with or without smoke so compositors could build an image blending several passes in different illumination to secure the precise effects they required in post. To secure the zombie-like appearance of the King of the Dead, Weta used a related technique, shooting an actor in prosthetics, scanning his face with and without them, carving a life-mask of the actor down to reveal an imagined skull beneath his features, digitising that, and combining the live performance with layers of both models and digital scans to present varying degrees of flesh and bone.

Not every effect required such high technology, however. The second unit director Geoff Murphy used the old trick of shooting Denethor's unlit pyre through a sheet of glass laid at 45 degrees to the camera, in which was reflected a fire off-camera, giving the basic effect of a flaming pyre (later digitally enhanced). At the low-tech end of the scale, costume-maker Matt Appleton raided Wellington charity op-shops for second-hand leathers and furs, which he shredded and dyed to dress Orcs. He also recollected that in battle scenes

> you're working closely with the other departments, making sure your fake blood doesn't stain the costumes or hair, for example, and with the amputations, you're just off-camera, pulling off this fake arm as the sword goes through, pushing the button at the same time for the blood pumps, hoping the spray doesn't cover the nearby actors too much. ('Designer dressing for Orcs' 2004)

In similar low-tech fashion, Rivendell's autumnal feel in the final film was achieved by powdering the miniature's leaves with curry, dry mustard, chilli, and paprika.

In addition to the live action sequences on location, in studio sets and against blue screen, and on top of the miniatures, locations, and effects units, the trilogy also made extensive use of motion capture shoots to produce digital doubles for all the major and many of the minor characters. Remington Scott directed the motion capture team, whose work fell loosely into three areas. First, there were shot-specific actions. The motion capture unit was charged with providing plates (photographic layers) that would be composited into the finished frames of action sequences. Here Scott provides an example from *Return*:

> When caught in the crossfire of an ambush, the Oliphants charge and many of the troops aboard fall off or hang on. In order to create this, we used the locked animation of the Oliphants as timing and motion factors. Then, using those rotation variables, we drove a rocking platform timed appropriately. Again, we captured several performers per session on the platform and motion editor Iwan Scheer integrated that motion into the scene. (Scott 2003)

Second, Scott's group produced motion capture footage of stunt performers for the forty-four classes of creature whose actions were programmed in the Massive artificial agent software. Stunt performers performed their actions in body suits equipped with various sensing devices whose movement through space could be captured both photographically and as computer data recorded on film. These actions then became the repertoire of activities that the characters generated in Massive could perform when attacking, attacked, fleeing, or seeking foes.

> Overall there were 12,011,729 frames of motion capture data that was processed, edited and delivered to the Massive technical directors (at 60 frames per second, this equals just over 55 hours of motion capture data for the Massive simulations if played end to end). (Scott 2003)

The most famous of the motion capture products, however, was Gollum. Over five weeks between February and June 2002, Serkis performed in a 'zone' first of sixteen cameras in a space 5 by 5 by 4 metres, then a larger one of 24 cameras covering 6 by 9 by 4 metres.

> Essential to the process of motion capture, a volume, or zone, is created using multiple high-resolution cameras. The suit Andy wears has a configuration of retro-reflecting spheres dotting the surface the placement of which corresponds to the rotations of his joints. When Andy is in the zone, the spheres, or markers, are recorded and triangulated into 3D space on a computer. A kinematics computer-generated skeleton is driven by the 3D marker data; this is referred to as the Source. Often the computer-generated skeleton is different in size and proportions; this is referred to as the Target. For the creation of Gollum, every subtlety and nuance of Andy's actions that were recorded through motion capture had to be retargeted to a three-foot six-inch tall creature. (Scott 2003)

Scott's team designed special digital 'character maps' that automatically distended Serkis's body-shape to conform to the distorted skeleton of the diminutive Gollum, including specialised maps for upright and all-fours motion. Other team members developed proprietary software, Nuance, to permit marrying the mo-cap sessions with the set and location footage of the other actors. The end result of the five-week mo-cap shoot was a total of eight hours of camera-ready footage, much of which ended up on the cutting room floor, though some edited shots made their way to the extended versions.

The trilogy made extensive use of locations in Aotearoa New Zealand not only for live action shoots but for digital mattes, backgrounds prepared from photographs by respected landscape photographer Craig Potton, and a dedicated scenic unit, removing that task from the tight schedule of location crews. Many of these would be digitally enhanced in post-production, but many were also used as they were, especially for skies and cloudscapes, notoriously difficult to trick digitally. Helicopter units shot some live action footage, and many locations could be reached only by helicopter, a mode of transport that Sean Bean disliked so much that he frequently tramped uphill to avoid using them. *The Making of 'The Lord of the Rings: The Fellowship of the Ring'* shows locations, intended to be shot in sunlight, dowsed in persistent rain. When the crew finally decided to use the location for a different sequence requiring rain, and hand-carried the required lighting, cameras, booms, recording equipment, and tracks out, the snow began. Unsurprisingly, given both the vagaries of weather and the fantastic nature of many of the settings, much of the film was shot in studio or on back lots where sets could be built, lighting controlled, accommodation provided, and some degree of control over the shooting schedule established.

Among the physical effects, few are as demanding as stunts. *LOTR* used extensive wirework and other trick effects to generate live elements. The battle of the wizards and the elven-rope-assisted descent from Emyn Muil both relied on suspending actors from wire rigs. Gandalf's battle with the Balrog and Arwen's flight from the Ringwraiths both demanded shots of Sir Ian McKellen and Liv Tyler respectively aboard bucking bronco machines. Matching the lead actors with stunt doubles was a key element of the project, but involved the leads in performing many elements of their own stunts.

The stunt specialist Bob Anderson, a seventy-seven-year-old sword-master, was responsible for designing fighting styles employing the weapons and armour supplied by Weta Workshops. Anderson's early involvement in films featuring Errol Flynn (the swashbuckling star of action films in the 1930s and 1940s), his performance as Darth Vader in the early *Star Wars* films, and his work on the *Highlander* series made him an eminent contributor to the *LOTR* films. He trained all of *LOTR*'s major stunt performers, who then trained the extras.

The stunt co-ordinator Bruce Brown has detailed not only the normal selection of horse, fire, fighting, and battle stunts, but some of the innovations required. At the Battle of Helm's Deep, stuntmen and stuntwomen fell as far as eighty feet on to industrial airbags. However, since every fall required a wait while the air was replenished, Brown's company Stuntworx commissioned the Auckland-based Boat Cover Company to produce more robust airbags using gym mats in their construction, which could be used for rapidly repeated shorter falls.

The production build-up used a 450 horsepower V8 wind machine. Air-rams (devices that throw stunt performers up twenty feet into the air and over sixty feet across the ground) and air-ratchets (wire rigs to which performers are harnessed so that they can free fall for up to forty feet and still be set lightly down on the ground) were specially purchased for the films. These rams and ratchets were used

> so that if someone is being thrown 50 feet through the air they can be spinning around and look like they're doing somersaults as well. That's what we use the air ram and air ratchets for. I brought some back from LA, and Steve Ingram is developing some new ones. Normally, they just fire one way, but he's developed one that'll fire in and out – he's got two-way control over it, which is pretty unique.
>
> You can have a scene where you're standing on the ground, and you're hit by, say, a magical staff which throws you at 45 degrees from the ground straight back and up, say 50 feet in the air, and then pulls you back 30 feet. And that's the end of the shot, then it just lets you down to the ground. (*Onfilm* 1999: 12)

Live-action shoots required major design work. Full-sized catapults and trebuchets flung objects far enough to get out of shot, and were matched with flaming footballs fired from mortars at full-scale sections of the walls of Minas Tirith (Fordham 2004b: 92, 96). Hero Orc characters close to camera wore full facial appliances, body prosthetics, and hands and feet, all made out of foam latex – ten thousand foam latex facial appliances in all, as well as silicone and gel prosthetics for two-thirds of the twenty-eight lead characters and their stunt and scale doubles, some of them, such as the Hobbits' feet, manufactured in industrial quantities. During the main shooting period, thirty-eight people were working on set dealing with five hundred people needing prosthetics each day. Some extremely delicate touches were required to match prosthetics to the actors' skin-tones, but, given the numbers of appliances involved, short cuts had to be devised. The on-set make-up supervisor Gino Acevedo came up with a recipe for gelatine-based prosthetic ears and nose-tips (normally made in silicon, which is more resistant to heat).

Most pieces were tinted 20% lighter than the actor's skin-tone, and we would paint them to match their actual color, once it was applied. Because I was training the other make-up artists, I developed a simpler coloring system than usual. I mixed up a creamy yellow and a very deep crimson red. Red for me has always been the most important color with prosthetics because it always drops out under the lights. Rather than just spraying the pieces, I did a lot of speckling with the Iwenta IIPC airbrush, which gave the illusion of little tiny freckles, and transferred the actor's own skin tone onto the prosthetic. Under the lights, gelatin actually absorbs light like human skin, rather than bouncing it back like foam rubber. (*Make-Up Artist* 2004)

The same combination of craft and industrial-scale organisation pitched to what is visible to a camera was critical to the work of costume designer Ngila Dickson.

Each Hobbit has shirts for each stage of their three-film journey – clean and tidy in Hobbiton, ragged and muddy on Mount Doom and plenty of variations in between. A shirt can begin fresh, then get retired to a grubbier stage later on . . .

Each character needs a set of five shirts for each scene – one each for the actor, his body double, stunt double, scale double (for the Little People) and horse double . . .

Dickson shows me human- and miniature-size copies of Merry's tweed coat and gold waistcoat. She explains that they use different weaves of cloth for big and miniature outfits, but each costume must be printed, buttoned and cut exactly to scale. (Forde 2000)

Dickson's workshop employed more than forty cobblers, embroiderers, jewellers, tailors, and designers, with more work freelanced away from the workshop as production deadlines neared. A typical process involves washing, bleaching, dying, and sandpapering Indian brocade to give the fabric texture, and to expose its infrastructure of metallic threads to achieve a subtle glitter for elven costumes. Equally detailed are the terracottas and reds for the Haradrim costumes, colours carefully co-ordinated with DoP Lesnie to ensure the best cinematographic result. One unusual aspect of the costuming involved making credible scale versions of fabrics, which would show up as oversized in cuts between lead actors and scale doubles:

At the end of it, I threw up my hands and went back to the craftsmanship of the time – to bring weavers on board and weave the fabric. To make the buttons ourselves so we could make them to scale – to make embroidery the method [to] embellish those costumes which worked brilliantly with the Hobbits. Not only did it give me the scale easily, but it gave me the right home-spun country naiveté which is integral to those little lads. (DVDFILE.com 2003)

Even the jewellery designer Jasmine Watson had to establish a substantial workshop: 'I had a team of 5 people and together we created over 300 pieces of jewellery, and of that about 80 were one off originals' (Xoanon 2003). Dickson also had to co-ordinate with Weta's creature shop, where more than 48,000 items, including a thousand suits of armour, five hundred of leather, and more than two thousand weapons were produced, all of which needed to be matched with appropriate costumes.

The long production schedule in 1999 to 2000 was undoubtedly fatiguing for all concerned. In an unusually revealing interview with fans, posted to ScoopNews, Jackson confessed

> physically I could just keep on going like a tortoise, just keep plodding along, but mentally I was realising my imagination was shutting down, and some days I'd come home at the end of shooting and think 'God, I just shot TV today' . . . So what I started to do was on Sundays – because I had Sundays off – I'd sit at home on Sunday afternoons and put movies on, movies that I felt where the directors had really used the medium of film making in imaginative ways. And they were all films I'd seen before, like *JFK*, *Goodfellas*, *Casino*, *Saving Private Ryan*, and I just watched these movies on Sundays, and it would be stimulating. It would just be like this is what good filmmaking really is, this is people who are imaginative, who are using the camera, and it would kind of get me excited and reinvigorate me and get my brain a bit more focused on it. (ScoopNews 2003)

Interviewed after the Oscars ceremony in 2004, Jackson is reported as saying, 'It nearly killed me, but right now it feels absolutely fine' (*One News Online*: 2004).

## Post-production

Another unusual characteristic of *LOTR* is that no firm line can be drawn to separate traditionally distinct phases of film-making:

> Visual effects supervisor Jim Rygiel notes that with *The Lord of the Rings* trilogy, there is no real post production. 'The making of the effects is not treated as post production', he says. 'It's actually part of the process itself, which is a very interesting way to work. We're all playing off each other'. (New Line 2002)

Similarly, editor Jamie Selkirk noted in an interview with *Onfilm* (2004) that editors on big productions are commonly hired during pre-production to work with the director on storyboarding, working through production checking footage and producing first passes at the cut, before settling into the traditional post-production edit. None the less, in what follows we continue to observe the traditional distinctions in order to make analytical sense of the available data. It is important to recall, however, that not only did post-production commence almost as soon as principal photography (and in the case of pre-visualisations, before), but all the different types of post-production were being undertaken on different timescales, among other things requiring that one department might have to alter its work to fit with developments in another. An example featured in the DVD appendices for *Return* is the co-operation between sound and digital effects departments on mutual inspiration for the look and sound of Shelob. From 740 effects shots in *Fellowship* to 950 in *Towers* rising to 1850 in *Return*, with storage rising from 7.5 terabytes for the first film to 72 for the third, some selection was necessary. Jackson also favoured a high shoot-to-print ratio:

> By the time the main shoot of the *Rings* trilogy came to an end, over five million feet of film had been shot. Of this, around 3.5 million feet – or roughly 650 hours – was printed. To give a comparison, Terrence Malick's three-hour *Thin Red Line*, which used perhaps the most film of any fictional movie production, shot 1.5 million feet of celluloid, and 1.3 million feet were printed for the infamous *Heaven's Gate*. With months of reshoots still to come, there was a lot of film. (Pryor 2003: 287)

With this in mind, this section selects some cases of specific scenes where collaboration was most important. It also foregrounds innovations in post-production techniques and technologies, in order to indicate the problems of maintaining a single look throughout a film whose production covered a period of intense evolution in film technologies.

Many sequences demanded co-ordination not only between departments but between Weta, Three Foot Six, and sub-contracting companies across Europe and North America. For example, the location for the Ford of Bruinen sequence for *Fellowship* was filmed at Skipper's Canyon, near Queenstown, but none the less remote. The crew and equipment were flown in by helicopter, while the horses walked in by trail. For the six shots required for the white horses that Arwen conjured to engulf the Ringwraiths, Digital Domain, the LA-based company founded by James Cameron, used initial reference footage of a New Zealand dam bursting. Further elements were shot at Niagara Falls and in Digital Domain's studios, using dump tanks dropping their loads of water forty feet, shot at between 72 and 96 frames per second to increase the sense of volume. Spray was mapped from glass beads poured over a dummy horse's head. Further live elements came from a second unit that filmed Ringwraiths charging at the camera, at some risk to operator Brian van't Hul. These charges were rotoscoped – a system for

**Figure 13** 2004 New Zealand Post stamp identified as 'Skippers Canyon (The Ford of Bruinen)'.

tracing outlines from projected film – and added to the effects shots. Since no animals could be injured during the shoot, Weta Digital supplied digital models of the mounted Ringwraiths in NURBS (Non-Uniform Rational B-Splines) format to Digital Domain, who converted them to polygonal format before adding cloth dynamics to emulate the movement of the Black Riders' soaked cloaks. Each rider was given a different behaviour as collectively they were hammered by the onrushing waters using keyframe animation – a technique also used for the oncoming white horses. This process involved volumetric modelling, fluid simulation, particle animation, and careful hand-generated shading and highlight effects. The whole sequence was then composited in Digital Domain's proprietary software Nuke, and rendered in Voxel-B, a plug-in for the Houdini 3D animation programme, which offered the efficiency of rendering only what was visible to camera (a capability that, unlike industry standard software RenderMan, it shares with Weta's Grunt programme). The six shots occupied Digital Domain for eleven weeks (Duncan 2002: 101–2). The processes involved here blend

**Figures 14** Frodo on a balcony at Rivendell.

photographed 'practical' elements such as real water with digital models to which the photographs are applied. The combination is known as a sprite.

The Rivendell miniature was built on casters, so the units could be moved to provide more variety. In this instance, the backdrop was filled with a CG cyc (computer-generated cyclorama – a physical cyclorama is a curtain high enough to mask the background, sometimes dyed or painted or constructed of colour xeroxes; a CG cyc is built from location stills and constructed exclusively in computer in a circle or hemisphere with some 3D elements to allow for parallax effects). Stills derived from yet another South Island location formed the majority of the canyon where Rivendell is set, with waterfalls provided by miscellaneous locations in the wake of the same bad weather that shifted the colour scheme of Rivendell from Mediterranean blues to autumnal yellows and oranges.

In many Rivendell shots, motion control was not used. Instead, Weta provided 'technical breakdowns' of Jackson's fluid camerawork, which could then be used to match the miniatures and CG unit elements. A programme called 3D Equalizer provided some of the technical breakdown, but skilled operators still had much work to do.

Zooms were particularly difficult, since data about the focal length of the lens are vital to the system's functioning, but a zoom by definition changes focal length. This became even tougher in shots, like that of the departure of the Fellowship from Rivendell, when a zoom in is matched with a helicopter move out, requiring immense skill and knowledge of the movie-making process (Duncan 2002: 103–7). Likewise, a follow-shot of Saruman and Wormtongue walking to the balcony to greet the assembled Uruk-hai was filmed hand-held, in part to give immediacy to the shot. To aggregate the live action with the digital and miniature elements required extensive hand-equalisation. The reverse shot that follows, with a huge and very fast fly-back of the camera from the Orthanc miniature to reveal the Uruk-hais' view of the tower, resulted in such lens distortion that the effects crew stripped everything from the shot except the surfaces of the tower and remade it as a 3D model, applying the miniature photographic elements as skins. The shot, still mobile, of Saruman viewing the wreckage of Isengard from his balcony contained no fewer than fifty plates including live action, digital cyc, miniatures at various scales, animatronics, CG characters, and Massive agents (individualised characters).

Massive agents have three senses – sight, sound, and collision detection. Sound emitted by agents identified good guys and bad guys; collision stopped them running into (or worse still, through) each other and also gave them a relation to terrain. The terrain could also supply flow-fields, effectively directions to the agents (such as Saruman's crows flocking into the caverns of Isengard) to move in a particular direction, and to start or stop fighting on a particular cue.

Thirty master agents were prepared in Massive, each of which had two hundred major actions and a subsidiary library of 350 smaller gestures, each of which was blended to produce a smooth flow of movements. These master agents were then reproduced across the battlefields of Middle-earth, and their behaviours subtly or broadly modified by adjusting their levels of 'aggression' – sensitivity to various virtual environment factors – while retaining varying degrees of autonomous movement and decision-making. In addition, the basic agents could be modified and morphed in Massive (made taller, thinner, or fatter, and operators could change elements of their costume to add variety to scenes featuring thousands of replications of the master agents. The rendering software, Grunt (Guaranteed Rendering of Unlimited Numbers of Things – also specially developed for the trilogy), included a procedural filter that made the Massive agents appear dirtier as a battle progressed (Duncan 2002: 84–9).

The Warg attack in *Towers* again mixed live action and digital creatures, in this case animals with no living relatives except the much smaller hyenas and Cape hunting dogs on whose anatomies they were modelled. To save render time, the hair, animated in detail, was made less translucent, but it still had to be blended with the riders' prop cloaks.

The animals were built up from the skeleton and then incorporated into
landscape passes with live actors miming interactions with them. Many
of the Rohirrim riders and horses were digital, which (as in the case of
Gandalf's dawn charge on the Orc armies at Helm's Deep) allowed the
two sides to clash with extreme violence. According to Randy Cook,
who was in charge of the sequence effects,

> There were a series of 'battle vignettes' that focussed on individual tus-
> sles. Peter Jackson, Christian Rivers and I blocked out each encounter,
> then layered them into the background – and sometimes, God help us,
> the *foreground* – of any given shot, allowing us to depict a ferocious clash
> of beasts with relative efficiency. The animation team did exemplary work
> in realistically conveying gruesome carnage. I've always respected my team;
> but now, seeing how bloodthirsty they can be, I *fear* them. (Fordham 2003:
> 120)

Similar effects were used to composite the charge of the Rohirrim on
the Pelennor Fields. Five hundred extras and 350 horses enacted the
charge over a six-week shoot in Twizel, but unlike Helm's Deep, which
occurs at night, the Battle of the Pelennor Fields takes place in full daylight. As a result, for the first time, the sequence required A-level Massive agents constructed, unlike the B- and C-level agents of earlier films,
not in polygons but in sub-division modelling, a more organic but more
processing-intensive mode of 3D animation (for a graphical demonstration
of these techniques see the subdivision modelling tutorial at www.
secondreality.ch/tutorials/modelling/head.html). To acquire sufficient
data to build realistic Massive horses passing close to camera, the crew
spent two weeks shooting horse movement, mapping the mud and dust
they kicked up, and shooting real horses' rumps to provide skins for the
3D models (Fordham 2004b: 115).

Even relatively innocuous effects required immense detail and inventiveness. To create the Palantir effect when Pippin steals it from Gandalf,

> 'We already had the Eye of Sauron as an asset from the earlier films', [the
> Weta compositor Charlie] Tait explained. 'I rendered that in the middle
> of a frame, placed it within the sphere using shading and bulging, then
> warped the opening of the iris. For the swirling fire elements, I figured
> the only way I could create spherical imagery in 2D was by rendering a
> ring, duplicating it, and spinning it around, like a gyroscope'. [The 2D
> programmer Shane] Cooper wrote colour filter nodes that Tait blended
> with fractal noise effects in Shake, creating directional blur based on
> the flow of noise around the spinning shape. 'I color-graded the noise
> to create a fiery appearance, placed Pippin's hands back on top, and revealed
> bits of fire coming through his fingers. We also added a time-lag effect
> to control the direction of smear in frame, so as Pippin shook the palantir

around, there was a "history" of flames lagging behind'. (Fordham 2004b: 73)

This effect required the use of a digital technology known as tracking, associating a digital effect with another digital object's motion, such as the digital effects tracked to the rotoscoped outline of Frodo as he enters the wraith world at Bree, the ghosting effect that follows the King of the Dead, and dust and flying debris from the feet of digital creatures like the Massive horses and the CG Mumakil on the equally digital terrain of Pelennor Fields.

An especially complex instance of tracking was achieved during Gollum's fight with Sam during the ascent of Mount Doom. Previously all motion capture sessions had been shot separately from the live-action elements, but, under pressure to complete the film for release, both were shot simultaneously, using infrared markers invisible to the live-action cameras to map Frodo, Sam, and Gollum, Sam and Gollum's hands, and Sam's sword as well as the other cameras throughout the scene. Using these markers, not only could the digital Gollum replace Andy Serkis, but Gollum's body could be tracked to the point of Sam's blade at the key moment.

The night-time assault on Minas Tirith posed several special problems, especially in designing believable fire effects. Some pyrotechnic elements were extended with 3D volumetric CG fire and smoke, and added to hand-assembled 2D Photoshop elements. Much of the work was done during multiple Mo-Co passes of the miniature.

> 'Wherever the city was supposed to be burning', explained Alex Funke, 'we inserted a small bulb on a long wire, and shot a series of positions of that bulb. Then, by dithering the bulb and moving the shadows, we created the illusion of a flickering fire'.
> For a low swooping angle, the camera gliding over the burning city and sailing out to Pelennor, Funke's team shot 200 positions of bulbs around the miniature. (Fordham 2004b: 96)

Composited, the shot also included burning fireballs hurled from beyond the walls, digital haloes, and additional orange colour applied to the firelight to emulate normal camera response to firelight at night, miniature buildings collapsing, and beyond the walls a Massive army of Orcs and their miniature siege tower, scanned and replicated across the battlefield.

It happens that films generate specific challenges requiring innovation at the technical level, but the scale and duration of the *LOTR* post-production made it unusually prolific in generating new technical elements. In addition to those mentioned, technical developments associated with post-production on *LOTR* included additional software for the Mental Ray plug-in for Softimage to provide the specific qualities of light radiating from Arwen on her first appearance; a proprietary muscle-building plug-in for Maya that allowed digital characters to be built up from their skeletons, musculature added, and a skin applied over it to provide convincing movement for often fantastical body-shapes; a hair simulation for digital doubles; and a physics-based fluid dynamics system designed for the fire and smoke produced by the Balrog. According to Chris Godfrey, in order to produce the watery effect in Galadriel's mirror, 'We rendered the rays effect in RenderMan; and once we had that, we positioned those in Maya, then took the majority of it to Shake where we did most of the distortion as an overlay through this simple programme that we wrote' (Duncan 2002: 128). *Fellowship* also led to the development of a virtual camera (Duncan 2002: 117) that allowed the director and animators to walk through a virtual set of Balin's tomb to select angles for the fight with the troll (a development that New Zealand Trade and Enterprise was pleased to showcase in promotional material it used when marketing Aotearoa New Zealand's creative industries overseas).

On *Towers*, Richard Addison-Wood developed custom code to translate Gollum from NURBS to the sub-division modelling system preferred for the later films. Joe Letteri abandoned sub-surface refraction modelling of skin tones in favour of techniques borrowed from silicon model painting imitated from the model of Boromir's corpse for *Fellowship*. New code was written for the wetness effect inside Gollum's lips, nostrils, and eyes. A new programme, Grove, was developed to 'grow' leaves and branches in Fangorn. Treebeard's beard required a custom-designed plug-in for RenderMan, largely to reduce rendering times for complex models, and a 'jitter' tool to give the digital Treebeard's movements a more staccato feel. Another suite of RenderMan tools and Maya plug-ins was developed specifically for Warg fur. To extend the Edoras set digitally, the production developed AutoTracker, a programme that allows a camera to record thousands of points in a plate derived from the real location that could then be converted to digital geometry, and thence as accurate reference for additional digital sets. And the dry-for-wet techniques pioneered in Sam's plunge into the river at the end of *Fellowship* were further enhanced by Sony Pictures Imageworks for Frodo's fall into the Dead Marshes, using a proprietary particle animation system to produce bubbles and a rendering system first developed for *Harry Potter*. New 'hair' plug-ins, initially developed for the Wargs' fur, also provided Shelob's stubbly covering and the remodelled Gwahir's wings in *Return*, for which 186 'hero' feathers were duplicated and provided with collision detection and aerodynamic ruffling (Fordham 2004b: 106, 131).

Many of the innovations had to meet two competing goals. The 3D lead Wayne Stables describes the challenges of the Massive agents at Helm's Deep:

> First, we had to make the CG characters look realistic; and second, we had to be able to generate the images simply. It was a huge computing task to render thousands of guys in a shot. I wrote all our Uruk shaders, which was an exercise in how to make them render as fast as I possibly could, while featuring as much detail as possible. (Fordham 2003: 126)

Despite the fact that Weta was adding workstations and processors throughout the shoot, and despite the sub-contracting of many shots to other specialist houses, rendering – the process of converting digital information to cinema-quality images – required increasing amounts of processing time as the number and detail of elements increased. Many of the innovations made in digital post-production on *LOTR* were specifically designed to ease, or at least to try to reduce the call on processing time while also increasing the level of realism and the choice of shots for the director and editors. For the fall of Barad-dur, Gray Horsfield initially created a 250,000 polygon model over Christmas 2002. This eventually increased to 250 million polygons for the final CG model

**Figure 15** Elrond and troops: Massive-ly impressive.

– since the miniature could be destroyed only once, if at all, and there-fore could not reliably provide enough detailed coverage for the final catastrophe. The critical problem was not just adding the interiors revealed inside the collapsing tower but controlling up to 2500 rigid objects col-liding and splintering into about ten thousand fragments. To make this possible in the time frame available, Weta collaborated with Jim Hourihan of Tweak Films in San Francisco to produce a dynamic spring simulation, in which objects could interpenetrate, but would spring apart according to the depth of their interaction (Fordham 2004b: 139). This new software, again, was dedicated to lowering the rendering and pro-cessing time required to secure the shot, while maintaining the degree of detail on which the project was premised.

The introduction on *Fellowship* of a digital scanner (Duncan 2002: 111), somewhat like a barcode reader, allowed technicians to scan the extremely detailed physical maquettes built by Weta into 2D and 3D computer programmes. As the *LOTR* Exhibition panel display-ing this hand-held scanner explained, Applied Research Associates of Christchurch developed this technology independently and approached Weta about its availability shortly before production on *Fellowship* began. The process of digital scanning, like rotoscoping and in some ways like sprites, suggests a changing relationship between cinema and the phys-ical world, one not necessarily locked into the camera, but in some ways equally or even more faithful to physical reality. The scanner logs the surface detail of a model or an actor's face in extreme detail. An ana-logue process widely used in the trilogy may cast light on this, as described by Richard Taylor:

> We went to the coastline around Wellington, which is only a two min-utes' drive from our workshop . . . and took massive silicone molds off the rock faces there. Then we brought these back to the shop and sprayed up libraries of insulation foam urethane sheeting, so we could create stock-piles of rock face. Through that process, we were able to very quickly build huge rock structures fitted to large steel frames. (Duncan 2002: 72, 77)

Similar processes applied to tree bark were used in generating the tex-tures of both Lothlorien and Fangorn. The moulding process 'records' the physical reality of surfaces in ways that photography can only aspire to: this is the goal of digital scanning.

Scans of double-sized Gollum statues (which allowed for finer detail) were sent to computer. Among uses were the generation of new maquet-tes based on scaled computer outputs of the original scans. The highly detailed version was reduced to a low-resolution version for animation, with the difference in detailing stored as a computer file until the final render, when it could be added to any shot. Serkis's face was also scanned as he performed a series of expressions, which could then be blended with clay models and production sketches, not least for transformations from Smeagol into Gollum. The final product, a computerised model of Gollum's face, included 675 sculpted expressions with nine thousand individually manipulable muscle shapes controlled by sliders, with some combinations saved for repeats.

The creature facial lead Bay Raitt, responsible for oversight of this process, faced a special problem, given the amount of dialogue Gollum had in the film. Attempts to automate the process produced an overly robotic effect, so the animation of Gollum's face while speaking was done using keyframe animation. Raitt devised three golden rules for lip-syncing animated speech:

> One: write out all your lip sync . . . It really helps to do a dope sheet and write out what phonemes you want where. Two: Don't try to hit every phoneme. Let them mush over each other. The 'plosives' – the 'm's, the 'b's, the 'p's and the 'th's – hold those for an extra frame or two. Three: When you're done with everything, grab all of your key-frames and slide them two frames forward. Trust me. It works. You make the shape before the sound. (Fordham 2003: 85)

Gollum's unusual body-shape and movements were based partly on an imitation of a lizard's spine, which can flex from side to side as well as bending forward like a human. His skin folds and slides over muscles, as with real animals. His designers added heartbeat and breathing behaviours, and permitted animators to use either 'forward kinematics', in which each joint is hand-placed, or 'inverse kinematics', where animators place hands and feet and the computer adds the corresponding skeletal dynamics.

Similar effects were applied across other creatures, among them the Mumakil or Oliphaunts which make their first appearance in *Towers*. The sheer weight of these four-storey animals had to be communicated in the resonance of each footfall reverberating through their whole bodies. For this, the creature design team included muscular dynamics and skin jiggle, responding to but autonomous from the muscular system that kicked in whenever the creatures' feet hit the ground. Integrating such actions with convincing detail, such as spurts of dust, splashes of water, or shaking terrain as imaginary creatures move over it, required extreme skill in compositing:

> Coordinating with camera, models and editorial, the motion editors were on the front line of integration because they composed the shots by importing

and arranging the WetaCam, plate, audio track, terrain obj, match moved Frodo and Sam, AMC, and of course the motioncaptured Gollum into Nuance. Once the shot was composed and arranged, the editors would blend or adjust the characters' elements as needed to fit the scene. (Scott 2003)

Unsurprisingly, Weta's digital equipment base included 'more than 230 SGI IRIX and SGI Linux OS-based visual workstations, 125 Silicon Graphics Octane workstations, several SGI Origin 2000 and SGI Origin 200 servers and three SGI Origin family servers' (SGINZ 2004). Milton Ngan of Weta Digital reported further equipment:

> 1600 × dual Processor Intel P4 Xeon 'corporate nodes' running Linux, 400 × dual processor P4 Intel Xeon workstations running Linux (and some running Windows), 30 × single and dual processor G4 PowerMac workstations running OS X, 10 × dual processor G4 PowerMacs for high resolution video playback, 10 × G4 Mac Powerbooks for various purposes, six dual processor Mac G4 Xserves for QuickTime generation, one G5 single processor PowerMac for FinalCut Pro. (Webster 2002: 22)

There were, in addition, two workhorse Mac G3s running OS8.6 for visual effects and two Avid PC-based Adrenaline suites, all connected to a 10 gigabit backbone.

Sound effects were produced in the main dubbing theatre, initially on an Otari Premiere console, and later on Euphonix System 5. By the time *Return* was in post, recalls Mike Hodges, there were two System 5s:

> On one, we had 70 inputs for dialogue and music, while Chris [Boyes] had 212 inputs for the effects part of the dub. Our biggest nightmare was conforming the automation package so that it would interlink with the Pro Tools automation, but the Euphonix agents along with our mixers – Lora Hirshberg and John Niell – came up with a solution and got it working really well. We finessed a little more in terms of knowing exactly what we required with reverbs and delay lines for *Return of the King*, plus we had Pro Tools running straight into the consoles. We had two effects Pro Tools linked to Chris' side of the console, two dialogue Pro Tools for Michael's final dub, one for the pre-dub, and another was dedicated to all the ADR choices. Peter wanted access to every line. If he wasn't happy with something, he could let us know right away. (Boyes *et al.* 2004)

The equipment included Tascam MMR8 and MM16, and a number of Pro Tools systems running between eight and thirty-two faders. Much equipment had to be hired overseas, since the New Zealand market was not big enough, for example, to provide 160 pairs of professional headphones for orchestral recording sessions (which were recorded direct to

ProTools in Wellington, and to Sony 3348 HR in London). According to Boyes, as re-recording mixer,

> the bottom line as far as the equipment was concerned was that I thought we needed a digital board. I knew from a sound effects point of view that I was going to have to 'marry' a tremendous amount of material because we weren't going to have enough inputs and enough playback machines to play them all back. There was a tremendous amount of panning, a tremendous amount of sweeping with EQ, and a lot of dynamics processing. I just don't think I could have done it with an analogue desk. (Mitchell 2002)

While Jackson was in London during the scoring of *Return*, his hotel room at the Dorchester was equipped to allow him to participate in the sound mixing sessions in Wellington.

> We set up a 'polycom': We had a TV monitor and a camera pointed at us, and he would have the same thing pointed at him in his hotel room in London. We would send a computer file via a fat pipe – an ultra-wideband Internet connection – and then he would sit at a Pro Tools system with Genelecs and a video monitor and listen to our pass at the final mix for any given reel. Then he would send us back his ideas. It wasn't a perfect situation, but better to have that than flying blind or getting typewritten notes and not being able to see him describe what he wants. (Jackson 2003d)

The films' epic nature and scale promoted the idea of big volume. This tendency was resisted in the first two films especially, partly to allow for a gradual crescendo in the huge scenes of the final film, partly on a philosophy of sound mixing adopted for the production:

> It was pretty obvious there would be moments in the movie that would be potentially very loud, but the level could be brought down considerably, if music and sound effects didn't hit the same events. We discussed that, most of the time, sound effects don't have a choice 'where' to put sound, but music does. For example, if we see the Balrog pounding on the wall, then we have to put a pounding sound in sync with the action. If that sound effect is something we want to hear, then music should play before or after it, but not hit it in exact sync. It was on that whole action/reaction theory, with the sound effects being the action, and the music being the reaction, that the soundtrack was built. (Mitchell 2002)

Boyes cites as an example the entry of the Ringwraiths into the bedroom at Bree, where Shore's choir-led nondiegetic score fades to nothing, allowing the silence to increase the suspense, and focusing on the sound of their armour, produced by recording metal prop armour from Weta Workshop.

The film's constantly changing edit demanded equally constant changes to the soundtrack. To manage this process, originally undertaken by an editor's assistant named Katy Wood, John McKay, supervising sound editor, devised a new tool for managing workflow:

> On completion of a cut, the *The Lord of the Rings* picture editor would export an EDL [Edit Decision List] from the Avid, and email this file to *The Lord of the Rings* sound department. Sound would compare with the previous version and update sessions to reflect changes well before digitized picture arrived from the cutting room. What was once 'dead' time was efficiently used to keep picture and sound in step.
>   From this, Virtual Katy evolved. Virtual Katy compared the differences between previous and current versions of *The Lord of the Rings* picture edits. We were able to import up to 36 EDLs to analyse (across multiple reels). Virtual Katy would produce a VK Change List that would automatically re-sync the Pro Tools session to reflect the changes in *The Lord of the Rings* picture. (McKay 2004)

In January of 2005, Virtual Katy was in a substantial partnership with Digidesign, the makers of ProTools, with plans for NZ$100m revenues within ten years from a dominant position in the market. McKay referred to this future position as 'the application that runs your post-production' (*New Zealand Herald* 2005).

Of particular concern early in the production process was the nature of the musical score. During 2000, Jackson told theonering.net,

> we have been talking to several composers about doing the soundtrack and have not yet made a decision, although we probably will very shortly. I'm imagining the score of the films to be orchestral, I'd also like to use interesting instruments, ancient instruments, to really evoke the cultures and the history of Middle-earth. I don't think it's appropriate to use existing music necessarily, I mean I know that bands like Led Zeppelin have written Tolkien-inspired songs, but I think just the nature of the music and the technology of their music would be inappropriate to the visual look of the film. I mean we have to make that, you know, we've taken a lot of care and time to give the films a very organic, real feeling and quality, and I think the music has to support that rather than act against it. So I don't think there's any room for electronic music or any modern-feeling music, it should have an oldness, and a sort of ancient feel. So really I think that at this point in time certainly, and we haven't started post-production yet, but I'm imagining that all of the music will be original and new to the movies, written especially for the film. (theonering.net 2000)

Attached to the film in July 2000, Howard Shore, whose previous scores included *Seven*, *Naked Lunch*, *Crash*, *Silence of the Lambs*, and *Looking for Richard*, worked closely with Boyens, particularly on the score's choral sections, using poems written by Boyens in the languages of Middle-earth. The musical resources were suitably large for the style Shore adopted, which was fundamentally operatic.

The ensemble was 200 pieces. There was a 100-piece symphony orchestra, the London Philharmonic, which is a great orchestra and one that I've worked with for 15 years and have a strong connection to. Then there was a 60-voice all male choir that sang the Dwarvish music, because Peter wanted all of the sounds in Moria to be male oriented due to the predominately masculine Dwarvish culture. A mixed choir was used for Rivendell and Lothlorien, they actually have quite different sounds as you can hear on the CD. They sang in Elvish (Quenya and Sindarin) and Black Speech – they did all of the Wraith singing. I used a 30-piece boy's choir to represent the innocence of Frodo and Sam . . . There are also some North African instruments, and an Indian bowed lute which I used in 'Lothlorien'. (Goldwasser 2001)

Other 'exotic' sounds used for the score include a Ney flute, Hardanger fiddle, sarangi, bodhran, Japanese taiko drums, metal bell plates, and chains beaten on piano wires for the Orcs' theme. In Wagnerian style, Shore used motifs for specific races and characters, a technique developed from Wagner's operas and nineteenth-century programme music.

'In actual fact there's probably 40 or 50 of them', he says, referring to the number of distinct themes he wrote for various portions of the filmscore. 'There's characters, there's culture and there's objects attached [to the music]. It's based on Wagner's storytelling and he was the first to do this kind of thing. He was the first to say "It's okay to feel something when you hear music and to attach motifs to characters". He did that over a 100 years ago'. (Goldwasser 2001)

Shore also worked on the three-act structure of the trilogy to produce a distinctive sound palette for each film:

The end of the film is important, and each song that Fran and I worked on (most recently with Annie) was written specifically for the end of the film, and for that particular artist. There was a progression in the storytelling, and Enya was part of *Fellowship*. The musical cast for each film has been very specific. In *Return of the King*, you have Annie Lennox, Renée Fleming, James Galway, and Ben Del Maestro. In *The Two Towers*, you have Elizabeth Fraser – who also sang in *Fellowship*, so there was some crossover – but essentially there was a new cast for each one. The first film had Enya, Miriam Stockley, and 'In Dreams' was sung by Edward Ross. So, there was a specific cast for each film. (Goldwasser 2003)

All three films were extensively re-scored for the extended edition DVDs, a complex task given that the additional running time is often made up of shots inserted in existing scenes, rather than whole new scenes. Shore's *Lord of the Rings Symphony* for orchestra and choirs received its world premiere in Wellington on 29 November 2004. Doug Adams, author of the forthcoming book *The Music of the Lord of the Rings Films*, described the music in the programme notes thus: 'Centuries of stylistic tendencies are treated with equal respect, creating a uniquely all-encompassing vision. Original folksongs stand proudly alongside diatonic hymns, chromatically complex tone clusters and seething, dissonant aleatoric passages' (2004). The score won Grammy and American Film Institute awards as well as Oscars. The soundtrack for *Fellowship* went Platinum internationally with over a million international sales, and Gold in the USA (over half a million units sold).

The Weta partner and long-term Jackson collaborator Jamie Selkirk led the editing team. The task of editing the footage required even more expert timing than the kind of parallel action made famous by *The Godfather*'s baptism-and-massacre sequence (cut by William Reynolds and Peter Zinner) because of the triple storyline. Selkirk reflected that

> there was obviously the Frodo story we had to push through. . . . Then there was the whole Minas Tirith battle and action with Gandalf. And then there was Aragorn's story, . . . [sic] trying to get the army of the dead. So we had to try to mingle all those stories without staying too long on any one particular. [If] you're with Frodo for too long, you forgot about what's going on down the other way. And then you got stuck into the Minas Tirith battle, which was one of those sorts of battles that was very hard to get out of once you got in there, because the momentum was pushing it along all the time. So we had to pick really good moments when we could actually cut away from that to follow the other story. (*Sci Fi Wire* 2003)

Selkirk supervised editing by John Gilbert on *Fellowship* and Michael Horton on *Towers*, with a team of fourteen editors. Selkirk himself edited *Return*, with Annie Collins. Selkirk's jobs included oversight of all handling of the negative masters, from colour timing to the film conform screenings (in which the electronic edit decision lists are matched to the master print), as well as financial and managerial oversight of the whole post-production system. Editing the 80 per cent printed footage from over seven million feet exposed gave a final product of about 60,300 feet or an editing ratio of 117:1. The cutting was done on six Avid ABVB 7.2 systems linked by three optical-fibre Unity storage and access systems, which allowed editors access to all stored footage simultaneously. The process was physically and technically demanding, as Selkirk says.

> The editorial assistant team very often had to contend with the synching up and preparation for screening of 40,000 feet from up to six shooting units per day, and we frequently had three or four hours to view. It was quite hilarious at times to hear the odd snore from the back of the cinema as one of the crew succumbed to the long day.
>
> This sheer amount of footage obviously slowed the editing process – it all had to be carefully viewed again and again in the cutting room by the editor and Peter during the performance selection process prior to editing a particular scene.
>
> In addition to the drama, we had to deal with the endless effects elements – sky plates, scenic backgrounds, miniatures, the various versions of effects shots from Weta Digital. No wonder the Avids occasionally decided to crash. (*Onfilm* 2004)

Selkirk notes in the same interview that, despite the centrality of the effects, he understood his job as editor to be driven by storytelling, while also noting that with that emphasis, what tends to get lost is backstory and character development, both of which are, in general, the scenes that find their way back into the extended versions of the trilogy.

In all, eleven companies were involved in effects work in addition to Weta Workshop and Weta Digital. They include EYETECH Optics, Motion Works (motion capture), Animal Logic, Hybrid Enterprises, Sony Pictures Imageworks, Oktobor, Rhythm & Hues, Rising Sun Pictures, Sandbox Pictures, Tweak Films (visual effects), and Digital Domain (visual effects for the 'Ford of Bruinen' sequence). Other companies involved in production and post-production included 4MC UK Ltd. (adr facilities), AFM Lighting Ltd, AON / Albert G. Ruben Insurance Services Inc. (additional insurance), Abbey Road Studios (music recording and mixing), Air Lyndhurst Studios (music recording), BBVC / Kelly's Eye Ltd (video assist design and build), Bank of New Zealand (investment services), Camperdown Studios (adr facilities), Chapman/Leonard Studio Equipment Inc. (cranes and dollies), Colorfront (digital film grading system), Colosseum, Watford (music recording venue), New Zealand Department of Conservation, Flying Trestles (catering), Giant Studios Inc. (motion capture), International Film Guarantors Inc. (completion guarantee), London Symphony Orchestra (LSO), London Voices, Mahony & Associates (insurance services), New Zealand Defence Force, New Zealand Symphony Orchestra, Pacific Title, Redline Sound Studios (foley recording), Spacecam Systems Inc.), The Film Unit (color and telecine dailies, re-recording facilities), The London Oratory School Schola,

The PostHouse AG (digital color grading), The Saul Zaentz Company (licensing), Upper Deck Film Services (negative cutting),Wellington City Council, Wellington Regional Council's Parks and Forests, Wellington Town Hall, and Wescam USA Inc. The soundtrack was published by Reprise Records, WMG Soundtracks, and Warner Music Group.

## Note

1 The *LOTR* exhibition includes a panel demonstrating how this technology works. If Gandalf and Frodo were sitting positioned in a certain way, then the prop Gandalf was sitting on would move under the camera's control in order to keep the distances and angles between each character and between the characters and the camera constant.

# 14

# Sonic resonances of nature and supernature in the *Lord of the Rings* trilogy

*Kevin Fisher*

This chapter examines sounds whose sources originate within the films' fictional world: diegetic sound, as opposed to nondiegetic sound sources (such as the musical score). *LOTR* provides a fictional world that operates on at least two levels – the natural and the supernatural. Sound both differentiates and bridges these realms via its relation with the images. Audiences often ignore this relation, prompting Chion to nominate the term 'audio-vision' as a challenge to the 'additive approach' to cinematic sound, which neglects the ways that sound transforms the moving image (1994: xxvi). *LOTR* allows us to study components of audio-vision through sound's transformative effects upon the visible and invisible modalities of Middle-earth's natural and supernatural realms.

*LOTR*'s representation of Middle-earth's natural world relies upon sound's ability to express the material attributes of visible objects and physical forces – to see *and* hear fires crackling adds dimension to the film image. However, Chion cautions against assuming that this enhanced audiovisual realism depends upon some pre-existing 'natural harmony' of sound and image (1994: 95). Rather, these additional dimensions reflect the phenomenon whereby any simultaneous audio and visual events produce the illusion of a spontaneous and irresistible bond, which Chion refers to as 'synchresis'.

'Synchresis is what makes dubbing, postsynchronization, and sound-effects mixing possible, and enables such a wide array of choices in these processes. For a single body and a single face on the screen, thanks to synchresis, there are dozens of allowable voices' (1994: 63). The sound effects editors must therefore choose carefully to make sound and image express the elements of the natural world in *LOTR*. The films cultivate what Chion identifies as 'sync-points' and 'visual-microrhythms' – factors that enhance the effects of synchresis.

Audiovisual sync-points foreground and enhance the correspondence between certain audio and visual events (1994: 58–60). In *LOTR* they frequently arise through a combination of audio and visual close-ups with cuts on action. For example, in sequences when Saruman's armies are marching, the image often cuts to close-ups of feet pounding the earth as the sounds of impact jump abruptly in volume. In such instances, the soundtrack performs something analogous to the isolation and foregrounding of the object within the visual close-up by diminishing all competing sounds within the mix and punctuating the contrast of volume and texture within the soundscape. The Supervising Sound Editor Ethan Van der Ryn describes how they also 'built in beats of silence' to punctuate the sound of the explosion of the castle wall at the battle of Helm's Deep (Jackson 2003d). Combined with a visual cut on the explosion, the momentary silence produces a 'dynamic contrast that heightens the aggression and visceral nature of the action' (ibid.).

Synchresis also demonstrates how the presence of sound always implies the passage of time within the image. There is no sonic equivalent to a still image, yet even a still image of a landscape seems to reanimate once the sound of falling water is added. Sound *is* motion, however slight or even invisible. How things sound is a product of their material resonance (literally the frequency at which sound vibrates within a given material), and expresses the sonic relation of movement and materiality. Cinema enhances this relationship by making the resonance of sound visibly animate in the 'microrhythms' of the image.

Chion writes: 'By *visual microrhythms* I mean rapid movements on the image's surface caused by things such as curls of smoke, rain, snowflakes, undulations of the rippled surface of a lake, dunes, and so forth . . . These phenomena create rapid and fluid rhythmic values, instilling a vibrating, trembling temporality in the image itself' (1994: 16). Visual microrhythms play a powerful if subtle role within synchresis throughout the trilogy. In the first shots of Mount Doom, the ground visibly shakes and pebbles roll as the volcano rumbles below. Elsewhere, visible ripples on surfaces of water corroborate the gentle splashing sounds of rowing oars, and whitewater microrhythmically dances to the crashing sound of waterfalls and deluges.

Sync-points and microrhythms synchretically reinforce the materiality and vitality of the natural world throughout the trilogy. They also narratively establish nature as the site of conflict between forces of good and evil. Within this context, synchresis works to create an audiovisual vocabulary of a natural order based loosely on the four elements in which sync-points and microrhythms become most intensified when this order is threatened. For example, Sauron's power over the wizard Saruman and the tower of Isengard overturns the natural harmony of the elements and redeploys them in unnatural ways to produce an army of evil. *Fellowship* and *Towers* both present elaborate montage sequences that alternate aerial establishing shots of Isengard with audiovisual close-ups of trees crashing to the ground and thrown into the pit at the foot of the tower. From inside the pit we see and hear trees ricocheting off walls and crashing on to pyres in order to fuel the forges below. Deeper inside the pit another series of audiovisual close-ups expresses a system of non-natural production, an industrial nightmare of the natural world literally turned upside-down. Audiovisual close-ups focus the transformation of wood, fire, and metal through violent action; sync-points emphasise physical force, while microrhythms of sizzling coals, molten metals, and vibrating steel pounded into crudely shaped weapons and armour visibly echo their audible resonances.

Synchresis forges correspondences between what is immediately present to hearing and vision. In philosophical terms, this perceptual immediacy defines the field of immanence as what is audible and visible for a particular subject, from a particular position, at a particular time. However, what is immanent within any given act of perception never exhausts the existence of the thing(s) perceived. For example, to see a thing is always to see it only partially, from one side, excluding facets available to other points of view. Within any given act of perception, immanence thus implies a degree of 'transcendence', whereby the existence of the perceived object exceeds its immediate presence within the perceptual field. This threshold of immanence and transcendence is structured differently across the various perceptual fields. In cinema, we regularly hear the presence of things, or aspects of things, that transcend the visual field within the frame. What is immanent to audition both overlaps (as in the phenomena of synchresis), and also *overextends* or transcends the reach of vision. Chion has pointed out that while the visual field of the film is contained within the frame, there is no corresponding audio container for its sound. Yet the power of synchresis and audiovisual illusion often obscures this difference. 'Visual and auditory perception are of much more disparate natures than one might think. The reason we are only dimly aware of this is that these two perceptions mutually influence each other in the audiovisual contract, lending each other their respective properties by contamination and projection' (Chion 1994: 9).

The 'audiovisual contract' characterises the more general phenomena of synaesthesia – which describes the processes whereby what is immanent within one of the five senses will invariably evoke a sense of presence within the others, even if the object in question is beyond their direct reach. As Merleau-Ponty explains: 'When I say that I see a sound, I mean that I echo the vibration of the sound with my whole sensory being . . . My body is a ready-made system of equivalents and transpositions from one sense to another. The senses translate each other without any need of an interpreter, and are mutually comprehensible without the intervention of an idea' (1962: 234–5). We thus fail to understand sound and vision as discrete precisely because their mutual 'contamination' occurs so automatically, prior to reflection.

The synaesthetic projection of visible structures through sound is most evident in offscreen space. For example, in *Fellowship* sound plays a large role in the passage through the mines of Moria – whose voluminous dimensions are visibly concealed through dark, enclosed, and winding passages. In the only clearly lit chamber of the mines, Pippin accidentally knocks a decapitated head (still wearing its helmet) down a dark hole. This audiovisual event begins with straightforward synchresis, as an audible 'clanging' matches the visibly metallic surface of the helmet as it bounces off the stone edge of the hole before disappearing. But 'out of sight' does not mean 'out of audition', as an irregular sequence of metallic sounds continues, transcending the visible field within the frame, and sonically expressing the helmet's descent through a series of unseen physical spaces.

The helmet has passed into the realm of what Chion describes as 'acousmatic' sound: lacking a visible source within the frame yet expressing a material presence within the fictional world. Furthermore, offscreen acousmatic sounds not only continue to resonate the materiality of the helmet, but also to 'reverberate' the materiality and dimensionality of the unseen spaces through which it falls. Each audible resonance of the helmet also expresses a distinctly resonant surface of contact within a distinctly reverberant spatial volume. Sharp tones evoke rock surfaces; dull, aspirated sounds evoke surfaces of dirt or sand; and a final cluster of metallic 'clangs' evokes a pile of other like objects. Equally significant are the intervening periods of silence, which measure the distance between surfaces. Finally, the descending volume of each successive crash announces that these spaces are becoming successively more distant.

Following the helmet's last audible crash, other ominous sounds emerge, beginning with shuffling movements punctuated by drumbeats. As with the helmet, the reverberant echo of each drumbeat sonically expresses the contours of its space. The locations of the drums and subsequent footsteps are also communicated through varying reverberations, relative volumes, and positional biases within the soundscape. The drumbeats precede multiple footsteps that likewise issue from different sonic locations, reverberate the spaces through which they pass, and reduce increments of spatial distance through increasing increments of volume. As the footsteps grow louder and more numerous, they assume a greater proximity and more decisive positionality in relation to the visible space within the frame. These acousmatic sounds culminate in a sync-point when visual microrhythmic vibrations upon the inner surface of the chamber door coincide with the resonant sound of wooden impact; 'they' are outside.

Through the interaction of resonance and reverberation, sound synaesthetically expresses not only the materiality of objects outside the frame, but also their surrounding physical environments. These spaces are uniquely audiovisual creations, existing neither on the image or sound track alone, but only through their strategic combination. The image 'magnetises' sound in space, but sound extends this space beyond the image, proving Chion's argument that audiovisual combinations are always experienced as more than the sum of their parts, a mutual and co-operative extension of the filmic world through sound and image that Chion calls the 'audiovisual superfield' (1994: 69).

The examples so far have illustrated sound's ability to express the material qualities of objects and spaces through the action of physical forces within the natural world. However, throughout *LOTR*, synchretic and acousmatic sounds regularly evoke qualities of things beyond their material presence through the activity of nonphysical and supernatural forces.

*LOTR* features various cultural artefacts fashioned from natural elements yet endowed with supernatural powers. The creation of the ring itself is represented as simultaneously an act of natural and supernatural craft as it is poured, pounded, and polished into shape through a series of audiovisual close-ups. The ring is made of more than natural materials, and the supernatural excess assumes distinct sonic forms. For example, the power of the ring to deceive individuals is belied by its otherwise modest visible appearance, yet audible in the sweet tonalities and incomprehensible whispers it emits in the hands of characters. The Sound Designer David Hopkins remarks: 'When I first started playing with ring sounds for Peter, we were going for an actual more physical ring sound, but that turned into the ring actually having a voice' (Jackson 2002c).

The transmission of the ring's immaterial, supernatural powers through audible voices elaborates upon more mundane functions of internal dialogue. Often we hear a character's voice during a shot in which she does not visibly appear to be speaking. A form of synchresis occurs, but one in which sound is understood as issuing not from any material forces acting upon or from within the character's physical body, but rather from immaterial forces within his psyche. We might think of inner speech being inside a character, but not in the same way that an object resides within a container. This explains why, for many philosophers, thought is not only transcendent (partially beyond the reach of a particular point of view or audition) but a form of 'transcendental' presence (situated categorically beyond the reach of sound and vision).

Cinema can, uniquely, express externally a character's inner dialogue and vision. The ability of internal dialogue to situate the immaterial psyche as both within and yet beyond the physical body provides a model from which *LOTR* extrapolates the habitation of supernatural entities within material objects and the natural world. This ability also helps to explain why audiovisual expressions of supernatural agency tend towards anthropomorphism by giving voice and agency to things that do not naturally speak. The supernatural powers lurking within the forest are personified through the talking Ents, the evil forces dwelling within molten lava are bodied forth by the roar of the Balrog, and the winds that blow out of the cave and through the canyons from Mount Dwimorberg vocalise the curses of the disembodied souls trapped inside. These modifications of internal dialogue demonstrate the presence of an inner as well as outer horizon of visibility transcended by sound within the audiovisual superfield. Lending a supernatural interiority to material objects such as the ring also organises them on a level beyond their material presence. As Gandalf narrates, Sauron poured all of his hatred and lust for power into the ring: 'He and the ring are one.' The ring's supernatural unifying power is evident in its material inscription: 'One ring to rule them all, one ring to find them, one ring to bring them all and in the darkness bind them.' Like a tuning fork, the ring induces natural and supernatural realms to vibrate at Sauron's frequency and reverberate with his will, and it can speak within – and ultimately possess – the mind of whoever bears or wears it.

A similar projection of internal dialogue occurs in *Towers* when Frodo hears an internal voice that is not his own, but that of the Elf witch Galadriel. She welcomes Frodo – 'the one who has seen the eye' – but her mouth and face remain motionless even as her words become audible within Frodo's point of view. As Galadriel speaks, the film cuts to a close-up of her eyes, synaesthetically transcoding the power of speech and audition to that of vision. The mutual exclusivity of eye contact is commuted to that of a voice heard only between the two, giving the impression that Galadriel speaks within Frodo's mind. She whispers from a physical distance and at a volume that would have been scarcely audible within the natural space of the sequence, and yet her voice mysteriously supervenes over all other sounds in the mix. Also, while the voices of others are spoken in the open air with little echo, her whispers reverberate as if tracing the dimensions of some unseen conduit of transmission.

The sequence exemplifies Chion's observation that 'a certain type of unrealistic reverberation, not commensurate with the place shown in the image, can also be coded as dematerializing and symbolizing' (1994: 116). This sort of incommensurability between reverberation and 'place' is cultivated in the experience of wearing the ring, whose most immediate dematerialising effect is a reversal of the terms of visibility. At the moment someone dons the ring s/he becomes invisible within the natural world, but simultaneously hyper-visible within a parallel, supernatural realm of darkness before the Eye of Sauron. The visual expression of this supernatural realm is sonically accompanied by a constant hissing sound, out of which the voice of Sauron emerges first like a murmur and then rises steadily to a loud echoing whisper: 'I can see you.' The ring, the eye, and the tower are all radiating structures that commute the omnidirectional nature of the auditory field to the otherwise limited directionality of point of view, implying a supernatural vision by which the Eye of Sauron, his servants, and the wearer of the ring can sense one another from any distance and any direction.

The ring is not only an object of perception for Sauron but also a transmitter of his subjectivity and will through a continuum in which the structures of natural visibility and audibility are transformed. Resonance and reverberation here assume a symbolic and poetic expression of ego, power, and influence. Whoever bears the ring covets it as his own, and mistakes the voice of Sauron for one's own inner voice and will. Bachelard observes a curious property in the transmission of the poetic image: 'The image offered us by reading the poem now becomes really our own. It takes root in us. It has been given us by another, but we begin to have the impression that we could have created it, that we should have created it' (1994: xxiii). Moreover, Bachelard describes this poetic transmission as a process of resonance and reverberation in which the subjectivity that created the image reverberates within the depths of the receiver's psyche, not unlike the way in which sound reverberates beyond the visible frame, stirring up hidden facets of reality through novel sonic structures.

# 15

# Howard Shore's ring cycle: the film score and operatic strategy

*Judith Bernanke*

## Prologue

From the outset, Howard Shore considered his score for *LOTR* to be a single, coherent, dramatic work – an opera – with each film an individual Act (Adams 2001). This concept influenced compositional aspects such as the orchestral scoring, choice of instrumentation, and size of musical forces; the development of thematic material to represent characters, ideas, and cultural groups; and the use and variation of musical material throughout the three films (Adams 2002). Comparing this film score with Wagner's four-opera Ring cycle is inevitable, and Shore acknowledges that he 'had to look into Wagner's great and amazing work and into the opera form' (Wolf 2003).

Shore has composed well over ten hours of music for the series, with the extended DVD versions totalling over eleven hours. Over 90 per cent of the three films has accompanying musical material.[1] Such extensive and almost uninterrupted scoring fits the tradition of the 'music-flooded' film scores of Korngold or Steiner, both of whom composed music tracks closely linked to their films' dramatic structures (Brown 1994: 97). This approach also recalls the *unendliche Melodie* of Wagner's Ring Cycle, the 'endless melody' resulting from motivic associations between music and action extended over an entire work to create a seamlessly flowing dramatic unity (Dahlhaus 1979: 114). Many classic Hollywood film composers purposely looked to the musical styles and techniques of composers such as Richard Strauss and Wagner who had addressed the problem of scoring and unifying extended dramatic narratives (Prendergast 1992: 39).

Shore borrows another aspect of this Hollywood tradition of film scoring, also derived from late nineteenth-century symphonic and operatic compositional techniques: the use of recurring and interrelated melodies, or leitmotifs. Leitmotifs play an important formal and dramatic role in *LOTR*'s music. Shore composed a considerable number of distinctive themes for each film: forty-four compositions for *Fellow-ship*, twenty-seven for *Towers*, and somewhat fewer for *Return* (Adams 2003: 20).

Paulin notes that achieving unity and synthesis is a challenge for film, 'almost always an art with "multiple authors" and the resultant risk of rupture' (2000: 62). While continuity editing, in pursuit of the semblance of a seamlessly coherent narrative, works to conceal the disruptive effects of film cutting and splicing, music can also contribute to a film's impression of coherency. In fact, music has qualities especially well suited to contributing to a film's sense of narrative unity. According to Gorbman, '[Music's] malleability, its spatial, rhythmic, and temporal values, give it a special and complex status in the narrative film experience. It bonds: shot to shot, narrative event to meaning, spectator to narrative, spect-ator to audience' (1987: 55). Still, *LOTR*'s narrative complexity and epic scope make sound and image coherency particularly challenging.

Shore's compositional approach in *LOTR* echoes four of Gorbman's seven theoretical principles (1987: 73) for how traditional Hollywood film music composition, mixing, and editing perform a supportive role in narrative continuity. His score creates atmosphere and conveys emo-tions; reveals characters' subjective experience and illustrates dramatic events through narrative cueing; maintains continuity by filling 'gaps' and providing transitions; and constructs formal and narrative unity through repetition and variation. The following analysis discusses the concept of the leitmotif and then traces how the Fellowship theme enhances dramatic content and contributes to formal and narrative unity throughout the trilogy.

## Musical representation and the leitmotif

Kivy (1991) argues that, despite music's limited capacity to convey fixed or semantic meaning, it can acquire such meaning by depicting exter-nal non-musical reality through imitation of sounds and motions (bird songs, flowing water) or by illustrating actions and emotional states (travel by horse, weeping). Such musical meaning through association devel-ops over time via cultural conditioning, and requires listeners with some prior knowledge and experience. Music can also acquire mean-ing through 'internal representations' or associations that may develop within the context of a particular musical work (ibid., 52). The most familiar example of this representational approach is the use of leitmotifs, or musical themes, which operate within a dramatic work according to an internal system of signification linked to narrative material. Listeners learn the extra-musical associations as the work unfolds and generally do not require prior knowledge or experience to understand the musical references. The use of leitmotifs, derived from Wagner's music dramas, thus became one of the most common techniques for structuring film scores (Neumeyer and Buhler 2001: 28).

In a leitmotivic score, a process of associating musically distinctive melodic or harmonic material with a character, place, situation, or concept occurs through usage and repetition (London 2000: 87). This association is usually established by presenting such material with the character's first appearance and then restating the musical material with each appearance or mention that follows. A leitmotif's meaning and function may remain the same throughout a film or change as it recurs in new contexts to reflect the character's development as the story progresses. Nor must a leitmotif be limited to representing only the immediate visual presence of someone or something; music can also connect the present with the past and the future (Dahlhaus 1979: 123).

Typically, in narrative film leitmotifs underscore the onscreen presence of a character, place, or thing; indicate memory or thought by signalling the psychological presence of someone or something that is absent (London 2000: 89); or foreshadow future events – all of which can be discerned in *LOTR*'s leitmotifs. The Fellowship theme illustrates Shore's use of these techniques in *LOTR*; it reflects and reveals dramatic meaning while providing formal and narrative unity.

### Narrative motivations: introducing the Fellowship[2]

*Fellowship*'s eight-minute Prologue operates narratively as an exposition of the ring's history leading up to the film's events. Musically, this continuously scored opening functions as an opera overture to introduce the audience to significant musical material and its narrative referent, and to establish the overall mood of what follows. The film begins mysteriously, in darkness with the sound of a chorus and two female voices, one whispering in Elvish and the other proclaiming, 'The world has changed'. The music (Figure 16) conveys a sense of sadness and longing, created by its exotic harmonic minor key; it also associates this theme with the concept of change linked to the ring. The theme's repetition throughout *Fellowship* and the subsequent films strengthens this connection.

Another theme emerges simultaneously with the onscreen appearance of the title *The Lord of the Rings*. As this leitmotif plays, the account of the ring's history continues in voice-over. The connection between this particular leitmotif and the Ring's history (Figure 17) is reinforced by the theme's three recurrences during the Prologue: first, when Isildur

**Figure 16** Lothlorien theme.

**Figure 17** History of the Ring theme.

**Figure 18** Shire theme.

**Figure 19** Fellowship theme.

gains the ring from Sauron; next, when Isildur loses the ring and it comes into Gollum's possession; and finally, when Bilbo acquires it. The historical account ends with the ring's unexpected possession by a Hobbit and uncertainty about what will happen next. This suspense is represented musically as the Prologue ends with a sustained E-flat minor chord that progresses to E-flat major as the next section, 'Concerning Hobbits', begins and the mood lightens. Both the scene and the narrator's voice change, and, as the camera glides past a map of the Shire, we hear the folk-like Shire theme (Figure 18). As this theme in D major cadences, it leads directly into a subdued, full statement of the Fellowship theme (Figure 19), which underscores the appearance on screen of this film's title.[3]

*Towers'* opening follows this same formal approach: separating the main title's two parts and underscoring their appearance with thematic material significant to the film's narrative focus. In this case, the *LOTR*

**Figure 20** Rohan theme.

title appears along with the History of the Ring theme and the *Towers* title is accompanied by a brief statement of the leitmotif associated with Rohan, the realm of the horsemen. However, this theme suggests something More. While the first film focuses on the formation and fragmentation of the Fellowship, the second film introduces the various realms of Men and explores their capabilities and frailties. These qualities are suggested symbolically in the melodic structure of this version of the Rohan leitmotif (Figure 20) and in its harmonic connection with other themes. Unlike its more heroic and powerful presentation later in the film, the Rohan theme's brief statement here (in A minor) is hesitant, communicating uncertainty not only by its thin scoring and slow tempo but also through the shape of its asymmetrical melody line, which moves upward ending on the submediant of the scale rather than resolving more emphatically on its tonic pitch. This melodic line, suggesting a question, reflects the uncertain future of Men, whose 'hearts . . . are easily corrupted' (Prologue, *Fellowship*). Whether Men have the moral will to resist the seduction of power underlies all the films; musically, the simple presentation of this leitmotif hints at the question.

According to London (2000: 87), main title cues of classic film scores were frequently binary forms consisting of an opening 'A' theme, usually identified with either a character or a setting, and a contrasting, more lyrical 'B' theme. Dividing the main film titles into their two parts and presenting each one separately, accompanied by a distinctive theme, recalls this classic approach to the binary treatment of main title cues. Also, this approach not only highlights some of the most important musical material to be heard in these films but also establishes the opposing forces of good and evil that will operate narratively and musically throughout all three.

### 'In the darkness bind them': thematic connections

Repetition and variation of melodic material help a leitmotivic score achieve coherency. Recurring leitmotifs are especially valuable in epic works comprising numerous characters and narrative elements. Such an approach can create a sense of interconnectedness in which 'everything seems to belong to everything else' (Dahlhaus 1979: 109).

Shore uses this technique most clearly in his varied treatment of the Fellowship theme, which appears frequently throughout all three films and serves structurally to identify connections between characters and to signify travel and action. After its initial statement as a main title cue in the first film, the Fellowship theme recurs, usually in fragmentary form, as the narrative unfolds and as various members join the Ringbearer's quest. The first brief statement of this sort follows directly after the Shire theme and occurs as Sam and Frodo leave the Shire. This moderately slow, poignant version of the theme, performed by a horn with orchestral accompaniment, contrasts with its next presentation underscoring Gandalf's urgent ride to Orthanc to seek Saruman's advice. Here, the theme's faster tempo is punctuated by crashing cymbals and accompanied by the percussion's rhythmic ostinato imitating the sound of Gandalf's galloping horse.

The leitmotif next appears as Aragorn leads the hobbits to Rivendell. Horns repeat the static first part of the theme while the string sections play a variation of the next portion of the melody accompanied by a timpani drumbeat matching the pace of Aragorn's footsteps. The constant, unrelenting sound of the timpani indicates the journey's increasing danger and difficulty as well as Aragorn's determination to lead the hobbits to safety. When, despite Aragorn's best efforts, the Ringwraiths locate and attack the travellers, Shore musically represents this battle by intertwining fragments of both the Fellowship and Ringwraith themes.

The first full, heroic statement of the leitmotif occurs at the Council of Elrond when the group, now formally identified as the Fellowship, sets out to destroy the ring. After this auspicious moment, the theme, like the Fellowship itself, breaks apart and occurs only in fragmentary form after Gandalf is lost at Khazad-dum and the Fellowship fractures into three separate groups. At the end of *Fellowship*, Shore uses counterpoint, a compositional technique combining several independent musical lines (most commonly demonstrated in a fugue, derived from the Italian word *fuga* meaning 'flight'), to represent Frodo's departure from the Fellowship and Sam's efforts to join him. This fuguelike musical material effectively matches the dramatic moment when Frodo attempts to leave the group. In addition, by developing and extending the thematic material and dividing it into independent musical lines, this brief bit of counterpoint creates tension and uncertainty to reflect not only 'the splintering of the group', as Shore refers to it but also the complexity of the narrative to come (Adams 2002: 22).

The fragmentation of the Fellowship theme resumes in *Towers*, as the three storylines continue independently. Only heard in relation to Aragorn, Gimli, and Legolas, the Fellowship theme often functions in

**Figure 21** The three hunters.

**Figure 22** Isengard theme.

**Figure 23** Trailing the Uruk-hai.

this film as a transitional device to bridge space and time. For instance, as the three companions track the Uruk-hai who took Pippin and Merry, the theme takes on a triple metre (Figure 21), particularly appropriate for a chase scene. Unlike a duple metre, the asymmetrical pulse of a triple metre creates a sense of forward momentum, especially when combined with a syncopated melody line, as here. The treatment of the leitmotif changes as the three hunters realise that the Uruk-hai are travelling towards Isengard and their own pace intensifies. Shore replaces the rolling motion of the triple metre with the awkward 5/4 rhythmic figure of the Isengard theme (Figures 22, 23) and merges the melodic material of both themes. In the earlier scene the rhythmic figure conveys determination and momentum and the theme, scored with trumpets and horns, evokes the sound of a hunt. The second rhythmic treatment, however, suggests this journey's ultimate destination by means of the percussive ostinato of the Isengard theme, and the hunt becomes a race as the pursuers grow desperate to save their friends.

As the film continues, the Fellowship theme increasingly fragments. For instance, when Legolas and Gimli believe Aragorn to be dead, we hear just the first notes and then a recurrence of this fragment when he is reunited with his companions at Helm's Deep. In these two cases, the theme does not merely underscore an event that affects the members of the Fellowship; it also conveys the characters' subjective emotional experience. In these scenes, the theme has been reduced to its simplest, most understated form. A full statement is unnecessary since the theme is easily recognised, but minimising the thematic material also restrains the emotional content for scenes with restrained dialogue and emotional expression, and prevents them from being overly melodramatic. The theme's simplified form here perhaps reflects what could be considered an appropriate masculine emotional expression as well as the kind of subtle, understated communication that often occurs between close friends.

The Fellowship theme continues in its primarily fragmentary form in *Return*, although the complete theme is also present at least three times. The most significant occurrence accompanies the reunion of the Fellowship after Frodo has destroyed the ring and Sauron is defeated. As Aragorn comes through the doorway of Frodo's room, a full statement of the Fellowship theme leads directly into the Shire theme that underscores Sam's appearance. These two themes presented together mirror their appearance in the first film when Frodo and Sam left the Shire to begin their journey. In both situations, the themes are in the key of C but they are presented in opposite order, serving as framing devices that signal the beginning and ending points of the Ringbearer's mission. These themes also link the narrative across the three films by providing a symmetrical structure for the entire work.

## Epilogue

As Shore's music demonstrates, a leitmotif can have a close connection to the dramatic narrative by underscoring events as they occur on screen and revealing the more subtle subjective experiences of characters. However, music also operates over time and through memory to unify a film's larger formal structure. Shore explains that his motifs can act as 'guideposts' directing viewers' attention to onscreen events as well as their relationship with other dramatic elements (Adams 2003: 19), just as Wagner refers to a music drama's 'melodic elements' as 'signposts for the emotions' operating as essential unifying devices for the epic dramatic form (Dahlhaus 1979: 108). The repetition of a theme can make it memorable and its association with narrative elements assigns meaning, but varied treatment of this familiar music also adds new layers of significance. According to Gorbman, 'The repetition, interaction, and variation of musical themes throughout a film contribute much to the clarity of its dramaturgy and to the clarity of its formal structures' (1987: 91). Tracing the Fellowship theme's journey throughout *LOTR* illustrates the added value and interest that a well-wrought film score can provide.

## Notes

1 The running time for the theatrical releases of each of the first two films is about 178 minutes, with 150 minutes of music in the first film and 160 minutes in the second, which equates to over eighty per cent of each film (Carlsson 2001; Barry 2002). The extended editions of each DVD were re-edited, and Shore composed and recorded new material for each of these longer versions. The longer version of the first film presents 30 minutes of extended and new material, the second film 44 minutes, and the extended version of the final film has 50 minutes of added material.

2 Analyses of *Fellowship* and *Towers* are based on the extended DVD versions of the film; however, analysis of *Return* is based on the theatrical release available at the time of writing.

3 The treatment of the main title cues is different in the theatrical version of *Fellowship*. While the two parts of the film's title are separated in the theatrical release as they are in the DVD version, the theatrical version lacks the added scene 'Concerning Hobbits' and the title, '*The Fellowship of the Rings*', appears on screen with the visual introduction of the character Frodo underscored by the Shire theme. Compared with the theatrical release, the DVD treatment is musically and formally more complex and reflects the film's narrative content more effectively.

# 16

# Realising Middle-earth: production design and film technology

## Sean Cubitt

Miniatures, bigatures, digital mattes, 3D animation, costume, set and prop design, forced perspective, location and studio shoots all contributed to the creation of Middle-earth. The panoply of visual effects *LOTR* uses to build Middle-earth's image has become familiar, not just from the films but also from television specials, websites, DVD appendices and commentaries, and the remarkable travelling Exhibition. Armour, prosthetics, stunt and miniature doubles, animal wranglers, blue screen, and the Massive intelligent agents are part of our language now. Weta Workshop and Weta Digital, with their army of collaborators, did more than visualise the most-read – and most-imagined – book of the twentieth century. They realised the script, made real the fictional world where the narrative would take place. The challenge of realisation is in some sense the challenge of cinema itself – the French even use the word *réalisation* to describe filmmaking. Realising Middle-earth is both a technical challenge and a special kind of problem in realism, the aesthetic field dealing with depictions of reality (as in documentary) and the illusion of reality (as in dramatic fiction). Most complicated of all is the realisation of a world whose highest technology, the explosive device in the culvert of the Deeping Wall, is portrayed as the work of Saruman's dark arts. Tolkien's hatred of industrialisation comes through in the firepits of Isengard. Yet the films depend on the use of and innovation in new media technologies, and much of our viewing pleasure comes from appreciating the craft that has gone into them. We watch entranced by a double magic: the fascination of illusion, and the fascination of how it has been achieved. The contest between the dark arts and white magic in the film is, among other things, a parable about the uses of technology, and it begins in the magic of illusion.

Few audiences can watch the films without sensing the immense effort that has gone into giving viewers the illusion of Middle-earth's reality. From Viggo Mortensen's repairs to his costume to the artificial ageing of sets and props, the filmmakers have been at pains to render the world

**Figure 24** Gandalf in Bilbo's home.

of Middle-earth as if it possessed a history as well as a geography. Actors and the dialogue tell us of the older days, but also and crucially the production design emphasises the used, the rusted, the cracked, and the windblown. Perhaps nothing shows this more than the depth of the film: the detail of the design work, the staging of scenes in depth, and the use of deep focus. The 'reality' of Middle-earth in the film trilogy is an effect, like magic, perhaps the most special of all the special effects the films deploy.

Kracauer, a pioneer of realist criticism, once wrote, 'The small random moments which concern things common to you and me and the rest of mankind can indeed be said to constitute the dimension of everyday life' (1960: 304). Such fragments of reality are for Kracauer the most important elements of film, enabling us to experience as if for the first time the rich detail of life that, through habit or culture, we have learned to ignore. The critical term here is 'random'. Because it is an automatic machine for gathering images, the camera will seize even on things its operator is unaware of filming. Though location shoots are notoriously fickle, snowing when you want sun, raining when you want snow, they also give the filmmaker those unrepeatable fragments of actuality that are clouds, riverscapes, the flicker of leaves in the breeze, or sunset on a mountain range. Cinematography grasps those sensations with a scientific and democratic lack of choice. Bazin, Kracauer's near contemporary, moved from the randomness of locations to a passion for deep focus, the use of wide-angle lenses, and light to allow all elements of a shot to appear in focus. These techniques gave audiences the freedom to look wherever in the frame they wish. Yet in 'An Aesthetic of Reality' he admits that 'realism in art can only be achieved one way – through artifice' (1971: 26). The problem, he notes, is that the illusion soon replaces reality itself, and mere technique replaces the redemption of the real. That is one of the commonest criticisms of *LOTR*, and it is the nub of the dialectic between natural and technological that governs technologies and design processes in the films.

Clearly the *LOTR* films are not realist in any useful sense of the word. Yet real things play a significant part in the movies' reality effect. A key difference between sets and locations is that locations, however prepared for shooting, always have some residual reality in the sense that they cannot be entirely planned. Randomness is a hallmark of reality, in the cinema as in life: Eowyn's hair flying round her face in the wind is both emotionally and pictorially convincing because it is random. Replicating randomness is a critical advance in CGI, as a comparison of the invading forces at Helm's Deep with the robot army of *Star Wars Episode One: The Phantom Menace* shows at a glance. Because randomness is a mathematical concept, it can be programmed. But CGI tends to be very clean: everything in perfect focus, surfaces pristine. Noise and dirt need to be added, for example, by using digital fog (software that dims 'distant' objects and shifts them towards the blue end of the spectrum) and adding motion blur to replicate human and cine-camera optics. Likewise, virtual objects created in 3D software can be wrapped in textures derived from photographs of actual textiles, skin, and rocks. In the case of sets and bigatures, mouldings from pohutekawa bark and boulders give fine grain to Treebeard and the cave at the Pool. Real grasses and sedges were planted all over the Dead Marshes, real leaves and branches in the Fangorn set. It is not so much the authenticity of the set dressing that counts as the random untidiness of natural objects, a randomness that also adds depth to the most successful synthespian to date, Gollum, orchestrated on Serkis's performance but also on the tripping, splashing, and tumbling that a real actor suffers, and that a wholly scripted CGI effect would lack.

To clarify some of these points, it is instructive to compare a couple of scenes, the first dominated by location and a set built on location, the other largely shaped by compositing bigatures and CGI. 'The King of the Golden Hall' (*Towers* extended DVD, disc 1, episode 20) brings us to the Edoras set. Running for 11 minutes and 6 seconds with a total of 206 shots, the average shot length (ASL) of just over 3.2 seconds is slightly misleading. At least four shots (Gandalf, Aragorn, Gimli, and Legolas riding over the plains of Rohan; Eowyn walking onto the look-out point outside the Golden Hall; the 17-second helicopter shot of the Edoras location; and Theoden's transformation scene) run well over ten seconds each, and several are reprised after embedded shots, indicating that the sheer length of the takes was not a technical problem. The ASL is so short because the scene is punctuated by two intensely edited sequences, the three heroes fighting their way to Theoden's throne, and the battle of wills between Gandalf and Theoden/Saruman. Absent these flurries of activity, the ASL settles somewhere above 4 seconds. External scenes are shot in natural light, and internal ones add a blue filter to give the impression of daylight as the Great Hall's main illumination.

By contrast, 'The Flooding of Isengard' (*Towers* extended DVD, disc 2, episode 59) runs a far brisker 2 minutes and 21 seconds, with 40 shots and an ASL of 3.5 seconds. Here the cutting is far more regular, with no shots running over five seconds. The rule so flamboyantly broken in the first film, that miniature shots should always be as brief as possible, is here more rigorously employed. Though there is a great deal of detail – tiny figures run across the top of the dam as the Ents tear it down, for example – none of it is dwelt on. The rhythms are subordinated to the rising crescendo of the film's last act, and the use of effects proliferates as the faster cutting predominates.

The Golden Hall sequence is marked by the detail of costumes, armoury, textiles, and architecture, all built at full scale. Though some of these elaborate props are merely glimpsed, the attraction of deep staging is both that it provides a sense of the depth of the story world, adding to its illusion of reality, and that it invites audiences to multiple viewings, a vital attractor for success in the DVD sell-through market. 'The Flooding of Isengard', by contrast, is dominated by bigatures, miniatures, animatronics, CGI figures, and the compositing of live action into multi-layered shots (for example, the image of Saruman peering from his window on to the chaos below). At the same time, both sequences share some aesthetic techniques. Dialogue in close-up is largely done with shallow focus, though rarely as shallow as that used for the romantic pick-ups set in Rivendell. Elsewhere, deep focus is the rule. In both sequences, despite the difficulties of matching the various plates in compositing, the camera is rarely static, from minor reframings to grand crane and helicopter passes. This constant reframing adds to the sense of the real by emulating, in a suitably stylised way, the movements of a documentary camera, which always follows its subjects.

It is interesting to note that the predominance of live action or location rather than its exclusivity seems to regulate the duration of shots. The wide shot of Edoras that begins the Golden Hall sequence has extensive digital 3D additions to the location build, and Lesnie notes on the DVD commentary that Gandalf's nose prosthetic needed frequent touch-ups in the digital grading process. None the less, these segments, where the wind tousles hair and beards or rips a banner from a flagpole, are touched with the randomness of the location, down to the wheat sprouting in the thatch as the four ride into the hilltop settlement, or the curling and twisting of smoke from the chimneys. Likewise Lesnie notes that the ambient daylight needed some supplement in the great hall of Edoras, and the film in general uses a great deal of fills, spots, and more effects-driven lighting tools such as 'practical fire' (piped gas flame used to illuminate interiors in this electricity-free world).

If, as Godard is supposed to have said, 'morality is a question of tracking shots', this is a highly moral film. Hand-held shots like those of Wormtongue's ejection from Meduseld, crane and helicopter shots, or the 360-degree swirl around Grima and Eowyn in Theodred's chamber are the more obvious, but even in the more portrait-like sequences, such as that depicting Theoden drawing his sword again, there are minor but significant reframings in almost every shot, except those that, like Theoden's transformation, require the camera to be locked off between takes of the different stages of the make-up. The use of 3D and bigatures makes similar mobility available in the Flooding of Isengard. The nine-metre dam model, supplemented with sixty tons of water in two shipping containers, and the one-sixth scale model that it floods allow the cameras an extraordinary freedom, with rare exceptions like the composite shot of Saruman at his window looking across the CGI compound, with its population of moving figures, to the cataract plunging into his domain. A slightly earlier shot of a very similar composite includes a pan up the side of the tower model to find Saruman, while also keeping the compound and the mountainside in frame and in focus, though without the additional problem of rendering digital water to hide the worst artefacts of scale, especially difficult to manage in the case of water. The busyness of the scene is echoed by the camera's constant movement, with the implication that the world of Middle-earth is never bounded by the frame and that, were the camera to swivel on its axis, we would see still more of it.

Ironically, the techniques of deep focus and the long take have become hallmarks of special effects cinema, where a new contradiction has arisen. Speaking of composited actual and virtual camera movements

– for example the swirling image of the gladiators in the Coliseum in *Gladiator* – Allen notes that 'they both confirm the spatial reality of the scenes in which they appear and simultaneously announce their amazing presence as illusion. This tension between the real and the illusory lies at the heart of the impact computer-generated images can have for their spectators' (2002: 114). Pierson's careful periodisation of digital effects in cinema suggests that special effects became increasingly embedded, and therefore less obviously wonderful, with films such as James Cameron's *Titanic* (see Pierson 2002). But with *LOTR* we are back in the tension described by Allen, the continuation, by other means, of the dialectic first analysed by Bazin between the technical redemption of reality and the triumph of technique. As if to emphasise the struggle, our most 'human' characters (the hobbits, elves, and men, Gimli, Aragorn, and Gandalf) do battle with the most fantastic (the Balrog, the Ringwraiths, Sauron), even though their victory will bring about the end of magic and the rule of men – or, we might say, the end of special effects and the beginning of realism.

And yet, to swing back to the other side of the dialectic, we have come to see the special effects, and once they are over, so is the film. The purpose of the design work is not entirely to tell the story but to establish the credibility of Middle-earth. Credibility demands detail, the multiplying of layer upon layer of simultaneous actions and objects in the majority of shots, and the detail of hero costumes, arms, hair, prosthetics, and jewellery in close-ups. For those details to be significant, we need some kind of orientation, both the kind offered by the map and the kind given by the type of contradictory establishing shot described by Allen. Writing in a much earlier period of cinema, Balász observed of the 'panorama' shot (now usually abbreviated to 'pan') that it 'makes the camera move so that in gliding past the objects it takes pictures of them in the same order as that in which they are aligned in reality'. As a result, 'space is not merely the place in which people and things can be shown; it achieves a reality of its own and has its own significance, independently of the objects which fill it' (1952: 139, 141). This space expands that discovered by Bazin to include both time and subjectivity: 'our time-sense measures the real distance which lies between the various objects', with the additional possibility of depicting 'in one and the same shot a man moving in space and the space this man sees out of his own eyes' (Balász 1952: 140). The elaborate dolly, track, crane, and helicopter shots of *LOTR*, including swooping sequences through and over miniatures and composite images, variously establish the world of Middle-earth as a discrete whole, and give us, for example in Gandalf's fall through Moria at the beginning of *Towers* and Frodo's vertigo at the foot of the stairs to Shelob's lair, an entirely subjective view of it, Middle-earth as a space that can be inhabited viscerally. So, for example, the slow tracking shots that follow Gollum, Sam, and Frodo across the Dead Marshes establish the temporal dimensions of this world, the days of walking, the hours of climbing. Middle-earth's tracking shots evoke both duration and extension to give it a physical presence that approximates what we would expect of a real geography. Unlike film, reality contains infinite detail. The first-time theatrical viewer's strong sense of having missed much of the detail suggests an evolving definition of realism: If reality is what exceeds perception, the realist film must constantly evoke an infinity of detail that a close-up or a wider pan would reveal.

The Exhibition's success touring panels on the production materials demonstrates some of this fascination with grasping a 'reality' that is essentially ungraspable, the desire for Middle-earth to exist, even though we know it does not and could, perhaps should, not. The detail of design serves many purposes, not least to do visually what the languages do in the book, demarcating each culture, building that series of homes – Meduseld, Hobbiton, Gondor, Rivendell – that tugs on the characters, what they defend, what they long for. There is immense daring here – as in the huge fly-through of the miniature for Saruman's armoury – and the immense pride of artisans in a job well done. That pride too becomes part of our fascination – there is almost as much pleasure to be had from identifying with the crew as with the heroes of the quest. The digital and craft guilds working in production have as perhaps their highest achievement a utopia of creative camaraderie which they offer as a model for the transformation of Aotearoa New Zealand from an agricultural to an information economy without traversing Saruman's industrialisation. This more than elvish magic articulates a potent, clean, green, digital economics with a fable about the dangers of technology. The power to make real, to defy destiny, and choose the world we want is acted out in the making of the films. We can only wait to see if that magic survives the departure of the elves.

**Part V**

# Reading for meaning: *The Lord of the Rings*, Middle-earth, and Aotearoa New Zealand

# 17

# Dossier: adapting a script

*Sean Cubitt and Barry King*

This section relies heavily on the words of the filmmakers themselves. What got discussed in all that interaction between Jackson and Tolkien fans on the Web before and during production of the trilogy? How did the scriptwriters go about adapting the script? What was their division of labour? What were the differences between preparing scripts for a two-film version and a three-film version of *The Lord of the Rings*? What was it like to be involved in writing the script while shooting was under way, and even into post-production? Is there a connection between the trilogy's limited psychological depth and the relative absence of female characters? What themes from the novel did they choose to emphasise?

The chapters that follow also explore the trilogy's themes, those originating in Tolkien's novel as well as those that seem to originate in the films. First, Ann Hardy ('There and back again: *The Lord of the Rings*, contemporary religiosity, and cinema', Chapter 18) argues that Aotearoa New Zealand's secular character has permeated *LOTR*, but also that *LOTR* offers its viewers a spiritual experience. While Allen Meek's 'Fantasising history as trauma' (Chapter 19) doesn't use the language of religion, he too looks at what sort of experience the trilogy can offer its viewers. Roy Parkhurst's 'The persistence of cacogenics in nationalist mythology: the case of *The Lord of the Rings*' (Chapter 20) looks especially at the Isengard episode, suggesting in passing that we compare it with other representations of mad scientists familiar to us from other films. Stephen Turner and Misha Kavka (Chapter 21) focus on the Magritte-like quality that Aotearoa New Zealand took on in the wake of Middle-earth. Ryan Reynolds, Henry Bial, and Kimon Keramidas ('Tourist encounters', Chapter 22) take a trip around parts of the South Island in search of Middle-earth, which they do and do not find. Finally, Alice Te Punga Somerville ('Asking that mountain: an Indigenous reading of *The Lord of the Rings*?', Chapter 23) sees through Middle-earth to Aotearoa on a homesick night in Ithaca, New York.

> Some days we were writing for seven different [film] units . . . if you ever
> get the yearning to shoot three films out of sequence with twenty-two main
> characters, there's a reason why it isn't done too often. (Philippa Boyens,
> quoted in Goldsmith 2004: 63)

The art of adaptation is integral to Hollywood and global film production.
Of the five films nominated for Best Picture Oscars in 2004, *The Lord
of the Rings: The Return of the King, Lost in Translation, Master and
Commander: The Far Side of the World, Seabiscuit*, and *Mystic River*,
only one, *Lost in Translation*, was an original screenplay. Also nominated for Best Adapted Screenplay alongside *The Return of the King*
were *City of God, American Splendor*, and *Seabiscuit*.

In many instances, adaptations have the benefit of developing
from already successful print and stage properties. As Barrie Osborne
explained to jubilant fans at the Oscar party for *Return*, this can also
be a liability.

> It's a strange relationship when you start a movie and you have such a
> wide fanbase. The book, as you know, was read by over a hundred mil-
> lion people, and when you set out to make a movie you want to keep it
> fresh. You want the audience to walk into the theater and be surprised
> by what they see, so it's a real tricky balance between what you let out
> during production and what you don't. And I remember at the beginning,
> we tried to keep some distance from TheOneRing.net, and then one day,
> we were shooting in Hobbiton and Peter said to me 'You know, why
> don't we invite Erica Challis in?'[1] And that started the greatest relation-
> ship, as you all know, and led to . . . well, you supported us from way
> before then, but I think that spirit of cooperation and the respect that all
> of you showed our film in controlling the information that was released
> and at the same time supporting us, was great, so thank you very much
> for that. (*West of the Moon* 2004)

Adaptation involves a complex system of rights, leasing, options, and
licensing. It also involves a dedicated labour of writing, bound by the
same expectations as original screenplays, but in varying degrees also
expected to respect the original source material. Certainly, Tolkien
himself would accept nothing less than what he thought appropriate.
In a letter to Rayner Unwin, Tolkien responded to an early script for
an animated version of the books: 'A proposed abridgement with some
good picture work would be pleasant, & perhaps worth a good deal
in publicity; but the present script is rather a compression with resultant over-crowding and confusion, blurring of climaxes, and general degradation' (Fuller 2002: 19).

Simply translating the original print text as is to a film text wouldn't
work. As the Tolkien critic Tom Shippey observed,

even in their extended versions, Peter Jackson's three *Lord of the Rings* movies will run to not much over twelve hours duration. Meanwhile, marathon public readings of *The Lord of the Rings* have shown that each volume takes some forty to fifty hours to complete, while even fast silent reading of the texts would take, at the very least, considerably longer than watching the movies. Nor is it always the case that pictures convey information faster than words. (2004: 235)

Adapting Tolkien posed specific problems for the scriptwriters Fran Walsh, Philippa Boyens, and Jackson. The process demanded abridging and even cutting many scenes, but determining what to cut was part of the scriptwriters' challenge. Their most notable choices include the Tom Bombadil chapters of the first volume and the 'Parting' and 'Scouring' chapters of the third.

There must have been times when the scriptwriters wished they could revise more radically. In one interview, Boyens notes that 'in an ideal world, if you sat down to write a movie, you'd never have a fellowship of nine people. You wouldn't need four hobbits; you'd have two. You wouldn't have two villains who are so similar, with their names sounding the same' (Ryfle 2002: 40). In another interview she said that 'you would never set out to write a script with eighteen main characters – not unless you want to drive yourself completely insane' (Watson 2002). Furthermore,

the villains, [Jackson] and Walsh said, were the most difficult thing of all. 'Tolkien evokes evil; he evokes Sauron. For most of the books, the only image of Sauron is a flaming eye. Let me tell you, to have your villain be a flaming eyeball for three whole movies is a difficult thing'.
    Even the Ring-wraiths that terrorize the hobbits at the beginning of the story are problematic. 'Think about it', said Fran. 'They can't see, they're afraid of fire, they're swept away by water . . . how frightening are they really on the screen?'
    They also disappear less than halfway through *The Fellowship of the Ring*.
    'No screenwriter would ever, ever get rid of his villain just after the first act', said Jackson. (MacNamara 2001–2)

None the less, as Jackson noted in an early interview, the spirit and especially the language of the novels were immensely important in the adaptation:

When we first started writing the scripts 3 or 4 years ago, we made an assumption at that time that we would have to simplify the language, that we'd have to modernize the language, that's really what a 'modern' film would require. And it's been a very interesting process because over subsequent drafts of the screenplays we have gone further and further into Tolkien's language, because it is beautiful, it's very evocative, and when spoken by good actors, it comes to life in a way that's really fresh and exciting. So the answer to the question is there is a HUGE amount of Tolkien's dialogue in the films. Every time we come to write a scene, or at the stage where we're revising scenes all the time, we always turn to the book – as our first part we either take dialogue from the book from that particular moment, or what we often do is, because in the film we sometimes have to portray a scene in a slightly different way, we may look at taking some lines from other places in the books and putting them in a scene where they originally didn't belong, but they're nonetheless still Tolkien's language, it's still his words. And so Tolkien's voice is heard throughout the movies very strongly – a lot of memorable lines from the books are in the films. And also what's happened is that over the three years we've been working on the scripts we've also become very familiar with Tolkien's writing style, his dialogue style, and so when it comes time for us to have to write original dialogue, you know, because there's nothing in the book that is appropriate, we've become able to at least write in a very similar style to Tolkien's. But the films very much evoke that language. (theonering.net: 2000)

*Creative Screenwriting* reported that the first, two-film version of the script – co-authored by Jackson, Walsh, and *Braindead* and *Meet the Feebles* collaborator Stephen Sinclair (who gets a script credit on *Towers*) – came in two 150-page segments. The first film's climax came with the battle of Helm's Deep, roughly half-way through the second volume of the book, requiring a great deal of structural manipulation of the text. The first drafts of the three-film version split these into three 110-page versions (normally, a page of script is expected to equal a minute of screen time, meaning that these first drafts were much briefer than the theatrical films).

Even in the three-film version, these structural issues demanded innovative responses in scripting:

We didn't feel we wanted to end [*Fellowship*] with a cliffhanger, because I didn't want people walking out of the cinema with a feeling of anxiety. That wouldn't have been a satisfying experience. If you were releasing your second film three or four months after the first, you could probably get away with that, but a year we thought was too long to leave people in that position . . .

Before we had written a word of the script we constructed a new ending built around the character of Frodo that will hopefully be emotionally satisfying . . .

Frodo needs to decide that he doesn't need the others or, more than that, that the others pose a danger to him, because the ring is starting to exert power with people around him. That's really the climactic moment in the film. (Bauer 2002: 10, 12)

Equally problematic is the structure of the first film. Boyens defines the issue:

'The first book in the trilogy is a lot of set-up', she says, 'and, of course, we also have to set up the story in our first film. We are introducing sixteen main characters, and we are also introducing an entire world. We try to do it in a very real way. Part of the wonderment, part of the experience of an epic film like this is that it takes you into such a complete world where you can just lose yourself for a few hours . . . We're taking people on a very long journey. In order for it to work, for the audience to be willing to invest the necessary time and energy to stay with the story, they have to have a sense of the ultimate payoff'. (Smith 2000: 6)

If anything, the problems increased with the 'middle story', Boyens explained:

It has its own flavor, with the introduction of the world of men . . . There are only two characters from the first story who do not appear in this one, Celeborn and Bilbo Baggins. So, we've got most every character who appears in the first film, plus about six or seven important new characters. So we had a lot of characters to deal with, and then we had the story splitting off, as it does in the book, into three distinct storylines – there's Merry and Pippin's story, there's Aragorn's story with the people of Rohan, and then there's Sam and Frodo and Gollum. Keeping those stories somehow talking to each other was a very difficult thing to do. (Ryfle 2002: 40)

Normally completed before shooting begins and only slightly modified by actors, scripts serve as a shoot's architecture, providing all production staff with the scaffolding on which the filming is organised. In this instance, however, the script remained in development throughout, even during post-production.

'It's hard to say what all will be in or out until the opening', said Boyens, refusing to answer a question about another character. 'When we were filming, it was just like this. We would be rewriting the night before and handing out pages. It got to be a joke. Fran said it was like laying train tracks even as the train bears down on us. She said that this was no way to make a movie, but it was the only way to make *this* movie'. (MacNamara 2001–2)

Walsh, who also acted as unit director for the sequence at the beginning of *Return* in which we see Smeagol's theft of the ring and the murder of Deagol, indicates some of the challenges and virtues of this practice in relation to the collaborative nature of scriptwriting:

What is really interesting about Gollum is that this is the first time that we've been engaged with writing a character that has so many authors. Obviously Tolkien is Gollum's first and primary voice – we've taken Gollum from the page and then made certain choices that inform his character in the writing of the screenplay. Then Andy Serkis, the actor who played the role, gave him life, and though Andy doesn't physically appear on screen he had a huge part in the authorship of Gollum. Andy's performance was the template for every animator who worked on shots in the movie. But i[t] doesn't stop there, because the animators have invested in the creation of this character. (Watson 2002: 44)

A combination of structural problems in adaptation with the collaborative process of scriptwriting emerged in the editing of *Fellowship*:

'Again, no screenwriter in his right mind would send the heroes into this timeless, quiet place at the end of the second act', [Jackson] said. 'But there was no way we could leave it out, so we just did the best we could'.

A key scene, between elf-queen Galadriel and Frodo, takes place in Lothlórien, added Walsh, although it too has been modified, and then the part in which Galadriel refuses to take the ring was excised in the editing room. 'I almost cried when we cut that', she said. A month later, however, that cut had been restored. (MacNamara 2001–2)

**Figure 25** Gollum reaching for ring, Wellington Airport, 2004.

The writers had a privileged access to post-production:

> On first cut, we would look at the movie and go, 'Oh my god, how do
> we fix this?' We were lucky enough to have a pickup shoot scheduled to
> do this. We brought the actors back and shot additional material because
> we just weren't able to adapt the three books into three scripts on the
> run . . . Philippa and I had ongoing roles in postproduction, and that has
> enabled us to be involved with ADR – the voice recording of the actors
> – and the edit. During this process, you become familiar with the story
> to the point where you understand by watching the scenes over and over
> again what's wrong with them . . . We were doing a huge amount of fixing
> at the ADR stage. (Feld 2004: 13)

Of particular concern was the relative lack of female characters of
major significance in the novels. As Boyens explained on the official movie
website,

> [Tolkien] wasn't writing about female characters. He was writing an epic
> saga . . . When he did come to a female character, such as Galadriel, I think
> he wrote them brilliantly. So we had fantastic source material for female
> characters. And with Arwen, we did as well because we had the appendix
> to draw on . . . it's given us a chance to write an extraordinary love story
> because it's a love story that's very, it's very tragic, very sad and has a
> lot of things about it that you don't normally explore. It has the great
> epic quality, but it has a lot of bitter sweetness to it . . . Then we have
> stunningly great characters like Eowyn. I think she's a fantastic charac-
> ter, played brilliantly by Miranda Otto. She's the one that I went for when
> I was a girl, when I read that book . . . To fall in love with someone who
> doesn't love you is a great source of material for us to write from and
> we have. The other thing is we have a lot of differences between our female
> characters. They are very, very different to each other, which is wonder-
> ful as well. And the female energy in the film is very strong. (lordofthe-
> rings.net: 2001)

Jackson agrees that the epic saga has little room for psychological
depth, and like Boyens singles out Eowyn and Miranda Otto's performance, adding:

> Arwen likewise, and Galadriel – they both fulfill their very important roles,
> I mean Galadriel was a very powerful character. She has immense
> strength, she bridges both good and . . . evil, or perilous, is what Tolkien
> describes her . . . she has a very strong presence. Arwen represents a
> very important value of Tolkien's world, which is love, and immortality
> versus death, and she really has that incredible decision to have to make,
> as to whether she should give up her immortality for the love of a
> mortal man, and these are very powerful story elements – and so I think
> that there certainly aren't very many female characters, but I think that

**Figure 26** Arwen in action.

the ones that are in the movies certainly are very vivid. (theonering.net 2000)

Script analysis is not only about process but about the structuring of narrative. Even professional journals rarely indicate the structures visible to script editors, but occasionally they become clear. Here is an example from an interview with Jackson:

> We had the event story, which we grappled with, and the ongoing process of whose story we were following at any one time, and the emotional throughline of the story, of characters, and of how they were woven together and connected to the whole . . . The old storytelling rules hold true: embed exposition in character as much as possible, find the right place to reveal it, and then use pace. (Feld 2004: 14, 15)

In the same interview, Jackson emphasises the frequently observed hobbit-centrism of the script:

> Your central spine is obviously the story of a hobbit who comes into possession of this dangerous ring, which he ultimately learns has to be destroyed, and he has to go on this journey to destroy it. If that's the spine of *The Lord of the Rings*, then we were fairly ruthless right at the beginning with any characters or events that didn't, either directly or indirectly, serve that spine. (Feld 2004: 15)

The character arcs and story arcs of each of the three films, the three-act structure of each, and finally the overall shapes of character, story, and narration in the whole trilogy are crucial to an understanding of the films' organisation. Equally, however, analysis should be informed by what the scriptwriters care to reveal about the themes that they address. A sample of such thematic statements from a variety of interviews indicates that, for the writers, a variety of major themes coexisted during the production process, including death, choices, good versus evil, innocence and bravery, freedom, and friendship.

*Return*'s press kit includes a headline – LOYALTY, DESTINY AND HOPE: THE HEART OF *THE RETURN OF THE KING* (New Line 2003; in the contents listing, this heading appears as *Destiny, Heroism and Hope*) – that contrasts with a statement Tolkien made to a television interviewer: 'Human stories are practically all about one thing, aren't they? Death, inevitably death. All men must die, and for every man his death is an accident, an unjustifiable violation. You may agree with these words or not, but they are the key spring of *The Lord of the Rings*' (Fuller 2002: 20). Boyens recalled this anecdote in 2002, saying that death

> is not something you want to pitch to a studio! But on certain levels, I certainly think of death – in terms of life, and how people live their lives. At the end of the first film, when Frodo says, 'I wish none of this had ever happened', Gandalf's reply is, 'So do all who live to see such times, but that is not for them to decide. All they have to do is decide what to do with the time that is given to them'. I think that is definitely one of the themes – the choices that you make, and how they reverberate. Very personal choices can reverberate on a huge scale. It's about being true to yourself, and to others. (Ryfle 2002: 42)

In Jackson's opinion,

> the books are universal in the sense that they are about good versus evil, about heroism, about innocent people who have to display courage and be brave in a way that they never thought they could. They talk about great friendship, about friendship under adverse conditions, friendship without strings attached. (Bauer 2002: 8)

In Boyens's opinion, Tolkien's fantasy

> asks some interesting questions of a modern day audience; one of which – for me – is the journey that Frodo takes to undo a huge evil. And could we do that in this modern day. Could we undo . . . could we knowingly unmake something that we know should never have come into being? It's a wonderful question to ask, and it's not just a straight allegory of the atomic bomb, for example. It encompasses a whole lot of broader issues I think . . . [Tolkien's] not somebody who is looking back saying, 'We must

destroy this and go back to a way of life'. He's fully aware that the age
has passed. But I think he asks the question and I hope these films ask
the question. The ring represents another kind of evil, and it's asking, to
me, could we do what Frodo does? (lordoftherings.net: 2001)

Jackson noted a sub-theme: 'The ring is a metaphor for the machine,
for the way that a piece of metal controls and dictates what you do. A
lot of *Lord of the Rings* is about protecting your freedom and the fight
against enslavement. [Tolkien] was passionate about all this stuff, so
we felt we should honour it' (Feld 2004: 14). Yet, according to Sir Ian
McKellen, 'Peter Jackson doesn't go for sub-text' (*Empire* 2005: 83).
As for Walsh, she has said that 'I've never really liked fantasy films'
(Feld 2004: 15).

## Note

1 Known as Tehanu on Theonering.net, which she co-founded, Erica Challis
  was a major influence on net fan coverage of the films, especially after being
  served a writ for trespass on the films' sets while photographing for the website. Recognising her commitment and talent, the producers were persuaded
  to make the most of their fans, rather than lock them out. She is also second French horn in the Auckland Philharmonia.
     Theonering.net was founded in May 1999 (though the earliest New
  Archives date from 10 April of that year) by Michael Regina (Xoanon) and
  Challis, and webmasters Christopher Pirrotta (Calisuri) and William R.
  Thomas (Corvar). A central site for fan discussion and planned leaks from
  the producers, Theonering.net remains active, as a Tolkien and Jackson fan
  site and especially in the realm of *LOTR* games.

# 18

# There and back again: *The Lord of the Rings*, contemporary religiosity, and cinema

*Ann Hardy*

Among the many ways in which this book frames *LOTR*, J. R. R. Tolkien would have endorsed a study of its religious character. For Tolkien, a lifelong Catholic, the 'Blessed Sacrament' was 'the one great thing to love on earth', and explanations of the saga in religious terms feature in his correspondence in the years around its publication.

## A religious text

'*The Lord of the Rings* is of course a fundamentally religious and Catholic work', Tolkien asserted in December 1953, 'unconsciously so first but consciously in the revision'. In a 1955 discussion with his publishers about a review, he noted that 'the only criticism that annoyed me was one that "it contained no religion" [whereas] it is a monotheistic world of natural theology'. Other letters elaborate on the parameters of this natural theology in which Middle-earth was created by the supreme God, Iluvatar or Eru, and its various peoples assisted both by a group of demi-gods called the Valar and by angelic beings known as the Maiar. Gandalf is a member of the Maiar as are Sauron and Saruman but these latter two are part of a corrupt lineage originating with 'the Diabolus Morgoth', a Valar who, initially motivated by pride and envy, gradually became a tyrannical destroyer within Eru's creation. Tolkien depicts each character in *The Lord of the Rings* as being in a dynamic relationship with these negative and positive forces; they confront a series of moral choices the outcome of which either sustains their integrity or takes them on a path of spiritual degradation. Even briefly sketched out, the parallels between Tolkien's imagined universe and the Biblical creation-myth – where the proposition that God has given sentient beings free will results in their ability to 'fall' and to rebel, although not perhaps to have ultimate triumph – are evident.

Why then, if Tolkien repeatedly described *The Lord of the Rings* as religious, should a critic of the time have asserted that 'there is no religion in it'? Why did a book with a religious 'heart' get translated into film at this particular time, fifty years later? Why, once filmed, should the text's religious qualities have received so little attention in the voluminous marketing and publicity surrounding the film-event that has been *LOTR*? Why, nevertheless, has this film-event, as much commercial campaign as aesthetic experience, been received by some sections of the audience with a passionate attachment usually reserved for commitments of the spirit?

The answers to these questions involve the slippery interface between 'author(s)' or 'producer(s)', and 'audience(s)', with both sides perceived as social subjects in constantly changing fields of discourse. Those answers also illuminate changes in the understanding of the nature, purposes, and value of religiosity: a general concept that encompasses both 'religion' and the more favoured contemporary term 'spirituality'.

The most comprehensive explanation of why Tolkien but not others might regard his work as religious rests on an extreme theory of the audience's power. It imagines a divide between those who create a text (or film) and those who read or view it, such that each audience member is free to interpret the text as she desires. My female friends, for instance, who have seen a *LOTR* film and dismiss it as merely 'a boy's movie' full of fighting are exercising a freedom of interpretation that ignores any more complex intentions on the filmmakers' part.

More commonly, as Hall, Corner, and others have argued, the meanings producers 'encode' into a work *do* influence and constrain readers and viewers to some degree. Creators of texts designed to appeal to large and broad audiences draw on a resource-base of meanings considered relevant in public discourse at that particular historical moment. In turn, audience members consider and evaluate these possible sets of meanings, deciding whether to adopt, modify, or reject them, and probably doing all three at different times. According to this model, the specific techniques that encode meanings into a work may make particular sets of meanings more or less prominent for an audience and more or less likely to figure in interpretive processes.

For example, Malone (1997) suggests that in assessing a film's religious significance it is useful to examine whether the religiosity of its content is explicit or implicit; that is, whether there are obvious signs of religiosity – religious people, objects, ceremonies, statements – displayed clearly on the text's surface, or whether ideas of a religious nature appear throughout the text, implied by symbols or played out in particular patterns of human behaviour. In Tolkien's case, it appears that he actively worked to make his writing implicitly rather than explicitly religious since his books omit the more distinctive markers of the Christian story. For instance, there is no reference to Christ's birth and crucifixion (but a number of characters – Gandalf, Aragorn, Arwen, Frodo – act in a Christ-like mode of self-sacrifice). Even in the detailed world-history of *The Silmarillion*, the underlying narrative of which, Tolkien indicated, *The Lord of the Rings* is 'simply [the] continuation and completion', there is no reference to these key events. Tolkien gave straightforward reasons for these lacunae. Both epics are set in a 'pre-Christian' world in which these events have not yet happened. Moreover, 'the odd fact that there are no churches, temples or religious rites and ceremonies is simply part of the historical climate depicted'. The result, he says, is that 'God and the "angelic" gods . . . only peep through in places', but this does not make the books any less religious at heart since 'the religious element is absorbed into the story and the symbolism'.

### Religiosity downplayed

It was appropriate that Tolkien should write in this implicit, allusive manner about a pre-Christian world since the mid-twentieth-century environment in which he published witnessed a rising tide of anti-religious sentiment and secularisation that seemed likely to deposit Europe into a post-Christian era. As Murdoch (1997), drawing on Weber, has argued, the Western world, insisting on the progressive qualities of secular reason, appeared increasingly after the Second World War to be disenchanted or, in Bauman's term, 'de-spiritualized'. Explicit presentations of religious faith were not called for in these circumstances.

New Zealand's public culture in the second half of the twentieth century also did not favour religious frameworks of meaning. The *LOTR* films therefore developed within a secular cultural milieu where it would have seemed natural to de-emphasise further the text's implicit religious references. Although Jackson's previous films had featured elements of the otherwordly – aliens in *Bad Taste*, ghosts in *The Frighteners* – these elements had been used to add a crazy power to the destruction of life rather than as part of any serious quest for its ultimate meaning. Only in *Heavenly Creatures*, which framed the young women's obsession with each other and Mario Lanza with the trappings of religious ritual, did Jackson move beyond his customary practice of constructing genre pastiche. Even then, it is tempting to attribute *Heavenly Creatures*' depth to a combination of the real-life nature of the material and Fran Walsh's substantial input into the project.

This is not to say that none of the implicit religiosity of Tolkien's writing made it into the films, since the patterns of temptation and redemptive sacrifice played out by Gandalf, Gollum, and the others are integral to the plot. However, it does mean that a combination of industry assumptions about audience expectations and Jackson's own taste shaped decisions about what to include and emphasise in the films. The opposition of good and evil still forms the trilogy's spine; it has even been strengthened by the addition of a pre-credit sequence for *Return* showing Sméagol murdering his friend for possession of the ring and beginning his process of decay into Gollum. Like the books, the films explore whether the process of becoming evil can be halted or reversed. The answer is 'no' in the case of Sauron, Saruman, and several others, and also 'no' in Gollum's case, although his obsession with the Ring is also the means of saving Frodo from his own corruption. The answer is 'yes' in relation to Middle-earth itself when Sauron is defeated.

Nevertheless, an opposition between good and evil does not have to be interpreted in religious terms, since the production industry views this form of opposition as a generator of basic story-material, polarising groups of characters and providing an inbuilt source of conflict and hence action. It is ubiquitous often to the point of invisibility. Or, when the dynamic *is* highlighted, it can be framed in humanist, moral terms rather than implying the existence of a transcendental or godly source of cosmic goodness. For example, in the book Gollum wavers in his ill-will towards the Hobbits because of a growing love for Frodo, even reaching out to caress him. This action and the pause around it suggest that a divine spirit flickers in even the most depraved character. However, in the film this event diminishes into part of an ongoing dispute between Sam and Gollum, as much about jealousy as about the possibility of redemption.

Missing from the films is Sam's epiphany in *Return*, when he looks up at the sky, gazing beyond the misery of Middle-earth to see a white star that reminds him there is 'light and high beauty' for ever beyond the reach of the (temporary) tyranny of the Dark Shadow. Missing, too, in other scenes are several of the more Christ-like of Aragorn's attributes such as his ability to heal. Instead, the Jackson version values the heroic, action-oriented elements of Sam's and Aragorn's personalities.

The writers' and director's commentary on the extended DVD of *Towers* provides glimpses of how the process of adapting Tolkien's work inevitably involved adjusting its encoded meanings, even though the production team maintained great respect for his work. For instance, despite the numerous battles in both versions, Jackson energetically rejected charges that either Tolkien or he himself is 'pro-war'. He said

**Figure 27** Sam's gaze.

he doesn't believe 'anyone in the world is pro-war' but that some wars are justified (the Second World War in particular) because 'occasionally there are these moments in time, moments in history where you do have to say this is not acceptable – we have to fight'. This decision rests on the defence of freedom, says Jackson; 'I mean Tolkien was all about defending freedom'. While Tolkien was involved in the 'complete mess' of the First World War and it is accurate to say he thought forces exist against which one must fight, the condensation of his complex thoughts on war into the phrase, 'Tolkien was all about defending freedom' is inaccurate. In his correspondence Tolkien is more likely to emphasise duty and responsibility (to God, to family, to Middle-earth) than any glib concept of 'freedom'.

A statement from Walsh suggests a similar process of meaning-shift involving a long speech near the end of *Towers* when Sam challenges Frodo about the value of their quest.

> In the end you have to think: what was this movie about? What was it doing and what was it saying? And this is the moment where, if ever it was going to crystallize into a theme or a single thought, then we should do it. I felt it was about storytelling, about the value of stories, why we need them and what we get from them and, I think, in the end it's about our need to feel there are universal values of good. Whether or not that's

true in the real world, who can say, but certainly in terms of drama that's why people need it.

The speech expands on material included in the books, but whereas the value of storytelling – stories transmitting culture by providing models of noble behaviour – is just one of many explanatory frameworks they provide, it has explanatory primacy in the film version. It is what the film, in Walsh's opinion, 'is about'. There is a particularly relativistic, postmodern spin to the formulation of this meaning as well in that it speaks of the representation of 'universal values of good' as desirable in entertainment and drama, but as possibly less relevant to 'the real world'. Such a statement would hardly come from someone with a religious point of view since believers see the values of religious systems as applicable both to real life and to all the ways in which it is represented, including the stories told about it.

Yet, while choices made in the context of a secular culture have shaped *LOTR*, its style and its treatment of ideas are nevertheless friendly to that flavour, or tendency, of contemporary life known as 'spirituality'.

### *LOTR* and contemporary spirituality

'Spirituality' means many things. Its use in public discourse has increased over the last few decades, arguably in a counter-cyclic relationship to the fall-off of Western involvement in religion. It may refer to the intense personal experience at the heart of a religious tradition but nowadays it more typically describes informal, eclectic beliefs and practices that provide focus on life's deepest motivations for people who consider themselves non-religious. Consequently, late-modern spirituality can be understood as overlapping with a secular worldview. In King's words:

> [Spirituality] suggests a non-reductionist understanding of human life. It is more firmly associated than religion with creativity and imagination, with change and with relationship. It is less associated in the popular mind with hierarchies of race, gender and culture. It indicates an engagement with, or valuing of human experience, and expression through art and music, through a response to nature and to ethical ideals as well as through the great religious traditions. It can embrace secular therapies and cosmologies as well as concerns with the environment. (1996: 345)

*LOTR* is not everybody's idea of a text redolent with spirituality. While it offers little to those who are interested in what Tipton (1982) calls 'utilitarian individualism' – a form of spirituality that urges one to marshal one's inner resources in order to prosper – it does offer a

nostalgic and 'expressive' form of spirituality that is stimulated by reinventing and imagining (historic or fictional) premodern cultures. In their
ideal form these cultures are envisaged as societies of harmony among
nature, humankind, and the divine. They are 're-enchanted' worlds where
goddesses (such as Galadriel) still walk the earth and where powerful
beings use magic to work with animals and the forces of nature. The
appeal of this type of spirituality, which counterbalances the harshness
of the everyday world, appears in popular literature on goddess-worship,
Celtic mythology, or the culture of shamanism, and probably contributes
to the international popularity of a film like *Whale Rider*, which brings
many of these characteristics into a modern setting.

According to Woodhead and Heelas (2000), those interested in expressive spirituality also value sociability, warmth, and understanding –
qualities amply demonstrated in the loyal fellowship of humans, Elves,
Dwarves, and Hobbits, and played out most intensely in Sam and Frodo's
relationship. There is a warm, expressive quality to the society depicted
as the most idyllic in Middle-earth – that of the Hobbits, who extract
pleasure from life in the Shire without exploiting the land or each other.
Bassham (2003) describes them, in a list that echoes the advice found
in popular self-help texts, as having found the 'six keys to happiness',
the first two of which are 'Delight in simple things' and 'Make light of
your troubles'.

It is a small step from this world-cherishing Hobbit ethos to the spiritual theme within *LOTR* that the filmmakers most readily identified:
the desirability of good environmental stewardship. Whereas other philosophical aspects of the books have been pared back or condensed, the
Ents and their defence of the forest receive a large amount of screen
time, while the scenes set in Lothlorien also evince a relationship of respect
and mutual dependence between the elves and the trees in and among
which they live. By contrast, the environment's destruction is one of
the strongest signifiers of the presence of evil in the films, from the time
that Saruman orders the trees to be torn down to fuel his furnaces. This
environmental destruction is usually linked to the use of machine-
technology whereas the more spiritually balanced Elf and Hobbit societies use artisanal methods to produce craft-objects of domestic utility
and delicate beauty, and where necessary, for the Elves at least, effect-
ive weapons of war.

In his comments on the Treebeard storyline, Jackson said he felt this
was the part of the project where he felt Tolkien's own voice speaking
most strongly – that Tolkien was obsessed, in a way of which Jackson
approved, with the defence of nature. Of course Tolkien demonstrates
his love of, and fear for, wild nature in his writing, but this is one instance

where the development of public discourse – the burgeoning late twentieth-century discourse of the environmental or 'green' movement – has encouraged a particular aspect of Tolkien's work to be given prominence.

## Cinema, communities, and religiosity

This chapter has been exploring how various kinds of meanings relating to religion and spirituality can be nudged towards, or away from, the viewer's attention, depending on the preferences and actions at a particular point in time of those who create the film-text. It is also possible, however, to look at a film not primarily in terms of what kinds of meanings it might offer, but instead in terms of what audiences, reacting to the film text, can do with the film-viewing experience. Hoover and Venturelli construct a persuasive argument by re-reading some of the supposed theorists of secularisation, Weber, Marx, and Durkheim: that, regardless of what they show and say, the media are 'an organic site of contemporary religious practice'. That is to say, it is in relation to the media nowadays that we have some of our strongest understandings of ourselves as members of a community bound together by shared values: a sense of community that Durkheim, for instance, feels is at the base of all religious experience. 'If the contemporary social order [is] in any sense a "sacred" one', say Hoover and Venturelli,

> then the mass media, the contemporary context within which the values, beliefs and practices of that order are expressed and celebrated become a site of contemporary religion. The media are the site of ritual celebration of the commodities which define, and are in a sense coextensive with, contemporary consciousness. (1996: 258)

This sense of ritual celebration of the things that we value is easy to see in relation to an event such as a large sports game where thousands of people gather to engage in time-honoured behaviours of appreciation (or dismay if their team is losing). It is harder to see the community-creating aspects of media products when so many of us experience them alone or in small groups. Nevertheless, many different interests appreciate and exploit this linking tendency of media products. It is the organising principle behind an anthology that uses the *LOTR* phenomenon to illustrate important issues in philosophy (Bassham and Bronson 2003). The Anglican bishop where I live hoped to achieve a renewed sense of Christian community when he published a small book on how the films could be used to develop an 'applied theology' (Moxon 2003); he also gave talks to packed halls on the trilogy's mythic and religious roots. New kinds of secular worshippers, building on the books' fan-base, have arisen among those who have contributed to *LOTR* websites, made documentaries about the films, or gone to premieres and screenings dressed as characters from Middle-earth. From my own experience, while we would never have gone together to see the more explicitly religious film *The Passion of the Christ*, for three years in a row a dozen members of three generations of our family went to see the latest *LOTR* film together – an unprecedented event and one that seemed more satisfying than Christmas itself.

Some people can draw the religious roots of Tolkien's work through into the film experience; others may find that aspects of the films resonate with their own sense of what matters in life – their own personal spirituality; and a substantial number of others do not enter into the *LOTR* conversation at all – it is irrelevant to the frameworks of knowledge and value that guide them. The viability of all of these positions, and others, indicates the complex and still-changing interactions possible among religiosity, culture, and the media in the early twenty-first century.

# 19

# Fantasising history as trauma

*Allen Meek*

The psychoanalytic theory of trauma provides a model for understanding the relation of a work of cinematic fantasy to the ways that we understand history. According to Freud, some experiences are so profoundly disturbing that they exceed the individual's ability to make sense of them. Unable to be assimilated into everyday experience, traumas elude conscious recollection and recur instead in the form of physical symptoms, repeated shocks, or compulsive behaviours. Freud's theory influenced the Frankfurt School critics Walter Benjamin and Theodor Adorno, whose analysis of culture and society understood certain experiences of modernity – including rapid urbanisation, technological warfare and, later, the Holocaust – as traumatic. These critics also saw mass media not only as failing to provide structures adequate to comprehending such experiences but also as replicating, through technological effects, the traumatic overwhelming of individual consciousness.

More recently Elsaesser has discussed how contemporary 'trauma theory' condenses and potentially advances several debates about representation and referentiality and thereby constitutes an 'important agenda for ... film and television studies' (2001: 194). Elsaesser observes that the question of trauma has directed psychoanalytic approaches to film away from the emphasis on desire and spectatorship (associated with *Screen* theory as formulated throughout the 1970s and 1980s) toward questions of memory and history. Elsaesser's own focus on historical trauma derives from his research on German film and the legacies of Nazism and the Holocaust. In the case of such modern catastrophes as technological warfare and genocide, trauma becomes part of larger problems of public commemoration and historical witnessing. Film and television play an increasingly important role in narrating and thereby mediating historical trauma. However, they also intensify the problematic (non)representability of traumatic events.

This chapter approaches Jackson's *LOTR* as a mediation, in the context of transnational modes of production and distribution, of the historical traumas registered both in Tolkien's imaginative fiction and in the public discourses of the postcolonial nation where Jackson lives and works. Distressed by the country of his childhood 'being shabbily destroyed' and surviving the mass slaughter of the First World War with 'all but one of my close friends . . . dead' (Tolkien 1968: 9–10), Tolkien invented Middle-earth, a mythic alternative to industrial modernity (Sale 2000: 27–8). Jackson's special-effects blockbuster presents a vehicle by which a globally dispersed audience can negotiate a 'memory' of trauma that is not located geographically or historically. In Aotearoa the legacies of colonisation, including the grievances of the indigenous Maori people, have been mediated through state policies of biculturalism and (to a lesser extent) by a small national film industry. Jackson's films displace this work of cultural mourning into new globalised contexts and technologically mediated forms.

## Trauma theory

Caruth writes that traumatised persons 'carry an impossible history within them, or they become themselves the symptom of a history that they cannot entirely possess' (1995: 5). Because the experience of trauma is delayed and displaced, the location of trauma as a physical event is complicated by its repetition and re-articulation as psychic event. This problem of locatedness is also endemic to various technological media that represent and reconstitute events in contexts that are always removed in space and time yet often experienced with a powerful sense of immediacy and involvement. Just as trauma is transmitted without reference to a clearly situated memory, media representations can become events in their own right, displacing access to any original context. The spectacular imagescapes of the cinema, live television transmission, and digital interactivity may all be considered in terms of this logic of displacement and simulation.

In trauma theory 'it is not the event itself – or its distortion – but its structure that is of chief interest': 'marked by deferral, unpredictability and incomplete knowledge, it is at once "real" and "spectral", "historical" and "virtual"' (Elsaesser 2001: 200). What psychoanalytic theories of trauma can help us to understand is how contemporary media cultures constitute us as subjects in historical narratives and how these narratives are complicated with respect to 'chronological time-frames and geographical co-ordinates' (Elsaesser 2001: 198). Different ways of understanding time and space are themselves the product of historical struggles, such as the appropriation of territories and the reorganisation of time in the imagined and virtual communities of the nation state and transnational capitalism. Thus in any historical situation that we might call postcolonial, identity would find its traumatic articulation in the conjunctures and disjunctures of these different spatial and temporal modes.

For Elsaesser the implication of these new complexities for the understanding of history is that 'to the degree that the culture is generating . . . new forms of media memory, the subject "invents" . . . or invokes temporal and spatial markers . . . which is to say, she/he fantasises history in the form of trauma' (2001: 198). For example, the Nazi state left the legacy not only of its own cinema and the productions of its culture industries but also visual records of the First World War and the Holocaust. Since then, in countless films and television programs Nazism has not only been documented but has also become a space of fantasy, transgression, and melodrama. In its continual replaying and reconstruction of history, media culture today forces us to confront the increasing difficulty of dissociating actual history from media representations, past and present, personal and public.

### Postcolonial trauma

Trauma theory considers how extremely violent or otherwise disturbing events both resist and compel representation. Jackson's *LOTR* presents an imaginary place – Middle-earth – that nevertheless evokes actual events and historical narratives, both ancient and modern. The representation of place, land, and territory has a particular significance in a society such as Aotearoa New Zealand, where processes of colonisation and decolonisation remain the basis of dispute and conflict. The violence of the colonial intervention can be called traumatic in the sense that it continues to have destructive effects among Maori and remains in significant ways unassimilated into the dominant pakeha understanding of national history.

Unlike so many films made in New Zealand, Jackson's films (for example, *Heavenly Creatures* or *The Frighteners*) do not explicitly focus on New Zealand's official biculturalism. Haunted by ghosts and horrors, Jackson's version of colonial Gothic has been removed from racial conflict. Virtual technologies and virtual capital enable Jackson to displace historical trauma at a new level. He provides the technological extension that Tolkien's traumatised response to modernity anticipates. Instead Jackson's *LOTR* negotiates numerous historical and cultural referents, evoking both the cosiness of Tolkien's Englishness, the mass destruction of the Second World War, 1960s pastoral fantasy, and nuclear age anxieties, as well as the technospace of contemporary cyberculture. These various audiovisual landscapes are not designed to cohere into a realist representation of history, but rather serve as signifiers by which a multiplicity of audiences can situate themselves in a narrative of sublime terror and redemptive community. In a country where local production has always struggled for visibility (even more so in the case of Maori film and television), the *LOTR* films are an unprecedented event, a giant step into the international mediascape. The New Zealand media have celebrated Jackson as a new kind of cultural hero, someone who has adapted the DIY (do it yourself) frontier ethic to conquer the virtual peaks of the global entertainment industry. Thus Jackson apparently vindicates national identity while successfully integrating locally based production with globalised forms of investment and distribution. *LOTR* is also New Zealand's most economically successful vehicle yet for plugging into global media's technologisation of historical trauma.

The massive production of ghouls and demons, the crowds of undead that have given Jackson's *LOTR* cult status (national and global), would appear to have banished the spectres of colonial violence. Yet one vehicle by which these ghosts can be seen to stage a kind of traumatic return is in the figure of the Orc warrior Lurtz, the product of ten hours of prosthetic construction on the body of the (Maori) actor Lawrence Makoare. Tolkien's book pays only the briefest notice to what will become the extensive sequence featuring Lurtz and his band of Uruk-hai in pursuit of the Fellowship of the Ring in the filmic version. As previously noted, the *LOTR* Exhibition features a video display of Makoare's transformation into the character of Lurtz. While Te Papa, the country's national museum, has faced public controversy and debate for its representations of colonial history (Brown 2002), the Exhibition (along with the Wellington premiere of *Return*) appears to have attracted relatively uncritical celebration. All of this suggests that one contemporary solution to the unmourned traumas of colonialism is the media fetishisation of the Indigenous body. The prosthetic body that Makoare so spectacularly exhibits is the armour of both the media-friendly techno-subject and the increasingly globalised postcolonial subject.

## Special effects

Trauma provokes a crisis of historical representation: an event so terrible that memory fails to recover it except as delayed effects. As the invention and consumption of media technologies accelerate and intensify, they appear to parry with ever greater mastery each return of traumatic memory, leaving that memory's shocking force further displaced and diffused in the mediascape. According to such a logic, special effects play a significant role in the mediation of trauma. Cubitt argues that the goal of the special effect is to transcend narrative and thereby present a contemporary manifestation of the sublime (1999: 127). When cinematic simulations of danger, catastrophe, loss, and death are more intense and memorable than the stories in which they are embedded, they are also likely to be dissociated from historical frames of meaning. According to psychoanalytic theory, only the ongoing negotiation of trauma by conscious practices of recollection can begin to confront its delayed effects. In place of this working through, special effects simulate the traumatic overwhelming of consciousness and thereby reinscribe trauma into an aesthetic of visual spectacle and an economy of pleasurable consumption.

In his critique of Wagner's Ring Cycle, Adorno argued that, while Wagner's compositions were musically advanced, they nevertheless revealed traces of the commodification of culture made possible by mass production (Huyssen 1983: 30). According to Adorno, by seeking to overwhelm his audience with spectacular musical and dramatic effects (the sublime), Wagner positioned his listeners as reified objects of calculation; mass-culture industries would later approach their customers similarly (Huyssen 1983: 31). Arguing along the same lines, Giddings notes that the overall accessibility of the *LOTR* narrative reveals its commodified structure and thus belies Tolkien's pretensions to great and timeless literature. Tolkien's success thus rests on his professional mastery of mass communication (Giddings 1983: 11).

Although Tolkien resisted selling his epic to Hollywood, he shared the Hollywoodian ambition of producing mythic heroes and sublime spectacles in an era of technological modernity. Alongside the elaborate invention of Middle-earth's various histories, mythologies, and languages, Tolkien presented a strangely hollow account of psychological motivation, which may be related to what Benjamin described as the inability of those who returned from the battlefields of the First World War to communicate their experience (1968: 84). Benjamin related this to a general decline in traditions of storytelling and the rise of the information media. Yet many people regard Tolkien, who survived trench warfare, as the greatest of modern storytellers. He exchanges traumatic modernity for a mythic heroism, something that Tolkien's books and Jackson's filmic adaptation share with other successful forms of mass entertainment. Like other contemporary blockbusters including *Titanic*, *The Matrix*, and the *Harry Potter* films, Jackson's *LOTR* films present heroes whose fate depends on sublime forces that threaten to submerge human agency ('the world of men'). Under Sauron's eye, Frodo's destiny as Ringbearer and Sam's indomitable good nature sentimentalise the weakening of individual autonomy in the modern world of advanced technology and market capitalism. What Tolkien's large scholarly book and Jackson's spectacular movies have in common is the resituating of certain traumas of modernity – colonisation, industrialisation, and technological warfare – in a mythic drama of sublime dimensions. The aesthetic of the techno-sublime allows the audience to negotiate historical trauma by means of commodity forms.

### Gollum

These issues associated with special effects and subjective experience are poignantly expressed in both the figure of Gollum and Serkis's performance. Gollum is the most explicitly traumatised character in Tolkien's text. He has been cast out, tortured, and deprived of his 'precious'. This posed numerous challenges for Serkis, as he stresses in his book *Gollum: How We Made Movie Magic* (2003). Serkis also worried about the CGI effects that would digitally enhance his acting, thereby giving his performance a further traumatic turn. These different dimensions of Gollum the character, the actor's performance, and the digital animation need to be read against the horizon of the global system within which they are articulated, or what Miller *et al.* have called the New International Division of Cultural Labour (Miller 2001: 44–82).

The name Gollum resonates with the Jewish legend of the Golem (a clay statue magically infused with life), and Gollum's origins and his original crime (evoking the story of Cain's murder of Abel) link him with a sense of primal guilt and Old Testament morality (in contrast with Bilbo's Christ-like carrying of the ring). As the one who possessed the ring before Bilbo and Frodo, Gollum is marked by its return as trauma – *it* possesses *him*. The image of Gollum in Jackson's film could also be seen as having Holocaust resonances (Serkis 2003: 11, 21). In a story packed with hoards of sinister and comic monsters, Gollum's otherness is the most difficult to dissociate from the preferred space of identification (he was once a Hobbit-like creature). Repellant and sympathetic by turns, he is the social outcast who becomes a sacrificial victim in the symbolic resolution of the narrative. There is much in all of this to recall the Nazi construction of the Jew as a figure of a modernity who must be purged for the rest to return to a mythic pastoral and Aryan idyll. Once the corrupt outsider is destroyed, the Hobbits can return to their *Heimat*.

Gollum became the site of an intensive use of CGI, and a major attraction in the promotion of *Towers*. CGI poses specific problems of integrating naturalistic, or even expressionistic, acting with digital animation within the (dominant) codes of narrative realism. And while as early as Disney's *Snow White* an actress was filmed for later modeling by animators (Cubitt 2002: 23), Jackson and his technicians constantly stressed their desire in their cinematic portrayal of Gollum to integrate CGI with the actor's psychological interpretation of character (Serkis: 8, 34, 37, 49, 86, 94). Allen has noted that CGI shots are rarely run together in a sequence as their artificiality must be framed and 'reconfirmed by the real' (2002: 115). CGI, then, always threatens to shatter the expectations of realism that persist despite the prominence of special effects. In the case of Serkis and Gollum, the attempt to integrate psychological portrayal with computer graphics suggests one way that the film fantasises history as trauma. That is, the hallucinatory edge of the special effect is presented as grounded by the physical performance of the actor.

Yet Benjamin's analysis (1968: 228–31) of the alienation of the actor's performance through the decontextualising, fragmenting, and commodifying processes of filming, editing, and exhibition was never so insistently supported as in Serkis's account of playing Gollum. Not only was Serkis, like all film actors, removed from direct engagement with an audience, he was shot acting the part on his own to capture Gollum's movements, then the scene was re-shot on set or location (with motion-controlled camera) but without him, as if to remove even the final vestiges of performative presence. It has long been standard Hollywood practice to use English character actors such as Serkis, along with European and Antipodean performers, not to mention technical labour of all kinds. Now Global Hollywood extends this strategy to 'attract or otherwise exploit talent developed by national cinemas to compete with it' (Miller *et al.* 2001: 54). Global Hollywood has assumed new levels of 'control over cultural labour markets, international co-production, intellectual property, marketing, distribution and exhibition' (Miller *et al.* 2001: 18). Thus Serkis's book can be read as an attempt to safeguard the actor's commodified labour in the face of advanced CGI (itself produced by a relatively invisible team of animators) that potentially erases his performance from public exhibition. The more radical development, as Miller *et al.* suggest, is that 'the coming generation of screen workers are synthespians or vactors – virtual actors' (2001: 79) – a possibility that Serkis's MTV award for 'best virtual performance' supports (Serkis: 115).

Behind the cinematic creation of Gollum, then, one can discern a new technological mode of representation allowing a more intensive alienation of labour under the regimes of multinational corporate power called Global Hollywood. Providing a business-friendly environment, small nations such as New Zealand offer up their skills base at rates that must undercut production costs in Los Angeles. Thus Miller *et al.* propose that 'the military domination of empire suffered by First Peoples is now experienced – in milder form – as corporate domination by former colonisers and colonised alike' (2001: 19). But such a gloss on global history seriously underplays the violences of colonisation that continue both as everyday realities throughout the world and as spectral images in today's mass entertainment. Not only labour but the representation of history is being transformed under this new regime of capital. Indeed the globalisation of Hollywood increasingly demands that postcolonial nations displace local histories with big international productions, leaving it up to the blockbuster (as *ghost*buster) to mediate the delayed effects of trauma with the special effects of the cinema.

# 20

# The persistence of cacogenics in nationalist mythology: the case of *The Lord of the Rings*

## Roy Parkhurst

### Cacogenesis of the nation state

Whether in fictional or real wars, conflicts are often about difference and identity, particularly ethnic or cultural identity. The importance of identity and, by extension, the concept of a nation state reflects a discourse of difference, often racial and ideological in character. Our popular culture, both historical and contemporary, repeats the discourse of difference explicitly or implicitly, sometimes allegorically, in its narrative structures. A structural analysis can usefully highlight these formations, and place them in a theory of discourse that aids our understanding of certain narrative features of the popular culture around us. The recent film adaptations of Tolkien's *The Lord of the Rings* illustrate a historical continuity of particular discourses that have been dismissed as either out of date or irrelevant. By extension, a structural discursive analysis provides insights into the interaction between larger historical discourses and the specific cases of individual films and the contexts in which they are produced and received. In following the discursive thread of identity and difference as it has been articulated through ideologies of race and breeding, a strong relation to the mythic formation of nation-states and similar identity programmes can be better understood.

A particularly strong pair of binary discourses that can help illuminate larger identity questions might be 'eugenics' and 'cacogenics'. Eugenesis, or good breeding, was an actively discussed subject throughout much of J. R. R. Tolkien's life; its counterpart, cacogenesis, or bad breeding, is rarely mentioned. The desire for eugenesis is often as much about a fear of the weak, the disabled, or simply the different, as it is about producing healthy citizens. While the concept of eugenics fell into ill repute after the Second World War, cacogenics, or the study of evil, damaged, or otherwise less than perfect offspring, is still likely to be found in association with stories of mad scientists, and it still serves a powerful function as a marker of difference.

Technologies of war are easily linked to modern industrial means and times, and since then they have formed part of the narratives of popular imagination, including fantasy as well as social realist fictions. While we have manufactured mass death since the early twentieth century, the identification of the mutagenic side-effects of radiation associated with nuclear weapons has raised larger questions about technology and the life-world. Yet, we have continued to engineer weapons that impact the life-world directly, from neutron bombs to genetically engineered killer microbes.

When, in *Fellowship*, the first Uruk-hai bursts from its mockery of an amniotic sack in the middle of Saruman's wastes, we are confronted with the image of a terrifying organism that has been genetically modified to function as the first new super-soldier of the War of the Ring in the Dark Lord's army of destruction. Tolkien is clear that these foul beings are not created, but bred: 'Treebeard does not say that the Dark Lord "created" Trolls and Orcs. He says he "made" them in *counterfeit* of certain creatures pre-existing' (Carpenter and Tolkien 1981: 190). The Orcs are 'creatures' who have been 'horribly corrupted'. The appearance of cacogenesis in Jackson's adaptation of Tolkien's trilogy deserves analysis.

While a 'racist' reading of the original *The Lord of the Rings* is possible, Tolkien's letters seem to undermine any such intentions, thus ameliorating any parallels drawn between the National Socialist adoption of Wagner and his *Ring* as the perfect nationalist myth of Aryan-Teutonism, on the one hand, and, on the other, of Tolkien's *The Lord of the Rings* as an attempt to forge an English nationalist myth. As Tolkien liked to point out when his epic was compared to the *Nibelungen*, 'Both rings were round, and there the resemblance ends' (Carpenter and Tolkien 1981: 306). However, a deeper structural similarity of narrative logic should be explored: the importance of the discourse of cacogenics, miscegenation, and racial 'degeneration' as a thematic feature that serves the structuralist function of nation-building and identity.

By contrast to Tolkien, Wagner's own racism is more explicit. His later thinking is directly influenced by a reading of the so-called 'father of racist ideology', Joseph Arthur, comte de Gobineau. In particular, Wagner wrote 'Hero-dom and Christendom' (1881) in response to de Gobineau's *Essay on the Inequality of the Human Races* (1853–55). Wagner's synthesis of Darwinism, racial philosophy, and the Romantic search for primitive origins and expression in 'myth, saga, and legend' (Biddiss 1970: 19) has its echoes in philological research that Tolkien undertook, particularly involving the Icelandic sagas and the Finnish *Kalevala*. A discursive continuity in the sources of late nineteenth-century nationalism makes it no surprise that some traces surface in subsequent work.

In the twilight of post-Romantic arts and letters, the pessimistic theme of 'decline' became prominent. Again, Tolkien seems to have inherited this nostalgia for the loss of a golden age. Late nineteenth-century thought produced various responses to this theme (e.g., Nietzsche, Spengler's *Decline of the West*, and Nordau's *Degeneration*; see Morton 1984). The dialectic between 'degeneration' and 'eugenics' that occurred in the first half of the twentieth century, and the associated theme of 'regeneration', can be observed in places as diverse as Nazi ideology and Tolkien's epic.

This discourse should not be confused with a more explicit racism. While critical responses to the films have suggested that *The Lord of the Rings* abounds with such racist ideas (Yatt 2002; Ibata 2003) or see race, class, and the support of 'Empire' (Dilday 2003) as troublesome features of Tolkien's world in general and hence of the film adaptations, this is really just another form of allegorical reading which Tolkien himself resisted adamantly. Even in the contemporary context of Tolkien's work, when Rütten and Loening of Potsdam were negotiating the publication of the German translation of *The Hobbit* in the late 1930s and wrote a letter of enquiry to Tolkien's English publisher, Allen and Unwin, asking about whether or not Tolkien was of 'Aryan' origin, Tolkien took strong offence at the unstated suggestion by responding: 'I do not regard the (probable) absence of all Jewish blood as necessarily honourable; and I have many Jewish friends, and should regret giving any colour to the notion that I subscribe to the wholly pernicious and unscientific race-doctrine' (Carpenter and Tolkien 1981: 37). On the other hand, it is also quite clear that the concept of 'races' has a prominent role to play among the denizens of Middle-earth, and some of these may have their precedents in the modern world. In another letter, Tolkien points out that 'I do think of the "Dwarves" like Jews: at once native and alien in their habitations, speaking the languages of the country, but with an accent due to their own private tongue' (Carpenter and Tolkien 1981: 229). Perhaps Gimli is related to Alberich after all. In this regard, it is worth reflecting on how the discourses of race and particularly genealogy and miscegenation play a narrative function at various points in the epic.

It is clear, for example, that the Elves play a poignant role in representing the waning of a golden age. The Age of Man has come to supersede them, but Men are easily corrupted and have as many weaknesses as strengths. The portrayal of the ineffectual, somewhat decadent 'stewardship' of Gondor and the regeneration of social order through the rightful king's ascendance highlight the ambiguous significance of genealogy. Aragorn himself, being directly descended from the deeply flawed Isildur who could not resist the One Ring's evil power, is unsure whether he has the nobility to take this charge. Throughout this portion of his life, he has hidden under the pseudonym Strider and only slowly comes to assume his rightful place in the order of things. The guarantee of blood hints at a nostalgia for a lost aristocracy, which, in common with class difference, is after all a matter of blood.

The Orcs' genealogy emphasises their cacogenic origins, an aspect explicitly retained in the film adaptations. Tolkien's explanation of the origin of goblin men, or Orcs as they come to be known in the epic, is that they were perhaps once men or Elves themselves but have been 'corrupted' by dark forces. The fall of the golden age and Middle-earth's regeneration in Tolkien is premised on the battle against evil. Tolkien seemed to perceive the modern world as this land Morgoth wrought. He thought that these forces of industrialisation and corruption could be overcome, but at a cost. As he explains to his son in a letter in 1944, 'The penalty is, as you will know, to breed new Saurons, and slowly turn Men and Elves into Orcs' (Carpenter and Tolkien 1981: 78). Later that year, Tolkien again writes to Christopher:

> There are no genuine Uruks, that is folk made by the intention of their maker; and not many who are so corrupted as to be irredeemable (though I fear it must be admitted that there are human creatures that seem irredeemable short of a special miracle, and that there are probably abnormally many of such creatures in Deutschland and Nippon – but certainly these unhappy countries have no monopoly: I have met them, or thought so, in England's green and pleasant land). (Carpenter and Tolkien 1981: 90)

The suggestion that nations can be largely corrupt is an interesting feature of the parallels Tolkien makes between contemporary events and his epic. In the reverse of Teutonic myth-making and its sense of nationhood, Tolkien is out to establish a proper order in 'England's green and pleasant land', a theme that is mirrored in the industrialisation of war of the Dark Power and particularly Saruman's stripping the land of its greenery to burn for the forges of war. Tolkien admits as much at one point in the mid-1950s when he writes: 'Having set myself a task, the arrogance of which I fully recognized and trembled at: being precisely to restore to the English an epic tradition and present them with a mythology of their own: it is a wonderful thing to be told that

I have succeeded, at least with those who have still the undarkened heart
and mind' (Carpenter and Tolkien 1981: 230–1). In an example of classical structuralist binarism, the mythological foundation of the 'beautiful state' is made in contrast to the corrupt and cacogenic state that
it is not (Germany, for example), itself also founded on a structurally
similar nationalist myth.

### Teratology and myth

In the Western tradition, teratology, the study of monsters, makes its
strongest appearance in the literature of mythology and fantasy to which
*LOTR* belongs. While this arcane science seems to have been superseded by more enlightened forms of biology, the term has made a rebound
in recent years in the field of genetics (see Daston and Park 1998). This
is no surprise because as far back as the ancient Greeks teratology was
almost always a matter of genetics, and of miscegenation in particular.
The vast majority of mythic monsters that appear in Greek mythology
are chimerical hybrids of species, and the most singular monsters, such
as the Minotaur, result directly from an 'unnatural coupling' of human
and beast.

Tolkien's great contribution to the literature of monsters is the invention of the Orc. This creature plays a central role in the battle for Middle-
earth. Tolkien explains its origins in a letter from 1954:

> Orcs (the word is as far as I am concerned actually derived from Old English
> *orc* 'demon', but only because of its phonetic suitability) are nowhere clearly
> stated to be of any particular origin. But since they are servants of the
> Dark Power, and later of Sauron, neither of whom could, or would, pro-
> duce living things, they must be 'corruptions'. (Carpenter and Tolkien 1981:
> 177–8)

These 'corruptions' indicate a possible link to the degeneration of the
race, brought on presumably by breeding and dark magic. Elsewhere,
Tolkien is clearer about who was corrupted: 'The Shadow that bred them
can only mock, it cannot make real new things of its own. I don't think
it gave life to the Orcs, it only ruined them and twisted them. In the
legends of the Elder Days it is suggested that the Diabolus subjugated
and corrupted some of the earliest Elves, before they had ever heard of
the "gods", let alone God' (Carpenter and Tolkien 1981: 191).

The recurring theme of physical and spiritual corruption and its
monstrous results sits well within the teratological tradition. The film
adaptations retain these points of Orc genealogy, although they are
unnecessary. Any process of adaptation retains some things and discards

others, but this particular retention also suggests some form of symptomatology. In fact, this ongoing discourse of teratology, particularly when it is founded on a genetic discourse, has become the lingua franca of contemporary fantasy and horror cinema. Many of the mythic functions of contemporary fantasy are justified through deference to genetics, especially genetic engineering. Many vampire films have their storylines driven by genetic subplots, whether it is the intermingling of vampire and lycanthrope blood in *Underworld* or the genetic engineering of a new breed of vampires in *Blade 2* or the more thriller-based storyline of the BBC series *Ultraviolet*. Even all the standby superheroes of comicdom coming to big screen are full of genetic implications, from the *X-Men*'s mutants to the genetically engineered Bruce Banner of *Hulk* to the mutant arachnoid blood of *Spider-Man*. Genetics has become the master discourse of a science to explain both the magical and monstrous, and reflects a deep-seated fear and fascination with genetic modification, cloning, and engineering in the popular imagination.

As morality tales of the dangers of intervening in the natural order, like Tolkien's *The Lord of the Rings* and Jackson's *LOTR*, these populist fantasies bring attention to the impact of industrialisation and technologisation of the life world. The new eco-disaster is a genetic one and these tales form a mythic continuity of sentiments and concerns.

## The wasting of paradise

The discourse of eugenics and cacogenics may seem incidental in the recent *LOTR* (a residue of its presence in Tolkien's original), but its New Zealand context may be influential. New Zealand has an ongoing debate about genetically modified organisms, and much discussion about New Zealand as the locale for the films is caught up in this discussion. Ian McKellen's comments on New Zealand's supposedly uncorrupted environment ('New Zealand is Middle-earth'), for example, tie in with the marketed image of the country as 'clean and green'. Evidence of this discourse occurs in such disparate sources as a Radio New Zealand *Ideas* show (aired 15 August 2004) entitled 'Eugenics in Paradise', which traces the strong presence of eugenic discourse in New Zealand history, and Martin Doutré's book, *Ancient Celtic New Zealand*, which posits an ancient Celtic culture that preceded the arrival of Maori to the country.

What do an embarrassing, historical phase of social philosophy and a pseudo-historical, Celtic fantasy indicate about an ongoing mythic construction of New Zealand? If *The Lord of the Rings* forms a mythic foundation of the English nation state, it is no less significant, in a New

Zealand where the English colonial past is ever-present in contemporary politics, that the film adaptation retains these connections. The anxiety of the 'settler nation' permeates the ongoing formation of New Zealand identity. In a land not rightfully its own, the settler culture needs such a foundation myth even more strongly than does England. If a mythic belief in an unspoiled and uncorrupted earth contributes to national identity, then Tolkien's epic provides a suitable reinforcement of just such a myth. It is no surprise that the films are populated by fair-skinned Europeans modelled on the ancient Celts. The swarthy armies of Sauron's human alliances come clearly from the Near East as they did in Tolkien's world, and the only presence of the Pacific Islander is in the form of the Orc hordes, less worthy races to inherit the land. They are a large, dark, and fearsome lot. The 'real' New Zealander is obviously a European one (and must always have been so).

While the themes of degeneration and biological perversion have a role to serve in the screenplay, the strongest visual statement about the myth of the land comes in the form of the New Zealand landscape itself. Endless commentary on the beautiful 'green and pleasant land' that is New Zealand has saturated the popular press and imagination, as much outside New Zealand as within. Spectacular images – helicopter shots over central Otago or the verdant Waikato that is transformed into the Shire – reinforce a mythic view of an uncorrupted land. Not until the dark pall hangs over Isengard are the real consequences of environmental destruction made clear. This murky place of shadows is filled with the smoke of burnt forests, its clouds of soot a result of Saruman's forge building the machinery of war.

The Isengard sequences illustrate this stark contrast through production design. This industrial hell, worthy of a Blakean vision, turns New Zealand into a fiery cauldron of a wasteland. In Isengard the most famous shot begins on the tower where Gandalf lies destitute and then plunges down into the underworld of Orthanc where the Orcs labour on forging weapons and hatching the 'perfected' Uruk-hai. Here it is perpetual night in a shadowy and cavernous netherworld of degenerate creation. The later films reprise this netherworld in the hellish land of Mordor with its literal volcanic fire and brimstone.

The narrative dialectic of 'good and bad aesthetics' that Levin (1998) views as a structural principal in Wagner's operas forms a similar structural logic of 'good and bad genes' that is found in Tolkien and reiterated in the film adaptations of the epic in its various 'good and bad environments'. Despite the protest that the only similarity between the ring tales is their roundness, there is clearly a discursive formation that propels the narrative logic and suggests the importance of paying closer attention to various discourses that transcend specific iterations to provide a broader context for understanding their function wherever they may appear, from ancient Greek islands to the islands of Aotearoa as well as in the popular imagination of the filmgoing public. It is through mythic formations of identity and nationhood that received and sometimes problematic ideas are passed down transparently and naturally rather than making us pause to consider their unnatural genesis.

# 21

# 'This is not New Zealand': an exercise in the political economy of identity

*Stephen Turner and Misha Kavka*

The New Zealand of *LOTR* is both the magical land of Middle-earth and a tourist paradise, a composite graphic where one map slides easily over the other. New Zealand *is* Middle-earth, tourist adverts proclaim. Other films have been shot in New Zealand with either non-NZ or collaborative crews and funding, but have not been branded by their shooting location. Only *LOTR* has served to foster a national image of New Zealand for the global population.

To take this seriously is to appreciate that *LOTR* has been an exercise in *two-way* branding, where New Zealand is not only branded as Middle-earth, but the epic realisation of Middle-earth is itself branded as New Zealand. The brand sticks even more effectively because the actual landscape of New Zealand has been cinematically denuded of its people and culture, emptied to accommodate the visiting casts of Middle-earth.[1]

As the man behind the superimposition, Peter Jackson would be the first to admit, Magritte-like, that 'this is not New Zealand'. Yet what happens when Middle-earth comes in the shape of the place itself?

The connection through landscape between film and place is unusually strong, even over-determined, for a film whose backdrop could just as easily have been computer-generated. Much has been made of Jackson's remarkable achievement in taking the production of *LOTR* outside Hollywood, and of the tax breaks that persuaded the project's financiers to make the film in New Zealand. It is unlikely that the financiers cared about the two-way branding of New Zealand as Middle-earth that in effect turned New Zealand itself into an element of the films' merchandising budget. Yet, the national Tourist Board's full co-operation with this merchandising suggests that the branding of New Zealand is neither a side effect nor an intervention from the outside.

Rather than reading New Zealand as a convenient and contingent backdrop for Middle-earth, it is worth taking the location seriously, because a physical place always carries the residue of its own history. By linking landscape with the history of place we will discover an economy at work beyond that of tax breaks or the price of Jackson's genius: namely, a logic of franchise capital constitutive of the business of settlement. We therefore offer a brief sketch of a political economy of identity as an approach to NZ-based cultural production (whether or not *LOTR* is a New Zealand film, it is, importantly for tourism, NZ-based). We argue that the country has been settled and the nation of New Zealand established by a capitalist logic of deterritorialisation that seeks to separate recognisable physical features – landscape, sea, and local peoples – from history, particularly the historical relations that stretch back to pre-contact New Zealand.

The de-linking of place from its full human history, as carried out by non-Maori settlement, is not unlike the production of the trilogy itself, captured in Jackson's modest admission that the 'real country' needed to be 'nudged over ever so slightly'[2] in order to inscribe Middle-earth on to New Zealand. *LOTR*'s *trompe l'oeil* effect suggests a magical realism, or more specifically a magical historicism, that is a cinematic synonym for the political logic of settler societies.

The managed relation between film-text and the actual country is key to the settler enterprise reflected in *LOTR*. This strategically funded and carefully staged relation of screen and place exploits a deeper tension between a settler idea of place and its actual, longer history. For the enterprise of settler New Zealand to succeed it has had to remove the place from its peoples and history – to reconstruct the land, not unlike the task of Jackson as the local-gone-global filmmaker. Our analysis attempts to recover the historical traces that have been written over in the (re)branding exercise synonymous with settlement, and to ask what relationship the film bears to the physical place of its production.

### Emplacement and emptying

If there is an extradiegetic weight to the *LOTR* trilogy, resonant in moments that prompt recognition of place among New Zealand's inhabitants, franchisers, and tourists, then this has to do with Jackson's insistence on using physical bodies, actual places, and 3D models to prop up the work of fantasy. 'Real' actors, landscapes, and settings are reworked: John Rhys-Davies wears three latex moulds on his head alone to become Gimli; a farm outside of Matamata is reconstructed, replanted, and regraded so as to become Hobbiton. Everyone and everything is heavily made up, made over, and/or masked in order to achieve the right phantasmatic effect, and yet, equally, nearly every fantastical place and creature has a physical original. This is notable in a film where the director estimates that 80 per cent of it has been digitally enhanced.[3] The physical details of body and place have been scrubbed away in order to overlay the history of another time and place. The result is the emplacement of Middle-earth and the emptying of New Zealand. The physical is over-ridden by the virtual and yet remains present as palimpsest. Hence Middle-earth comes into being *as* New Zealand.

The cinematic effect is to add greater texture and realism than could be provided by digital manipulation alone. Jackson's avowed reason for using 3D bodies and extensive modelling was that Middle-earth would be made all the more real, and convincingly historical. In the extended edition DVD appendices he recalls an important early speech to his crew in which he said that *LOTR* will not be a 'fantasy movie, not Holly-wood', but 'actually history', hence the need 'to shoot in the real loca-tions, where these events happened'.[4] This un-Hollywood and, dare we say, New Zealand feel for the reality of place is what we call the mag-ical historicism of *LOTR*. The magical historicism of *Forgotten Silver*, with its 'discovery' of an invented history of place, employs a similar realism. The real place, however scrubbed and burnished, carries the residue of real history.

Rebranded as a mythical and timeless place, New Zealand's histor-ical configuration none the less remains stubbornly stuck to *LOTR*. As a settler colony, New Zealand is historically a franchise of first-world capital; in a similar fashion, Jackson is today's franchise manager. *LOTR* thus strikes both national and international chords, for its pro-ject of transplanting history is recognisable as both deterritorialising pro-cess and franchise product of settlement. Importantly, New Zealand is signalled in *LOTR* in ways other than landscape, which plays less and less of a 'character' role as the trilogy develops. Though Jackson may speak of himself as little more than Tolkien's aesthetic handmaiden, *LOTR* signals its cultural provenance through motifs or tropes recognisable from other New Zealand-based productions.

### The stereotrope

One such 'signal' moment, symbolic for New Zealanders, comes in the final battle of *Fellowship* with the appearance of the Uruk-hai, a sort of *über*-Orc race moulded by the black wizardry of Saruman out of the earth. Makoare plays Lurtz as primal, savage, and animalistic. For all that Makoare's performance appears to reprise roles in *Crooked Earth* and *What Becomes of the Broken-Hearted*, with added latex, he is not here strictly a stereotype, as there is little besides the heavy-set Makoare himself and distinctive topknot to associate this figure with anything specifically Maori. Makoare may have brought bulk and a practised snarl

**Figure 28** Lawrence Makoare as Lurtz.

to the role, but a Maori stereotype could not be sustained in New Zealand, and only with difficulty would it be readable to international audiences.

Lurtz is rather a composite figure of the barbarian; the bare thighs and biceps and simian features suggest a semi-naked, half-human brute. Following Jo Smith's work on the plasticity of the ethnic type in Hollywood film, in particular her focus on Maori men as global film-workers whose labour is used to recode an excessive or primal mas-culinity,[5] we consider the Uruk-hai figure to be a stereotrope, a filmic trope that distils and reduces a wide range of historical forms and sema-phores of barbarism. The composite works through viewers being unable to associate his features and attributes with any single race – 'barbarian' peoples – a careful avoidance of allegory, evident throughout the film and in line with Tolkien's thinking. For New Zealanders this means he is and is not Maori, since his masking distils a range of characteristics from peoples who have for others been savage or barbaric.

This Uruk-hai figure started in *LOTR*'s design workshop as an oscil-lation between an orientalised Saracen and a foetal roundling before being literally unveiled – the Arab Ninja's veil removed – and recon-structed to expose the lineaments of the more primitive savage or wild barbarian.[6] The symbolic moment for New Zealanders, that which local culture has contributed to this reconstruction and the horror it represents, is its autochthony, the fact that it emerged from, or has been moulded out of, the earth. This distinguishes it from the other inhabitants and races of Middle-earth. Even the major race of villains, the Orcs, are fallen angels of Elven lands. At the start of *Towers*, we see this mucky birthing process in action, with Orcs digging amniotic sacs of full-grown Uruk-hai out of the mud and rocks that make up Isengard's mines. And in the extended edition DVD version of *Fellowship*, footage of Makaore himself in a mucus sac makes clear his character's primitive birth from the bowels of the earth.

These Uruk-things are not just of the earth; they are in some sense earth itself, and therefore utterly without 'culture', or the virtues of the races of men (even the Orcs seem comparatively chatty and human-like). They are too inhumanly all the same, as indistinguishable as barbarians must be, though the Uruk-hai we do see up close is individualised to establish his savage credentials (so the stereotype contradictorily merges many historical peoples but must use their differences to establish savagery). The Uruk-hai is a pure barbarian, an uncultivated, unthinking, and uniform apparition, a creature from outside the city walls, or the gated community of civilisation.

This super-barbarian, we suggest, carries something of the real nature of place – a residue or residual element of the filming location that helps to make Middle-earth more real. Created on and out of Makoare's body, the Uruk-hai refracts New Zealand's own history: This snarling, dripping, stripped-down yet made-up figure is a prosthetic projection of phantasmatic history that articulates a culturally specific dread. Interestingly, in Tolkien's version, the Uruk-hai are not authochthonous creatures; their emergence from within the mines of Isengard is a grace note to the chronicle of Middle-earth that comes with its transplantation to New Zealand. Tolkien's chronicle itself, of course, is a history that never was, and yet as an imagining of history it too is the product of a particular place (an England loaded with myths that constitute its own Anglo-Saxon past). When this imagined history is brought to New Zealand, and here made real, it takes on the outlines of the physical body under the mask, in this case a particular version of the savage who lives to fight.

### Settler dread

*LOTR* is not necessarily a 'New Zealand film' simply because it has Maori in it. *LOTR* is less a New Zealand film, understood in terms of national cinema, than a film marked – even haunted – by New Zealand tropes. To be precise, the film does *not* have Maori in it; rather, it has a dread figure standing in where Maori might be. This stereotrope works negatively, signifying the dense absence of Maori in a virtualised landscape. The absence of Maori is only weakly signalled by the physiognomic correspondence between the Polynesian actor Makoare and Uruk-hai; it is signalled, more strongly, by the meta-filmic correspondence of indigeneity and autochthony. In a film where nothing is actually 'of the earth' of New Zealand – the scenery, too, when not directly computer-generated, is digitally coloured and enhanced – the earth is important because it disgorges the horror of the indigene.

New Zealand films typically raise up such a dread figure in order to discharge the psychological burden of, or debt to, history. This is the precise function of Makoare's characters in *Crooked Earth* and *What Becomes of the Broken-Hearted*; this dread 'bad' Maori, a criminal and/or separatist opposed to the 'good' Maori in each film (played in both by Temuera Morrison), is necessarily killed off. The others of history – especially that other history that exceeds non-Maori settlement – must be made dreadful to assuage settler anxieties of origin. Though arrival in Aotearoa remains an implicit memory, the prime historical anxiety for non-Maori settlers is that they did not come out of the ground, but from somewhere else. (Maori did not come out of the ground either, but settler anxiety loads them with this charge.) The 'thing' that is the dread figure emerges quite literally out of the land as its dark or dense spot, something seemingly from outside the picture-perfect landscape that then turns up inside it. That Maori may consciously wield the dread image thrust upon them by settler anxiety helps to explain the plasticity or elasticity of the stereotrope, the way the trope is manifest in new forms, yet loaded with a familiar, felt resonance. The form of the Uruk-hai could hardly look like what it does without a whole chain of related representations in New Zealand film and television; this chain of 'dread' associations itself functions as part of a wider network of associations, made global by the work of colonialism, that link the indigene with savagery and 'human' prehistory.

This chapter might suggest that for New Zealanders *LOTR* is New Zealand after all. But our point would be that the symbolic moment of the Uruk-hai is one that New Zealanders misrecognise. As a figure of misrecognition the Uruk-hai leader is not so much a displaced image of Maori (because not properly recognisable as Maori) as a figure for the misrecognition of place and history. This is why we say that the Uruk-hai is a projection of phantasmatic history, as this is an imagined or reconstructed past that strives to discharge the burden of the actual past. This fundamental and originary misrecognition is the historical basis of a political economy of identity. For the ideal condition of a viable economy in this part of the world is a place and history that can be made-over, reconstructed at will, to meet the demands of larger markets. The real place and real peoples that settlers encountered had to be misrecognised for their settlement to take place, so that the place could be made available for the investment of others' interest in it. Representations of place are strictly synonymous with this logic of settlement; thus, filmic stereotropes do not mark actual historical peoples but rather the workings of political economy.

### The settler franchise

New Zealand's settler economy historically depends on human and financial capital from elsewhere. Indeed, such an economy must bind people and place within or to international circuits of investment and opportunity as defined in the first instance by the nineteenth-century British Empire. The settlers' original idea of New Zealand as a 'Britain of the South' (Park 1999: 184–5) makes the place precisely a first-world franchise. It is a replicant or agent operating under the terms and conditions of the British Empire and the global economy it oversaw. This franchise economy describes both the settler economy during the decline of the British Empire's colonial hold and the rise of the European Union, and the current predicament of settler society, which seeks to maintain a first-world sense of self through retaining first-world alliances while finding alternative markets.

In both financial and aesthetic terms, *LOTR* repeats this original logic of investment opportunity, capital, and production. The production's success, from a local point of view, exemplifies the *modus operandi* of settlement: *LOTR* uses the place as raw material for an export initiative, so that the local place and peoples may be fully de-linked from the screen image. New Zealand history is evident in the logic of settler franchise rather than in the content of representation (as representation, New Zealand history is misrecognised). The franchise economy of which *LOTR* is an instance describes the way settlers have internalised and promulgated the original conditions of the nation's establishment, or, more accurately, of the settling of place by non-Maori.

A key component of the film's *modus operandi*, quite in keeping with the historical settler economy, is the tax break afforded *LOTR*'s financiers. The nature of the tax subsidy and the relative advantages to the national economy of bringing such productions to New Zealand have been much discussed in local popular journalism, especially as against industries not so helped by the government. At its most pessimistic, the government is accused of leaving the New Zealand public with a $225 million bill to pay for the production; at its most generous, the tax breaks are considered a risky but worthwhile investment (Campbell 2000). The wisdom of providing such incentives to non-national film production continues to be hotly debated. Still, if the New Zealand public has carried the production's risk, such as it was, then Jackson's speculation has paid off handsomely, with real though hard-to-calculate benefits to the country's economy and sense of identity (at once 'profile' and 'pride of place').

Tax breaks for film productions suggest the crucial role of representation, or symbols, in the context of today's local economy. Symbols matter more for the settler collective than the non-symbolic goods of other industries because only through representations or symbols can history be discharged. The idea that the settler economy works as a first-world franchise suggests why the argument for carrying the risk of investors' capital could support the making of *LOTR*. This is just because film in general, and *LOTR* as a successful instance of franchise capital, is best able to discharge, or de-charge, the historical debt of Maori, whose land is thus virtualised, mediatised, and made profitable for first-world capital. In so doing, the thing that is the historical place is blotted out, leaving precisely a blot, a dark spot that resonates with Maori presence but is not clearly Maori.

### Historical prosthesis

In *LOTR* the transformation of place and peoples (the 'thing' as above) that we have ascribed to the less-than-visible political logic of settlement is made visible through filmic prosthesis, that is, a lot of latex. If the identities of the peoples of Middle-earth are prosthetic, produced out of latex applications, then the political economy of settler identity seen at work in this film production is similarly prosthetic; the settler franchise (think 'better Britain' as 'settler Starbucks') is an extension of first-world or metropolitan economy, the result of making over an existing place – a local latex job, if you will. The magical historicism of *LOTR* is exemplary. Whether *LOTR* is or is not New Zealand is a somewhat redundant question, given that this place as settler territory is in the first instance a metropolitan extension. So the object of settler dread and this metropolitan mould are inseparable, but the longer history of place remains part of the mix as something to be discharged.

Jackson is not simply erasing or even colonising Maori by using New Zealand's picturesque landscape to create Middle-earth; rather the *modus operandi* of the production repeats a logic that underpins settler economy viability. The double branding of New Zealand / Middle-earth accrues returns on investment while it serves to discharge the debts of history: The place may be sold to the first world as a history-free product, offering a canvas for Middle-earth, while the first world is brought to the place to justify the evacuation of history from its earth, providing a first-world grounding for New Zealand.

The discharging of history in *LOTR* is strongly aided but fiercely contested off-screen. While tax breaks for film use of the land attract capital, consolidate settlement, and increase tourism, the long history of Maori reclaims time and place, disputing settler ownership and settler imagery. While Maori open out a different future of place, one that demands a break from the pathologies of white dread, they are more usually accorded the Halloween role of *über*-Orc, or otherwise sentimentalised as traditional peoples in spiritual rehab, viz. *Whale Rider*. The twin imperatives of the Dread Native and Ethno-Disney,[7] carrot and stick of global film investors and funding agencies, will determine New Zealand-based use, or lease, of the place and peoples. Time and place, that is, history itself, remains for settlers to tell and sell, although Maori dispute this settler licence and would send the mould back to the mines. In any case, *LOTR* is a lesson in contemporary economies of representation: how settler society works as an offshore first-world franchise.

## Notes

1 At the 2004 Oscar ceremony Ian McKellen gave as one of the main reasons for the success of the trilogy not only Jackson's talent, but the 'delights of the New Zealand countryside'.
2 See 'Digital Grading' in the Appendices to the extended edition DVD of *Fellowship*.
3 Ibid.
4 See 'Designing Middle-earth' in the Appendices to the extended edition DVD of *Fellowship*.
5 We are indebted to her seminar paper 'The Plasticity of Ethnicity' (16 October 2003).
6 See 'Design Galleries', and follow 'Designing and Building Middle-earth', 'Peoples of Middle-earth', 'Isengard', 'Isengard – the fighting Uruk-hai' in the Appendices to the extended edition DVD of *Fellowship*.
7 For an intelligent and unfavourable review along these lines from a non-New Zealand perspective see Bradshaw 2003b: 'This sentimental crowd-pleaser about a young Maori girl facing her tribal destiny is somewhere between whale music and world music, or maybe a cross between *Free Willy* and a 90-minute Benetton ad . . .' etc.

# 22

# Tourist encounters

*Ryan Reynolds, Henry Bial, and Kimon Keramidas*

## On the performative nature of *Rings* tourism

The relatively recent phenomenon of movie-location tourism presents a new wrinkle in the fabric of audience reception theory. Conventional film theory and cultural studies suggest that the viewer's experience of films such as *LOTR* is a virtual one: mentally and emotionally active but physically passive. The spectators, alone in the dark, project their desires on to the performers' images, imagine themselves into the filmic landscape, experience pity and fear at the perils of the protagonists, and swell with exultation at the heroes' triumph. And then, of course, the lights come back on and the spectators are returned to their everyday lives.

But what happens when the passive interaction is insufficient? Some people purchase talismans of the film: the poster, the keychain, the souvenir calendar. The 'Earrings of Arwen', for example (available via catalogue and online), are part fetish – on to which the owner can project some of the same fantasies and desires evoked by the film – and part totem, the display of which marks the owner publicly as a member of a particular interpretive community. Stenger has analysed Planet Hollywood as an example of a place in which moviegoers seek out the fulfilment of their film-inspired fantasies (1997: 54). He writes that 'it explodes the two-dimensional reality of cinema by deploying all the signifiers of Hollywood into a three-dimensional, inhabitable space, a hands-on experience that is at once unavailable at the movies and yet wholly dependent on its unavailability' (1997: 48). It is doubtlessly true that the very incompleteness of the filmic experience is exploited as niche market, but the success of this exploitation depends upon *how* complete the fictional world appears to be. That is, the near-completeness of Middle-earth in the films – bolstered by the unified world depicted, the ten-hour duration, the stunning digital effects, the entire Tolkien mythology legitimising it – is precisely what seduces people to complete the experience. The film's affective power is so great that, for some viewers at least, the lure of the fantasy persists, spilling beyond the boundaries of screen and theatre. For these viewers, the next logical step is to grab their passports and head for New Zealand to tour 'Middle-earth'.

Within months of the release of Fellowship, HarperCollins New Zealand published Brodie's The Lord of the Rings Location Guidebook. By the time Return premiered two years later, the Guidebook had been through six printings, suggesting that the number of tourists choosing to follow in Frodo's footsteps is significant indeed. Brodie lists thirty-two sites, referring to them by both real and virtual names, and in most cases providing latitude and longitude co-ordinates, allowing those tourists equipped with a GPS-locator (or a sextant) to orienteer their way to sites that are otherwise unmarked and indistinguishable from the surrounding landscape.

As our contribution to the April 2003 Performance Studies international conference, PSi9: Field Station, New Zealand, the authors of this chapter set out to investigate the performance of tourism that has sprung up around LOTR.[1] Armed with a copy of Brodie's Guidebook, a hand-held GPS-locator, and a broad array of maps, as well as a DVD copy of Fellowship, we found our way to the following South Island locations (actual name / virtual name): Kawarau River / The Pillars of the Kings, Arrowtown / The Ford of Bruinen, The Remarkables / Dimrill Dale, Poolburn / Rohan. We also took one of the 'Trilogy Trail' tours offered by Glenorchy Air of Queenstown, a chartered aeroplane flight that provided overviews of numerous sites, and included a landing at Dan's Paddock / Isengard and a leisurely stroll through Paradise Forest / Amon Hen.

If the films (as well as video games, DVD special releases, and other technological derivatives) offer spectators a virtual reality in which to play out their LOTR fantasies, touring the locations where the film was made offers what we might call a 'real virtuality' in which they can do

Figure 29  Merry and Pippin adventuring through New Zealand,
home of Middle-earth

the same thing.[2] *LOTR* lends itself well to this particular form of imaginative play, because the films' narrative is strongly reminiscent of the tourist experience: a fantastic departure from a bourgeois quotidian existence (the Shire), a journey across a strange and unfamiliar landscape, a tireless battle where the most perpetually daunting foe is geography. For tourists, this struggle with the landscape therefore becomes a way of inscribing themselves into the films' obstacle-presented or obstacle-surmounted economy. Furthermore, because many of the *LOTR* locations do not bear on-site markers, the tourist (not unlike Aragorn, Legolas, Frodo, *et al.*) must employ knowledge of forgotten lore, experience as a traveller, and the occasional dose of expert assistance to induce the landscape to surrender its secrets. This form of tourism is inherently dramatic or performative: The location becomes a 'site' and attains significance only in the presence of a spectator-tourist.

In a manner of speaking, then, the tourist space is transformed by and through performance: the performance of the narrative (in this case, *LOTR*), which animates the space, as well as the performances of the tourists who move through it.[3] This transformation is social rather than physical, but powerful none the less. Just as ritual performances are commonly employed to consecrate otherwise ordinary space for sacred purposes, tourist performances mark, delimit, and authenticate the sites on which they take place.[4] The location tourism engendered by *LOTR* functions as such a performance, one that draws inspiration from and builds upon the performances of the actors, sets, costumes, camera, effects, etc., embedded in the films themselves. The difference is that ritual performances create liminal spaces whereas *LOTR* has created a liminoid space, supersaturated and commodified – similar in this respect to the most prevalent modern sacred space, the shopping mall. The 'real virtuality' of this tourist experience already blurs boundaries between real and virtual in a unique way; rather than enact their fantasy on a video screen, *LOTR* tourists enact it upon and within the real New Zealand landscape. The performative and social nature of this tourism has the potential to transform the environment, like religious ritual, in such a way that the transformation persists beyond the stay of any one tourist. The present chapter rests in part on this first-hand experience of *LOTR* tourism; it investigates the varied relationships between fantasy and reality encountered at several sites.

## On the transformative potential of tourism reliant upon memory

Tourist attractions are always a blend of the perceptible and imperceptible. MacCannell, author of *The Tourist: A New Theory of the Leisure Class*, uses the example of a moon rock on display to demonstrate that the allure of certain tourist sites is the marker more than the site itself. He quotes a newspaper article: "'It looks like a piece of something you could pick up in Central Park', one 13 year-old boy said. "But it's cool that it's from the moon"' (1976: 113). The physical properties of the rock itself are not the attraction, but rather the sign explaining it and the claims made about it: the markers.

MacCannell describes situations in which a site is *obliterated* by its markers. A common example is the historical battlefield, which often bears no physical evidence of the battle, but is littered with markers: claims about what happened there, replica cannons, reconstructed forts, etc. This allows for a variable definition of the place: change the markers, and the site is changed. A clear example is Normandy Beach, which MacCannell observed was 'giving up as an ex-battlefield and taking on a new identity as a suburban resort community' (1976: 129) by swapping markers, replacing cannons with deck chairs and umbrellas.

That this experience of 'real virtuality' is a hallmark of nearly all tourist encounters is not insignificant. Extending MacCannell, Kirshenblatt-Gimblett has noted that tourism 'deal[s] in the intangible, absent, inaccessible, fragmentary, and dislocated' (1998: 167). Many, if not most tourist sites derive their attraction not from their actual properties, but from the virtual environment generated by guidebooks, tour operators, and other discursive practices. The tourist travels to an actual site, but the appeal of that site rests on a story: this place is the first, the largest, the only . . . As Kirshenblatt-Gimblett writes, 'Tourists travel to actual destinations to experience virtual places' (1998: 9).

While the appeal may be generated externally of the site, a typical tourist site is none the less attentive to its role as a tourist destination and acknowledges it via on-site markers: signs, brochures, admission fees, and so on. The *LOTR* sites are unique, however, in that most are defined by markers not present at the sites. New Line Cinema's deal with the New Zealand Department of Conservation (DoC) ensured that no evidence of the filming remained on public land. There are no signs marking the spot where Boromir died; no structure remains at *Amon Hen*. Instead, tourists bring the markers with them. Brodie's *Guidebook* is a popular resource, giving directions to many sites and leaving the tourists to authenticate the sites themselves. Guided tours are popular too, and in some cases guides can confirm precise filming locations.

But most *LOTR* tourists are not interested in a site because they are told that Viggo Mortensen and Sir Ian McKellen filmed a scene in that exact spot; they are drawn because Aragorn and Gandalf had an exchange there in Middle-earth.[5] That is, the 'official' markers (the guidebook and tours) are secondary to the most important marker, which is the film itself. If the specified location is not recognisable from the film, then it is not a successful *LOTR* tourist experience. Since most tourists do not have a copy of the movie with them at each site, the authenticating mechanism becomes a combination of 'official' claims and their *memory* of the film – a very unstable marker. Memory always involves interpretation, and in this case the tourist faces the daunting task of matching a real environment to a memory of a fictional event. Even if the tourist does, as our team did, have a DVD of the film and the means to play it on-site, authentication is still difficult. There are numerous obstacles to definitive site identification, ranging from the gross physical similarity between one mountain or another to the film's technological underpinnings (complex editing, light filtering, digital enhancement), to the tourist's inability to reach the viewpoints offered by a camera-crane or helicopter.

When the success or failure of each tourist site (that is, the success in discovering Middle-earth) depends upon tourists' memories, there is potential for a blindness to, or erasure of, the real landscape. This erasure is less than complete in places where a distinct feature from the film (especially if digitally added, such as the *Pillars of the Kings*) is sought; it is similarly less than complete if real features, such as roads and buildings, interfere. But the potential exists, in the more remote and featureless locations, to lose oneself in the fantasy, or to ignore reality while searching for the fantasy. Once, we were searching for the location of a short helicopter shot of the Fellowship traversing the landscape. Unable to find a recognisable location with the directions given, we turned to the GPS. In the midst of a beautiful New Zealand landscape, our eyes were on the digital output of the GPS, relying upon it to guide us to Middle-earth. Thus it seems that, for animating a landscape, stories are superior to traditional markers, as tourism is a fundamentally dramatic or performative action. A ten-hour fantasy spectacle (and one in which geography features highly) is the trump card of such stories. The real landscapes activate these stories held in the tourists' memories and engage the imagination – with the potential, if reality is not too obtrusive, to alter the significance of the land.

### On the uneasy relationship between fantasy and reality

In *Destination Culture*, Kirshenblatt-Gimblett writes about the development of heritage in New Zealand. 'New Zealand tourism projects an imagined landscape that segments the history of the country into three hermetic compartments. The nature story stops with the coming of people. The indigenous story stops with the coming of Europeans. And the Europeans (and later immigrants) have until recently not been convinced that their story is very interesting' (1998: 141).

Kirshenblatt-Gimblett's theory continues to be relevant to discussions of New Zealand tourism, especially now that a new level of cinematic heritage generated by the *LOTR* phenomenon portends a new impact on the real and the historical by the virtual and the popular. This impact is aided by the readiness of the New Zealand government, the national airline, and tourist agencies to advertise their nation as 'Middle-earth'. Within the negotiation and creation of this *LOTR* heritage, the landscape becomes a site of struggle and poses questions concerning virtuality, simulacra, erasure, authenticity, and the real and hyperreal. The land is at once Aotearoa / Middle-earth / New Zealand. As a tourist walking through the forests and climbing mountains one must ask the question: Where am I standing?

The tourist's encounters with the hyper-real while trekking across New Zealand are greatly influenced by the digital remapping of the landscape. As a tourist the struggle with geography becomes an important part of the journey, especially since the only remnants of Middle-earth are those physical spaces in which filming took place. Moviegoers connect the images constructed from this altered New Zealand landscape and apply it to the map of Middle-earth, which ultimately becomes the map by which *LOTR* tourists guide their trip. But places cinematically juxtaposed are in fact far away in the physical landscape of New Zealand; a chronological tour, in terms of the *LOTR* narrative, would be incredibly inefficient. The reality of a particular New Zealand geography rather than an illusory Middle-earth continuity exposes the hyperreality of the filmscapes, whose collapse can result in a highly unsatisfactory tourist experience.

This virtual–real disjointedness came to light in our own travels. The movie locale *Dimrill Dale* was located in the Remarkables, a mountain range near Queenstown, which provided our most physically taxing trek. After an afternoon hiking up the trail-less, boulder-strewn mountainside in search of the correct GPS location, we yielded to the difficulty of the terrain without having found our site. To add to this disappointment, the splendid vista that Aragorn looks out upon in the film – containing the mountains that form the *Spine of the World* and the forest of *Lothlorien* – was absent. These features had been digitally generated and had replaced what we were now looking at: a large, grey, featureless mountain. The images in the film of *Dimrill Dale* are diffuse and elusive if you are searching for them in the real world because that is not where they are meant to exist. In this way the portrayal of

New Zealand as Middle-earth is deceptive, because Middle-earth as a simulacrum can only ever be seen on a screen in two dimensions; it cannot be experienced in the real. But millions none the less try to experience Middle-earth in three dimensions and, judging from entries in tourist registers,[6] most feel that they succeed to some degree.

Our trip to Dan's Paddock, despite a similar lack of signification, put the virtual and real in contestation for our attention. Dan's Paddock rests by a beautiful riverbed with forests, open fields, tree-covered slopes, snow-capped peaks, and rolling hills. This luscious landscape functioned as the backdrop for the digitally constructed city of *Isengard* with its solitary black spire *Orthanc*, and we were able to discern where the digital spaces had been created within the natural locale. Why did Dan's Paddock seem so much more beautiful to our 'fellowship' than did *Dimrill Dale*? Perhaps because once we had accomplished our nominal mission – to identify the film location – we could relax and enjoy the landscape for its 'real' virtues. Though the inherent beauty of New Zealand's landscape was not generated by Tolkien's myths, *LOTR*, after all, had brought us there. Sightseeing must wait until the quest is complete. Or perhaps, to access the real, the tourist must first identify the virtual – for the appeal of the real is enhanced by contrast to the virtual. Dan's Paddock was not-virtual, and hence beautiful. *Dimrill Dale*, because we never conclusively identified its virtual location, continued to haunt our experience of the Remarkable mountain range, denying us the pleasure of experiencing a real landscape.

Yet another type of experience was offered by the filming site for the *Pillars of the Kings*, creating a strangely disjointed blend of pleasure and disappointment. The pillars, two monoliths guarding the entrance to *Gondor*, were digitally created and blended in with landscape filmed on the Kawarau River. The site was none the less recognisable from the film and sparked the imagination to picture the fellowship's boats passing by. But it was only a spark. This site plainly revealed the type of erasure through simulacra that can occur as the *LOTR* heritage develops and supersedes a precursor. In the film, after passing through the pillars, the fellowship goes around a bend and comes out of the ravine on to a lake with a waterfall. Although the digital rendering in the film is impeccable, when standing there in person it was impossible not to notice that beyond the spot where the *Argonath* had been inserted was the Kawarau River Bungy Jump. This bungee jump, the world's oldest commercial bungee jump, has its own cultural significance as, prior to *LOTR*, adventure sports were New Zealand's premiere global attractions. The films' digital space erases this preceding landmark, but the *LOTR* tourist confronts both heritages simultaneously.

and cannot resolve the stark contrast between Middle-earth and New Zealand, fantasy and reality.

## On the cultural impact of the *LOTR* film-event

At a site where no outstanding features are noticeable (and no outstanding digital features are noticeably absent), however, the contrast between Middle-earth and New Zealand is indistinct. Robert Rutherford of Glenorchy Air, our pilot and tour guide through the Paradise Forest, waved his arm in a 90-degree arc along the horizon to indicate the *Amon Hen* hillside, where Boromir died and the Fellowship split. Despite the imprecision, or more likely *because* of it, this was a highly rewarding site. The mossy beech forest was highly evocative of those scenes from the film, as we remembered them. Every clump of trees and patch of moss was redolent of the film; we found ten different spots that were 'definitely' from the film, willing as we were to forget that the forest had had two years of growth since the filming. This site was a success in terms of discovering Middle-earth because it relied upon our memories of an extended sequence in the film, a sequence in which the only distinctive features of the location are moss and beech trees on a slight slope.

This tourism is by nature repeatable, and spots such as this put the landscape into flux and attempt to abolish parameters. Since such sites, being unmarked, have the freedom to resonate differently for each tourist, *all* of Paradise Forest (for instance) becomes synonymous with *Amon Hen*. From the 1998 press release announcing New Zealand as the site of filming, to the repetitive recognition of New Zealand at the 2004 Oscars, to the release of the final DVD in 2006, the worldwide associative link between Middle-earth and New Zealand is so strong, and so frequently reinforced, that the whole country becomes a potential 'unmarked site' that can become Middle-earth at the tourist's will – particularly in remote areas. On the road to Poolburn (Central Otago) is an expanse of rocky tussock not used in *LOTR*. But being, as we were, in a Middle-earth mindset, it was easy to picture the Fellowship trudging for days through this endless countryside. This region, not used in the films, can none the less be appropriated – through tourism – by the *LOTR* legend. Of course, this phenomenon also indicates that *LOTR* does not *own* the landscape, which could be appropriated for other means. However, and this is the key issue, the dominant interpretation of (in this case) the landscape is determined by the prevailing and most public proclamations. To this end, Hollywood money, popularity, and ubiquity will always outweigh other interpretations, particularly those of only local significance in a nation of roughly four million people.

For this reason, *LOTR* tourism has difficulty existing concurrently with other (earlier) forms of tourism. While Glenorchy Air, for instance, still regularly runs scenic tours to *LOTR*-unrelated sites, it does not combine 'normal' tourism with *LOTR* tourism. Perhaps because of the wide-eyed awe with which we first consumed the spectacle, perhaps because of its status as 'ancient' folklore, *LOTR* mythology supersedes any existing significance of the landscape. Whether Paradise Forest has any importance in ecological terms or in Maori mythology is irrelevant to the busloads of *LOTR* tourists. Prior to entering Paradise Forest, Rutherford sat us down and briefly discussed the history of the land. He was pointing out interesting things about the landscape around us, including some small gnarled trees estimated to be more than five hundred years old, i.e., old enough to have shared air with the moa, an extinct native bird. Worried about losing his audience, he abruptly changed tack. Saying 'but that's all beside the point', he started instead telling stories of flying *LOTR* cast members to remote locations. His perception of our desires as tourists clearly altered the importance of this location, as he narrated it.

While many sites reveal the uncomfortable relationship between fantasy and reality, and the impossibility of complete landscape transformation, countless others, from the film or not, reveal a possibility for erasing history and the existing significance of the land. Existing connotations can be replaced by a mythology invented by Tolkien and reinterpreted (for commercial means) by the filmmakers. It is not an implausible stretch to consider this event in terms of a second colonisation of New Zealand. The millions of viewers who associate this fantasy with New Zealand (whether they visit or not) are all colonisers to some degree. In the global context, New Zealand is now first and foremost known as Middle-earth. Even homegrown Kiwis begin to see their land in this new manner, and it is (paradoxically, perhaps) a source of great national pride.

Is the 'authentic' New Zealand (or its representation) under siege? Conversely, has the *LOTR* filming, screening, and tourist experience catapulted the island nation (and the tourist industry in general) into a new age of inescapable postmodernity, where any site can signify anything, and every site is a blank slate on to which tourists inscribe their own desires? We may perhaps find a clue in the idea of fantasy.

The sites that tourists find most rewarding are those in which their own fantasies are enhanced and encouraged by the harmonic convergence of the location, the experience of getting to that location, and the animating narrative. How the landscape *performs*, in other words, is more important than what the space *is*. This suggests that for the

*LOTR* tourist, the patent artificiality of the experience is, on some level, central to the pleasure taken therein. By abandoning one's mundane existence, by wilfully setting aside one's everyday relationship to space and time, by expending money and other resources in the service of an experience with no commodifiable value whatsoever, the tourist enters a world of play that offers 'the illusion of mastery over life's circumstances' (Sutton-Smith 2001: 53). Or to put it another way, *LOTR* tourism does not offer the 'real Middle-earth' as much as it offers a Middle-earth every bit as *unreal* – and therefore pleasurable – as the landscape presented in the film.

## Notes

1 Rob Smith and Dr Alan Wright were involved in this phase as well.
2 The term 'real-virtuality' is also used by Castells in *The Information Age, Vol. 1: The Rise of the Network Society* and elsewhere to indicate the collapse of the real-virtual distinction in a globally networked society. As used here, however, 'real-virtuality' specifically indicates a *physical* environment that is animated in the mode of play by the virtual environment of the *LOTR* films.
3 Cf. Bachelard 1964, Bennett 1995, and elsewhere.
4 In a modern, artistic context, Schechner's *Environmental Theater* (1973) details his conscious exploration of the links between ritual and contemporary performance in order to transform an environment.
5 Brodie's *Guidebook*, as evidence, contains nearly three hundred photographs, and of these only a handful feature the film crew or Jackson; none features the actors out of costume. The 'making-of' shots are confined to the introduction and the end matter; on the pages dedicated to particular sites, images are limited to film scenes or photos of nearby tourist attractions.
6 See, for instance, tourists' comments at www.glenorchy.net.nz.

# 23

# Asking that mountain: an Indigenous reading of *The Lord of the Rings*?

*Alice Te Punga Somerville*

Toitu te whenua, toitu te iwi.

I watched the first film of the *LOTR* trilogy on a snowy December night in upstate New York with my sister, three friends, and a baby. All of us were from New Zealand, and either didn't live there or had spent significant time away. When the lights came on, a friend who had attended the same session looked at the five-and-a-half of us perched in the back row, and laughed out loud. 'I thought you must be here, Alice', he explained. 'I could hear the groans and gasps you made whenever there was a wide shot of the scenery, no matter what was happening in the narrative'. As expatriate New Zealanders, we had decided to see the film together in order to catch a view of 'home'. As a Maori person, however, I recognise the extent to which Indigenous peoples can be considered 'expats' (or perhaps refugees, fugitives, exiles, migrants) within the very nationstate of which they or we are citizens. When I lived in Ithaca, I was disconnected from New Zealand; in Aotearoa New Zealand, there is still disconnection from turangawaewae[1] as long as the right to exercise te tino rangatiratanga[2] over it is refused.

I wonder if it is useful to think of non-Indigenous and Indigenous as distinct (perhaps ultimately competing) ways of reading *LOTR*. If Indigeneity is tied to a particular kind of relationship with land, might there be a particular way of reading land, including when that land is projected onto a screen? How would this reading of a film be different from a non-Indigenous reading? What would such a reading look like? What would it make possible?

## An Indigenous reading

As I write about the possibility of an Indigenous reading, I am reminded that, because 'Indigenous' has multiple, dynamic, and overlapping meanings, we must consider some caveats around the term's use. First, 'Indigenous' is simultaneously used to describe a comparative category (when it refers to all Indigenous people everywhere, as in Smith (1999), which focuses on colonised people everywhere) and a specific category (where it is used as a substitute for a local term for a specific local group, as in Moreton-Robinson (2000), which uses 'Indigenous' and 'Aboriginal' – the specific Australian term – interchangeably). Additionally, because a shared Indigenous identity rests on a claim to specificity, defining the comparative use of the term can become oxymoronic: How do you find things you share when the basis of your connection is your insistence on uniqueness?

The (unmarked) oscillation between the comparative and the specific, crucial when formulating reading practice, necessarily inflects any discussion about an Indigenous reading of film. For example, an Indigenous reading of *LOTR* might attempt to read the text from a position that centres the (comparative) Indigenous; it would centre those things that are imagined as pertinent to all Indigenous communities. This might consider issues of connection to land, or perhaps a specific experience of colonialism marked by alienation from land and resources, issues around language retention, genealogies, and so on. But equating a set of particular issues or aspects as Indigenous sets up a generic Indigenous that seems in danger of replicating the European-imagined Native. On the other hand, an Indigenous reading of *LOTR* might centre the (specific) Indigenous; it might emphasise specific land, specific place, specific peoples and bodies, and modes of representation in the film.

Then why wouldn't this be called 'a Maori reading' instead of the more ambiguous 'an Indigenous reading'? One reason is that I do not believe the term 'Maori' can ever be fully substituted by 'Indigenous'. A Maori reading might be Indigenous, but it also might be Pacific, Postcolonial, Minority, New Zealand, Southern, and so on. 'Maori' necessarily exceeds and challenges each of these categories as well; a Maori reading would need to take into account cosmological, cultural, and aesthetic considerations specific to Maori. (Iwi, hapu or rohe-specific readings would complicate and enrich this further.[3]) In the current reading of *LOTR*, I will focus on those aspects of Maori that might be described as Indigenous; for the sake of producing parameters for my discussion, I specifically engage with the dimension of land. Tied to this point is the second reason for calling this an Indigenous reading: Ambiguity, as critical theory reminds us, can be productive. Indeed, it serves the critical and political purpose of my work to take advantage of the slippage between the specific and the comparative in order to enable the kinds of claims I make about *LOTR* to be extrapolated to other Other contexts. An Indigenous reading might seem more mobile, more exportable, more – well – more like the very films with which we grapple in this volume. Rather than signalling complicity with a market-driven kind of criticism, this recognises the simultaneous specific and comparative contexts in which *LOTR* circulates, and perhaps suggests the possibility of collaborative readings across Indigenous communities.

Furthermore, there is a difference between an Indigenous reading of film and a reading of Indigenous film (or, indeed, an Indigenous reading of Indigenous film). Indigenous film and cultural production continues to be theorised, explored, and challenged by thinkers and practitioners, including the Maori scholars and filmmakers Barry Barclay, Merata Mita, Sam Cruickshank, Leonie Pihama, and others.[4] I would not argue that *LOTR* or *The Last Samurai* are Indigenous films, but it is possible to imagine an Indigenous reading of them. Similarly, unlike work about the representation of Indigenes in non-Indigenous texts, such as *Celluloid Indians*, I am not reading the representation of Indigenous peoples in film; *LOTR* and *The Last Samurai* do not include a single Maori character.

Instead, I am suggesting a reading of film that privileges land to the extent that real land – and the histories of identification and colonialism embedded in that land – cannot be absented from existing film texts that include images of that land. Indeed, this project is not about a re-reading of Indigenous representation in film as much as it is about the impossibility of Indigenous *non*-representation in films that are shot on Indigenous land. So, if land really is crucial to – even constitutive of – what it means to be Indigenous, how might this inflect our Indigenous reading of film?

## Asking that mountain

For some readers, this chapter's title might seem a little abstract, while for other (perhaps Other) readers, the genealogies and implications of the phrase 'Ask that Mountain' will be clear. In short, the knowing reader will recognise this phrase from Parihaka (see below). Perhaps in some way this parallels my claims about the reading of film. While the immediate context of this book invites a focus on this chapter's subtitle, which engages explicitly with *LOTR*, for some readers the earlier phrase necessarily roots this discussion in the context of the history of Aotearoa New Zealand, the violence of the colonial project, the multiple and complex forms of resistance to that project (including the specific resistance to colonial forces in New Zealand by Te Whiti, Tohu Kakahi, and Titokowaru), the issue of sovereignty over land, and the politics, suppression, and maintenance of these histories. According to Scott's *Ask*

*That Mountain: The Story of Parihaka* (1975), William Baucke (a Pakeha
journalist, farmer, and commentator) sat with Te Whiti o Rongomai,
the pacifist prophet whose passive resistance to colonialism in the later
nineteenth century resulted in some of the darkest hours in New
Zealand history.[5] By the time he met with Baucke, Te Whiti had returned
from his imprisonment, and lived again at Parihaka. Scott writes: 'The
old man's eyes blazed as he spoke of the evil of war and blessing
of peace. But suddenly he pointed back to the mountain, "Ask that
mountain", he said, "Taranaki saw it all!" ' (186–7). After the telling
of histories (and specific, gruesome, embarrassing, shameful histories)
through language, the ultimate witness to and narrator of those histories is Taranaki. In this context, Taranaki is not merely a feature of the
landscape, or the background, or setting. Nor is this strictly a kind of
personification in which an 'inanimate object' is ascribed human traits;
'Taranaki' is, and remains, a 'mountain'. This *agency* of the land is key.
The anecdote above about watching *Fellowship* in Ithaca[6] allows a
distinction between an expat viewing of the film in order to see the
New Zealand landscape and an Indigenous reading of the film. While
the former might emphasise the extent to which the representation or
presence of the landscape as a part of the setting or backdrop is recognisable to the knowing viewer as 'New Zealand' or perhaps 'Otago High
Country' at the same time that it is Middle-earth or Mordor, the latter
suggests a more active role of the land.[7]

I first started to think about how a particular understanding of land
might inflect the Indigenous reading of a film while watching *The Last
Samurai*. Conveniently for *The Last Samurai*'s filmmakers, the mountain we know as Taranaki looks very similar to Fujiyama. Like Fuji,
Taranaki looks eerily like a perfect triangle, with a sharp pointy peak
and glossy white snowy sides that turn into rolling green hills near the
base. Unlike the twenty-first century Fuji, though, Taranaki's rolling hills
are not covered by signs of 'development' such as homes, buildings, power-
lines, and roads. *The Last Samurai* is set – for the film's purposes –
in Japan, and Taranaki stands in for Fujiyama precisely because of its
difference from the 'real' Fujiyama. However, for the viewer of *The Last
Samurai* who retains an identification with Taranaki and the history of
Parihaka, it is impossible to ignore the messy spectral presence of the
bloodshed and violence of Parihaka. The mountain is simultaneously
Fujiyama and Taranaki. The rolling hills are not only trodden by the
horses of Japanese troops; they are simultaneously the hills over which
horses moved as a part of the colonial attack on the pacifist settlement.
The film's landscape thus also suggests the history that has taken place
in that real place where it has been filmed.

There are some compelling parallels between *The Last Samurai* and *LOTR*. They both capitalise on the landscape and labour of the 'local' in order to produce a film that is explicitly about the *non*-local. Aotearoa New Zealand is neither Japan nor Middle-earth, but in these films it is substitutable for both or either of these. Both Japan and Europe require a setting for their pasts, and while imagined (and literally filmed) temporal travel may be impossible because of the literal marks of (what is recognised by a global audience as) modernity on the landscape of those places, spatial travel can provide exactly the kind of disconnect required. This landscape is unknown and uninhabited to the extent that it can stand in for nineteenth-century Japan and historical Middle-earth. For the global audience, these temporal spaces are projected on to the blank slate of the landscape. Indeed, Aotearoa New Zealand is able to stand in for these Other places precisely because of its difference and – significantly – its emptiness. While New Zealand's landscape was understood in the later nineteenth and early twentieth centuries as 'Maoriland', now it is empty. The transition from a populated – and specifically populated – landscape at the beginning of the twentieth century to a depopulated and repopulated landscape at the end of that century can only be marked as colonial. But – and this is where an Indigenous reading comes in – while much of the non-local commentary around *LOTR* was about the 'otherworldliness' of the landscape, for some people this land is not about 'otherworld' or 'anotherworld': this is the turangawaewae, the place to stand. These films can represent Japan and Middle-earth only when they can successfully produce a blank slate of landscape by countering two things: the actual presence of Indigenous people (and, indeed, a contemporary settler nation state), and the representational presence of Maoriland. This kind of historical erasure might be called representational genocide.

Finally, there is also an economic dimension to the use of the New Zealand landscape (and New Zealand bodies or labour) for the production of 'international films'.[8] Films are made here because it is cheap and because of the famed local skill at innovation. First, the 'cheapness' of resources here needs countering by the recognition that there is no such thing as a free lunch. Films are cheap to make in New Zealand because it is a settler colony, and because of the displacement of Indigenous peoples. The colonisation of New Zealand since Cook first encountered Aotearoa in 1769 brought these islands into the world capitalist system, but in particular ways. Since the early whalers and traders, visitors to these islands have come to take advantage of available resources and ultimately to take them home. The large cost of these big-budget films is still paid, but because of the mechanisms by which this small settler nation participates in the capitalist economy, these costs are either already accounted for (displaced Indigenous people have 'paid' for the land, for example) or are siphoned differently into the global public (the cheapness of the NZ dollar compared to the US dollar is ultimately paid for by those who do not earn US dollars). Second, the idea of settler innovation is inseparable from the violent process of colonialism upon which it depends for open space and resources. The number 8 fencing wire that stands metaphorically for Kiwi ingenuity marks out the land that has been alienated from its original owners.

### Allegories of Indigenous resistance

To what kind of work might this idea of an Indigenous reading of *LOTR* be put? Although the multiple possibilities of Indigenous readings of film – and LOTR in particular – cannot be treated here, it is instructive to test one possible direction for this kind of critical work. Remembering that Te Whiti charges us to 'ask that mountain [who] saw it all', and holding as a crucial point that it is impossible to pay attention to this specific land (these islands, Aotearoa New Zealand) without recognising the bloodshed and violence of colonialism,[9] I suggest the possibility of reading *LOTR* as a series of overlapping (unconscious) allegories of the imperial project in this place. This is not to reduce *LOTR* to a series of fables, or to suggest that the books on which the films are based treated (or didn't treat) the specific process of colonialism as it happened here, but it is to argue that, if an Indigenous reading of *LOTR* advocates recognition of the land's agency, then the films cannot help but intersect with that land's specific histories. That two competing – or perhaps compellingly simultaneous – readings exist of the possible allegories suggested by the relationship between those who dwell in the Shire and the Orcs points, for me, to a crucial dimension of a settler colony such as Aotearoa New Zealand. One reading would suggest that the Hobbits are Indigenous, and under threat by the hyper-industrial and violent colonising Orcs. The opposite version would read the Shire as a Settler space, and the space beyond the Shire as a projected anxiety about the Indigenes of the land occupied in part by the Hobbits. A third reading, tied to the second, would take as a specific parallel the journey into the psychological heart of the European coloniser staged in Conrad's *Heart of Darkness*.

### *Hobbits as Indigenous*

The Hobbits who inhabit the Shire could be understood as standing in for an Indigenous community or, to be clear, a (European-imagined)

Native community. They are balanced, subsistent, keen agriculturalists; indeed, these Indigenous people are so authentic they even talk to trees! In this version, the threat issued from Sauron and manifest by the Orcs and other 'forces of darkness' is tied explicitly to colonialism's destructive industrialism and violence. According to this reading of *LOTR*, the Hobbits are engaged in resistance to an apparently more powerful enemy and, with the leadership of Frodo and his fellow-travellers, they ultimately succeed in their resistance because of their commitment to pure principles and their unique ability to place communal integrity over personal gain. Within the context of the nation state of New Zealand, this seems to be a compelling reading, both because of the relative sizes of the communities (Maori are outnumbered by non-Maori, as Hobbits are by Orcs) and because of the aggressors' hyper-industrialisation. However, the Hobbits' simplicity, childlikeness, and innocence parallel colonial representation of Indigenous peoples – especially Noble Savage ones! – and so, while the viewer is encouraged to value and cheer for the Hobbits, this is all from a position of paternalism. We are proud of Frodo, after all, but we fall in love with Legolas or Arwen. This reading is also limited by the cultural and phenotypic markers of Europeanness (and perhaps Anglo-Saxonness): the built environment, lived culture, modes of recorded history, and agricultural styles are European; and, of the New Zealand actors who worked on the films, the Hobbits and their allies are acted by the most blonde.

## Hobbits as settlers

So if the bodies of the 'goodies' on screen resist this reading of the Hobbits as Indigenous, the bodies of the 'baddies' resist the reading even more so. The Orcs may be involved in a kind of anti-environmental industrialisation predicated on surplus resource accumulation and the exploitation of increasing amounts of land and labour, but they are also black. The Orcs (and their *über*-versions, the Uruk-hai) are explicitly racialised, and the Hobbits are thereby represented as even more vulnerable – and thus even more deserving of audience sympathies – to the violence these forces of darkness threaten. Like all film, *LOTR* trades in representational shortcuts in order to evoke race, gender, hierarchies of power, and so on. Specifically, Orc and especially Uruk-hai bodies are large, grotesque, and marked by scarification and painted skin; they are clumsy and work as a simple-minded mob; their bodies are disposable and replaceable, which ultimately denies them the possibility of individualisation; they are infinitely substitutable. Further – and this is where the specificity of the land of *these* islands becomes crucial – I would argue that these baddies are also represented as Indigenous. There is a moment of literal autochthony when they are pulled from the land, and in the context of New Zealand the paint on the faces compellingly suggests the moko[10] that is associated not only with whakapapa[11] but also (particularly in the European imagination) with war. It is no coincidence that all of the Polynesian (including Maori) actors used in *LOTR* are either Orcs or Uruk-hai.

This reading, then, evokes the white settler colony's ultimate anxiety. The Hobbits' greatest fear – so great as to be necessarily erased from that community's lived culture and popular histories – is of the Native communities beyond the pale. The Hobbits live in a self-contained (and ultimately ignorant) world of agriculture and intra-community relationships. However, their pristine environment demands multiple forms of maintenance: First, a small number of men – this is all gendered, after all – venture out to defend that space; second, the suppression of histories (both through lack of interest in 'real' histories, disrespect for their tellers, and marginalisation of the communities for which the tales have most meaning) maintains the ignorance of the 'real', violent context of the settlement. Third, an overriding nostalgia arises for the peacetime and innocent status of that community within the host landscape.

In New Zealand, as Elleray argues, this feared space is the space of the bush, into which men travel in order to create a kind of (colonial, civilised) order, but in which they are in danger of going Native.[12] Furthermore, the 'bush' (the place beyond the Shire, both in the internal narrative of *LOTR* as well as the filmed locations of the various spaces) is feared precisely because of racialised or indigenised bodies. According to this version, the Hobbits are innocent only through suppression of histories and social or physical context, and the imagined malevolent, wild, cannibalistic, and violent aggressors are perhaps performing a kind of resistance, or at least are engaged in exacting a kind of territorial justice for the act of settler colonialism by which the Hobbits have produced their apparently pristine home. This reading of the narrative as settler anxiety about what is lurking in the shadow has clear articulations in the context of Aotearoa New Zealand.

### Frodo as Marlow

Finally, after previously reading the Shire as Settler space, and Frodo and the other Hobbits' journey as part of the mechanism that maintains the innocence of that space, a reading of Frodo as Conrad's narrator-hero Marlow might be productive. After all, Frodo is an explorer who remains untainted by his movement into the 'heart of darkness', which is simultaneously a physical journey into the heart of geographical landscape populated by grotesque black threatening beings, and a psychological journey into the heart of the explorer. Both Conrad's novel and *LOTR* suggest that, in journeying to the most remote and unfamiliar, we journey into the most intimate and internal. Both value the explorer who ventures beyond the pale and not only survives that journey untainted by the violence and savagery encountered there (whether Frodo/Marlow is untainted is debateable), but who also returns and writes or recounts histories in multiple ways for the multiple home audiences. Indeed, both texts also emphasise the tension between the desire to relate the journey's experiences and the impossibility of relating those experiences upon return to the space of the metropolitan centre, which can function 'as usual' precisely because it does not engage with those histories upon which it relies.

## Conclusions, beginnings

An Indigenous reading of these films insists that neither *The Last Samurai* nor *LOTR* is filmed in an empty space. The land on which they are shot is already imbued with a complex of Indigenous identification and settler violence. An Indigenous reading of *LOTR* is not a simple condemnation of the films or an attempt to undermine their success; instead, it is one way to account for the specific historical, geographic, social, and political contexts in which the films have been produced. The simultaneous possibilities of the three readings I gesture towards in the final move of this exploration produce a productive tension that lies, ultimately, at the heart of what it means to inhabit a place that is both settler colony and Fourth World nation. Te Whiti directed Baucke to 'ask that mountain', and this discussion of an Indigenous reading of the film attempts to follow that directive.

## Notes

1 Turangawaewae = literally, a place to stand; the place of belonging.
2 Te Tino Rangatiratanga = a phrase used in the Treaty of Waitangi / Te Tiriti o Waitangi, by which Queen Victoria (and, by extension, the emerging New Zealand government) guaranteed 'absolute sovereignty' or 'chieftainship' over natural and cultural resources.
3 Iwi = tribe; Hapu = subtribe; Rohe = region.
4 Important texts include Barclay (1990), Mita (1992), Pihama (1994), and Cruickshank (2002). See also Barclay 2003 and 2005.
5 Parihaka is the pacifist village or town where the methodical and peaceful lifting of surveyors' stakes in the surrounding land brought upon the people the full violence of the colonial military and ideological machine; colonial troops stormed, ransacked, and disbanded the pacifist settlement

in November 1881. The role of Parihaka in New Zealand's national consciousness has been fraught. The events surrounding Parihaka have been a
suppressed history in New Zealand. Although some writers commemorated
the events at the time (e.g., Jessie Mackay's parodic poem 'The Charge of
Parihaka'), it was then omitted from the histories taught at schools and
universities, popular histories, and so on. The suppression of this history
is treated by a number of contemporary Maori writers and musicians. The
first English-language play by a Maori playwright, Harry Dansey's 1972
play *Te Raukura* (1974), deals specifically with the storming of Parihaka.
Apirana Taylor writes about the suppression of this history in his poem
'Parihaka' (2004). Scott's popular *Ask that Mountain* was for many Maori
and non-Maori their first introduction to the events there. Tim Finn and
Herbs collaborated on a widely played song entitled 'Parihaka' that was
released in 1989. An exhibition entitled *Parihaka – The Art of Passive
Resistance* was held at the City Gallery in Wellington from August 2000
until January 2001, and is now on permanent display at Puke Ariki, the
Museum in New Plymouth, Taranaki (the New Zealand province where
Parihaka is located). A book and CD were produced in relation to this exhibition; the CD collects a number of compositions pertaining to Parihaka
(including the Herbs and Tim Finn song), along with a number of poems
and stories by Maori and non-Maori writers.

6  *Ithaca* – another example of a mythical place overlaid on an Indigenous
   landscape.

7  For a striking parallel, this agency of land is of central importance to the
   narrative and visual components of Rotuma-born Vilsoni Hereniko's
   recent film, *Pear Ta Ma 'On Maf / The Land Has Eyes*.

8  By this I mean that the films are largely conceived, funded, and distributed
   outside New Zealand, and explicitly work *against* the use of the local 'as itself'.

9  In *Cinema of Unease*, Sam Neill and Judy Rymer's contribution to the British
   Film Institute-sponsored series of documentaries on national cinemas produced to mark a centenary of film, Neill comments: 'And the question I
   ask myself is, does a resonance remain? Is soil forever stained by blood?'
   Although his comment is ostensibly about the murder later memorialised
   in *Heavenly Creatures*, a question about the resonance of blood in the soil
   must surely include the blood spilled as part of the colonial project in these
   islands.

10 Moko = Maori tattoo; related to the Polynesian tatau. The facial moko in
   particular has circulated widely around Europe and Euro-America since the
   popularity of late eighteenth-century engravings of Polynesians, and inclusion
   as markers of race and indigeneity in texts such as Melville's *Moby-Dick*.

11 Whakapapa = genealogies. The design of any moko is specific to the person; it includes reference to genealogical, ancestral, and historical information.

12 A reading of Gollum as a Settler who has gone Native is compelling. His
   moral and then physical degeneration results from a moment located away
   from the Shire, in the bush.

## Part VI

# There, back again, and beyond: production infrastructures and extended exploitation

# 24

# Dossier: corporations, lawyers, small domestic economies, technology, and profits

## Sean Cubitt and Barry King

This section returns to *LOTR*'s corporate pedigree in greater depth, examining *LOTR*'s importance for both international and domestic economies. It also looks more particularly at how *LOTR* has generated profits. Brett Nicholls's 'The ludic integration of the game and film industries: *The Lord of the Rings* computer games as entertainment meritocracies' (Chapter 25), which completes this section, explores just one small component of the merchandising associated with *LOTR*, finding once again something unique associated with the trilogy.

According to Jackson's unofficial biographer, Ian Pryor, while Jackson was completing his debut Hollywood feature film, *The Frighteners*, in 1995 and considering the possibility of directing the remake of *King Kong*, the idea began to cross his mind that it would be worth investigating who owned the rights to Tolkien's fantasy masterpiece. In an interview with *Pavement* (a local magazine), he indicated that

> the thinking at that time was that we'd have to create an original fantasy film. But we kept referring to the fact that it would be *Lord of the Rings*-like. I wasn't at the place where I had a lifelong ambition to make a film of *The Lord of the Rings*. I'd read the book once and really liked it. But I felt it would be out of my reach . . . You just naturally assume it's an impossibility. (McDonald 2001–2)

It very nearly was. The rights belonged to Saul Zaentz, a film producer who made his money as the agent for the 1960s rock band Creedence Clearwater Revival. Zaentz's film credits include *The English Patient*, a project that had been rescued from cancellation by Harvey Weinstein, one of two brothers whose independent film production house Miramax had an impressive record of hits, including *Platoon*. In January 1998, after meetings with Weinstein, Zaentz agreed to sell the rights, and Miramax gave Jackson and partner Fran Walsh the go-ahead to start work on a script. This was to be a two-part version, but then the Walt Disney Company, anxious to expand its base into more adult-oriented feature films from its own brand (Touchstone Films), bought Miramax. Disney was reluctant to budget the US$75 million project, and Weinstein began an elaborate search for other studio backers. In June 1998, the lack of results from this search led Weinstein to tell Jackson there was enough money for only one movie. Jackson and Walsh flew to Los Angeles from Aotearoa New Zealand to tell Miramax they could not countenance doing the film on that basis.

During the long flight, however, Jackson's American agent Ken Kamins had negotiated a deal with Weinstein: Jackson had four weeks to find a backer for the two-film version who would also pay for Weinstein's US$12 million costs on acquiring rights, plus script, design, and technical development. Miramax also negotiated executive producer credits for the Weinstein brothers and 5 per cent of the box office gross (the takings before tax).

Returning to Wellington, Jackson and Walsh produced a 26-minute showreel of test CGI and landscape shots. They took this back to Los Angeles, but their first meeting with Polygram collapsed because the film wing was being sold to Universal. Their last chance was a meeting with Bob Shaye, founding director of New Line. This is how Pryor takes up the story:

> The meeting did not begin promisingly. Shaye felt the need to tell Jackson that whatever was about to happen, he would love to work with him on other projects. He also mentioned that he didn't like *The Frighteners*. Jackson and Walsh sat nervously with their agent as the tape rolled, half-expecting Shaye to press stop before seeing any of the video. Here was Jackson, sitting next to a precipice, armed only with a 36-minute [*sic*] promotional tape, and Bob Shaye was the last man in Hollywood who might build a bridge to the dream waiting on the other side.
>
> When the tape finished, Shaye's comment was, 'I don't get it. Why would you want to do two *Lord of the Rings* films?'
>
> At first Jackson did not know what Shaye could possibly be meaning. But when it became clear that the *Rings* might work better as three movies rather than two, Jackson began to kick his agent under the table. (Pryor 2003: 235–6)

(An alternative version of this anecdote has Shaye asking, 'So tell me why someone would pay $9 to see this when they could pay $27?' (MacNamara 2001–2).) Jackson and Walsh flew back to Wellington to start work.

Shaye established New Line in 1967 as a non-theatrical distributor, one specialising in films for schools and universities, and for film societies, catering particularly to the campus special event market, like the 1936 kitsch classic *Reefer Madness*. Moving into theatrical distribution in 1973, Shaye focused on a combination of art house and cult movies with a mix of rock documentaries and queer cinema. From 1978, New Line began investing in pre-production deals to secure distribution rights to films still in production. The breakthrough came with the 1984 low-budget horror *A Nightmare on Elm Street*, which not only made a significant profit but spawned a series of increasingly profitable *Elm Street* films. Another franchise that became a runaway success was *Teenage Mutant Ninja Turtles*, the most successful independent film ever made, and its two sequels. Lewis notes that

> New Line's franchises recall Paramount's adherence to 'tent pole' movies: in the mid-1980s, Paramount built their release schedule around commercial tent poles like the *Indiana Jones*, *Star Trek* and *Beverley Hills Cop* movies, which could support less viable projects. For New Line, the franchise permitted two developments: the creation of a home video division, and a separate distribution division, Fine Line Features, devoted to more specialised, hard-to-market films. While many New Line films had been distributed through RCA / Columbia Pictures Home Video, the benefits of retaining video rights were clear: control of another window of release and the advantage of further coordination of the theatrical-video release programme.
>
> As early as 1983, New Line announced that they would split their product into mainstream and specialty items . . . The move has allowed New Line to produce more commercial fare and to have stars as insurance for their films. Most conspicuously, in 1994, New Line's product included two Jim Carrey vehicles, the comedy / special effects movie *The Mask* and another film for which they paid $7 million for his talents, *Dumb and Dumber*. Ridiculed in the press at the time . . . both films became blockbusters, with *The Mask* making $119 million and *Dumb and Dumber* $127 million domestically. (1998: 78)

Among more recent franchise successes are the *Austin Powers* and *Rush Hour* series.

Fine Line meanwhile struggled with a series of flops, but made significant inroads with *The Player* and the unexpectedly successful *Shine*. One can see a shared aesthetic between New Line and Jackson, whose earlier splatter films included a tongue-in-cheek humour, but whose *Heavenly Creatures* was a surprise art-house hit. The company's success was sealed in 1993 with its US$600 million purchase by Ted Turner, founder of CNN, who was looking for content for his new cable channels, TBS and TNT. As with Miramax, purchased the same year by Disney, New Line were to keep their own production slate, and control over releasing and distribution, although in some instances – for example, David Cronenberg's controversial *Crash* – there were rumours of Turner's intervention in releasing. The Turner Corporation was then the subject of a merger with Time-Warner at the millennium's close. As a wholly owned subsidiary of Turner Broadcasting, now embedded in the largest media conglomerate on earth, New Line retained enough independence to engage the three-film project, and enough capital to see it through.

Fruit of a merger between Warner Communication and Time Inc. in January 1990, Time-Warner

> is divided into several divisions: AOL, Cable, Filmed Entertainment, Networks, Music and Publishing ... *Warner Brothers Pictures* had sales of nearly $7 billion in 2001, thanks to top-grossing *Harry Potter and the Sorcerer's Stone*, as well as other notable hits ... Turner Broadcasting also owns *Castle Rock Entertainment*, a production company responsible for *When Harry Met Sally*, *A Few Good Men*, and *The Shawshank Redemption*. The company also produces television programming, including *Seinfeld*. (Wasko 2003: 63–4)

Wasko's comprehensive listing of the company's holdings includes, among other notable brands, the CNN network and HBO (Home Box Office, a pay-per-view cable station that produces both films and highly successful television like *The Sopranos*); the Warner, Elektra, Atlantic, and WEA record labels; Little Brown and Warner Books publishers, and hundreds of magazines including *Time*, *Fortune*, *People*, *Sports Illustrated*, *Woman's Weekly*, *Woman's Own*, and *Marie Claire*. Time-Warner was one of the first big media companies to take a major interest in the Internet and the World Wide Web. Having burned their fingers with an earlier attempt to replicate their successful magazine formats online, in 2001 the company moved to acquire AOL (America Online), the largest service provider and most popular internet gateway in the US. Unfortunately, the purchase predated the dot.bomb crash: as with so many other Internet-based companies, AOL had over-estimated its revenues. On 24 October 2002, well into the release period of *LOTR*, the *Hollywood Reporter* noted that

> AOL Time Warner on Wednesday posted a third-quarter profit and reaffirmed its projections for full-year 2002 but said it will restate two years of financials after an accounting review at its America Online unit uncovered improperly recorded sales.
>
> The restatement will reduce the AOL division's revenue by $168 million and cash flow by $97 million for the period, which extends from third-quarter 2000 through second-quarter 2002.

The adjustments account for 1% of AOL's total revenue and 1.9% of its cash flow for the two-year period.

In addition, other AOL TW divisions will see a $22 million downward revision in revenue for advertising they delivered in cooperation with AOL.

. . .

Analysts have said that weakened momentum at AOL and falling cable valuations will force AOL TW to write down the value of its holdings by billions of dollars.

. . .

AOL TW's third-quarter results were mostly in line with Wall Street expectations, with net income of $57 million, compared with a loss of $997 million. Both figures exclude results from cable systems whose management AOL TW recently handed to Advance/Newhouse.

The world's largest media conglomerate also said revenue rose 6% to $10 billion, while cash flow fell 1% to $2.2 billion.

While growth momentum at the film, cable and TV network units was strong, AOL continued to exhibit weakness.

. . .

AOL TW's filmed entertainment unit saw revenue grow 25% and cash flow rise 8% thanks mainly to strong home video releases, including *The Lord of the Rings: The Fellowship of the Ring* and *Harry Potter and the Sorcerer's Stone*. DVD sales doubled year-over-year, the company said. ('AOL TW posts profitable Q3' 2002: 1)

The tribulations of the conglomerate involve sums that put *LOTR's* budget in the shade. The year 2003 was a good one for top music acts Linkin Park and the Red Hot Chili Peppers, but AOL, anxiously awaiting the impact of new software and of Microsoft's competition for new subscribers, experienced a significant downturn. In February 2003, the *Hollywood Reporter* ran another headline: 'AOL TW skids into record books: conglomerate registers $98.7 billion loss for 2002'. The only light for the troubled company was that

AOL TW's revenue for the fourth quarter came in at $11.4 billion, up 8% when adjusted for recent transactions and slightly ahead of most analysts' expectations. The gain was driven by 16% growth in the company's film business thanks to such blockbuster releases as *Harry Potter and the Chamber of Secrets* and *The Lord of the Rings: The Two Towers*. (Harris 2003: 53)

Things did not improve for Time-Warner in 2003, with a 25 per cent decline in magazine sales and the loss of 700,000 AOL subscribers. In this climate, the success of New Line's *LOTR* films was all the more significant:

The 'Lord of the Rings' film trilogy from subsidiary New Line is a tentpole franchise that could contribute $1.5 billion in profit to Time Warner's corporate coffers over time . . .

'Once you have a successful movie, it drives revenue down the line', says Mark May, senior analyst with Kaufman Brothers. ' "Lord of the Rings" has driven a 150% increase in DVD sales' for Time Warner . . .

Peter Mirsky, media analyst at Oppenheimer, said the payoff from the trilogy will be 40% box office, 35% home video, 5% to 10% TV and 15% merchandise.

Mirsky's calculations begin with a worldwide box office figure of $2.5 billion for the three films. 'The Fellowship of the Ring' has earned more than $860 million (7th all time biggest take) since its 2001 release, while 'The Two Towers' has earned $918.6 million (5th all time) since its 2002 release. .

'Return of the King' must only come in third to its two predecessors – making $800 million (80 million admissions at $10 a ticket) and taking the trilogy to a $2.5 billion total. Half the box office revenue goes to theater owners, according to Mirsky, who estimates production and marketing costs for the three films at $600 million.

That leaves Time Warner with a tidy $650 million profit from box office alone.

And Marcy Magiera, editor of VideoBusiness, expects each of the three films will probably deliver around $400 million in video sales and rentals, plus another $100 million bump from the eventual release of the three-film deluxe box set.

'The Two Towers', for example, sold a cool 3.5 million DVDs (list price $29.95) and VHS tapes in one day on its August 26 debut.

Mirsky, who noted 'DVD is mostly pure profit', added that ABC bought broadcast rights to 'Fellowship' and 'Two Towers' for a tidy $135 million. Even toy sales will bring in an estimated $30 million to $40 million. (Goldstein 2003)

The accounting procedures behind these figures are more complex than they seem. For example, *Broadcasting & Cable* reported on 4 February 2002, 'AOL Time Warner nets The WB, TNT and TBS Superstation will pony up at least $75 million for New Line Cinema's *Lord of the Rings: The Fellowship of the Ring* and two upcoming sequels', observing that New Line as well as the three cable stations were all AOL-Time-Warner subsidiaries (Albiniak 2002: 19). Indeed, TNT and TBSD are part of the same division within the company. Further complexities enter the picture when co-production companies enter the scene, in the case of *LOTR* even quite late in proceedings. *Variety* reported in October 2000 that

A German investment company is offering local investors with at least $43,000 to spare the chance to share in the magic and glamour of Hollywood.

Hannover Leasing is establishing a DM350.5 million ($150 million) fund to finance *The Return of the King*, the third installment of New Line Cinema's $270 million *Lord of the Rings* Hobbit trilogy.

Such investment schemes are usually offered toward the end of the financial year to high-bracket earners looking to bring down their taxable income. (Meza 2000)

Commenting on the fact that the trilogy's third film had already completed principal photography by the time Hannover came on board, Michael Cullen responded thus to a question posed by the Aotearoa New Zealand weekly *The Listener*:

Does it bother Cullen that the first two films are being written off against our tax base as New Zealand films, while one third of the trilogy is serving in Germany as a German tax vehicle? 'Mmmm', Cullen says, thinking the matter over. 'It concerns me but we cannot do anything about it. The law was absolutely clear under which the *Lord of the Rings* financing structure was created. . . .' So if New Line can take tax benefits from two countries while playing the rules in each jurisdiction then . . . lucky old them? 'That's exactly right'. (Campbell 2001: 19)

Like all film companies and perhaps with more reason, New Line was ready to make the most of any tax loopholes available.

Investments like those established through Hannover Leasing require a return, which may be calculated in a number of ways. One is through tax write-offs, where even a failure to break even brings financial benefits to investors. For other investors, a profit is essential. As we have seen, Harvey Weinstein secured a 5 per cent (often referred to as 5 points) interest in the gross. This participation may fall before or after breakeven. This is the point at which a film's earnings move into 'net profit', a term defined by Daniels, Leedy, and Sills as 'Gross receipts, less 1. Distribution fees, 2. Distribution expenses, and 3. Production costs (which may include overhead, interest, and gross participations); plus, deferments out of first net profits or participants in gross receipts before breakeven' (1998: 227). As Wasko notes,

The industry uses highly unusual procedures including reporting accounts differently for profit participation and other purposes (tax accounting etc.). Thus, the claim that Hollywood keeps 'multiple sets of books for the same picture' is technically true. For profit participants, studios regularly report revenue when it is collected (cash accounting) and expenses when they occur (accrual accounting). In all other industries, either one method or the other is used, but not both. While claims are made that this policy is necessary because of the nature of the industry and that profit participants are not cheated, it is a highly controversial issue which even accountants disagree on. As one accountant concludes, 'Generally accepted accounting principles for financial reporting have little effect on reporting motion picture results to outside participants'. (2003: 99–100, citing Leedy 1980: 14)

Figures are used to advertise the film (especially when setting box-office records or passing the symbolic US$100 million mark in receipts), to attract investors, and to reassure stockholders. They are also used to minimise tax liabilities, and to guide the share of revenues going to investors, distributors, and other companies with an interest in the film. Zaentz, who acquired the rights to Tolkien's books from United Artists in 1976 and optioned the rights to Miramax with significant profit participation clauses, took out a legal case against New Line in August 2004 for up to US$20 million.

> According to the complaint, Zaentz was to receive a percentage of adjusted gross receipts of New Line and New Line's sales agents, distributors and distributing agents, without deductions for fees and other expenses.
>
> Zaentz claims that New Line's calculations have been based on receipts that the studio receives after the foreign distribs take their cuts. The difference, Zaentz says, is $198 million, and he says 10% of that is owed to him. Zaentz also seeks an additional $700,000 in compensatory damages.
>
> Zaentz claims that New Line has failed and refused to provide his auditors 'with documentation necessary to determine whether other monies are due' under the license agreement. According to the complaint, Zaentz and New Line began mediation last month, but that the studio 'continues to fail and refuses to acknowledge its obligation'. (Harris 2004: 1, 10)

All Hollywood figures should therefore be taken with a grain of salt.

Moreover, many of the legal, contractual, and financial arrangements surrounding Hollywood films are fiercely guarded trade secrets. It is unclear, for example, how much Burger King paid to secure merchandising rights for *Fellowship* in its ten thousand outlets, a deal set three months before the release of the first film (McNary and Swanson 2001: 55), nor how much the major sponsors JVC, Barnes & Noble, and General Mills paid for their involvement. Unlike the majority of big Hollywood films, *LOTR*'s fantasy setting did not permit product placement. (New Line is believed to hold the record for the number and value of product placements in the second *Austin Powers* movie.) Merchandising was therefore all the more significant, but the sums involved are usually extremely difficult to ascertain. The movie merchandising year's key event is Licensing International, which celebrated its twenty-fifth anniversary in 2005. The 2004 show featured New Line still working its massive franchise licensing campaign for *LOTR*, a franchise licensing programme, which

> has generated more than $750 million in retail sales worldwide.
>
> The latest onslaught of J. R. R. Tolkien-inspired tie-ins will include a board game, action figures and collectibles.

Hasbro, which has already issued 'Rings' versions of Trivial Pursuit, Monopoly and Risk, will introduce 'Stratego: The Lord of the Rings' next month.
Several lines of action figures will be coming from NECA/Reel Toys, Play Along and Toy Biz. ('Return of the "Rings" merch' 2004: 13)

Vivendi Universal, the conglomerate formed during the brief ownership of Universal Studios by the French Vivendi Group, acquired rights to develop games from the novels, while New Line licensed Electronic Arts (EA) to produce film-related games, starting with *Towers*. Also known for its games franchised from the world's leading sport associations (FIFA, NHL, NBA, and others), 'on 29 January 2003 EA announced that it would build a large new studio in Los Angeles, reporting that it had nearly doubled its profits for the last quarter of 2002 based on its movie-linked games tied to the James Bond, Harry Potter and *The Lord of the Rings* franchises' (Thompson 2003: 59).

Collectibles include Toy Biz's Coronation set of figures in the costumes worn exclusively in the scene of Aragorn's ascent to the Gondorian throne in the third film, and NCEA/Reel Toys figurines that speak lines from the trilogy. In an unusual deal, Weta Workshop, the company that provided the physical effects for the trilogy and that Jackson part-owns, was able to use this aspect of marketing to help establish itself as a viable business. Jackson reported that

> in the middle of the *The Lord of the Rings* shoot we flew to New York for the day to pitch a new project to New Line that would provide us with continuity of work. The guy we were meeting with literally said 'Hit me son, you've got 10 minutes'. Five hours later the meeting finished and we'd secured the right to produce the merchandising for the *The Lord of the Rings* trilogy. We're doing this with US company Sideshow, because we lack their expertise in mass production and product marketing. This is unique in the film world – that the effects house is producing the merchandise – and it's allowed 48 people to continue working at the workshop. (*Onfilm* 2002: 15)

Meanwhile Jackson had returned to Wellington to begin work.

> When New Line announced *Rings* in August 1998, the proposed budget [for the trilogy] was 'more than $130 million', a figure that in reality sat closer to $US180 million. By the time the shoot began in October 1999, and Barrie Osborne (*The Matrix*) had signed on as producer, the figure stood at a more realistic $US270 million. The total is now thought to be closer to $US320 million, a figure in line with three medium/large Hollywood effects movies. (Pryor 2003: 279)

According to Pryor, New Line's new corporate boss Richard Parsons was already considering amalgamating New Line to Warner Bros. Pictures. A lot was riding on the success of *Fellowship*.

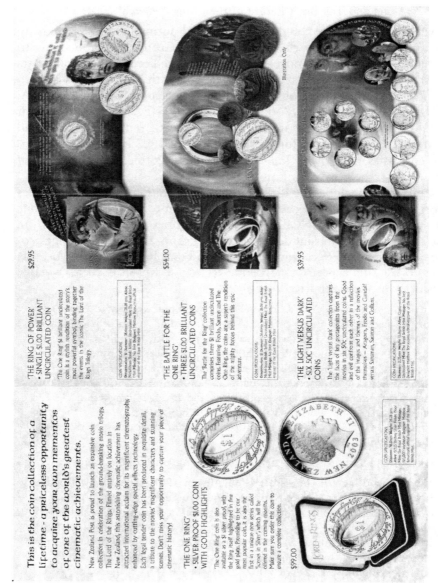

**Figure 30** State-sanctioned collectibles: New Zealand coins commemorating *The Lord of the Rings*.

### Production infrastructure

In this context, one can see why the production needed the services of lawyers. Working thousands of miles away from Los Angeles added to the legal problems, as happens with all runaway productions. Three Foot Six, Jackson's production company, hired the services of the Auckland firm Simpson Grierson to provide legal advice for the New Zealand end of the business. According to the law firm's website, their tasks typically involve

- employment and contractor issues with New Zealand and overseas cast and crew
- health and safety laws and risk minimisation strategies
- immigration and customs issues
- assisting with production exigencies
- New Zealand taxation issues (including GST and income tax issues for key cast and crew)
- intellectual property issues, including rights acquisition and in-market protection
- location issues including environmental law, local government issues and advising on Department of Conservation issues
- financing and funding agreements. (Simpson Grierson 2004)

MarketNewZealand.com, an official website of New Zealand Trade and Enterprise (NZTE), the country's trade and economic development agency, reckons that 'screen production industry turnover is now worth between NZ$1 billion a year' (*sic*). NZTE also supports overseas productions shot in the country:

> Through its Large Budget Screen Production Grant for medium and large budget international screen productions, the Government offers a 12.5% rebate on New Zealand production spending over NZ$15 million. Economic Development Minister Jim Anderton, announcing the scheme in December 2003, said it would add to the attractiveness of New Zealand as a screen production location.
> 'Our creative edge, our technological innovations, our skills base and scenery already make an attractive package as a film production location. While there are no guarantees in this world, the Government believes this scheme will increase the chances that major productions will choose New Zealand as a film production location', he said.
> Anderton also pointed out that major productions are important for New Zealand's screen industry as they provide continuity of employment, accelerated skills development and technology transfer.

Another NZTE document of 2003 specifies the agencies most attuned to overseas film production. In addition to the NZFC (see below),

Investment New Zealand's *Screen Production in New Zealand* brochure promotes two main bodies:

> Film New Zealand aims to ensure that everyone has a satisfying experience when filming in New Zealand, and will do everything in its power to ensure this happens.
>
> Film New Zealand's network reaches throughout the country, and can provide a fast and educated response to any inquiry from its comprehensive database and information resources – whether for a feature film, a telemovie, a miniseries, a commercial, or an extended location shoot.
>
> Film New Zealand can also liaise with and coordinate contacts with New Zealand's growing network of regional film offices who can provide further on-the-spot assistance. Its website can give you a quick and exciting introduction to filming in New Zealand. Check out its substantial section on locations. www.filmnz.com
>
> Investment New Zealand, the country's investment promotion agency, is the primary link between international filmmakers and the New Zealand public sector. It has a dedicated Creative Investment Manager charged with helping filmmakers cut through red tape, obtain the answers they need, and commence filming as quickly as possible. Via its partnerships with New Zealand Trade posts and the Ministry of Foreign Affairs and Trade – with more than 50 locations round the world – Investment New Zealand can help you begin your New Zealand research from your home base. New Zealand Trade Commissions can also help with inquiries about immigration.

Although film productions are erratic sources of income, the amount of spending associated with them is significant to local and national economies, so much so that many European and North American cities now boast film commissions whose task is to attract and serve incoming shoots, if necessary deploying tax breaks as an incentive, as well as finding locations and negotiating with local law enforcement, fire, health and safety, and other regulatory bodies. *LOTR* established Wellington firms Weta Digital and Weta Workshop and the Jackson co-owned Stone Street Studios and Park Road Post, as well as specialist effects house Oktobor. Governments around the world encourage such high-value and highly visible firms, both to secure prestigious and high-paying employment, and to form the centre of new economic sectors. The values associated with these policies are summarised in a report commissioned from the New Zealand Institute of Economic Research by the New Zealand Film Commission. In their summary, the authors argue that,

> with the release of *The Fellowship of the Ring*, and the continuing post-production of the next two features, transitional effects include the following highlights (all in NZ dollars):

- $352.7 million expenditure by the production company in New Zealand (to March 2002). The above New Zealand expenditure includes:

  - labour costs of $187.7 million
  - digital effects costs of $99 million
  - miniatures and creature costs of $36.5 million
  - location costs of $31.3 million
  - construction costs of $25.1 million
  - transportation costs of $12 million

- This level of expenditure produced peak period employment of around 1500 people per week (This number does not include any day labour or extras).
- It is about 3,200 person years employment of New Zealand tax residents for the four years from 1997 to 2001.
- Around 5000 vendors were used, most of them in New Zealand.
- Expenditure will continue as the next two films are prepared for release. (Yeabsley and Duncan 2002: vi)

A year later, however, as the production of *LOTR* wound down, another taskforce warned that

> foreign productions that are attracted principally by the low cost of New Zealand as a filming location are commonly known as 'runaways' – they are often controversial. They bring both risks and benefits to the domestic industry.
>
> The benefits of 'runaway' productions include: employment opportunities; adding value to the craft skills of industry practitioners through working on larger budget productions and in a wide variety of teams; expenditure in peripheral industries (e.g. rental vehicles, accommodation, catering); generating a worldwide knowledge of the skills and talents available in New Zealand; and providing cashflow for infrastructure in New Zealand – this in turn means service providers can offer expanded services to the domestic industry.
>
> The risks attached to 'runaway' productions are that crew prices can become inflated for domestic users; and where local production partners or personnel are not involved, local working conditions, safety and legal requirements can be overlooked. Managing these risks is important for the industry. (Screen Production Industry Taskforce 2003: 40)

Jackson's relationship with these government-led initiatives has often been fraught. In a 2004 interview with the *Hollywood Reporter*, he makes a typically robust case:

> I feel that the N. Z. film industry has been floundering without strong direction from the film commission or support from the government. You can only judge an industry by the films it produces each year, and in my

mind, the New Zealand films of the past 10 years have seemed less interesting than the decade before that. Or maybe I'm just getting older.
A decade ago, the film commission made a policy of trying to create a
producer-led industry in New Zealand. Unfortunately, there are very few
producers in this country who know anything about developing good screenplays or making good movies. On the other hand, develop a great screenplay under the supervision of a good director, and there will be any number
of competent producers who can make the thing happen. It was a policy
that has hobbled, restrained and frustrated the country's writers and directors, whilst all these people walk around calling themselves producers, soak-
ing up development money and achieving nothing. It has produced 10 years
worth of weak films. A film industry should be built on its talent, i.e. writers and directors. They should be identified, nurtured and supported. In
my opinion, most of the tiny N. Z. Film Commission budget should be
targeting the country's six best writers and six best directors, investing in
their talent. Unfortunately, such a focused strategy flies in the face of the
film commission's mandate to support anybody who can fill out the forms
correctly and jump through the hoops. ('Peter Jackson: Filmmaker' 2004)

When cultural and financial arguments arose over the debts owed to
one of Jackson's companies by Kahukura, a small New Zealand production company, Jackson responded in part by rescinding the NZFC
representatives' invitations to the Wellington premiere of *Towers* (see
Pryor 2003: 201–18). He also told the Aotearoa New Zealand trade
magazine *Onfilm*,

now what's worrying me a little bit is that we're shifting into this mode
where there's huge emphasis on co-productions – these British producers
came over and everyone's got very excited about the possibilities of co-
productions. Which in themselves are great, but too much emphasis on
that is going to mean New Zealand actors don't get much work because
they're going to import their actors, New Zealand post-production facilities are not going to get much work because they're going to shoot their
films here and take them back to Britain to do the post production – it's
always a one-way street too, we never see British shot movies coming over
here to do their post production, it's always one way traffic. So the New
Zealand film industry is effectively going to become a service industry for
British co-productions. And that's not healthy either. (Grant 2003: 2)

Later in the same interview, however, Jackson seems to contradict this
doubtful view of international productions in relation to the development of production and post-production infrastructure in Wellington:

I'm taking a gamble because I'm building a post production facility that
I know is not financially viable in New Zealand – I'm being foolhardy in
what I'm doing in some respects, and I'm hoping like hell that, by presenting a world-class mixing facility and laboratory and digital grading

and all the video post production, it'll be attractive to films from outside of the country – like Asian movies, some Australian films perhaps.

If I can build a facility that's better than anything in Australia, better than anything in Korea, better than anything in Hong Kong – which is my aim, I'm trying to make it as good as I can – I'm hoping it'll be attractive to other people. If that doesn't happen then I'm stuffed, because the New Zealand films that are being made will never sustain the sheer scale and cost of what I'm doing.

What I'm trying to do is make overseas productions the bread and butter of the facility, so New Zealand films can benefit from the fact that there's one of the best mixing facilities in the world here. (Ibid.)

The strategy appears to have been to use some of the spend on the films to establish the existing Weta companies, plus what would become Stone Street Studios. Prior to starting work on the trilogy, Jackson bought what was left of the National Film Unit, a resource whose facilities and services included film processing. On the one hand, this obviated the need to send materials overseas for processing and post-production, a costly and slow way of working. On the other hand, it maximised the amount of work staying onshore and going to companies in which Jackson himself had a major interest. The result: world-class production resources and a group of skilled film technicians based in Wellington.

Not everyone in Aotearoa was convinced of the strategy's virtue, however. Regretting the absence of tax breaks for cinema, Jackson only briefly mentions the breaks *LOTR* received, which became the object of public scrutiny during 2001.

The fact that New Zealand has shouldered the risks in making *The Lord of the Rings* has been well documented . . . Essentially the deals meant that the Americans did not have to finance the escalating budget. New Line could take its own money elsewhere until it buys back the *The Lord of the Rings* project some years later, by then from the box-office receipts. The deals also involve double dipping: whereby deductions are taken on film expenditure and also when the shell companies involved are sold later – even though, in the IRD [Inland Revenue Department]'s view, the same moneys are circling round this loop.

Belatedly in 1999, the government stopped the mechanism that made *The Lord of the Rings* possible, but – against strong IRD advice – the politicians then lost their nerve and chose to retain or 'grandparent' this tax mechanism for major film projects already underway. The needs of *The Lord of the Rings* became paramount. 'It was helped by the fact that it was election year', Cullen explains, 'and no-one wanted to look like they were out to destroy hobbits in election year' . . .

So how much taxpayer money are we talking about? Michael Lynn of New Line told *Hollywood Reporter* in July that our tax incentives helped

to minimise the risks posed to his company by the $NZ600 million tri-
logy – to the tune of about $US10–12 million for each film. 'How can I
say this?' Cullen muses, when queried about the accuracy of Lynn's
figures. 'Let's hope he's right. I would feel quite happy', he says wryly,
'if that figure was the final and accurate one'. (Campbell 2001: 19)

In addition to the trilogy's controversial, and probably unrepeatable,
tax breaks and services offered by government agencies acting to promote
runaway productions in Aotearoa New Zealand, other benefits included
the labour force's flexibility and ingenuity along with some unexpected aid.

> All that stuff at the Black Gates, all that stuff when Viggo's on the horse
> doing the speech to the soldiers, they're all kiwi soldiers, we were shoot-
> ing it on that live firing area up by Ruapehu, it was the only place in New
> Zealand we could find flat desert terrain, we needed that sandy desert,
> but we found it, the army let us on their land in Waiouru, you know, the
> land that you're never allowed to go on, and we found this perfect bloody
> spot which was all just flat. And they said well, this is full of unexploded
> bombs. This is our live firing area, we've used this for 40 years, since WWII
> and there's so much unexploded munitions there, and we couldn't find
> anywhere else, and so the Govt ordered the army to go in and clear it all
> out for us, and they did all this minesweeping of this whole big area, and
> they just took away all this unexploded ordinance, old rusty old bloody
> bombs, and then we had a big lecture on the day that we arrived there,
> the army had a table out, and they had all these bombs on the table, and
> they said listen, these are all things that we've recovered from this area,
> so if you see any of these, don't move, just put up your hand and one of
> our bomb disposal guys will come over, and that was pretty surreal!
> (ScoopNews 2003)

The army, which also did major construction work for the Hobbiton
and Edoras sets, belonged to the low-tech end of the enterprise. Equally significant was the development of a communications infrastructure
allowing the numerous second units to communicate with Jackson during the shoot, and then Weta Digital with Jackson while he worked in
London on the music edit.

> Although the video conferencing system was originally conceived for
> video communications only, the ability to integrate phone and network
> services became a critical part of the operation. The production crew used
> high frequency radio transmitters and military grade fiber optic cable to
> connect crews operating at great distances. Once the signal was received,
> it was fed through the analog video inputs on the back of the Polycom
> video conferencing system and was ready for transmission. The footage
> was then transmitted over satellite to the director, whether he was in the
> central studio or out on-location. (*Power Meetings Update* 2004)

On a smaller scale, Richard Taylor told *American Cinematographer* that 'for the four years of production, I wore a radio telephone that had an earpiece and a mouthpiece. I could be talking to a group of people while other information was coming through the earpiece, and I could hold other meetings using the "yes" and "no" button on the RT' (Magid 2001b: 61). This information and communication technology infrastructure was integral to the success of the trilogy's complex production procedures during the shoot, as were the trans-Pacific capabilities of the Southern Star cable and telecommunication satellites that allowed Jackson to make use of the time differences between Aotearoa New Zealand and Los Angeles, sending dailies electronically to New Line during the Wellington night to receive responses from the producers the following day.

### Profits

New Line and Warner Bros undertook major distribution of the trilogy, with rights licensed for both cinema and video or DVD release to specialist companies for each of the territories in which the movies played. The trilogy's budgets, estimated by IMDb Pro at US$93 million for the first and US$94 million for each of the other two films, may have been as large as $US320 million.

> Around $US160 million of this budget was covered by a series of pre-sales deals which New Line had arranged with distribution companies around the globe – with the companies agreeing to exhibit all three films, sight unseen. *Harry Potter* was released in most countries by Warner Brothers, which helps explain why it might have been a little more devoted to its success than to *Rings*. *Variety* compared the distribution of *Fellowship* to 'a guerrilla campaign fought by a loose network of local tribes with an unrivalled knowledge of the terrain'. Some of these local companies were in danger of going out of business if their gamble on the *Rings* failed. (Pryor 2003: 279)

As ever, all the figures that follow must be taken with a grain of salt. *Fellowship* grossed $314,776,170 in the domestic (US and Canada) market, and $556,592,194 overseas, for a total of $871,368,364. *Towers* took $341,786,758 domestic and $584,500,642 overseas, for a worldwide total of $926,287,400. *Return*'s domestic gross was $377,027,325, which with overseas takings of $741,861,654 brought it to worldwide box office receipts of $1,118,888,979. The films placed respectively ninth, fourth, and second among all-time worldwide box-office successes, and sixteenth, eleventh, and seventh in the domestic all-time listings. In their Wednesday and Thursday previews, *Return* took

$51,470,821, *Towers* $40,038,684, and *Fellowship* $27,917,978, with first week figures of $120,199,783 for *Return*, $111,143,998 for *Towers*, and $89,248,852 for *Fellowship* (figures in US dollars from boxofficemojo.com). boxofficemojo's Brandon Gray reported that '*The Lord of the Rings: The Return of the King* raked in an estimated $34.1 million domestically on 7,205 screens at 3,703 theaters on its opening day, according to distributor New Line Cinema' (Gray 2003).

IMDb Pro indicates US video rentals for the first week of release for each film at $17,200,000 for *Fellowship*, $22,890,000 for *Towers*, but a surprisingly low $9,790,000 for *Return*, with totals from US rentals in the region of $83m for the first, $66m for the second, and $39m for the third film, reflecting a shift from store rentals to video-on-demand and other delivery services. The DVD format became a critical profit centre for the trilogy when they were released in both theatrical and extended versions. The release to home formats began well: 'Currently, a sales record for the first day has been set in the UK with *The Lord of the Rings* selling 1.27 million copies' (New Line 2002). Also in the UK the British Videogram Association announced that 2003 total sales of 140 million units, featuring *Towers* and continuing sales of *Fellowship* in the top five, were up 75 per cent from 2002. The announcement also noted the advance of DVD over VHS formats, as compared with figures from Aotearoa New Zealand distributor Roadshow Entertainment who expected to ship 185,000 units of *Fellowship* for its November 2002 release; instead, it shipped 130,000 units on VHS and 85,000 on DVD. In Australia, Roadshow announced the biggest first week of sales in the history of DVD, a 49.1 per cent market share for the week in DVD plus a 54 per cent market share in VHS, resulting in the highest recorded market share for a distributor in the history of either format. According to DVDanswers, 'UK distributor "Entertainment in Video" reported that *The Lord of the Rings: The Fellowship of the Ring* sold 1.27 million units on August 7, compared to Potter's 1.25 million sold within 24 hours on May 11' (DVDanswers 2002). Hollywood.com repeated *Hollywood Reporter's* story that 'The DVD and VHS release of *The Lord of the Rings: The Two Towers* on Tuesday picked up the record for the best first day of any home video released so far this year, selling 3.5 million and taking in an estimated $60–$70 million' (Bowen 2003). There were fears that the third title might not be so lucky:

> The two previous extended-edition DVDs of the first two *Rings* installments arrived in mid-November at the beginning of the holiday shopping season. But this third DVD required more time to complete because of the scope of the project, says Stephen Einhorn, president of New Line Home

Entertainment. New Line may miss some holiday shoppers, but die-hard fans 'will buy it no matter when it comes out, especially this final Oscar-winning episode', says *DVD Exclusive* editor Scott Hettrick. (Snider 2004)

However, *Hollywood Reporter* had already noted in June that the theatrical version sold more than 6.3 million copies in its first week on VHS and DVD in the US. Preliminary data for the home video release of the extended version of *Return* seem already spectacular, with Amazon noting that DVD sales in the week ending 12 December set a one-week record. 'Lord of the Rings, Return of the King Extended Edition' made a single-title, one-day record of 13,000 orders on 14 December (*Yahoo News* 2004).

All in all, the profit associated with the trilogy and its spin-offs has dwarfed the gambles made at the project's start. There remain yet more avenues for exploitation as well, for example, in the form of computer games, to be discussed in the chapter that follows.

# 25

# The ludic integration of the game and film industries: *The Lord of the Rings* computer games as entertainment meritocracies

*Brett Nicholls*

The movie-licence games *The Lord of the Rings: The Two Towers* and *The Lord of Rings: The Return of the King* offer insights into the operation of the computer games industry and its location within contemporary media. EA (Electronic Arts) Games, producers of the *LOTR* games, entered into a contractual arrangement with New Line Cinema as copyright owners of the *LOTR* films for the right to use the *LOTR* films as the basis for the *LOTR* games. This franchise directly links the games to the event film phenomenon. At the same time the games are aesthetic accessories to these event films, using and remaining faithful to images of the landscape, characters, diegetic and nondiegetic sound, narrative structure, and cinematographic style of *LOTR*. The games also offer additional unlockable features in the form of screen shots, pre-production artwork, interviews with the films' stars, and previews of the films.

The contractual arrangement between EA Games and New Line Cinema sought to benefit both companies. In addition to the hefty licensing, for New Line Cinema the front-loading of the games added to the projected audience's anticipation of the release of the films and extended the reach of the films' promotions. EA Games, on the other hand, got the opportunity to cash in on the *LOTR* event as a cultural phenomenon.

The packaging of the games clearly buys into the films' success. To play the *LOTR* games, as the packaging declares, is to 'DECIDE THE FATE OF MIDDLE-EARTH', 'be the hero of Middle-earth', 'live the movie', or 'live the power of the epic movies'. Players are thus not invited to extend their knowledge of the *LOTR* universe; they are situated as participants in a structure that promises to deliver the pre-constituted world of the films.

**Figure 31** Integrating the film and computer game industries.

This chapter explores the 'design problem' that marks *Towers* and *Return* across the PS2, Xbox, Gamecube, PC, and Gameboy Advanced platforms (EA offers two other *LOTR* games – *The Battle for Middle-earth* and *The Third Age*). This chapter also considers the media's political economy and, by drawing on the critical vocabulary that has emerged within game studies, it traces the relationship between the production context and the form of the games. The design problem in question emerges in the relationship between what can be delineated as the filmic and the 'gamic' elements of the games. The term 'design problem' is meant to suggest that a clear link exists between the form of the games and the franchise arrangement between EA Games and New Line Cinema. The design task occurs in the tension between the franchise's responsibilities and the gaming market's expectations. The games' interfaces resolve this tension by situating game play in relation to a manufactured image of the world of film production. The games' interfaces are structured in terms of an ideology of entertainment as a reward for labour.

First, let us look at the production and reception of computer games. The demand for more intricate and interesting game designs, the difficult process of production, and highly competitive marketing and distribution networks exert budgetary pressures upon games' production teams. These pressures have produced a streamlined games industry dominated by three major distributors, EA Games being one of the large players along with Ubisoft and Microsoft. The gaming environments that this industrial complex produces for the most part reproduce conditions that resemble the competitive context in which games production teams are embedded (Stallabrass 1993). The *LOTR* games, for instance, lend themselves to what Jenkins calls a video game culture that parallels nineteenth-century forms of boy culture, where recognition among peers is gained competitively through 'daring as demonstrated in the virtual worlds of the game, overcoming obstacles, beating bosses, and mastering levels' (1998: 271). It is tempting to say that the competitive production environment has produced a homogeneous game market, and the industry does seem to be dominated by a 'play as power ethic', to borrow a term from Sutton-Smith (2001: 7–17). However, attention to the nuances and specificity of the production and form of games suggests otherwise. Computer games do not all produce the same types of competitive environments and reward systems. In effect, computer games act as specific sites for the exercise of power by multifaceted global media.

Within the games production environment the movie-licence game produces a particular design problem because computer games and cinema offer different aesthetic experiences. How can the film be successfully transformed into a game when, relative to cinema, which offers the spectator a pre-configured form to interpret, computer games are complex systems that offer dynamic pathways and trajectories through virtual spaces (Aarseth 1997)? The games player interprets the game's elements and makes the necessary decisions (by moving the avatar via the controller or keyboard and mouse) to configure, negotiate, and advance through the pathways that the game system offers. As Eskelinen puts it,

> the dominant user function in literature, theatre and film is interpretative, but in games it is the configurative one. To generalize: in art we might have to configure in order to be able to interpret whereas in games we

have to interpret in order to be able to configure, and proceed from the beginning to the winning or some other situation. (2001)

Within the gaming environment, narrative takes a back seat to the active process of the player negotiating the spatial field. Along with the games' backstory, narrative merely functions to provide the player with the necessary information to interpret the elements in the spatial field before proceeding to configure these elements in meaningful ways. In the case of the *LOTR* games the *LOTR* films function in this manner, providing, as Nicholls and Ryan put it, 'information in the form of *rules of orientation*' that enable players to 'engage successfully in the action of the game' (2004). Players make sense of screen objects, including the representation of the player on-screen, and then consider the relationship between objects in order to perform actions: to battle, solve, avoid, direct, etc. This process of making sense and decision-making within a structured spatial field constitutes the competitive gaming experience.

For many, this experience heralds the interactive revolution. Yet the process of configuring, for the most part, is not open-ended, but predetermined in that, to advance through the levels of the game, the player must master a set of predetermined tasks via the controlling mechanism. Players rarely pass levels the first time; they fail often (and may even resort to the cheat codes available online or in games magazines). They must repeat levels in order to gain sufficient mastery to succeed. The gaming experience frames the process of repetitive play within a system that measures and rewards performance. The *LOTR* games offer nothing unusual in so far as such systems operate widely within a range of games. But there is something unusual about the way that this system directs players to the world of the *LOTR* films. The games' interface sets up a relationship between game play and the unlockable features. This relationship directly relates to the franchise agreement between EA Games and New Line Cinema, an agreement that seeks to establish a seamless and profitable link between films and games. However, conclusions about this relationship depend on considerations of the games' formal aspects.

Newman provides a useful way to think about the relation between the measuring or reward system and the unlockable features. He identifies 'two fundamental states of engagement' within computer games, termed 'On-Line' and 'Off-Line'. Broadly, he writes:

On-Line refers to the state of ergodic participation[1] that we would, in a commonsense manner, think of as 'playing the game'. So, I'm On-Line when I'm actually playing *Metal Gear Solid* – when I'm Mario in *Super*

*Mario 64*; when I'm hurtling round a track in a souped-up Skyline in *Gran Turismo 3*. Off-Line engagement, could be seen as equating with non-ergodicity, and while it is important we do not allow ourselves to confuse this with passivity [*sic*] . . . Off-Line describes periods where no registered input control is received from the player. (2002)

We can extend this vocabulary in the case of the *LOTR* games. They offer two kinds of virtual pathways, most visible in the PC and console versions of the games. These interrelated pathways are structures that enable the games' producers to overcome efficiently the problem that the contractual arrangement between EA Games and New Line Cinema sets up. The online and offline elements of the games effectively connect the space of game play to the event of the films.

The first pathway functions online, that is, it enables the ergodic participation of the player in the actual space of game play. Cybertexts such as video games are 'ergodic' because the player works within a dynamic virtual space. This space is not purely interpretive, as is the cinema text, since the player must also work to configure the narrative space (Aarseth 1997: 64). The online pathway offers players the chance to play the roles of the key *LOTR* characters drawn directly from the film; they possess, as in conventional adventure narrative forms, unique characteristics and skills. In *Towers*, the player follows one path with Aragorn, Gimli, or Legolas, and can repeat this path with Isildur, who is unlocked when the Secret Level is passed. The Secret Level is itself unlocked when the last level, the Tower of Orthanc, is passed with at least one character at Level 10. In *Return* the player follows three distinct paths: that of the King (Aragorn, Legolas, or Gimli), the Wizard (Gandalf), and the Hobbits (Frodo or Sam). Passing the last level of the game, 'The Crack of Doom', with at least three characters at Level 10 unlocks a secret level, 'Saruman's Palantir'. This level can be played with any of the six existing characters or with the additional unlocked characters (Faramir, Pippin, or Merry).

On the online pathway the player begins with a basic skill set that can be expanded with the addition of specific weaponry at each level of the game. The game's object is to follow the path of the film characters and the part they play in the battle against Middle-earth's enemies. The stages of the films' epic journey give way to levels in the games. In the *Towers* game, for example, the player, in the form of a specific character, battles against enemies – Orcs, Ringwraiths, Uruk-hai, Wargs, etc. – and advances, from Weathertop, to the Gates of Moria, Balin's Tomb, to Amon Hen, through other key locations and finally to the Tower of Orthanc (which is structured with twenty floors of sublevels). At each level the aim is to defeat the enemies, keep 'life points' intact, and score 'attack points' through battle. These points enable the player to expand the character's skill set with 'upgrades' before advancing to the next level.

In the fray of battle at each level, the player receives an immediate indicator of the skill level of a particular battle move. An attack rating – 'fair', 'good', 'excellent', or 'perfect' – appears as text on screen as the player executes moves against the enemies. When Gimli is at Level 2 on the experience points rating in *Towers*, a move such as 'Balin's War Rush' consists of the player hacking at the enemy with Gimli's axe, then smashing his or her axe handle into the enemy's face, and finally driving the sharp point of the axe into the enemy's stomach (this move can be executed with X O R2, on the PS2 controller). The level of performance in executing such a move earns the player an attack rating that scores points on the skill meter. The points accrued via the skill meter can then be *spent* upon upgrading the attacks at the end of each level. Upgrades are then measured in terms of a level rating for each character: the higher the level, the wider the range of battle moves.

The basic structure of play along the online pathway is complemented by a visual style that attempts to recreate the film's epic thrust. The player engages visually with Middle-earth via a high-angle long shot throughout the game. This god-like point of view (POV) is standard for console, PC, and Gameboy Advanced versions of the games. Unlike a first-person shooter game, with its unsettling immediacy and limited POV that demands spatial decision-making, the god-like POV allows players to remain detached from the action. The *LOTR* games are strictly hack-and-slash affairs. Players simply wield their weapons against the forces of evil; strategising is unnecessary since there is never any doubt about direction, or any disorientation in space. The games are content to locate each battle within the films' larger narrative structure. In the films, we see each battle as a discrete task and each character as a contributor to the major task of destroying the ring and freeing Middle-earth from evil's tyranny. The part takes on meaning only in terms of the whole. In the *LOTR* games, each hack-and-slash battle is less about decision-making than performing a discrete task that fits into the overall scheme. The player never really gets to 'decide the fate of Middle-earth', as the games' packaging promises.

If the online pathways link the films and games formally, the offline pathways reveal the outcomes of the EA Games / New Line Cinema franchise. Three kinds of offline elements appear in the *LOTR* games. The first, embedded in the structure of online play, involves moments within the play environment over which the player has no control. These

include the loading of levels and narrative sequences that provide information. In the *LOTR* games the narrative sequences introduce levels
in the form of actual footage from the films. These film images then
transform into animated images before players can proceed through the
game level with their game character. Thus a clear relationship is set
up between the games and the film in that the player proceeds into action
in a space that is drawn directly from the film.

The second type of offline element, although outside the structure of
online play, directly affects it. These elements include breaks to configure
and reconfigure characters or vehicles, accessing the codes screen that
is unlocked when the game's levels have been completed, and accessing the game menu to advance to the next level. Separated from the
online play, the third type of offline element functions as an optional
extra in the form of unlockable features that players access via the game
interface in the form of a map. The Gameboy Advanced versions of
the games do not include a game map. The unlockable features, in the
form of screen shots from the film, are automatically included between
levels. And previews of the films are unlocked upon clocking each of
the *LOTR* games.

These offline elements enable the games to legitimate themselves by
drawing on the status of the *LOTR* films. As players proceed through
the levels of the game they are rewarded with access to pathways that
lead to virtual collectibles of the event films: screen-shots from the films,
pre-production artwork, film previews, and interviews with the films'
stars. The player does not proceed along these pathways as a character from the online space of game play. These offline elements do not
function in terms of the logic of the game play. They merely lift the
game's product beyond gaming into the world of entertainment commodities. As a reward for reaching specific levels in the game, the player
obtains access to images of film production and film stars at work. Elijah
Wood, Billy Boyd, Dominic Monaghan, Ian McKellen, and John Rhys-
Davies, among others, work and play on the games, and comment upon
the *LOTR* films and games.

The problem of producing a game version of the film while remaining faithful to the *LOTR* film product is engendered by the contractual
agreement between EA Games and New Line Cinema. The problem
that the *LOTR* games design throws up for media analysis is how to
understand critically the relation between the online and the offline
elements of the games. In other words, what is the relation between the
reward system in the field of play and the unlockable features that the
games offer in the form of virtual collectibles from the films?

The start of an answer lies in the function and the nature of ergodic participation. If to play is to master a set of skills that advance the player through the levels of the game and, as is the case with the *LOTR* games, open access to unlockable rewards, then the *LOTR* computer games work to direct ergodic participation toward specific ends. The structure of this direction reflects what Beller has called the 'Cinematic Mode of Production' (2003). He summarises this concept thus: 'Cinema develops a completely new method of value production and extraction by projecting the dynamics of political economy into the visual arena and by colonizing bodies by inducing them to labor in what amounts to a deterritorialized factory' (1998: 77). The development of cinema marks a shift from industrial capital, which gives rise to the social realist literary form, to an image-based capital, where the visual proliferates and dominates our understanding of the world of social relations. The technological basis for this shift situates subjects in new relations to their bodies and others. Indeed, discussions on contemporary experience must consider the technological structuring of the world of social relations. Information technologies, for instance, structure practices such that little or no distinction remains between work and play. This emphasis upon technological structuring is not technological determinism; it points out that social practices are inseparably linked to technological forms.

In the case of the computer games as a structuring technology, players quite literally configure the game's visual space directly with the body working upon the controlling mechanism. Ergodic participation is akin to working in a technical and formal structure that measures and rewards performance much like the world of work. It does not follow, of course, that to play computer games is to be positioned always as a cog in the capitalist machine. The range of computer games available today is varied and contradictory.

The *LOTR* games, however, clearly work to allegorise the split between work and leisure, with leisure (in the form of virtual collectibles) operating as a reward for successful work. The unlockable features function as virtual money in a labour system. In this instance, the *LOTR* films operate as entertainment commodities. They are, literally, functioning as a reward for work. The *LOTR* games are thus structured as meritocracies that reward labour with the spectacle of the *LOTR* films. They work not to enhance our knowledge of the *LOTR* universe through the creation of a critical distance but to funnel the player into the circuits of the *LOTR* films' event marketing. The games situate the player in the controlled and preconstituted circular world of work, exchange, and accumulation, or ergodic participation, rewards in the form of points, and access to film collectibles.

## Note

1 'Ergodic literature . . . requires special effort to comprehend or read, perhaps due to a "non linear" [*sic*] structure . . . Ergodic literature demands an active role of the reader, such that they become "users" who may need to perform complex semiotic operations to construct the reading' ('Ergodic literature' 2006).

# Part VII

# *The Lord of the Rings*: credits, awards, reviews

# 26

# Dossier: credits (courtesy of Internet Movie Database)

*Lord of the Rings: The Fellowship of the Ring, The* (2001)
Directed by: Peter Jackson

**Writing credits**
J. R. R. Tolkien: novel *The Fellowship of the Ring*
Frances Walsh: screenplay (as Fran Walsh)
Philippa Boyens: screenplay
Peter Jackson: screenplay

**Figure 32** Interior, Wellington airport, 2004: Banners promote *The Lord of the Rings* stamps, with OCEANIC ARTS in bottom right hand corner.

**Production**
Peter Jackson: producer
Michael Lynne: executive producer: New Line Cinema
Mark Ordesky: executive producer: New Line Cinema
Barrie M. Osborne: producer
Rick Porras: co-producer: WingNut Films
Tim Sanders: producer
Jamie Selkirk: co-producer: WingNut Films
Robert Shaye: executive producer: New Line Cinema
Ellen Somers: associate producer (as Ellen M. Somers)
Frances Walsh: producer (as Fran Walsh)
Bob Weinstein: executive producer
Harvey Weinstein: executive producer

**Cast (in credits order)**
Sean Astin: Sam Gamgee
Sala Baker: Sauron
Sean Bean: Boromir
Cate Blanchett: Galadriel
Orlando Bloom: Legolas Greenleaf
Billy Boyd: Pippin
Ian Holm: Bilbo Baggins
Ian McKellen: Gandalf
Christopher Lee: Saruman
Lawrence Makoare: Lurtz
Brent McIntyre: Witch-King
Sarah McLeod: Rosie Cotton
Dominic Monaghan: Merry
Viggo Mortensen: Aragorn
Ian Mune: Bounder
John Rhys-Davies: Gimli
Andy Serkis: Gollum
Harry Sinclair: Isildur
Liv Tyler: Arwen
David Weatherley: Barliman Butterbur
Hugo Weaving: Elrond
Elijah Wood: Frodo Baggins
Alan Howard: The Ring (voice)

**Original music**
David Donaldson: song 'Flaming Red Hair'
Enya: songs 'Aníron' & 'May It Be'
David Long: song 'Flaming Red Hair'

Steve Roche: song 'Flaming Red Hair' (as Stephen Roche)
Janet Roddick: song 'Flaming Red Hair'
Howard Shore: (also song 'In Dreams')
Cinematography: Andrew Lesnie
Film editing: John Gilbert
Production design: Grant Major
Art direction: Joe Bleakley, Philip Ivey, Rob Outterside, Mark Robins
Set decoration: Alan Lee (uncredited)
Casting: Victoria Burrows, John Hubbard, Amy MacLean, Liz Mullane, Ann Robinson
Costume design: Ngila Dickson, Richard Taylor

**Makeup Department**
Margaret Aston: hair stylist
Margaret Aston: makeup artist
Marjory Hamlin: prosthetics supervisor
Richard Taylor: supervisor: special makeup, creatures, armour, and miniatures

**Second Unit Director or Assistant Director**
John Mahaffie: second unit director
Ian Mune: additional second unit director
Geoff Murphy: second unit director
Guy Norris: additional second unit director
Barrie M. Osborne: additional second unit director
Rick Porras: additional second unit director
Frances Walsh: additional second unit director

**Art Department**
Alan Lee: conceptual designer

**Sound Department**
Nancy Allen: music editor
Brent Burge: sound effects editor
Jason Canovas: dialogue editor
Peter Cobbin: scoring mixer
Malcolm Cromie: sound recordist
David Farmer: sound designer
John McKay: sound effects editor
Suzana Peric: music editor
Ken Saville: sound recordist
Chris Todd: dialogue editor
Craig Tomlinson: sound effects editor
Ethan Van der Ryn: supervising sound co-designer

Ethan Van der Ryn: supervising sound editor
Ray Beentjes: sound editor (uncredited)
Andrew Dudman: music editor (uncredited)
Mick Gormaley: assistant music editor (uncredited)
John McKay: sound mixer (uncredited)
Hammond Peek: production sound mixer (uncredited)
Michael Price: music editor (uncredited)
Susan Shufro: assistant music editor (uncredited)
Mirek Stiles: assistant scoring mixer (uncredited)
Dave Whitehead: sound effects editor (uncredited)
Toby Wood: assistant sound recording engineer (uncredited)

## Special effects
Gino Acevedo: prosthetics supervisor: Weta Workshop
Steve Ingram: physical effects supervisor
Gary Mackay: head of armour weapons: Weta Workshop
Tania Rodger: manager: Weta Workshop
Richard Taylor: supervisor: special makeup, creatures, armour, and
  miniatures

## Visual effects
Matt Aitken: digital models supervisor: Weta Digital
Greg Allen: motion capture supervisor: Weta Digital
Tony Anderson: visual effects director of photography: Digital Domain
Elizabeth Arko: 3D technical director: Weta Digital
Felix Balbas: senior creature technical director: Weta Digital
Steen Bech: visual effects supervisor: Oktobor
Kelly Bechtle-Woods: 3D technical director: Weta Digital
Jeremy Bennett: visual effects art director
Nancy Bernstein: visual effects executive producer: Digital Domain
Lee Bramwell: senior camera technical director: Weta Digital
Stephen A. Buckley: senior animator: Weta Digital
Greg Butler: 3D sequence lead: Weta Digital
Julian R. Butler: 3D technical director: Weta Digital (as Julian Butler)
Andrew Calder: senior animator: Weta Digital
David Cole: lead digital colourist: The PostHouse AG
Peter Doyle: supervising digital colourist: The PostHoust AG
Yannick 'Botex' Dusseault: senior matte painter: Weta Digital (as Yanick
  Dusseault)
Mark O. Forker: visual effects supervisor: Digital Domain
Alex Funke: visual effects director of photography: miniature unit
David R. Hardberger: director of photography: miniature unit (as David
  Hardberger)

Gray Horsfield: conceptual digital visualization: Weta Digital
Florian Martin: lead digital colourist: The PostHouse AG (as Florian 'Utsi' Martin)
Erik Pope: visual effects co-ordinator: Digital Domain
Murray Pope: visual effects executive producer: Animal Logic
Kelly Port: digital effects supervisor: Digital Domain
Bay Raitt: senior creature technical director: Weta Digital
Ramon Rivero: lead performance animator: Weta Digital
Christian Rivers: visual effects art director: Weta Digital
Carlos M. Rosas: senior animator: Weta Digital (as Carlos Rosas)
Chuck Schumann: director of photography: miniatures unit (as Chuck Schuman)
John Sheils: digital effects supervisor: preproduction, Weta Digital
Brian Van't Hul: visual effects cinematographer: Weta Digital

**Stunts**
Daniel W. Barringer: assistant stunt co-ordinator
Alice Capper-Starr: stunt co-ordinator: sword master
Casey O'Neill: stunt co-ordinator: horse
George Marshall Ruge: stunt co-ordinator
Paul Shapcott: stunt rigger

**Other crew**
Liz Mullane: casting: New Zealand

**Production companies**
New Line Cinema [us] (an AOL Time Warner company)
The Saul Zaentz Company [us] (licensor) (d/b/a Tolkien Enterprises)
WingNut Films [nz]

**Distributors**
A-Film Distribution [nl]
Alexandra Video Club [bg]
Alliance Atlantis Communications [ca]
Argentina Video Home (AVH) [ar] (Argentina) (DVD)
Argentina Video Home (AVH) [ar] (Argentina) (VHS)
Aurum Producciones S.A. [es] (Spain)
Entertainment Film Distributors Ltd. [gb]
Karo Premiere [ru] (Russia)
Medusa Distribuzione [it]
Metropolitan Filmexport [fr] (France)
New Line Cinema [us] (an AOL Time Warner company)
New Line Home Video [us]
Premier Video Film [ru]

Svensk Filmindustri (SF) AB [se]
Warner Bros GmbH [de] (Germany)
Warner Bros [ar] (Argentina)
Warner Bros [us]
Warner Roadshow Film Distributors [gr] (Greece)

### Special effects
Animal Logic (visual effects)
Digital Domain [us] (visual effects: 'Ford of Bruinen' sequence)
EYETECH Optics [ca] (uncredited)
Oktobor [nz] (visual effects)
Rhythm & Hues [us] (visual effects)
Weta Digital Ltd. [nz] (digital visual effects designer and creator)
Weta Workshop Ltd. [nz] (special makeup, creatures, armour, weapons, and miniatures)

### Other companies
4MC UK Ltd. [gb] adr facilities
AFM Lighting Ltd. [gb] lighting facilities
AON / Albert G. Ruben Insurance Services Inc. [us] additional insurance
Abbey Road Studios [gb] music mixed at
Abbey Road Studios [gb] music recorded at
Air Lyndhurst Studios, London [gb] music recorded at
BBVC / Kelly's Eye Ltd. video assist design and build (uncredited)
Bank of New Zealand [nz] investment services
Camperdown Studios [nz] adr facilities
Colorfront [hu] digital film grading system
Colosseum, Watford [gb] music recorded at
Department of Conservation thanks
Flying Trestles catering
Giant Studios Inc. motion capture technology provided by
International Film Guarantors Inc. completion guarantee
London Voices music performed by
Mahony & Associates [nz] insurance services: New Zealand
New Zealand Defence Force [nz] thanks
New Zealand Symphony [nz] music performed by
Pacific Title [us] titles designed by
Redline Sound Studios [au] foley recording
Spacecam Systems Inc. [us] spacecam aerial camera system provided by
The Film Unit, Wellington [nz] color and telecine dailies
The Film Unit, Wellington [nz] re-recording facilities
The London Oratory School Schola [gb] music performed by
The London Symphony Orchestra [gb] music performed by

The PostHouse AG [de] digital color grading
The Saul Zaentz Company [us] licensor
Upper Deck Film Services negative cutting
Wellington City Council [nz] thanks
Wellington Regional Council's Parks and Forests [nz] thanks
Wellington Town Hall [nz] music recorded at
Wescam USA Inc. [us] Wescam provided by

Also known as:
*Fellowship of the Ring, The* (2001) (USA) (short title)
*Lord of the Rings: The Fellowship of the Ring: The Motion Picture, The* (2001) (USA) (promotional title)
MPAA: Rated PG-13 for epic battle sequences and some scary images.
Runtime: 178 min / USA: 208 min (special extended edition) / Sweden: 209 min (special extended edition)
Country: New Zealand / USA
Language: English / Sindarin
Color: Color (DeLuxe)
Sound Mix: DTS / Dolby EX 6.1 / SDDS
Certification: UK: PG / Argentina: 13 / Australia: M / Brazil: 12 / Canada: 14A / Denmark: 11 / Denmark: 15 (special extended edition) / Finland: K-11 / Finland: K-15 (special extended edition) / France: U / Germany: 12 (w) / Germany: 16 (special extended edition) / Ireland: PG / Italy: T / Mexico: B / Netherlands: 12 / New Zealand: M (special extended edition) / New Zealand: PG / Norway: 11 / Peru: 14 / Portugal: M/12 / Singapore: PG / South Korea: 12 / Spain: 13 / Sweden: 11 / Switzerland: 12 (canton of Geneva) / Switzerland: 12 (canton of Vaud) / USA: PG-13

## *Lord of the Rings: The Two Towers, The* (2002)

**Production**
Peter Jackson: producer
Michael Lynne: executive producer
Mark Ordesky: executive producer
Barrie M. Osborne: producer
Rick Porras: co-producer
Jamie Selkirk: co-producer
Robert Shaye: executive producer
Frances Walsh: producer
Bob Weinstein: executive producer
Harvey Weinstein: executive producer

**Cast (in credits order, additional to the cast listed for *Fellowship*)**
Bernard Hill: Theoden
Miranda Otto: Eowyn
David Wenham: Faramir
Brad Dourif: Grima Wormtongue
Karl Urban: Eomer
Jed Brophy: Sharku/Snaga
Paris Howe Strewe: Theodred, Prince of Rohan
Nathaniel Lees: Ugluk
Stephen Ure: Grishnakh
Billy Jackson: Cute Rohan Refugee Child
Katie Jackson: Cute Rohan Refugee Child
Peter Jackson: Rohirrim Warrior (uncredited)

**Original music**
Frances Walsh: song 'Gollum's Song' (as Fran Walsh)
Film editing: Michael Horton, Jabez Olssen, Loren Squires
Production design: Grant Major
Art direction: Joe Bleakley, Dan Hennah, Philip Ivey, Rob Outterside,
    Christian Rivers, Mark Robins
Set decoration: Dan Hennah, Alan Lee
Costume design: Ngila Dickson, Richard Taylor

**Makeup Department**
Peter King: hair designer
Peter King: makeup designer
Peter Owen: hair designer
Peter Owen: makeup designer
Jeremy Woodhead: makeup artist

**Second Unit Director or Assistant Director**
John Mahaffie: second unit director
Geoff Murphy: second unit director
Guy Norris: second unit director

**Art Department**
Jules Cook: assistant art director
Chris Hennah: art department coordinator
John Howe: conceptual designer
Alan Lee: conceptual designer
Richard Taylor: WETA workshop supervisor

**Sound Department**
Ray Beentjes: sound editor

Brent Burge: sound effects editor
Jason Canovas: dialogue editor
David Farmer: sound designer
Malcolm Fife: music editor
Mark Franken: sound editor
Mike Hopkins: supervising sound editor
John Kurlander: scoring mixer
Raphaël Mouterde: music editor
Jason Poss: music editor
Michael Price: music editor
Matt Rocker: music editor
Fabian Sanjurjo: sound effects editor
Nigel Stone: adr supervior
Craig Tomlinson: sound effects editor
Ethan Van der Ryn: supervising sound editor

**Special effects**
Mike Asquith: designer
Mike Asquith: sculptor
Felix Balbas: senior creature technical director
Blair Foord: special effects co-ordinator
Chad Moffitt: senior animator
Mike Morasky: senior massive technical director
Jason Schleifer: senior animator

**Visual effects**
Matt Aitken: digital models supervisor
Jim Berney: visual effects supervisor: SPI
Benjamin Cinelli: senior animator
John Clinton: visual effects producer: SPI
Aaron Cowan: visual effects co-ordinator
Christian Cunningham: technical director
Marion Davey: visual effects art department
Steve Demers: CGI look designer
Peter Doyle: supervising digital colourist
Theresa Ellis: 3D lead TD
Alex Funke: visual effects director of photography: miniature unit
Steven Hornby: senior character animator
Sharon James: motion combat choreographer
Heather Knight: senior character animator
Roger Kupelian: senior matte painter
Joe Letteri: visual effects supervisor
Matt Logue: senior animator

Stephen Regelous: Massive software developer
Jim Rygiel: visual effects supervisor
Remington Scott: motion capture and motion edit supervisor

**Stunts**
Daniel W. Barringer: assistant stunt co-ordinator
George Marshall Ruge: stunt co-ordinator

**Production companies**
Lord Zweite Productions Deutschland Filmproduktion GmbH & Co. KG [de]
New Line Cinema [us]
The Saul Zaentz Company [us] (licensor) (d/b/a Tolkien Enterprises)
WingNut Films [nz]

**Distributors**
A-Film Distribution [nl]
Alexandra Films [bg] (Bulgaria)
Argentina Video Home (AVH) [ar] (Argentina) (DVD)
Argentina Video Home (AVH) [ar] (Argentina) (VHS)
Cinergia Ltd. [ua]
Entertainment Film Distributors Ltd. [gb]
FS Film Oy [fi] (Finland)
Herald Film Company [jp] (Japan)
Karo Premiere [ru] (Russia)
Medusa Distribuzione [it]
Metropolitan Filmexport [fr] (France)
New Line Cinema [us]
New Line Home Video [us]
Shochiku Films Ltd [jp] (Japan)
Svensk Filmindustri (SF) AB [se]
Warner Bros. GmbH [de] (Germany)
Warner Bros. [ar] (Argentina)
Warner Home Vídeo [br] (2003) (Brazil) (DVD)
Warner Home Vídeo [br] (2003) (Brazil) (VHS)
Warner Roadshow Film Distributors [gr] (Greece)

**Special effects**
EYETECH Optics [ca]
Oktobor [nz]
Sony Pictures Imageworks [us]
Weta Digital Ltd. [nz]

**Other companies**
AFM Lighting Ltd. [gb] lighting rental facility
Colorfront [hu] digital film grading system
Flying Trestles catering

Also known as:
*Two Towers, The* (2002) (USA) (short title)
MPAA: Rated PG-13 for epic battle sequences and scary images.
Runtime: 179 min / USA: 223 min (special extended edition) / Sweden: 224 min (special extended edition) / USA: 235 min (special extended edition)
Country: USA / New Zealand
Language: English / Sindarin
Sound Mix: DTS-ES / Dolby EX 6.1 / SDDS
Certification: Argentina: 13 / Australia: M / Brazil: 12 / Canada: 14A / Denmark: 11 / Finland: K-11 / France: U / Germany: 12 (bw) / Ireland: 12 / Italy: T / Netherlands: 12 / New Zealand: M / Norway: 11 / Peru: 14 / Portugal: M/12 / Singapore: PG / South Korea: 12 / Spain: 13 / Sweden: 11 / Switzerland: 14 (canton of Geneva) / Switzerland: 14 (canton of Vaud) / Switzerland: 14 (canton of the Grisons) / UK: 12A / USA: PG-13 (certificate #39418) / Singapore: PG (extended version) / Finland: K-15 (special extended edition) / USA: PG-13 (extended version)

*Lord of the Rings: The Return of the King, The* (2003)
Director: Peter Jackson

**Writing credits (WGA [Writers' Guild of America])**
J. R. R. Tolkien: novel *The Return of the King*
Frances Walsh: screenplay (as Fran Walsh)
Philippa Boyens: screenplay
Peter Jackson: screenplay

**Production**
Peter Jackson: producer
Michael Lynne: executive producer
Mark Ordesky: executive producer
Barrie M. Osborne: producer
Rick Porras: co-producer
Jamie Selkirk: co-producer
Robert Shaye: executive producer

Frances Walsh: producer (as Fran Walsh)
Bob Weinstein: executive producer
Harvey Weinstein: executive producer

**Cast (in credits order, additional to the casts listed for *Fellowship* and *Towers*)**
Lawrence Makoare: Witch King / Gothmog
John Noble: Denethor
Paul Norell: King of the Dead
Thomas Robins: Deagol
Harry Sinclair: Isildur

**Original music**
Annie Lennox: song 'Into the West'
Frances Walsh: song 'Into the West' (as Fran Walsh)
Film editing: Annie Collins, Jamie Selkirk
Casting: Victoria Burrows, John Hubbard, Amy MacLean, Liz Mullane, Ann Robinson
Art direction: Joe Bleakley, Simon Bright, Dan Hennah, Philip Ivey, Christian Rivers
Set decoration: Dan Hennah, Alan Lee
Costume design: Ngila Dickson, Richard Taylor

**Makeup Department**
Peter King: makeup designer
Peter Owen: hair designer
Peter Owen: makeup designer
Jeremy Woodhead: makeup artist

**Second Unit Director or Assistant Director**
John Mahaffie: second unit director
Geoff Murphy: second unit director
Guy Norris: second unit director

**Art Department**
Jules Cook: assistant art director
Chris Hennah: art department coordinator
John Howe: conceptual designer
Alan Lee: conceptual designer
David Scott: previz artist
Richard Taylor: WETA workshop supervisor

**Sound Department**
Ray Beentjes: dialogue editor
Beau Borders: sound effects editor

Brent Burge: sound effects editor
Jason Canovas: dialogue editor
Hayden Collow: sound effects editor
David Farmer: sound designer
Mark Franken: dialogue editor
Mike Hopkins: supervising sound editor
John Kurlander: scoring mixer
Polly McKinnon: dialogue editor
Peter Mills: foley editor
Timothy Nielsen: sound effects editor (as Tim Nielsen)
Addison Teague: sound effects editor
Craig Tomlinson: sound effects editor
Ethan Van der Ryn: supervising sound editor

**Special effects**
Mike Asquith: designer
Mike Asquith: sculptor
Rich E. Cordobes: special effects set co-ordinator
Blair Foord: special effects co-ordinator
Chad Moffitt: senior animator
Mike Morasky: senior massive technical director
Tim Wigmore: miniatures model maker
Alain de Zilva: special effects contact lens artist: EYETECH Optics

**Visual effects**
Matt Aitken: digital models supervisor
Chris Burn: lead digital compositor: Weta Digital
Ian Cope: visual effects co-ordinator: Rising Sun Pictures
Tim Crosbie: visual effects supervisor: Rising Sun Pictures
Adam Dotson: senior character animator
Peter Doyle: supervising digital colourist
Theresa Ellis: digital effects supervisor
Theresa Ellis: head of the shots department: Weta Digital
Eric Fernandes: technical director
Frederic Fortin: creature technical director
Fiona Foster: visual effects co-ordinator
Alex Funke: visual effects director of photography: miniature unit
Mark Gee: lighting technical director: Weta Digital
Paul Griffin: senior character animator
Steven Hornby: senior character animator
Sandy Houston: lead digital artist
Dave R. Howe: technical director: Massive
John Huikku: environment technical director: Weta Digital Ltd.

Bridgitte Krupke: visual effects co-ordinator
Roger Kupelian: senior matte painter
Joe Letteri: visual effects supervisor
Mark Tait Lewis: 2D sequence supervisor: Weta Digital
Tibor Madjar: lead modeller: Weta Digital LTD
Ivan Moran: lead compositor
Jim Rygiel: visual effects supervisor
Eric Saindon: CG supervisor
Mahria Sangster: Massive co-ordinator
Mahria Sangster: motion capture co-ordinator

**Weta Digital**
Erik Winquist: lead compositor: Weta Digital, Ltd.

**Stunts**
Daniel W. Barringer: assistant stunt co-ordinator
George Marshall Ruge: stunt co-ordinator

**Production Companies**
New Line Cinema [us]
The Saul Zaentz Company [us] (licensor) (d/b/a Tolkien Enterprises)
WingNut Films [nz]

**Distributors**
A-Film Distribution [nl]
Alliance Atlantis Communications [ca] (Canada)
Aurum Producciones S.A. [es] (Spain)
Cinergia Ltd [ua] (Ukraine)
Karo Premiere [ru] (Russia)
Medusa Distribuzione [it]
Metropolitan Filmexport [fr] (France)
New Line Cinema [us]
Svensk Filmindustri (SF) AB [se]
Warner Bros GmbH [de] (Germany)
Warner Bros [ar] (Argentina)

**Special effects**
EYETECH Optics [ca]
Weta Digital Ltd. [nz]

**Other companies**
AFM Lighting Ltd. [gb] lighting rental facility

Also known as:
*Return of the King, The* (2003) (USA) (short title)

MPAA: Rated PG-13 for intense epic battle sequences and frightening images.
Runtime: 201 min
Country: USA / New Zealand
Language: English / Sindarin
Colour: Color
Sound Mix: DTS / Dolby EX 6.1 / SDDS
Certification: New Zealand: M / UK: 12A / Australia: M / Netherlands: 12 / Singapore: PG / South Korea: 12 / Finland: K-11/9 / Switzerland: 14 (canton of Geneva) / Switzerland: 14 (canton of Vaud) / Canada: 14A / Norway: 11 / Sweden: 11 / Argentina: 13 / Brazil: 12 / Portugal: M/12 / Germany: 12 (bw) / Hungary: 16 / USA: PG-13 (certificate #40415) / Philippines: PG-13

# 27

# Dossier: awards

*Fellowship* was nominated for thirteen Oscars (only *All about Eve* and *Titanic* – with fourteen each – have received more nominations), including Best Picture, Director, Actor in a Supporting Role, Writing (Adapted Screenplay), Art Direction, Costume Design, Film Editing, Best Song, and Sound. In March 2002, *Fellowship* won four: Cinematography, Makeup, Music, and Visual Effects. *Fellowship* also won Picture of the Year, Digital Effects Artist, and Production Designer of the Year at the American Film Institute Awards. Nominated for thirteen British Academy of Film and Television Arts (BAFTA) Awards, it won five: the Audience Award, Best Film, Best Achievement in Visual Effects, Best Makeup/ Hair, and the prestigious David Lean Award for Direction. In addition, the Director's Guild of America nominated Peter Jackson for Best Director, and Ian McKellen received the Screen Actors Guild Award for Best Actor in a Supporting Role. The film also won awards from the National Board of Review, ASCAP, the Broadcast Film Critics Association, critics' organisations from Chicago, Florida, Las Vegas, Kansas City, Los Angeles, and Motion Picture Sound Editors; it won an MTV Movie Award and was nominated for four Golden Globes, including Best Score and Best Song.

In the poorest Oscar showing of the three films, *Towers* took Oscars for Best Sound Editing and Best Visual Effects, with nominations for Best Art Direction-Set Decoration, Best Editing, Best Sound, and Best Picture. At the 2003 BAFTAs, the film took Best Achievement in Special Visual Effects, Best Costume Design, and the Children's award for Best Feature Film. Howard Shore's score won a Grammy for Best Score Soundtrack Album, and the film won the key science fiction awards, a Hugo and a Nebula. With a near-clean-sweep at the Visual Effects Society, and many Best Foreign Film awards, including awards from Japan and Australia, the entire cast was nominated for a Screen Actors Guild award. The film won several popular votes, including the MTV and *Empire* magazine best film. Significantly, the DVDs also won awards from the new DVD specialist consumer press.

The categories and winners in the 2004 clean-sweep at the Oscars were:

Best Art Direction-Set Decoration: Grant Major (art director), Dan Hennah (set decorator), Alan Lee (set decorator)

Best Costume Design: Ngila Dickson, Richard Taylor

Best Director: Peter Jackson

Best Editing: Jamie Selkirk

Best Makeup: Richard Taylor, Peter King

Best Music, Original Score: Howard Shore

Best Music, Original Song: Frances Walsh, Howard Shore, Annie Lennox (for the song 'Into the West')

Best Picture: Barrie M. Osborne, Peter Jackson, Frances Walsh

Best Sound: Christopher Boyes, Michael Semanick, Michael Hedges, Hammond Peek

Best Visual Effects: Jim Rygiel, Joe Letteri, Randall William Cook, Alex Funke

Best Writing, Screenplay Based on Material Previously Produced or Published: Frances Walsh, Philippa Boyens, Peter Jackson

In addition, the final film in the trilogy was honoured by the Art Directors Guild, BAFTA (Best Achievement in Special Visual Effects, Best Cinematography, Best Film, and Best Screenplay [Adapted]), Costume Designers Guild, Directors Guild of America, and Directors Guild of Great Britain; there were Golden Globes for Best Director, Best Motion Picture – Drama, Best Original Score, and Best Original Song. Other awards included the Hollywood Makeup Artist and Hair Stylist Guild award, the Screen Actors Guild award for ensemble cast, four prizes from the Visual Effects Society, another Hugo, the MTV and *Empire* popular awards, as well as many other prizes and nominations in almost all the key professional associations.

# 28

# Dossier: critics and reviews

*Sean Cubitt and Barry King*

The sampling below of online threads from *LOTR* fans includes an unexpected comparison between Jane Austen and *LOTR*, on the one hand, and Jane Austen and *The Lord of the Rings*, on the other. One enthusiastic fan writes that *LOTR* 'is to my film viewing what Jane Austen is to my reading', meaning, as any Janeite would immediately recognise, that Jackson's trilogy is eminently watchable, over and over.

From the corporate point of view, that's the only kind of response that matters. Not all professional reviewers of the trilogy were so enthusiastic. Most critics focused on the films' length and their narrative structure. Response to the technical achievement that the trilogy represents was overwhelmingly positive.

Within this framework – universal acceptance of the technical achievement and general acceptance of the films overall, tempered by occasional criticism of the depiction of violence and narrative pace (criticism often influenced by the critic's prior response to Tolkien's work) – we have selected examples of responses to *LOTR* from professional and non-professional viewers of the films. These responses suggest reasons why the films have appealed to viewers far beyond the exceptional technical work.

It is traditional when providing samples of viewers' readings of a film to focus on professional viewers such as newspaper- and journal-based reviewers. However, given the Web's importance for the development and reception of *LOTR*, it seems importance here to include the less official (because non-professional) response of fans who have expressed their opinions via the Web for an audience of other non-professionals.

Much of what is published at the time of a film's release forms part of its marketing. In this instance, the films are produced by a corporation whose interests also include television stations and magazine publishing, ventures that can both promote the movie and attract viewers and readers by offering them interviews, documentaries, and news items tied to the films. For this reason, much of what is published needs to be read with a careful eye for interpretation. Not only other companies in the AOL-Time-Warner conglomerate but many individuals and companies were egging the films on to succeed for reasons of national pride and sheer enthusiasm, let alone commercial gain. So the scholar needs to leaf through the files of material with as much attention to the motivations and effects of selective emphases, omissions, and repetitions among the data as in interpreting the films themselves.

Publicity and promotion did not follow in an orderly progression from production through to distribution and exhibition but rather demonstrated that all these phases are often contemporaneous. Practically, there was no primary text that did not draw on the collateral textual processes and sources in its formation, no individual film that did not talk to and about other media forms, from trailers to parodies, collectibles to computer games. Moreover there was a sense in which the films were not primary texts. This is particularly evident in the handling of Tolkien's *The Lord of the Rings* as a source. Influenced by the popularity of the books, Boyens, Walsh, and Jackson followed the creative rule that they would faithfully render as much as possible of Tolkien's writing on screen. It was obvious that, at best, the screenplay would be a more or less successful approximation and that numerous Tolkien fans were an important base-line market segment to satisfy.

Important, too, was the new culture of participation that various writers have identified as a feature of contemporary popular culture (Jenkins 2003). Fans increasingly want to customise their engagement with popular cultural products. Given that *The Lord of the Rings* has many fans and devotees, it was important to create a space for their psychic investment as a hedge against market uncertainty. So it emerged that the reviewing process for *LOTR* began before the primary text was formed – indeed, before a final working script was completed. Although it is quite usual for story ideas to be pre-tested through focus group methods, what happened was much more 'participatory' – Jackson submitted to a fan review of his creative intentions. The online discussion, moderated by Harry Knowles on the Aint-it-cool-news website, is worth citing as the first kind of review:

> Q: In the last twenty years the fantasy film has nose-dived into granite. What is wrong with the modern fantasy film, what is missing, and how is this going to be different from the parade of fantasy duds that have been kicking sand in the face of fantasy lovers for a generation now?
>
> PJ: One of my chief reasons for wanting to spend nearly 5 years of my life making these films has been that I don't think that fantasy has been well served by the cinema. Either the style has been wrong, or often the scripts have been terrible. Starting out with strong scripts (and we are obviously

dealing with great material) will put us ahead of a lot of other fantasy films. Not making the movies self-consciously fantasy will help too. (Aint-it-cool-news)

This discussion, revealing a director willing to listen to and filter suggestions, also demonstrates that there was no primary text of *LOTR* that was not actively (as opposed to passively) transtextual. *LOTR* is unusual in its use of the Internet and the staging of consultation as public event. Intentionally or not, Jackson corralled a significant audience as a cybernetic resource.

*LOTR*'s release strategy, with its prolongation of theatrical releases during the peak Christmas season over three consecutive years, deepened its transtextuality. Each film's release was timed for the last possible moment for inclusion in the Oscar nominations. Whatever the fate of the individual films, the success or failure of the trilogy itself existed for a long time in a state of inconclusiveness. Promotion and publicity campaigns exploited the anticipation to know how the trilogy's own story would turn out. Would Jackson get an Oscar for Best Director? Would the individual films get Best Film awards?

The release strategy had other effects. Milestone markers such as the first box-office returns could be changed by subsequent releases and indeed by release into sell-through markets for video and DVD. A poor box-office for the first film might be compensated for by succeeding films, or a good box-office for the first film (the actual outcome) might be undercut by the performance of the second and the third.

In fact, box-office for each film was consistently very good. Because New Line regarded each film in the trilogy as a potential Oscar winner, it invested heavily in campaigns over the three-year cycle of release (Hammond 2004: S64). Along with the timing of the release cycle there was what was released. The nominal primary texts – the films as released – were subject to retextualisation and dispersal even before the three-year theatrical release cycle was complete. Special DVD releases of *Fellowship* and *Towers*, containing extra footage and interviews with cast and crew, as well as advance trailers for the next film in the cycle, produced an ahistorical layering of versions existing within the present. Consumers are used to a 'director's cut' as the 'anniversary' re-release of an established hit. The instant repackaging of *LOTR* in DVD and videocassette was not a director's cut, Jackson insisted, but simply (though it's not that simple) an extended edition including scenes cut from the theatrical version. The studied deferral of closure to develop new 'niche' markets was a brilliant marketing ploy, increasing the number of purchases by projecting incompleteness backwards into the first purchase. This positioning drew on the fan's desire for a definitive rendition even as it implicitly denied that a definitive rendition had yet to be given.

What this meant for the reviewing process was that a judgment on a particular film was qualified by what was to come or what had been. The success of *Fellowship* affected evaluations of *Towers* and *Return* just as the later film(s) coloured previous evaluations of the one or ones before. Overall, reviews were predominantly positive, although they were not all positive in the same way.

It is impossible here to do justice to the diversity, range, and even eccentricity of published opinion on the films. The reviews selected here for illustrative purposes have been grouped in three categories: Internet-based discussion threads; film reviews in newspapers and broadcast media; and op-ed pieces. An additional critical perspective arose because several major participants set up personal websites, promoting their own performances. This was particularly true of the actors, e.g., Serkis and McKellen. Here's a sample from Serkis's website:

> Frodo and Sam continue to be guided by the fretful Gollum . . . the deformed former Ringbearer whose intended treachery is superbly revealed in a schizophrenic soliloquy delivered to his reflection in the water . . . Serkis gets to expand the remarkable Gollum with unexpected complexity. – Todd McCarthy, *Variety*

> Bad as the little bipolar devil is. You cannot take your eyes off Gollum, and if there is any justice, one of the dozen or so Oscars 'The Return of the King' deserves will go to Serkis. – Jack Matthew, *New York Daily News*
> (Both samples from www.serkis.com)

Other cast members' pages are similar. In addition, Astin and Serkis produced book-length memoirs of their participation in the project.

### Internet-based discussion threads

Internet discussion threads became the main public forum before, during, and after the films' production and release. Theonering.net, forged by and for Tolkien fans, contains various threads. One of the more interesting threads asks whether *Fellowship*, *Towers*, and *Returns* are important films.

> Crispycreme: The eclectic Éclair first, an Administrator Second:
> People on this site (and I'm sure others) have been saying for some time that the *The Lord of the Rings* films are the first important films of this century. But important how? Because of the nifty special effects? The marketing techniques? The way in which they were filmed? Or is there more

to it? Is there something beyond the craft itself that people will look at in years to come when critiquing *The Lord of the Rings*? Will there be a consensus that these films were successful in conveying an important message at an important time? . . . An important study in how to make and market films for the early 21st century? Important social commentary about our post-modern culture? Both? Neither? You decide!

Semuta: The Nameless One:
I'm sure they will be remembered primarily for 'The Big Gamble', filming all three simultaneously and for the huge amount of money they made. Some other things could be the break-through special effects (Gollum, Massive).

I think a lot of fans attach such importance to them solely because they are films of their favorite book. How can the films claim such importance when the books have been out for so long? Or does the question need to be looked at as if the book never existed?

Mammo: Changing her name to Calypso:
I agree with Semuta that PJ's ability to film all movies at once is worthy of kudos. For a director to be able to delegate parts and yet retain control of the whole to this extent is amazing . . . I like the ensemble cast. The score is amazing . . . The incredible detail in costumes, weapons, jewellery etc. stands out. Gollum brings new depth to CG.

Farawen: faraway:
People often think of fantasy or mythology as mere escapism, unimportant in the real world. What this new movie phenomenon reminds people is that fantasy can touch us very deeply. What the masses seem to be telling us is that good mythology is needed in these 'modern' times. High quality films of myths that take us far from our everyday world and yet stir us deeply are important.

BoleaII: shield bearer:
To me, artistic or social value is all that's relevant when deciding the film's importance . . . not how it affects the entertainment industry economically . . . But *The Lord of the Rings* at least has the potential for social ramifications (individual selflessness, heroism, stewardship of the natural world) in ways that few other Blockbusters have (except for *Jaws* which caused widespread fear and extermination of Great White Sharks).

Because *The Lord of the Rings* is the most-beautifully rendered story ever put on film, it should be regarded as important, even if it never has any discernible social ramifications. Its artistic greatness is already there for posterity.

Primula_Baggins: Sailing the Luminiferous Ether:
Everyone trots out *Citizen Kane* when 'importance' is mentioned with respect to film. *Citizen Kane* will probably be the most assiduously dusted DVD on most shelves. But watched?

But I know I haul out *Fellowship* or *Two Towers* for fun viewing, or comfort viewing or when I'm tired or sick – it is to my film viewing what Jane Austen is to my reading . . .

Semprini: Ranger of the North:
They are important in terms of success, use of the Internet as a successful media support for advertising films etc. but from an artistic point of view, the only great achievement of the movies is to be found in their special effects. Apart from this there is nothing innovative in PJ's direction . . .

Jnyusa: Ranger of the North
Great thread, Crispy!
   I thought that the amount of attention devoted to bad guys was about special effects. If orcs and cave trolls, etc., had not been such great fodder for horror-style fx production, I doubt that PJ would have given them as much screen time as he did . . .
   . . . in terms of the coherence that Jackson and his team brought to this film I think that one of the questions that will be asked in the future is how a set of films that were done so poorly could receive so much acclaim and make so much money.

Ersehkigal: The Quest achieved:
. . . Jackson may end up being more important than Tolkien, whose written work was accessible only to a few . . . But I believe it will be because of these movies that the legends of Tolkien's world will enter into our culture . . .

Theonering.net also featured Ringer Reviews – 8,836 reviews and still counting! Some examples:

Chip Douglas (Age 31) Tolkien fan level 6, review of *The Return of the King*:
Against all hopes, Peter Jackson managed to make a film out of a book with no beginning, an endless parade of battle scenes and a very extended epilogue. However it takes forever before the story finaly [*sic*] starts, the conclusion is dragged out in endless slow motion scenes and there are about 6 endings desparately [*sic*] in need of a voice-over . . . If only John Gilbert who was responsible for the first one, had been allowed to edit all three. He might have been able to fit every important plot point in without lingering on people standing at the edge of a cliff.

Nimbrethil028 (age 27) Tolkien Fan level 7 – gave ratings of 1 out of 5 for directing, editing and screenplay:
What the?!? And this is Jackson's favorite film, his favorite book? My heart feels broken. I couldn't even enjoy this movie because it made no sense! Who could follow such madness and not have a billion questions about the plot, regardless of whether you have read the books or not? The editing was terrible, the character development cheap, and the movie

itself a complete mockery of film and book logic . . . Why did we have such a dire urgency at Helm's Deep . . . when the next day Theoden can amass thousands of Rohirrim? I guess Gandalf's staff only works part of the time because he sure does use his power rarely. Likewise, Eomer is turned from a noble hero into a roughshod soldier with no real role. . . .

Megan (Age 18) Tolkien Fan Level 10:
Perfect. That's all I can say. Perfect. I'm speechless.

## Film reviews

In general, film reviews were very favourable. Of the 180 reviews for *Fellowship* on rottentomatoes.com, for example, only five warranted a rotten tomato; for *Towers*, 196 were good and only five rotten; for *Return*, of 216, eleven were rotten. Some illustrative reviews follow. Elvis Mitchell, writing on *Fellowship* in the New York *Times* of 19 December 2001, spoke of the anticipation:

> There are two groups probably sharing the same dread about the film adaptation of J. R. R. Tolkien's ornate and busy *Lord of the Rings: The Fellowship of the Ring* – its most loving adherents and those who have spent their lives avoiding the books. But neither side is likely to be disappointed by the director Peter Jackson's altogether heroic job in tackling perhaps the most intimidating nerd/academic fantasy classic ever . . .

Sounding a note of op-ed criticism, Mitchell continues:

> Mr. Jackson apparently feels that the way to keep each of the fighting groups separate in the audience's minds is to provide them with hairstyles reminiscent of 1970's bands. The Hobbits all have heads of tossed curls – they're like members of Peter Frampton's group. Aragorn and Boromir have the long, unwashed bushes of Aerosmith and the flaxen-maned Legolas has the fallen-angel look of one of the Allman Brothers. (The tubby, bibulous and bearded Gimli could be a roadie for any of them.) 'Fellowship' plays like a sword and sorcery epic produced by VH-1.

The same critic on *Towers*:

> The director Peter Jackson's scrupulous devotion to the spirit of J. R. Tolkien's 'Lord of the Rings' trilogy manifests itself in a gripping intense fashion for the second of the film adaptions. . . . The most incredible accomplishment of 'Towers' is that at its heart it is a transition film that lasts nearly three hours and holds the viewer's attention.

And on *Return* (finally, an entirely positive review):

> After the galloping intelligence displayed in the first two parts of 'The Lord of the Rings' trilogy, your fear may be that the director, Peter Jackson,

would become cautious and unimaginative in the last episode . . . But Mr Jackson crushes any such fear. His 'King' is a meticulous and prodigious vision made by a director who was not hamstrung by heavy use of computer special-effects imagery.

Covering *Fellowship* for the *Chicago Sun-Times*, Roger Ebert wrote in the 19 December 2001 edition:

If the books are about brave little creatures who enlist powerful men and wizards to help them in a dangerous crusade, the movie is about powerful men and wizards who embark on a dangerous crusade and take along the Hobbits. That is not true of every scene or episode, but by the end 'Fellowship' adds up to more of a sword and sorcery epic than a realization of the more naïve and guileless vision of J. R. R. Tolkien . . .

On *Towers*, Ebert opined:

With 'Lord of the Rings: The Two Towers', it's clear that director Peter Jackson has tilted the balance decisively against the hobbits and in favor of the traditional action heroes of the Tolkien trilogy. The star is now clearly Aragorn (Viggo Mortensen) and the hobbits spend much of the movie away from the action. The last third of the movie is dominated by an epic battle scene that would no doubt startle the gentle medievalist J. R. R. Tolkien.

The task of the critic is to decide whether this shift damages the movie. It does not. 'The Two Towers' is one of the most spectacular swashbucklers ever made, and, given current audience tastes in violence, may well be more popular than the first installment, 'The Fellowship of the Ring'. It is not faithful to the spirit of Tolkien and misplaces much of the charm and whimsy of the books, but it stands on its own as a visionary thriller.

'The Two Towers' will possibly be more popular than the first film, more of an audience-pleaser, but hasn't Jackson lost the original purpose of the story somewhere along the way? He has taken an enchanting and unique work of literature and retold it in the terms of the modern action picture. If Tolkien had wanted to write about a race of supermen, he would have written a Middle-earth version of 'Conan the Barbarian'. But no. He told a tale in which modest little hobbits were the heroes. And now Jackson has steered the story into the action mainstream. To do what he has done in this film must have been awesomely difficult, and he deserves applause, but to remain true to Tolkien would have been more difficult, and braver.

Finally, Ebert on *Return*, in the *Chicago Sun Times* for 17 December 2003:

At last the full arc is visible, and the 'Lord of the Rings' trilogy comes into final focus. I admire it more as a whole than in its parts. The second film was inconclusive, and lost its way in the midst of spectacle. But the 'Return of the King' dispatches its characters to their destinies with a grand and eloquent confidence. This is the best of the three, redeems the earlier meandering, and certifies the 'Ring' trilogy as a work of bold ambition at a time of cinematic timidity.

That it falls a little shy of greatness is perhaps inevitable. The story is just a little too silly to carry the emotional weight of a masterpiece. It is a melancholy fact that while visionaries of a generation ago, like Coppola with 'Apocalypse Now', tried frankly to make films of great consequence, an equally ambitious director like Peter Jackson is aiming for popular success . . .

There is little enough psychological depth anywhere in the films . . . and they mostly exist as surface, gesture, archetype and spectacle. They do that magnificently well, but one feels at the end that nothing actual and human has been at stake; cartoon characters in a fantasy world have been brought along about as far as it is possible for them to come, and while we applaud the achievement, the trilogy is more a work for adolescents (of all ages) than for those hungering for true emotion thoughtfully paid for.

An anthology of UK press reviews of *Return* compiled by BBC News provides a snapshot of the British Press opinion (http://news.bbc.co.uk/1/hi/entertainment/film/3313097.stm (accessed 6 January 2005)):

*The Times*:

And so it ends, the greatest film trilogy ever mounted, with some of the most amazing action sequences committed to celluloid. *The Return of the King* is everything a Ring fan could possibly wish for and much more.

*The Independent*:

Tolkien's *The Lord of the Rings* trilogy has morphed from being a quirky gamble – a fantasy adventure too frightening for kids and possibly too silly for adults – into the surest thing in town . . . And then – disaster! Having stroked and stimulated us into submission, Jackson just can't think how to wrap things up. I came out of *The Two Towers* feeling like I'd been converted to the Church of Tolkien; I emerged from the *Return of the King* on the side of the gargoyles.

*The Guardian*:

for about four fifths of its run, I had *The Return of the King* confidently filed as masterpiece – a big, stirring orchestral epic of a movie, full of blood and heroism and sacrifice and soul. The trouble is that it is hellishly long, frequently preposterous and humourless as a cat.

*Daily Mail*:

Disappointing. Overblown. Anti-climatic. Bungled. These are just some of the adjectives I shall not be using to describe the third part of *Lord of the Rings*. How about amazing, stupendous, jaw-dropping and overwhelming.

*Daily Express*:

'The Return of the King' is the great coming together of Tolkien's myth, where journeys end in vast battles and where incident is piled upon incident, climax on climax. And director Peter Jackson has more than done justice to his material.

Again and again the film places unblushing emphasis on old virtues – self-sacrifice, courage, steadfastness and faith.

*Daily Mirror*:

So as the much-hyped production is released simultaneously around the world today, is it worth the fuss? Was I bored by the *Rings*, or awed by the *Rings*. Well both to be honest . . . will Jackson at last win an Oscar for this towering achievement? No ifs. No buts. The answer is unequivocally yes. And about time too.

These capsule reviews are not surprisingly inflected by the market standing (tabloid versus broadsheet) and political (left to right) orientation of the newspapers in which they occur. The *Daily Express*'s commitment to the unblushing 'old values' is just as indicative as the less favourable judgements of *The Independent* and *The Guardian* or the breezy populism of the *Mirror*.

## Op-ed

The key themes concern matters of racism, sexism, nationalism, class, religion, cultural value, and aesthetic integrity.

### Racism:

'Lord of the Rings' unleashes debate on racism

There's an ugly war raging amongst the Tolkien faithful, those lovers of Hobbits and Elves and the magical lands of Middle Earth. 'The Lord of the Rings' trilogy – both the films and the books – is rooted in racism, say critics, a white supremacist fantasy where the good guys are white, the bad guys black and behaviour is predetermined by race.

PC-poppycock, say Tolkien supporters and the films' executive producer, who insist that those who see racial undertones in the epic tale are misinterpreting the half-century old classic that has turned into a series of blockbuster movies that have earned more than $600 million so far.

The latest skirmish in a debate Tolkien scholars say has tailed 'The Lord of the Rings' since the 1960s began last month with the publication of an article by journalist John Yatt in the British newspaper *The Guardian*.

'The Lord of the Rings is racist . . . the races that Tolkien has put on the side of evil are given a rag-bag of non-white characteristics that could have been copied straight from a (British National party) leaflet. Dark,

**Figure 33** Boromir.

slant-eyed, swarthy and broad faced – it's amazing he didn't go the whole hog and give them a natural sense of rhythm . . .

'They're seeing things that are not there', says Brandon Curtis, a University of New Mexico senior. 'It's a fantasy epic not a research paper'.

The executive producer of 'The Two Towers' on Monday denied the film or Tolkien was racist. 'It's an exploration of good and evil, not a racist commentary', Mark Ordesky says. (*Albuquerque Journal*, 26 January 2003)

### Social order

The racial perception of individuals having qualities defined by their appearance and skin colour is an example of the rule that social position is fixed by inherited or acquired personal characteristics. In a much quoted article, 'Tolkien and the New Medievalism', Dilday treats the imaginary world of *LOTR* as an evocation of a pre-capitalist social order in which the moral worth of an individual is defined by an ascribed social rank fixed at birth:

> By the time the second part of the saga, *The Two Towers* was released last year, the invasions (Iraq) had begun and the nascent 21st century had become eerily similar to Middle Earth. Now, *The Return of the King* opens around the world at the same time that global news media display images of a defeated enemy undergoing public, intimate, physical inspection as a symbol of his complete submission and degradation.

We are living in times when the public rhetoric is medieval. Politicians and pundits invoke the words good and evil casually, as if the age of reason never happened. They speak proudly of killing, bullet-ridden corpses are triumphantly paraded. And like in *Lord of the Rings*, we define evil by demographics. The bloodline, the colour of skin, the ethnic background or nationality makes someone immediately suspect.

Can one judge a film with the morals of politics? Is *Lord of the Rings* seen differently in the United States than it is in Europe where the majority of people were against the invasions of Afghanistan and Iraq? A fable is 'a narration intended to enforce a useful truth'. When I look at *The Lord of the Rings* as the fable its author, J. R. R. Tolkien, intended it to be, I see a world clearly divided into races and regions of leader and followers, I see Calvinist pre-determinism and I see the vindication and veneration of empire unfolding in frame after frame. And I feel the quick burn of shame that I always feel when realising that as a child I was taken in by a 'useful truth' that now seems odious. (Dilday 2003)

### Sexism

It's not that the film invented the warrior princesses Eowyn and Arwen. They're in the book too, but Tolkien always seemed a little theoretical in his presentation of women. Here the actresses playing them make them specific, mercurial and commanding. When Eowyn confronts the Lord of the Nazgul, he who cannot be killed by any man, with the fact that 'I am no man', and then thrusts her sword in his face, I could feel battalions of women cheering her on. I cheered too. (Richard Alleva, *Commonweal*, 131, 30 January, 2004, p. 20)

'Towers' is like a family-oriented E-Rated video game, with no emotional complications other than saving the day. Women have so little to do here that they serve almost as plot-device flight attendants, offering a trough of Diet Coke to refresh the geek-magnet story. (Elvis Mitchell, New York *Times*, 19 December 2001)

### Nationalism

I relished the way that Peter Jackson and his largely local crew, in making *The Fellowship of the Ring* (2001), had transformed the familiar yet spectacular rivers, mountains, paddocks and forests into locations for Middle-earth or Mordor. I heard that at the end of some screenings in New Zealand, audiences broke into 'God of Nations', the national anthem. But as the trilogy has rolled on, towing films like *Samurai* in its wake my pleasure has been replaced by a deepening unease about the way in which New Zealand continues to tout itself as a cheap and diverse background for Middle-earth, Japan, India, America, Scotland or wherever. . . . But what happens when the locations of your personal, provincial and national pasts are rented out to global corporations such as Warner Bros. as sites for their imagined Japanese–American histories? (Rachael Buchanan, *Meanjin*, 63, March 2004, p. 54)

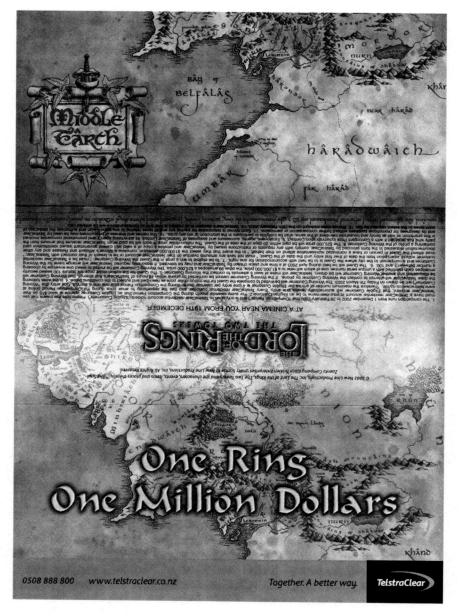

**Figure 34** International telecommunication company TelstraClear
incorporating the *LOTR* map into promotional material for
a sponsored competition.

## Morality

Scott Thill, Maybe that's a good thing.

Watching a young, Hobbit-like Smeagol (the amazing Andy Serkis) bait a hook on an idyllic pastoral pond in the first scenes of Peter Jackson's brilliant *Return of the King* is instructive – embroiled in a delirious metafiction of Paradise Lost, viewers are preparing for the ultimate sucker's ride. A three-hour-plus roller-coaster ride stuffed to the gills with extravagant visuals, breathtaking battles, and New Zealand's peerless environments, but – fitting, considering Jackson's character choice to kick off his much-anticipated film – a deceptive one to be sure.

After all, those familiar with Tolkien's now-canonical narrative will understand from the outset that, even though it ends well for most involved, *Return of the King* is not about special effects, martial triumphs, and monarchial victories, but rather irreconcilable loss and defeat. More than anything, the famed professor's fairy tale is about how one noble but draining quest can destroy anything resembling a normal life forever. For the entire world.

Tolkien knew this tragedy well, having spent months on a World War I battlefield before succumbing to trench fever and witnessing the death of all but one of his closest friends. He was unlucky enough to be involved in the Battle of the Somme, an artillery offensive – as well as a logistical failure – masterminded by Lt. General Sir Douglas Haig that cost the British 420,000 lives. And though he spent much of his postwar life railing against allegorical interpretations of his 1,000-page tome, it is impossible to separate Tolkien's battlefield from his bible of fantasy literature.

The specter of Haig is dredged up – if not by Tolkien then at least by Jackson – in the form of Denethor (John Noble), the mad steward of Gondor who sends Faramir (David Wenham) back on a similarly suicidal attack of Osgiliath, from which his brave but underappreciated son had just barely returned with his life. Jackson packs that Quixotic mission with poignancy, cutting across several meaning-laden events – a horse-borne Faramir galloping and gritting his teeth in preparation for inevitable doom; Pippin's (Billy Boyd) angelic rendition of 'The Steward of Gondor'; the orcs at Osgiliath lying in wait (much like the Germans did in the Battle of the Somme); and most importantly, the feasting Denethor (in extreme close-up) suggestively shoving meat and grapes in his mouth, the juice of the latter running down his chin like blood. It's a Caligula or Kronos moment, to be sure, the father eating his unwanted progeny; it's also one of Jackson's most powerful montages and comments on the interpersonal ravages of war. (www.brightlightsfilm.com)

## *Christian values: or the eyes of Ned Flanders*

Positive – One year ago, I walked into *The Fellowship of the Ring*. When I walked out, it was with a renewed respect for J. R. R. Tolkien. As a Christian, I'd seen far more than mere mythology. I'd seen profound truth in the most unexpected of places. With high hopes, I went into *The Two Towers*. I didn't come out disappointed. If you were impressed with the first film, prepared to be floored by the second. The filmmaking is spectacular, the acting stellar, and the CGI-created characters (including Gollum) are incredible. I never once felt I was watching a computer-generated actor. But beyond that, the true worth lies in the spiritual parallels. Tolkien originally claimed not to have written the novels as an allegory, but admitted later in his life that '[they] are a profoundly religious and Catholic work. . . . the religious element is absorbed into the story and symbolism'. Thus said, 'symbolism' abounds, some of it unabashedly blunt: such as the obvious Gandalf 'Christ-figure' emphasis. There are parallels to the valley of death, the second coming of Christ, and the eternal message that hope will always prevail. Seeking for these parallels has become something of a passion for me. I encourage others to try it: you may be surprised at what you find. My Ratings: [Good / 5] – Charity Bishop, age 19.

The special effects were great. The movie is very violent and parents should use discretion when allowing children to view this movie. I liked the way evil was portrayed by its ugly appearance in the Orcs, Uruk-hai, Wormtongue, and Gollum. This was unrealistic yet refreshing. The serpent in the Garden was quite beautiful as I recall. Wouldn't it be wonderful if we could spot evil so easily in our lives? The war between good and evil at Helms Deep was impressive and inspiring. Churchill said nothing is as exhilarating as being shot at without effect. I felt this through the triumph of Aragorn in the great battle. Gandalf assumes even a more powerful and angelic role than in the *Fellowship*. Whether this is suppose to be Christian imagery or not I do not know. Nevertheless, it certainly made me think of the spiritual realm. My Ratings: [Average / 5] – Mark L. Gilliam, age 41 (www.christiananswers.net/spotlight/movies/2002/thetwotowers.html).

### *Creative integrity:* The Lord of the Rings: The Return of the King *by Clint Morris, 18 December 2003*

Peter Jackson is so much more the filmmaker than George Lucas. . . . when you put Jackson's *Lord of the Rings* trilogy side by side with Lucas's *Star Wars* prequel trilogy, the latter's a mere pebble being skimmed across a huge mass stream that the New Zealand filmmaker has crafted. Whilst Lucas's back-story of Anakin Skywalker has been just as highly anticipated, the end result is an inferior, rather lifeless series of films – nothing unlike the original *Star Wars* trilogy which incongruously, resembles Jackson's grand series. There are some great special effects in the new *Star Wars* flicks but other than that, there's nothing much else. Jackson's *Lord of the Rings* trilogy on the other hand is seemingly perfect. Extremely well written with larger than life landscape, fantastically created sets and characters, as well as spot-on pacing, they're an immaculate bunch of films. (www.filmthreat.com).

### Finally, closer to Middle-earth

Here in the land of tall-poppy cutters . . . I have limitless respect for Jackson's managerial capacities and showman's instincts. I admire him as much as I'd admire any local entrepreneur who cracked, say, the international tomato sauce market.

So when I add that *The Lord of the Rings* trilogy is, as a work of cinematic art, ham-fisted, shallow, bombastic and laughably overrated, don't get me wrong. I'm not criticising Jackson but the degraded state of popular movies.

The *Rings* trilogy is an unremarkable boys' own action-adventure trilogy. Take away the frenetic effects and there isn't enough on the screen to keep even a subnormal human brain alive. (Dutton, *New Zealand Herald*)

This small sample of reviews of *LOTR*, from the creative establishment and from fans stealing employers' time to let loose their thoughts, suggests the diversity of opinion that *LOTR*'s hypermediated marketing drive released into the many sphericules that compose the cultural public sphere. The Movie Review Query Engine (mrqe.com) lists 379 reviews for *Fellowship*, 348 for *Towers*, and 335 for *Return*, ranging from Roger Ebert to evangelical Christians, *The Hindu* to *This Is Lancashire*, Gorilla Pants and The Juicy Cerebellum. Nor is the American Humane Association slow to provide its own review of the film's patchy animal husbandry – four horses died in the production and electric shock collars were used. Theonering.net alone counts 14,959 fan reviews for *Fellowship*, 12,487 for *Towers*, and a smaller but still daunting 4,589 for *Return*, ranging from the wrathful to the ecstatic. Twenty-five thousand respondents filled in the Lord of the Rings Research Project's online questionnaire (www.lordoftheringsresearch.net/) in more than a dozen languages. Among the preliminary results reported by the project leader Martin Barker on the public website is this table of responses to the question, 'What kind of story is The Lord of the Rings for you? *Please choose up to three*'.

| | | |
|---|---|---|
| Allegory: | 2586 | 3.8% |
| Epic | 13044 | 19.2% |
| Fairytale | 2808 | 4.1% |
| Fantasy | 9885 | 14.5% |
| Game-world | 531 | 0.7% |
| Good versus evil | 10734 | 15.8% |
| Myth/legend | 8897 | 13.1% |
| Quest | 8288 | 12.2% |
| SFX film | 5572 | 8.2% |
| Spiritual journey | 1877 | 2.8% |
| Threatened homeland | 1688 | 2.5% |
| War story | 2174 | 3.2% |

The sheer scale of such responses and the blurred boundaries between professional, semi-professional, and amateur reviewers makes generalisations difficult. In *Making Meaning*, Bordwell suggests that professional reviews usually comprise a condensed synopsis, some background information, a set of abbreviated arguments about the film, and an evaluation (1989: 38). Expanding on Bordwell's work, Buckland distinguishes three key objects of evaluation: the motivation of the film (plot logic, plausibility, intertextual motives such as fidelity to a literary source, and aesthetic), entertainment value, and social value, adding that many critics look for redeeming features of even the films they otherwise dislike (2003: 159–64).

Professional reviews of the trilogy focus typically on faithfulness to Tolkien, spectacle, acting, and narrative. Fan reviews do not have the responsibilities of professional reviewers to empathise with their readers' values (political, moral, social, and cultural) or to maintain a relationship with readers whose trust they hope to develop. Amateur reviewing frequently uses the language of radio shock-jocks, producing a rhetorical entertainment rather than attempting an accurate evaluation of the film; and fan reviews are often spiky, peppered with in-crowd language, and often written in pursuit of peer approval rather than personal kudos or professional service. Yet here, too, fidelity to the source material, spectacle, narrative, and performance are the key issues.

The intimate reliance of *LOTR* on the Internet is a factor in the diversity and scope of reviews. Promoting a kind of collective automatic writing, the Internet assembles a multiplicity of opinions in a common space. This universe of reviews is a shape-shifting totality in which any opinion – positive or negative, idiosyncratic or common, asserted or well argued – has equal visibility. 'Flame'-retardant expressions such as IMHO (in my humble opinion) are more a hedge against disagreement than a commitment to open dialogue. As a result, the sheer mass of materials, urged on by sheer adjacency, will push towards the horizontal equation of all aesthetic and cultural-political values. Yet reviews are not equal and visibility does not equate readily with relevance. This flattening of values results partly from formations of reviewing and even the funnelling effects of questionnaire response, but also from a production and marketing process in which the cultural object anticipates and fosters diversity in the pursuit of niche markets and fresh marketable meaning. *LOTR* thus emerges as the textual equivalent of an accident, witnessed by all but reported differently by many.

# Filmography

*Alfie*. Lewis Gilbert, Sheldrake Films / Lewis Gilbert, 1966, UK, 114 mins
*All about Eve*. Joseph L. Manciewicz, 20th Century Fox, 1950, US, 138 mins
*American Splendor*. Shari Springer Berman and Robert Pulcini, Good Machine
    / Home Box Office, 2000, US / Canada, 100 mins
*Apocalypse Now*. Francis Ford Coppola, Zoetrope Studios, 1979, US, 153 mins
*Austin Powers: International Man of Mystery*. Jay Roach, Capella Interna-
    tional / Eric's Boy / Juno Pix / KC Medien AG / Moving Pictures / New Line
    Cinema, 1997, US, 95 mins
*Austin Powers: The Spy Who Shagged Me*. Jay Roach, Eric's Boy / Moving
    Pictures / New Line Cinema / Team Todd, 1999, US, 96 mins
*Austin Powers in Goldmember*. Jay Roach, New Line Cinema / Gratitude
    International / Team Todd / Moving Pictures, 2002, US, 94 mins
*Bad Taste*. Peter Jackson, WingNut Films / New Zealand Film Commission,
    1987, NZ, 91 mins
*Basic Instinct*. Paul Verhoeven, Carolco Pictures, 1992, US, 123 mins

**Figure 35** Gandalf (temporarily) nearing journey's end.

*Beowulf*. Robert Zemeckis, ImageMovers / Shangri-La Entertainment, 2007, US, 113 mins

*Beverley Hills Cop*. Martin Brest, Eddie Murphy Productions / Paramount Pictures, 1984, US, 105 mins

*Beverley Hills Cop II*. Tony Scott, Eddie Murphy Productions / Paramount Pictures, 1987, US, 103 mins

*Beverley Hills Cop III*. John Landis, Eddie Murphy Productions / Paramount Pictures, 1994, US, 104 mins

*Blade 2*. Guillermo del Toro, Amen Ra Productions, 2002, US, 117 mins

*The Blair Witch Project*. Daniel Myrick and Eduardo Sanchez, Haxan, 1999, US, 86 mins

*The Bourne Supremacy*. Paul Greenglass, Hypnotic / Ludlum Entertainment / Motion Picture THETA Produktionsgesellschaft / The Kennedy/Marshall Company / Universal Pictures, 2004, US / Germany, 108 mins

*Braindead* (aka *Dead Alive*). Peter Jackson, WingNut Films, 1992, NZ, 104 mins

*Casino*. Martin Scorsese, Universal Pictures / Syalis DA / Légende Entreprises / De Fina-Cappa, 1995, US, 178 mins

*The Chronicles of Narnia: The Lion, the Witch, and the Wardrobe*. Andrew Adamson, Walt Disney / Walden Media / Lamp Post, 2005, US, 140 mins

*The Chronicles of Riddick*. David Twohy, Primal Foe Productions / One Race Productions / Radar Pictures / Universal Pictures, 2004, US, 119 mins

*Cinema of Unease*. Sam Neill and Judy Rymer, British Film Institute / New Zealand Film Commission / New Zealand on Air / TV3 (exec. prod. Vincent Burke, Colin MacCabe, and Bob Last), 1995, New Zealand / UK, 52 mins

*Citizen Kane*. Orson Welles, RKO, 1941, US, 119 mins

*City of God / Cidade de Deus*. Walter Salles, O2 Filmes / VideoFilmes / Globo Filmes / Lumiere Productions / Studio Canal / Wild Bunch, 2003, Brazil, 124 mins

*Cleopatra*. Joseph L. Mankiewicz, 20th Century Fox, 1963, US, 192 mins

*Cleopatra: The Film That Changed Hollywood*. Kevin Burns and Brent Zacky, Prometheus Entertainment, 2001, US, 119 mins

*A Clockwork Orange*. Stanley Kubrick, Hawk Films / Polaris Productions / Warner Bros., UK, 1971, 136 mins

*Conan the Barbarian*. John Milius, Dino De Laurentiis Productions / Universal Pictures, 1982, US, 129 mins

*Cowboys of Culture*. Geoff Steven, Vidcom, 1991, NZ, 46 mins

*Crash*. David Cronenberg, Alliance Communications / Recorded Picture / The Movie Network / Téléfilm Canada, 1996, Canada, 100 mins

*Crooked Earth*. Sam Pillsbury, Pandora Film, 2001, NZ, 107 mins

*Crush*. Alison Maclean, Hibiscus Films / Movie Partners / New Zealand Film Commission / New Zealand On Air, 1992, NZ, 115 mins

*Doom*. Andrzej Bartkowiak, Babelsberg Film GmbH / Di Bonaventura Pictures / Distant Planet Productions / Doom Productions / John Wells Productions / Reaper Productions / Stillking Films, 2004, UK / US / Czech Republic / Germany, 100 mins

*Dumb and Dumber*. Peter Farrelly, Motion Picture Corporation of America / New Line Cinema, 1994, US, 107 mins

*El Cid*. Anthony Mann, Samuel Bronston, 1961, US / Spain, 184 mins

*The English Patient*. Anthony Minghella, J&M / Miramax / Tiger Moth, 1996, US, 162 mins

*A Few Good Men*. Rob Reiner, Castle Rock Entertainment / Columbia Pictures Corporation / New Line Cinema, 1992, US, 138 mins

*Finding Nemo*. Andrew Stanton and Lee Unkrich, Walt Disney / Pixar, 2003, US, 100 mins

*Forgotten Silver*. Costa Botes and Peter Jackson, WingNut, 1995, NZ, 54 mins

*The Frighteners*. Peter Jackson, Universal Pictures / WingNut Films, 1996, NZ / US, 110 mins

*Frodo Is Great . . . Who Is That?!!* Stan Alley, Hannah Clarke, and Nick Booth, 2004, NZ, 60 mins

*Gladiator*. Ridley Scott, Dreamworks SKG / Universal / Columbia TriStar, 2000, US, 155 mins

*The Godfather*. Francis Ford Coppola, Paramount Pictures, 1972, US, 168 mins

*Goodfellas*. Martin Scorsese, Warner Bros Pictures, 1990, US, 145 mins

*Harry Potter and the Philosopher's Stone* (aka *Harry Potter and the Sorcerer's Stone*). Chris Columbus, 2001, US / UK 147 mins

*Heavenly Creatures*. Peter Jackson, Fontana Productions / Miramax / NZ Film Commission / Senator Film / WingNut, 1994, NZ, 98 mins

*Heaven's Gate*. Michael Cimino, Partisan Productions / United Artists, 1980, US, 219 mins

*Hidalgo*. Joe Johnston, Touchstone / Hidalgo / Casey Silver / Dune, 2004, US, 136 mins

*Highlander*. Russell Mulcahey, 20th Century Fox / EMI Films Ltd. / Highlander Productions Limited, 1986, UK, 116 mins

*Highlander II – The Quickening*. Russell Mulcahey, Lamb Bear Entertainment, 1990, US, 100 mins

*Highlander III – The Sorcerer*. Andy Morahan, Fallingcloud / Initial Groupe / Miramax Films / Transfilm, 1995, Canada / France / UK, 98 mins

*A History of Violence*. David Cronenberg, New Line / Bender-Spink, 2005, US, 96 mins

*Hulk*. Ang Lee, Good Machine, 2003, US, 138 mins

*Indiana Jones and the Raiders of the Lost Ark*. Steven Spielberg, Lucasfilm / Paramount Pictures, 1981, US, 111 mins

*Indiana Jones and the Temple of Doom*. Steven Spielberg, Lucasfilm / Paramount Pictures, 1984, US, 114 mins

*Indiana Jones and the Last Crusade*. Steven Spielberg, Lucasfilm / Paramount Pictures, 1989, US, 122 mins

*Jaws*. Steven Spielberg, Universal / Zanuck-Brown, 1975, US, 124 mins

*JFK*. Oliver Stone, Alcor Films / Camelot / Canal+ / Ixtlan Corporation / Regency Enterprises / Warner Bros Pictures, 1991, US, 189 mins

*Jurassic Park*. Steven Spielberg, Universal / Amblin, 1993, US, 127 mins

*Kill Bill Vol. 1*. Quentin Tarantino, Miramax / A Band Apart / Super Cool ManChu, 2003, US, 111 mins

*King Kong*. Peter Jackson, Universal / WingNut, 2005, US / NZ, 187 mins

*Last Man Standing*. Walter Hill, One Wolf / New Line Cinema, 1996, US, 101 mins

*The Last Samurai*. Edward Zwick, Warner Bros / Bedford Falls / Cruise-Wagner / Radar, 2003, US, 154 mins

*Looking for Richard*. Al Pacino, 20th Century Fox / Chal Productions / Jam Productions, 1996, US, 112 mins

*Lost in Translation*. Sophia Coppola, 2003, US / Japan, 102 mins

*Luther*. Eric Till, Eikon Film / NFP teleart / Thrivent Financial for Lutherans, 2003, Germany, 121 mins

*The Making of 'The Lord of the Rings'*. Costa Botes, 2002, NZ, no definitive running time

*The Mask*. Charles Russell, Dark Horse Entertainment / New Line Cinema, 1995, US, 101 mins

*Master and Commander: The Far Side of the World*. Peter Weir, 20th Century Fox / Miramax Films / Universal Pictures / Samuel Goldwyn Films LLC, 2003, US, 132 mins

*The Matrix*. Andy and Larry Wachowski, Groucho II Film Partnership, 1999, US, 130 mins

*The Matrix Revolutions*. Andy and Larry Wachowski, Warner Bros / Village Roadshow / NPV Entertainment / Silver Pictures, 2003, US, 129 mins

*Meet the Feebles*. Peter Jackson, WingNut, 1989, NZ, 97 mins

*Mystic River*. Clint Eastwood, Warner Bros Pictures / Village Roadshow Pictures / NVP Entertainment / Malpaso Productions, 2003, US, 137 mins

*Naked Lunch*. David Cronenberg, Film Trustees Ltd / Naked Lunch Productions / Nippon Film Development and Finance Inc / Record Picture Company (RPC) / The Ontario Film Development Corporation / Telefilm Canada, 1991, UK / Canada, 115 mins

*A Nightmare on Elm Street*. Wes Craven, Medium Home / New Line / Smart Egg, 1984, US, 91 mins

*Once Were Warriors*. Lee Tamahori, Communicado / New Zealand Film Commission / Avalon Studios / New Zealand on Air, 1994, NZ, 102 mins

*The Passion of the Christ*. Mel Gibson, Icon, 2004, US, 127 mins

*Pear Ta Ma 'On Maf / The Land Has Eyes*. Vilsoni Hereniko, Te Maka Productions Inc., 2004, Rotuma, 87 mins

*The Piano*. Jane Campion, CiBy 2000, 1993, Australia / New Zealand / France, 121 mins

*The Pirates of the Caribbean*. Gore Verbinski, Walt Disney / Jerry Bruckheimer / First Mate, 2003, US, 143 mins

*Platoon*. Oliver Stone, Cinema 86 / Hemdale, 1986, US, 120 mins

*The Player*. Robert Altman, Avenue Pictures / Guild / Spelling, 1992, US, 124 mins

*The Quiet Earth*. Geoff Murphy, Cinepro / Mr Yellowbeard Productions, 1985, NZ, 91 mins

*Reefer Madness*. Louis Gasnier, George A. Hirliman / G & H Productions, 1936, US, 67 mins

*Rush Hour*. Brent Ratner, New Line Cinema / Roger Birbaum Productions, 1998, US, 98 mins

*Rush Hour 2*. Brent Ratner, New Line Cinema, 2002, US, 90 mins

*Saving Private Ryan*. Steven Spielberg, Amblin Entertainment / Dreamworks SKG / Mark Gordon Productions / Mutual Film Corporation / Paramount Pictures, 1998, US, 170 mins

*Scary Movie 3*. David Zucker, Dimension / Brad Grey, 2003, US, 84 mins

*Seabiscuit*. Gary Ross, Universal Pictures / Dreamworks SKG / Spyglass Entertainment / The Kennedy / Marshall Company / Larger than Life Productions, 2003, US, 141 mins

*Seven*. David Fincher, New Line Cinema, 1995, US, 127 mins

*The Shawshank Redemption*. Frank Darabont, Castle Rock Entertainment / Columbia Pictures Corporation, 1994, US, 142 mins

*Shine*. Scott Hicks, Australian Film Finance Corp / Film Victoria / Momentum, 1996, Australia, 105 mins

*Shrek*. Andrew Adamson and Vicky Jenson, DreamWorks SKG / Pacific Data Images, 2001, US, 90 mins

*Silence of the Lambs*. Jonathan Demme, Orion Pictures Corporation / Strong Heart / Demme Production, 1990, US, 118 mins

*Sleeping Dogs*. Roger Donaldson, Aardvark Films / New Zealand Development Finance Corporation / Broadbank Corporation / Television One / Queen Elizabeth II Arts Council, 1977, NZ, 107 mins

*Smash Palace*. Roger Donaldson, Aardvark Films / Moviescripts / New Zealand Film Commission, 1981, NZ, 100 mins

*Snow White and the Seven Dwarfs*. David Hand, Walt Disney Pictures, 1937, US, 83 mins

*Spider-Man*. Sam Raimi, Laura Ziskin Productions, 2002, US, 121 mins

*Spy Kids 3D: Game Over*. Robert Rodriguez, Dimension Films / Los Hooligans Productions / Troublemaker Studios, 2003, US, 84 mins

*Star Trek – The Motion Picture*. Robert Wise, Century Associates / Paramount Pictures, 1979, US, 132 mins

*Star Trek II: The Wrath of Khan*. Nicholas Meyer, Paramount Pictures, 1982, US, 114 mins

*Star Trek III: The Search for Spock*. Leonard Nimoy, Cinema Group Ventures / Paramount Pictures, 1984, US, 105 mins

*Star Trek IV: The Voyage Home*. Leonard Nimoy, Paramount Pictures, 1986, US, 119 mins

*Star Trek V: The Final Frontier*. William Schatner, Paramount Pictures, 1989, US, 107 mins

*Star Trek VI: The Undiscovered Country*. Nicholas Meyer, Paramount Pictures, 1991, US, 110 mins

*Star Trek: Generations*. David Carson, Paramount Pictures, 1994, US, 118 mins

*Star Trek: First Contact*. Jonathan Frakes, Paramount Pictures, 1996, US, 111 mins

*Star Trek: Insurrection*. Jonathan Frakes, Paramount Pictures, 1998, US, 103 mins

*Star Trek Nemesis*. Stuart Baird, Paramount Pictures, 2002, US, 117 mins

*Star Wars Episode IV – A New Hope*. George Lucas, Lucasfilm, 1977 / 1997, US, 120 mins

*Star Wars Episode V – The Empire Strikes Back*. George Lucas, Lucasfilm, 1980 / 1997, US, 124 mins

*Star Wars Episode VI – Return of the Jedi*. George Lucas, Lucasfilm, 1983 / 1997, US, 131 mins

*Star Wars Episode 1 – The Phantom Menace*. George Lucas, Lucasfilm / 20th Century Fox, 1999, 2000, US, 132 mins

*Teenage Mutant Ninja Turtles*. Steve Barron, 888 Productions / Golden Harvest Company Ltd / Limelight Entertainment / Mirage Productions / New Line Cinema / Northshore Investments, 1990, US, 93 mins

*Teenage Mutant Ninja Turtles II: The Secret of the Ooze*. Michael Pressman, Golden Harvest Company / New Line Cinema / Northshore Investments, 1991, US, 87 mins

*Teenage Mutant Ninja Turtles III*. Stuart Gillard, Clearwater Holdings / Golden Harvest Company, 1992, US, 96 mins

*Thin Red Line*. Terrence Malick, Fox 2000 Pictures / Geisler – Roberdeau / Phoenix Pictures, 1998, US, 170 mins

*Thirteen Days*. Roger Donaldson, Beacon Communications / New Line Cinema / Tig Productions, 2000, US, 145 mins

*Titanic*. James Cameron, 20th Century Fox / Paramount / Lightstorm Entertainment, US, 1997, 195 mins

*Toy Story*. John Lasseter, Walt Disney / Pixar, 1995, US, 81 mins

*Ultraviolet*. Joe Ahearne, BBC / World Productions, 1998, UK (series)

*Underworld*. Len Wiseman, Lakeshore Entertainment, 2003, US, 121 mins

*Whale Rider*. Niki Caro, South Pacific Pictures, 2002, NZ, 97 mins

*What Becomes of the Broken-Hearted*. Ian Mune, 1999, NZ, 103 mins

*When Harry Met Sally*. Rob Reiner, Castle Rock Entertainment / Nelson Entertainment, 1989, US, 95 mins

*Das Wunder von Bern / The Miracle of Bern*. Sönke Wortmann, Little Shark / Senator / Seven, 2003, Germany, 118 mins

*X-Men*. Bryan Singer, Donners' Company, 2000, US, 104 mins

# References

## Primary sources

Jackson, Peter (2001) *The Lord of the Rings: The Fellowship of the Ring* New Line Cinema / WingNut Films 178 min. Feature release
—— (2002a) New Line Home Entertainment 178 min. DVD
—— (2002b) New Line Home Entertainment 208 min. Extended DVD
—— (2002c) 'The sound-scapes of Middle-earth', New Line Home Entertainment 208 min. Extended DVD
—— (2002d) *The Lord of the Rings: The Two Towers* New Line Cinema / WingNut Films 179 min. Feature release
—— (2003a) New Line Home Entertainment 179 min. DVD
—— (2003b) New Line Home Entertainment 208 min. Extended DVD
—— (2003c) 'Sound Design', New Line Home Entertainment 208 min. Extended DVD
—— (2003d) *The Lord of the Rings: The Return of the King* New Line Cinema / WingNut Films 201 min. Feature release
—— (2004a) New Line Home Entertainment 201 min. DVD
—— (2004b) New Line Home Entertainment 250 min. Extended DVD
Tolkien, J. R. R. (2002) *The Lord of the Rings*. HarperCollins Publishers, London

## Secondary sources

Aarseth, Espen (1997) *Cybertext: Perspectives on Ergodic Literature*. The Johns Hopkins University Press, Baltimore
*Action Adventure* (2004) http://actionadventure.about.com/cs/weeklystories (accessed 2 March 2004)
Adams, Doug (2001) 'Learning new hobbits'. *Film Score Monthly*, October–November, 6.9: 22–6
—— (2002) 'Towering achievements'. *Film Score Monthly*, December, 7.10: 20–4, 48
—— (2003) 'Seven days in September'. *Film Score Monthly*, December, 8.10: 16–26
—— (2004) 'The Lord of the Rings Symphony: six movements for orchestra and chorus – composed by Howard Shore', programme notes, world premiere,

*The Lord of the Rings Symphony: Six Movements for Orchestra and Chorus, Music from the Motion Picture*, Michael Fowler Centre, Wellington

Ain't-it-cool-news (nd) 'Peter Jackson answers THE GEEKS!!! 20 questions about Lord of the Rings!!!'. www.aint-it-cool-news.com/lordoftherings.html (accessed 5 July 2005)

Aksoy, Asu, and Kevin Robins (1992) 'Hollywood for the 21st century: global competition for the critical mass in image markets'. *Cambridge Journal of Economics*, 16.1: 7–20

Albiniak, Paige (2002) 'If networks went shopping'. *Broadcasting & Cable*. 4 February, 132.5: 19

Allen, Michael (2002) 'The impact of digital technologies on film aesthetics', in Dan Harries (ed.), *The New Media Book*. British Film Institute, London, 109–18

Altman, Robert (1992) *The Player*, quote reference from the Internet Movie Database, www.imdb.com/title/tt0105151/quotes (accessed 24 August 2004)

Ansen, David (2001) 'A "ring" to rule the screen: Peter Jackson's fierce, imaginative movie takes high-flying risks and inspires with its power and scale'. *Newsweek*, 10 December, 75

'AOL TW posts profitable Q3: but media giant forced to restate 2 years of financials' (2002) *Hollywood Reporter*, 24 October, 375.39: 1

Astin, Sean, with Joe Layden (2004) *There and Back Again: An Actor's Tale*. Allen Unwin, Sydney

Atkinson, Michael (1995) 'Earthly creatures'. *Film Comment*, May–June, 31: 31–7

audiocareers (2004) 'David Farmer'. www.audiocareers.info/index.cfm (accessed 20 December 2004)

Aumont, Jacques (1997) 'The variable eye or the mobilization of the gaze', in Dudley Andrew (ed.), *The Image in Dispute*. University of Texas Press, Austin, 231–58

Austin, Thomas (2002) *Hollywood Hype and Audiences: Selling and Watching Popular Film in the Nineties*. Manchester University Press, Manchester

Bachelard, Gaston (1964) *The Poetics of Space*, trans. Maria Jolas. Orion Press, New York.

Baigent, Robert J. (1998) 'We need some real men here: issues of masculinity in the films of Peter Jackson'. University of Auckland, Auckland, NZ, unpublished MA thesis

Bakalis, Anna (2003) 'It's unreel: DVD rentals overtake videocassettes'. *Washington Times*, 21 June, http://washingtontimes.com/business/20030620-113258-1104r.htm (accessed 20 January 2005)

Balázs, Béla (1952) *Theory of the Film (Origin and Growth of a New Art)*, trans. Edith Bone. Denis Dobson, London [reprinted 1972 by Arno Press, New York]

Balio, Tino (1998) ' "A major presence in all of the world's important markets": the globalization of Hollywood in the 1990s', in Steve Neale and Murray Smith (eds), *Contemporary Hollywood Cinema*. Routledge, New York and London, 58–73

Barclay, Barry (1990) *Our Own Image*. Longman Paul, Auckland
—— (2003) 'Celebrating Fourth Cinema'. *Illusions* 35: 7–11
—— (2005) *Mana Tuturu: Maori Treasures and Intellectual Property Rights*. Auckland University Press, Auckland
Barker, Martin (2003) 'The Lord of the Rings international research project', *Prom* 15, www.prom-aber.com (accessed 31 May 2004)
Barker, Martin, and Ernest Mathijs (eds) (2008) *Watching The Lord of the Rings: Tolkien's World Audience*. Peter Lang, New York
Barker, Martin, Kate Egan, Stan Jones, and Ernest Mathijs (2008) 'Introduction: researching *The Lord of the Rings*: audiences and contexts', in Martin Barker and Ernest Mathijs (eds), *Watching The Lord of the Rings: Tolkien's World Audience*. Peter Lang, New York, 1–20
Barr, Jim, and Mary Barr (1996) 'NZFX: the films of Peter Jackson and Fran Walsh', in Jonathan Dennis and Jan Bieringa (eds), *Film in Aotearoa New Zealand*. 2nd edn. Victoria University Press, Wellington, 150–60
Barrett, Victoria (2003) 'I don't want to play the fat guy or friend all my life'. *Guardian*, 19 December, http://film.guardian.co.uk (accessed 11 March 2004)
Barry, Matt (2002) 'Analyzing *Lord of the Rings: The Two Towers*'. 17 November, www.soundtrack.net/features/article/?id=100 (accessed 4 March 2004)
Bartos, Otomar J. (1996) 'Postmodernism, postindustrialism, and the future'. *The Sociological Quarterly*, 37.2: 307–26
Bassham, Gregory (2003) 'Tolkien's six keys to happiness', in Gregory Bassham and Eric Bronson (eds), *The Lord of the Rings and Philosophy*. Open Court, Chicago, 49–60
Bassham, Gregory, and Eric Bronson (eds) (2003) *The Lord of the Rings and Philosophy*. Open Court, Chicago
Bauer, Erik (2002) '"It's just a movie": Erik Bauer speaks with Peter Jackson'. *Creative Screenwriting*, January–February, 6–12
Bazin, André (1971) 'An aesthetic of reality: neorealism (cinematic realism and the Italian school of the liberation)', in *What Is Cinema? 2*, trans. Hugh Gray. University of California Press, Berkeley, 16–40
BBC News Online (2005) 6 January, http://newsvote.bbc.co.uk (accessed 1 June 2005)
Beller, Jonathan (1998) 'Capital / Cinema', in Eleanor Kaufman and Kevin John Heller (eds), *Deleuze & Guattari: New Mappings in Politics, Philosophy, and Culture*. University of Minnesota Press, Minneapolis, 77–95
—— (2003) 'The cinematic mode of production: towards a political economy of the postmodern'. *Culture, Theory and Critique*, 44.1: 91–106
Benjamin, Walter (1968) *Illuminations*, trans. Harry Zohn. Schocken, New York
Bennett, Tony (1995) *The Birth of the Museum: History, Theory, Politics*. Routledge, London
Berger, Peter (1967) *The Sacred Canopy: Elements of a Sociological Theory of Religion*. Doubleday, Garden City, NY
Biddiss, M. (ed.) (1970) 'Introduction to J.-A. comte de Gobineau'. *Gobineau: Selected Political Writings*. Cape, London

Bing, J. (2002) 'Actors savor star bucks'. *Variety*, 1–7 April: 1 and 75

Black, Joanne (2006) '100% urgent'. *New Zealand Listener*, 24 June, 26–9

Blair, Helen (2003) 'Winning and losing in flexible labour markets: the formation and operation of networks of interdependence in the UK film industry'. *Sociology*, 37.4: 677–94

Bordwell, David (1989) *Making Meaning: Inference and Rhetoric in the Interpretation of Cinema*. Harvard University Press, Cambridge, MA

Bordwell, David, Kristin Thompson, and Janet Staiger (1985) *The Classical Hollywood Cinema: Film Style and Mode of Production to 1960*. Columbia University Press, New York

Bowen, Kit (2003) ' "Two Towers", "Simpsons" Top DVD Sales'. *Hollywood. com*, 28 August, www.hollywood.com/news/detail/article/1726269 (accessed 30 December 2004)

Boyes, Christopher, Michael Hedges, Michael Semanick, and Hammond Peek (2004) '*Lord of the Rings: The Return of the King*'. *Editors Guild Magazine*, May–June, 25.3, republished at www.editorsguild.com/Newsletter/MayJun04/best_sound_mixing/lor_sound_mix.htm (accessed 20 December 2004)

Bradshaw, Peter (2003a) 'The Lord of the Rings: The Return of the King'. *Guardian*, 19 December, www.film.guardian.co.uk/News_Story/Critic_Review/Guardian_Film_of_the_week/0,4267,1109755,00.html (accessed 11 March 2004)

—— (2003b) 'Whale Rider'. *Guardian*, 11 July, www.guardian.co.uk/arts/fridayreview/story/0,,995301,00.html (accessed 9 July 2005)

Braund, Simon (2002) 'Battlefield Middle Earth'. *Empire*, January: 60–84

Brawn, David (2002) *The Lord of the Rings: The Two Towers Movie Photo Guide*. Houghton Mifflin Company, New York

—— (ed.) (2003) *The Lord of the Rings: The Return of the King Photo Guide*. Houghton Mifflin Company, New York

Brodie, Ian (2002) *The Lord of the Rings Location Guidebook*. HarperCollins Publishers, Auckland

—— (2004) *The Lord of the Rings Location Guidebook: Extended Edition*. HarperCollins Publishers, Auckland

Bronson, Eric (2003) 'Farewell to Lorien: the bounded joy of existentialists and elves', in Gregory Bassham and Eric Bronson (eds), *The Lord of the Rings and Philosophy*. Allen Court, Chicago, 72–84

Brookey, Robert Alan, and Robert Westerfelhaus (2002) 'Hiding homoeroticism in plain view: the *Fight Club* DVD as digital closet'. *Critical Studies in Mass Communication*, March, 19.1: 21–43

Brown, Marie (2002) 'Representing the body of the nation: the art exhibitions of New Zealand's National Museum'. *Third Text*, 16:3, 285–94

Brown, Royal S. (1994) *Overtones and Undertones: Reading Film Music*. University of California Press, Berkeley

Bruce, Steve (1989) *A House Divided: Protestantism, Schism and Secularization*. Routledge, London

Bruno, Giuliana (2002) *Atlas of Emotion: Journeys in Art, Architecture, and Film*. Verso, New York

Bruzzi, Stella (1995) '*Heavenly Creatures*'. *Sight and Sound*, February, 5: 45–6

Bryant, Rick (1995) '*Forgotten Silver*'. *Metro*, December, 174: 165

Buckland, Warren (2003) *Teach Yourself Film Studies*, 2nd edn. Hodder and Stoughton, London

Burger, Dennis (2001) 'What makes DVD "special"? An interview with *Terminator* DVD producer Van Ling'. 2 October, www.dvdangle.com/fun_stuff/interviews/van_ling/index.html (accessed 4 February 2004)

Calder, Peter (2003) 'The hoard of the Rings'. *New Zealand Herald*, 29 November, www.nzherald.co.nz/entertainment/entertainmentstorydisplay.cfm?storyID=3536697 (accessed 10 May 2004)

Campbell, Gordon (2000) 'Lord of the Rings'. *New Zealand Listener*, 21 October, 18–25

—— (2001) 'Planet Middle Earth'. *New Zealand Listener*, 15 December, 17–24

—— (2004) 'Ring cycle'. *New Zealand Listener*, 17–23 January, 192.3323, www.listener.co.nz/default,1328.sm (accessed 5 July 2005)

Campbell, Russell (1995) 'Dismembering the Kiwi Bloke: representations of masculinity in *Braindead, Desperate Remedies* and *The Piano*'. *Illusions*, 24: 2–9

Carlsson, Mikaell (2001) 'The journey into Middle-Earth: Howard Shore talks about his score for the *Lord of the Rings: The Fellowship of the Ring*'. November, www.musicfromthemovies.com/pages/shore_rings.html (accessed 9 December 2003)

Carpenter, Humphrey, and Christopher Tolkien (eds) (1981) *Letters of J. R. R. Tolkien*. George Allen and Unwin, London

Caruth, Cathy (ed.) (1995) *Trauma: Explorations in Memory*. Johns Hopkins University Press, Baltimore and London

Catherall, S. (2002) 'Extra slams the sting in the Ring'. *Sunday Star Times*, 17 February, www.theonering.net (accessed on 30 May 2005)

Caves, Richard E. (2000) *Creative Industries: Contracts between Art and Commerce*. Harvard University Press, Cambridge, MA and London

Chesters, Paul (2004) 'Letters to the Editor'. *The Guardian Review*, 9 January, 3

Chin, Bertha, and Jonathan Gray (2001) 'One ring to rule them all: pre-viewers and pre-texts of *The Lord of the Rings* films'. *Intensities: The Journal of Cult Media*, Autumn–Winter, 2, www.cult-media.com/issue2/Achingray.htm (accessed 4 January 2005)

Chion, Michel (1994) *Audio-Vision: Sound on Screen*, trans. and ed. Claudia Gorbman. Columbia University Press, New York

Chisholm, D. (1997) 'Profit-sharing versus fixed-payment contracts: evidence from the film industry'. *Journal of Law, Economics and Organization*, April, 13.1: 169–201

Clark, Helen (2001a) *Some Facts about Lord of the Rings*. Wellington: New Zealand Government announcement, 7 November www.executive.govt.nz/minister/clark/lor/lor.htm (accessed 4 January 2005)

—— (2001b) *Maximising Spin-offs from Lord of the Rings: Questions and Answers*. Wellington: New Zealand Government announcement, 7 November. www.executive.govt.nz/minister/clark/lor/qa.htm (accessed 4 January 2005)

—— (2002) *Growing an Innovative New Zealand*. Office of The Prime Minister, Wellington, www.executive.govt.nz/minister/clark/innovate/ (accessed 20 January 2005)

Cohen, David (2004) 'Thirty burning media questions for 2004'. *The National Business Review*, 5 March, www.nbr.co.nz/print/print.asp?id=8405&cid=0&cname=Search (accessed 4 February 2005)

Conrich, Ian, and Roy Smith (1998) 'Fool's gold: New Zealand's *Forgotten Silver*, myth and national identity'. *British Review of New Zealand Studies*, 9.2: 57–65

Corliss, Richard (2001) 'Lord of the films: without a single cute kid or flying broom, the movie of J. R. R. Tolkien's fantasy comes to thrilling life'. *Time International*, 24 December, 158.25: 64

Corner, John (1995) *Television and Public Address*. Edward Arnold, London

Counsell, C. (1996) *Signs of Performance: Introduction to Twentieth-Century Theatre*. Routledge, London

Crary, Jonathan (1999) *Suspensions of Perception: Attention, Spectacle, and Modern Culture*. MIT Press, Cambridge, MA

Creed, Barbara (1996) '*Heavenly Creatures*'. *Midwest*, 10: 20–1

Cruickshank, Samuel G. (2002) 'From a Scary Black Bastard: Thoughts from a Post-Graduate Maori Film Student'. MA thesis. University of Auckland, Auckland

Cubitt, Sean (1999) 'Introduction. *Le réel, c'est l'impossible*: the sublime time of special effects'. *Screen*, 40.2: 123–30

—— (2002) 'Digital filming and special effects', in Dan Harries (ed.), *The New Media Book*. British Film Institute, London, 17–29

—— (2004) *The Cinema Effect*. MIT Press, Cambridge, MA

Cunningham, Stuart (2004) 'The creative industries after cultural policy: a genealogy and some preferred futures'. *International Journal of Cultural Studies*, 7.1: 105–15

Dahlhaus, Carl (1979) *Richard Wagner's Music Dramas*, trans. Mary Whittall. Cambridge University Press, Cambridge

Daniels, Bill, David Leedy, and Steven D. Sills (1998) *Movie Money: Understanding Hollywood's (Creative) Accounting Practices*. Silman-James Press, Los Angeles

Dansey, Harry (1974) *Te Raukura: The Feathers of the Albatross*. Longman Paul, Auckland

Daston, Lorraine, and Katherine Park (1998) 'Monsters: a case study', in *Wonders and the Order of Nature, 1150–1750*. MIT Press, Cambridge, MA, 173–214

Davies, H. (2003) 'Lord of the Rings rebels in bonus row'. *Daily Telegraph*, www.telegraph.co.uk (accessed 1 June 2005)

Davison, Scott (2003) 'Tolkien and the nature of evil', in Gregory Bassham and Eric Bronson (eds), *The Lord of the Rings and Philosophy*. Allen Court, Chicago, 99–109

DCMS (Department for Culture, Media, and Sport, United Kingdom) (1998) *Creative Industries: Mapping Document, 1998*. DCMS, London, www.culture.gov.uk/global/publications/archive_2001/ci_mapping_doc_2001.htm (accessed 9 July 2005)

—— (2001) *The Creative Industries Mapping Document 2001*. DCMS, London (accessed 23 December 2004)

De Frantz, Monika (2003) 'Cultural regeneration as discursive governance: some lessons from the conflictive process of constructing a new "museums quarters" in Vienna'. Paper read at European Urban Development, Research and Policy and the Future of European Cohesion Policy, 28–30 August, at Budapest, Hungary

Deleuze, Gilles (1989) *Cinema 2: The Time Image*. University of Minnesota Press, Minneapolis

'Designer dressing for Orcs' (2001) *Massey News*, http://masseynews.massey.ac.nz/_2001/publications_2001/Massey_News/August/Aug_13/stories/lord_of_the_rings.html (accessed 28 December 2004)

De Vany, A. (2004) *Hollywood Economics: How Extreme Uncertainty Shapes the Film Industry*. Routledge, London

Dibdin, Michael (1992) *Cabal: An Aurelio Zen Mystery*. Faber and Faber, London

Dilday, K. A. (2003) 'The Return of the King: Tolkien and the New Medievalism'. www.opendemocracy.net/articles/ViewPopUpArticle.jsp?id=1&articleID=1653 (accessed 5 January 2004)

Dixon, Greg (2004) 'Seeking out the unsung heroes'. *New Zealand Herald*, 23 February (Newstext Plus subscription database)

Dolan, John (2003) 'Galadriel and I: a fatwah against Peter Jackson'. *Landfall*, May, 205: 5–11

Donald, Darroch (2003) *Footprint New Zealand*. Footprint, Bath

Doyle, Audrey (2003) 'The Two Towers'. *Computer Graphics World*, February, 26.2: 28–32

Du Gay, Paul (1991) 'Enterprise culture and the ideology of excellence'. *New Formations*, 13: 45–61

Duncan, Jody (2002) 'The Lord of the Rings: The Fellowship of the Ring: ring masters'. *Cinefex*, April, 89: 64–131

Durie, John, Annika Pham, and Neil Watson (2000) *Marketing and Selling Your Film Around the World*. Silman-James Press, Los Angeles

DVDfile.com (2003) 'In the round – Return of the King: interview with Ngila Dickson'. www.dvdfile.com/news/special_report/in_the_round/lordoftherings/returnoftheking/costumes.html (accessed 28 December 2004)

Dyer-Witheford, Nick (1999) *Cyber-Marx*. University of Illinois Press, Urbana and Chicago

Ebert, Roger (2001) [Review]. *Chicago Sun-Times*, 19 December, http://rogerebert.suntimes.com/apps/pbcs.dll/article?AID=/20011219/REVIEWS/112190301/1023 (accessed 6 January 2005)

—— (2002) [Review]. *Chicago Sun-Times*, 12 December, http://rogerebert.suntimes.com/apps/pbcs.dll/article?AID=/20021218/REVIEWS/212180301/1023 (accessed 6 January 2005)

—— (2003) [Review]. *Chicago Sun-Times*, 17 December, http://rogerebert.suntimes.com/apps/pbcs.dll/article?AID=/20031217/REVIEWS/312170301/1023 (accessed 6 January 2005)

Eco, Umberto (1976) *A Theory of Semiotics*. Indiana University Press, Bloomington

Elleray, Michelle (1999) '*Heavenly Creatures* in Godzone', in Ellis Hanson (ed.), *Out Takes: Essays on Queer Theory and Film*. Duke University Press, Durham, NC, 223–40

—— (2001) 'Unsettled Subject: The South Pacific and the Settler'. Unpublished dissertation. Cornell University

Ellis, John (1992) *Visible Fictions: Cinema, Television, Video*, rev. edn. Routledge, London

Elsaesser, Thomas (2001) 'Postmodernism as mourning work'. *Screen*, 42.2: 193–201

*Empire* (2005) '*The Lord of the Rings*: the untold story'. January, 76–87

'Ergodic literature' (2006) *Wikipedia*. http://en.wikipedia.org/wiki/Ergodic_literature (accessed 25 April 2006)

Eskelinen, Markku (2001) 'The gaming situation'. *Games Studies*, 1.1, www.gamestudies.org/0101/eskelinen/ (accessed December 2001)

Feld, Rob (2004) 'The one true ring: ring bearers Peter Jackson, Fran Walsh and Philippa Boyens live to tell the tale'. *Write Up* (New Zealand Writers Guild), Autumn, 10–15

filmsound.org (2004) '*The Lord of the Rings: The Return of the King*'. www.filmsound.org/articles/notes.htm (accessed 4 January 2005)

Fisher, Jude (2002) *The Two Towers Visual Companion: The Official Illustrated Movie Companion (The Lord of the Rings)*. Houghton Mifflin Co., Boston

—— (2003) *The Lord of the Rings: The Return of the King. Visual Companion*. Houghton Mifflin Co., Boston

Fiske, John (1987) *Television Culture*. Routledge, London, 108–25

Flusser, Vilem (2000) *Towards a Philosophy of Photography*. Reaktion Books, London

Forde, John (2000) 'Out of the closet with hobbits, elves and wizards'. *E!online*, www.eonline.com/Features/Specials/Lordrings/Location/000601.html (accessed 17 July 2001)

Fordham, Joe (2003) '*The Lord of the Rings: The Two Towers*; Middle-earth strikes back'. *Cinefex*, January, 92: 70–142

—— (2004a) 'Q&A: Peter Jackson'. *Cinefex*, January, 96: 55–61

—— (2004b) '*The Lord of the Rings: The Return of the King*: journey's end'. *Cinefex*, January, 96: 66–142

Frank, R., and P. Cook (1995) *The Winner Take All Society*. Free Press, Glencoe

Fried, J. (1995) '*Heavenly Creatures*'. *CineAste*, 21: 4

Friedberg, Anne (2000) 'The end of cinema: multimedia and technological change', in Christine Gledhill and Linda Williams (eds), *Reinventing Film Studies*. Oxford University Press, London and New York, 438–52

Friedman, Wayne (2002) 'Mittweg, Schwartz expand "Rings" fan base'. *Advertising Age*, March, 73.12: S-6

Fritz, Ben (2005) 'Rings' bling ding: Jackson sues New Line over product profits'. *Daily Variety*, March 2, 286.46: 1

Fuller, Graham (2002) 'Trimming Tolkien'. *Sight and Sound*, February: 18–20

—— (2004) 'Kingdom come'. *Film Comment*, January–February, 40.1: 24–9

Gardiner, James (2004) 'PM joins ecstatic fans for LOTR triumph'. *The New Zealand Herald*, 1, www.nzherald.co.nz (accessed 4 January 2005)

Gay, Charles, and James Essinger (2000) *Inside Outsourcing: An Insider's Guide to Managing Strategic Outsourcing*. Nicholas Brealey Publishing, London

Genette, Gérard (1992) *The Architext: An Introduction*, trans. Jane E. Lewin. University of California Press, Berkeley

Gibson, William (1996) *Idoru*. Putnam, New York

Giddings, Robert (ed.) (1983) 'Introduction', in *J. R. R. Tolkien: This Far Land*. Vision and Barnes and Noble, London, 7–24

Gill, A. (2004) 'Who's the richest in the land?' *Waikato Times*, 2 July 2004, www.global.factiva.com (accessed 6 June 2005)

Goldsmith, Jeff (2004) '"Return of the King": Jeff Goldsmith's definitive interview with "Lord of the Rings" screenwriting team Peter Jackson, Fran Walsh and Phillippa Boyens'. *Creative Screenwriting*, January, 11.1: 62–8

Goldsmith, Russell (2002) *Viral Marketing: Get Your Audience to Do the Marketing for You*. Financial Times Management, London

Goldstein, Michael (2003) 'Time-Warner's brass ring'. *New York Daily News*, 3 November, www.nydailynews.com/business/story/133182p-118772c.html (accessed 4 January 2005)

Goldwasser, Dan (2001) 'SoundtrackNet interview: Howard Shore – Lord of the Rings'. 20 November, www.soundtrack.net/features/article/?id=89 (accessed 21 September 2004)

Gorbman, Claudia (1987) *Unheard Melodies: Narrative Film Music*. Indiana University Press, Bloomington

Graham, J. (2005) 'Trainer has chance to star again'. *New Zealand Herald*, 24 January, C8.

Grainger, David (2005) 'The ring masters'. *Fortune*, 7 February, 151.3: 68–74, http://infotrac.galegroup.com (accessed 16 February 2005)

Granovetter, Mark (1985) 'Economic action and social structure: the problem of embeddedness'. *American Journal of Sociology*, 91.3: 481–510

Grant, Barry Keith (1994) '*Heavenly Creatures*'. *New Zealand Journal of Media Studies*, 1.2: 28–30

—— (1999) *A Cultural Assault: The New Zealand Films of Peter Jackson*. Kakapo Books in association with Nottingham Trent University, Center for Asia-Pacific Studies, Nottingham

Grant, Nick (2003) 'Interview with the ring master: writer/director/producer Peter Jackson on what's next after LOTR, the need for tax incentives, what ails the NZ industry, and his desire to create a world-leading post facility in Miramar'. *Onfilm*, March 2003, 20.3: 2

Gray, Brandon (2003) '*Return of the King* rakes in $57.6M worldwide on opening day'. *boxofficemojo*, 18 December, www.boxofficemojo.com/news/?id=1284&p=.htm (accessed 30 December 2004)

Gray, Simon (2002) 'A fellowship in peril: Andrew Lesnie, ACS and director Peter Jackson take on *The Two Towers*, the second installment of New Line's epic *Lord of the Rings* trilogy'. *American Cinematographer*, December, 36–40, 42, 44–53

Griggs, Kim (2001) 'New Zealand embraces Rings'. http://news.bbc.co.uk/1/hi/entertainment/film/1719103.stm (accessed 11 July 2005)

Gripsrud, Jostein (1995) *The Dynasty Years: Hollywood Television and Critical Media Studies*. Routledge, New York and London

—— (1998) 'Film Audiences', in John Hill and Pamela Church Gibson (eds), *The Oxford Guide to Film Studies*. Oxford University Press, Oxford and New York, 202–11

—— (1999) *Television and Common Knowledge*. Routledge, New York and London

Gruner, Stephanie and John Lippman (nd) 'Harry Potter fan web sites can't shake off Warner Bros'. www.harrypotter-buch.de/k4hpb/index.php?area=1&p=static&page=wallstreetjournal (accessed 23 June 2005)

Halasz, Franka, and Mayer Schwartz (1994) 'The Dexter hypertext reference model', *Communication of the ACM*, 37.2: 30–9

Halliwell, Leslie (1985) *Halliwell's Film Guide*. 5th edn. Charles Scribner's, New York

Hammond, P. (2004) 'Jewel in the crown'. *Variety*, August, 396.1: S6468

Hardy, Ann (1997) 'Heavenly Creatures and transcendental style'. *Illusions*, 26: 2–9

—— (2003) 'Sites of Value? Discourses of Religion and Spirituality in the Production of a New Zealand Film and Television Series'. Unpublished Ph.D. thesis. Waikato University, Hamilton, New Zealand

Harley, Ruth (2002) 'How we created world class performance'. *Innovate*, 2 March, www.innovate.org.nz/speakers-notes/harley.html (accessed 16 June 2005)

Harris, Dana (2003) 'AOL TW skids into record books: conglomerate registers $98.7 billion loss for 2002' (Week in Review). *Hollywood Reporter*, 4 February, 377.10: 51, 53

—— (2004) 'Zaentz seeks "Lord" loot'/'Zaentz seeks "Rings" coin'. *Daily Variety*, 20 August, 1 and 10

Harris, Dana, and Adam Dawtrey (2001) 'Can B.O. Postman "ring" twice?' *Variety*, 26 November, 1

Hastings, Bill (2003) Email correspondence with Geoff Lealand, 17 November

Hedetoft, Ulf (2000) 'Contemporary cinema: between cultural globalisation and national interpretation', in Mette Hjort and Scott Mackenzie (eds), *Cinema and Nation*. Routledge, London and New York, 278–97

Hendershot, Heather (2004) *Shaking the World for Jesus: Media and Conservative Evangelical Culture*. Chicago University Press, Chicago

Hight, Craig, and Jane Roscoe (1996) 'Silver magic: Colin McKenzie takes his place in New Zealand history'. *Illusions*, Winter, 25: 14–19

Hochschild, Airlie (1983) *The Managed Heart: Commercialization of Human Feeling*. University of California Press, Berkeley

'Hodgson confirmed as Minister of the Rings' (2001) *The New Zealand Herald*, 7 September, 10

hooks, bell (1994) 'Gangsta culture – sexism, misogyny', in *Outlaw Culture: Resisting Representations*. Routledge, New York, 115–23

Hoover, Stewart, and Shalini Venturelli (1996) 'The category of the religious: the blind spot of contemporary media theory'. *Critical Studies in Mass Communication*, 13: 251–65

'How is DVD doing? How can I get statistics' (nd) www.dvddemystifiedcom/dvdfaq.html#1.9 (accessed 20 January 2005)

Huffstutter, P. J. (2003) 'Hobbit movies make magic for New Zealand economy'. *Los Angeles Times*, 2 November, www.boston.com/news/world/articles/2003/11/02/hobbit_movies_make_magic_for_new_zealand_economy (accessed 5 July 2005)

Huyssen, Andreas (1983) 'Adorno in reverse: from Hollywood to Richard Wagner'. *New German Critique*, 29, 8–38

Ibata, D. (2003) 'Lord of racism? Critics view trilogy as discriminatory'. *Chicago Tribune*. www.chicagotribune.com/features/arts/chi-0301120067jan 12,1,3622646.story?coll=chi%2Dleisurearts%2Dhed (accessed on 5 January 2004)

Jeffcutt, Paul, and Andy Pratt (2002) 'Managing creativity in the cultural industries'. *Creativity and Innovation Management*, 11.4: 225–33

Jenkins, Henry (1998) 'Complete freedom of movement: video games as gendered play spaces', in Justine Cassell and Henry Jenkins (eds), *Barbie to Mortal Kombat: Gender and Computer Games*. MIT Press, Cambridge, MA, 262–97

—— (2003) 'Quentin Tarantino's *Star Wars*? digital cinema, media convergence, and participatory culture,' in David Thorburn and Henry Jenkins (eds), *Rethinking Media Change: The Aesthetics of Transition*. MIT Press, Cambridge, MA, 281–312

Johnson, Ann-Marie (2004) 'Frodo economy grows stronger'. *Dominion Post*, 27 May, 2nd edn, 5

Johnson, Ross (2005) 'The lawsuit of the rings'. *New York Times*, 27 June, Business Section, 1

Jones, Candace, and Robert J. DeFillippi (1996) 'Back to the future in film'. *Academy of Management Executive*, 10.4: 89–103

Jones, Stan (2003) 'Middle-Earthly creatures: some local comments on the cinematic Ring cycle so far'. *Metro Magazine*, 136: 62–6

Joyce, Hester (2003) 'In Development: Scriptwriting Policies and Practice in the New Zealand Film Commission 1978–1995'. Unpublished Ph.D. thesis. University of Auckland, Auckland, Aotearoa New Zealand

Jutel, Thierry (1996) '*Forgotten Silver*'. *Midwest*, 10: 22

—— (2004a) '*The Lord of the Rings*: landscape, transformation and the geography of the virtual', in Claudia Bell and Steve Matthewman (eds), *Cultural*

*Studies in Aotearoa/New Zealand.* Oxford University Press, Melbourne, 54–65

—— (2004b) 'Studying media texts', in Luke Goode and Nabeel Zuberi (eds), *Media Studies in Aotearoa/New Zealand.* Pearson, Auckland, 32–45

Kilpatrick, Jacquelyn (1999) *Celluloid Indians: Native Americans and Film.* University of Nebraska Press, Lincoln

King, Anna (1996) 'Spirituality: transformation and metamorphosis'. *Religion*, 26: 343–351

King, Barry (2005) 'Strutting and fretting'. *Onfilm*, February, 24

Kipnis, Laura (1998) 'Film and changing technologies', in John Hill and Pamela Church Gibson (eds), *The Oxford Guide to Film Studies.* Oxford University Press, London and New York, 595–604

Kirkland, B. (2003) 'The Lord of the money machine'. *Toronto Sun*, 19 December, www.canoe.ca (accessed 6 January 2005)

Kirshenblatt-Gimblett, Barbara (1998) *Destination Culture: Tourism, Museums and Heritage.* University of California Press, Berkeley

Kivy, Peter (1991) *Sound and Semblance: Reflections on Musical Representation.* Cornell University Press, New York

Kiwi Hobbit (2002) 'Kiwi Hobbit's guide to Middle Earth – New Zealand: culture'. www.geocities.com/kiwihobbit2002/NZculture.html (accessed 4 February 2005)

Kleiser-Walczak Studios (2005) 'KW Info'. www.kwcc.com/splash_resources/KW_Info.pdf (accessed 5 July 2005)

Knox, Sara (1995) 'Heavenly games: re-telling the Parker–Hulme case'. *Meanjin*, 54.4: 677–90

Kracauer, Siegfried (1960) *Theory of Film: The Redemption of Physical Reality.* Oxford University Press, New York

Krasny, Michael (1997) 'Stephen Jay Gould: interview'. *Mother Jones*, January–February, www.motherjones.com/commentary/columns/1997/01/outspoken.html (accessed 4 February 2005)

Latour, Bruno (1993) *We Have Never Been Modern*, trans. Catherine Porter. Harvard University Press, Cambridge, MA

Leedy, David J. (1980) *Motion Picture Distribution: An Accountant's Perspective.* [self-published]

Lesnie, Andrew (2002) 'The Empire Interview'. *Empire*, www.empireonline.com.au/new/html/inter/content.html#andrew (accessed 11 November 2004)

Levin, D. (1998) *Richard Wagner, Fritz Lang, and the Nibelungen: The Dramaturgy of Disavowal.* Princeton University Press, Princeton, NJ

Lewis, Justin (1998) 'The formation of the "major independent": Miramax, New Line and the New Hollywood', in Steve Neale and Murray Smith (eds), *Contemporary Hollywood Cinema.* Routledge, New York and London, 74–90

London, Justin (2000) 'Leitmotifs and musical reference in the classical film score', in James Buhler, Caryl Flinn, and David Neumeyer (eds), *Music and Cinema.* Wesleyan University Press, Hanover, NH, 85–96 lordoftherings.net (2001) 'Philippa Boyens (writer)'. www.lordoftherings.net/film/filmmakers/fi_pboye_interview.html (accessed 27 June 2003)

Louisson, S. (2003) 'OECD knocks "Rings" films' multimillion tax subsidies'. *New Zealand Herald*, www.nzherald.co.nz (accessed 10 June 2005)

Lyman, Rick (2001) 'Lord of the Rings trilogy taps the internet to build excitement'. *New York Times*, 11 January, E1

MacCannell, Dean (1976) *The Tourist: A New Theory of the Leisure Class*. Schocken, New York

McCarthy, Todd (2001) 'Tolkien's trilogy likely to grab the brass "Ring"'. *Variety*, 10–16 December, 385.4: 31

McDannell, Colleen (1995) *Material Christianity: Religion and Popular Culture in America*. Yale University Press, New Haven and London

McDonald, Bernard (2002–3) 'Peter Jackson: the visionary'. *Pavement*, December–January, 56: 114–16

McDonald, Bernard D. (2001–2) 'The Director: Peter Jackson'. *Pavement*, December–January, 50: 116+

McKay, John (2004) 'Virtual Katy and Lord of the Rings'. dmn forums, www.dmnforums.com/cgi-bin/viewarticle.cgi?id=29198 (accessed 20 December 2004)

McKellen, Ian (2001–4) 'The grey book'. 21 May 2001. www.mckellen.com/cinema/lotr/journal.htm (accessed at various dates)

McKenzie, J. (2001) *Perform or Else: From Discipline to Performance*. Routledge, London

McLean, T. (2004) 'Sean Astin, Ian McKellen and Viggo Mortensen'. *Variety*, 6 January, www.variety.com/index.asp?layout=print_story&artcliid+VR1117897930&cat (accessed 16 March 2004)

MacNamara, Mary (2001–2) 'Ring of fire: Philippa Boyens, Peter Jackson and Fran Walsh reach for Tolkien's *Rings*'. *Written By*, December–January, www.wga.org/WrittenBy/1201/rings.html (accessed 4 February 2005)

McNary, Dave, and Tim Swanson (2001) 'Burger King to serve up New Line's *Rings*'. *Variety*, 11–17 June, 383.4: 55

McRobbie, Angela (2002) 'Clubs to companies: notes on the decline of political culture in speeded up creative worlds'. *Cultural Studies*, 16.4: 516–31

Maddox, Garry (2004–5) 'The lure of event cinema'. [Sydney] *Morning Herald Movie Guide*. Summer, 10–11

Magid, Ron (2001a) 'Lord of the realm: interview by Ron Magid'. *Film Comment*, December: 52–9

—— (2001b) 'Imagining Middle-Earth'. *American Cinematographer*, December, 82.12: 60–9

*Make-Up Artist* (2004) 'The Lord of the Rings: The Return of the King'. 46, www.theonering.net/scrapbook/group/446 (accessed 28 December 2004)

Mallinson, Jeffrey (2002) 'A potion too strong? challenges in translating the religious significance of Tolkien's *The Lord of the Rings* to film'. *Journal of Religion and Popular Culture*, Spring, 1, www.usask.ca/relst/jrpc/tolkienprint.html (accessed 12 August 2003)

Malone, Peter (1997) 'Jesus on our screens', in John May (ed.), *The New Image of Religious Film*. Sheed and Ward, Kansas City, 57–71

Maltby, Richard (1998) '"Nobody knows everything": post-classical historiographies and consolidated entertainment', in Steve Neale and Murray Smith (eds), *Contemporary Hollywood Cinema*. Routledge, London, 21–44

Manovich, Lev (2001) *The Language of New Media*. The MIT Press, Cambridge, MA

Margolis, Harriet (2003) 'Janeite culture: what does the name "Jane Austen" authorize?', in Gina Macdonald and Andrew Macdonald (eds), *Jane Austen on Screen*. Cambridge University Press, Cambridge, 22–43

MarketNewZealand.com (2004) 'Multimedia, publishing, film, tv, music'. October, www.marketnewzealand.com/MNZ/MarketIntelligence/sectors/4594/11632.aspx (accessed 12 November 2004)

Martin, David (1978) *A General Theory of Secularization*. Basil Blackwell, Oxford

Marx, Karl (1990) *Capital*. Volume One, Penguin Classics, Harmondsworth

Masters, C., and K. Hoby (2002) 'Richest man in NZ tops a billion'. *New Zealand Herald*, 19 July, www.global.factiva.com (accessed 6 June 05)

Mathijs, Ernest (2006) '*The Lord of the Rings* and family: a view on text and reception', in Ernest Mathijs and Murray Pomerance (eds), *From Hobbits to Hollywood: Essays on Peter Jackson's Lord of the Rings*. Rodopi, Amsterdam, 41–63

Mathijs, Ernest, and Murray Pomerance (eds) (2006) *From Hobbits to Hollywood: Essays on Peter Jackson's Lord of the Rings*. Rodopi, Amsterdam

Matthews, Philip (2002) 'The Road to Middle Earth'. *New Zealand Listener*, 23–9 March, 14–21

May, Christopher (2000) 'Information society, task mobility and the end of work'. *Futures*, 32: 399–416

—— (2002) *The Information Society: A Sceptical View*. Polity Press, Malden, MA

Merleau-Ponty, Maurice (1962) *Phenomenology of Perception*, trans. Colin Smith. Routledge, New York and London

Metcalfe, J. Stanley, and Ian Miles (eds) (2000) *Innovation Systems in the Service Economy*. Kluwer Academic Publishers, Boston and London

Meza, Ed (2000) 'German fund seeks Hobbit investors'. *Variety*, 25 October, www.tolkienonline.com/docs/1385.html (accessed 13 August 2004)

Mikos, Lothar (2000) 'Big Brother als performatives Realitätsfernsehen – Ein Fernsehformat im Kontext der Entwicklung des Unterhaltungsfernsehens', in L. Mikos, P. Feise, K. Herzog, E. Prommer, and V. Veihl (eds), *Im Auge der Kamera. Das Fernsehereignis Big Brother*. Vistas, Berlin, 161–78

Mikos, Lothar, Susanne Elichner, Elizabeth Prommer, and Michael Wedel (2007) *Die 'Herr der Ringe'-Trilogie: Attraktion und Faszination eines populärkulturellen Phänomens*. UVK, Constance

Miller, Toby, Nitin Govil, John McMurria, and Richard Maxwell (2001) *Global Hollywood*. British Film Institute, London

Mirams, Gordon (1945) *Speaking Candidly: Films and People in New Zealand*. Paul's Book Arcade, Hamilton, New Zealand

Mita, Merata (1992) 'The soul and the image', in Jonathan Dennis and Jan Bieringa (eds), *Film in Aotearoa New Zealand*. Victoria University Press, Wellington, 36–54

Mitchell, Elvis (2001) 'Hit the road, Middle-Earth gang'. *New York Times*, 19 December, http://query.nytimes.com/search/article (accessed 6 January 2005)

Mitchell, Julian (2002) '*The Lord of the Rings*'. audiomedia.com/archive/features/uk-0102/uk-0102-lotr/uk-0102-lotr.htm (accessed 4 January 2005)

Moore, L. (2004) 'What makes a celebrity in New Zealand?' *New Zealand Fashion*, Spring, 54–6

Moreton-Robinson, Aileen (2000) *Talkin' up to the White Woman: Indigenous Women and White Feminism*. University of Queensland Press, St Lucia, QLD, Australia

Morris, Paul (1999) 'Fragments of faith: religion in contemporary New Zealand'. *New Zealand Studies*, 9.1: 15–21

Mortensen, Viggo (2001–2) [Interview]. *Pavement Magazine*, 108

Morton, P. (1984) *The Vital Science: Biology and the Literary Imagination, 1860–1900*. Allen and Unwin, London

Moxon, David (2003) *A Once and Future Myth: An Applied Theology of J. R. R. Tolkien's The Lord of the Rings*. Office of Anglican Bishop of Waikato, Hamilton, New Zealand

Murdoch, Graham (1997) 'The re-enchantment of the world; religion and the transformations of modernity', in Stewart Hoover and Knut Lundby (eds), *Rethinking Media, Religion and Culture*. Sage Publications, Thousand Oaks, London, and New Delhi, 85–101

Murphy, Geoff (1992) 'The end of the beginning', in Jonathan Dennis and Jan Bieringa (eds), *Film in Aotearoa New Zealand*. Victoria University Press, Wellington, 130–49

Netherby, Jennifer, and Laurence Larman (2002) 'New Line runs rings around retail'. *Video Business*, 22.32: 1

Neumeyer, David, and James Buhler (2001) 'Analytic and interpretive approaches to film music (I): analysing the music', in K. J. Donnelly (ed), *Film Music: Critical Approaches*. Edinburgh University Press, Edinburgh, 16–38

New Line (2001) '*The Lord of the Rings: The Fellowship of the Ring*, production notes'. http://movieweb.com/movies/download.php?id=1&q=notes.htm (accessed 12 December 2004)

—— (2002) '*The Lord of the Rings: The Two Towers*, production notes'. http://movieweb.com/movies/download.php?id=2&q=notes.htm (accessed 12 December 2004)

—— (2003) '*The Lord of the Rings: The Return of the King*, production notes'. http://movieweb.com/movies/download.php?id=3&q=notes.htm (accessed 1 December 2004)

Newman, James (2002) 'The myth of the ergodic videogame: some thoughts on player–character relationships in videogames'. *Games Studies*, 2, 1, www.gamestudies.org/0102/newman/ (accessed October 2002)

Nicholls, Brett, and Simon Ryan (2004) 'Playing in the zone: thirdspace in *Jet Set Radio Future* and *Shenmue II*'. *Scan: Journal of Media Arts Culture*, 1.1, www.scan.net.au/scan/journal/display_article.php?recordID=22 (accessed February 2004)

Nichols, Bill (1991) *Representing Reality: Issues and Concepts in Documentary*. Indiana University Press, Bloomington

Nichols, Peter M. (2003) 'Taking the children'. *New York Times*, 26 December: B26.

Noose, T. (1979) *Hollywood Film Acting*. T. Yoseloff, New York

NZ Film Commission (2003) *Taskforce Report: NZFC response*. Wellington: NZFC, www.nzfilm.co.nz/pdfs/NZFC_TaskForce_Response.pdf (accessed 16 June 2005)

NZPA (2001) 'It's lord of the mags'. *New Zealand Herald*, 22 November

NZTE (New Zealand Trade and Enterprise) (2003–4) *Developing Creative Industries in New Zealand*. Wellington, New Zealand Trade and Enterprise, www.nzte.govt.nz/section/11756.aspx#pub (accessed 16 June 2005)

OECD (Organization for Economic Co-operation and Development) (1996) *Employment and Growth in the Knowledge-based Economy*. OECD, Paris

Ohmann, Richard M. (1996) *Making and Selling Culture*. University Press of New England, Hanover, NH

O'Leary, Clare, and Paul Frater (2001) *The Business of Filmmaking in New Zealand: A Scoping Study of the Film Industry in New Zealand*. A scoping document commissioned by Industry New Zealand. Innovation and Systems Ltd, Wellington

*One News Online* (2004) 'Tribute Mooted for Jackson'. 2 March, http://one-news.nzoom.com/National.html (accessed 1 April 2004)

*Onfilm* (1999) 'Lords of the Lance'. *Onfilm*, October, 12

—— (2002) 'Taylor-made: at long last, an Onfilm interview with Oscar-winner Richard Taylor of Weta Workshop'. *Onfilm*, December, 15

—— (2004) 'Setting the benchmark: the special extended Onfilm website dance remix' [interview with Jamie Selkirk]. October, www.onfilm.co.nz/ (accessed 28 December 2004)

Oram, Rod (2001–2) '[Ring-leading] Brand New Zealand'. *Unlimited*, December–January: 40–5

Ordesky, Mark (2003) [Interview]. *Pavement Magazine*, Summer, 126

Osborne, Thomas (2003) 'Against "creativity": a philistine rant'. *Economy and Society*, November, 32.4: 507–25

Otto, Jeff (2003) 'Interview: Peter Jackson'. *FilmForce*, www.filmforce.ign.co (accessed 24 January 2005)

Pakes, Justin (2004) 'The King is crowned by Oscar!' [Lord of the Rings Fanclub]. lotr.fanhq.com/Articles/Article.aspx?ID=168 (accessed 16 June 2005)

Park, Geoff (1999) 'Going between goddesses', in Klaus Neumann, Nicholas Thomas, and Hilary Ericksen (eds), *Quicksands: Foundational Histories in Australia and Aotearoa New Zealand*. University of New South Wales Press, Sydney, 176–97

Patterson, Colin, and AAP (2004) 'Rings-style mask-making speeds up cancer treatment'. *Dominion Post*, 23 January, A4

Paulin, Scott D. (2000) 'Richard Wagner and the fantasy of cinematic unity: the idea of the *Gesamtkunstwerk* in the history of film music', in James Buhler, Caryl Flinn, and David Neumeyer (eds), *Music and Cinema*. Wesleyan University Press, Hanover, NH, 58–84

Perrin, Alisa (2001) 'Sex, lies and marketing: Miramax and the development of the quality indie blockbuster'. *Film Quarterly*, 55.2: 30–9

'Peter Jackson: Filmmaker' (2004) *Hollywood Reporter*, 24 February

Phillips, Jock (1987) *A Man's Country? The Image of the Pakeha Male*. Penguin Books, Auckland

Pierson, Michele (2002) *Special Effects: Still in Search of Wonder*. Columbia University Press, New York

Pihama, Leonie (1994) 'Are films dangerous? A Maori woman's perspective on *The Piano*'. *Hecate*, 20.2: 239–42

Pinflicks Communications and NZIER (New Zealand Institute of Economic Research) (2003) *Capability Study: The New Zealand Screen Production Industry. Report to Industry New Zealand*. Industry New Zealand, Wellington, www.nzte.govt.nz/common/files/exec-summarycapability.pdf

Portes, Alejandro, Manuel Castells, and Lauren A. Benton (1989) *The Informal Economy: Studies in Advanced and Less Developed Countries*. Johns Hopkins University Press, Baltimore

*Power Meetings Update* (2004) '*Lord of the Rings* director relies on Polycom to film three movies concurrently'. www.ivci.com/newsletter0104.html (accessed 16 June 2005)

Prendergast, Roy M. (1992) *Film Music: A Neglected Art*, 2nd edn. W. W. Norton and Company, New York

Prichard, Craig (2002) 'Creative selves? Critically reading "creativity" in management discourse'. *Creativity and Innovation Management*, 11.4: 265–76

[Programme Notes for *The Making of The Lord of the Rings, Part One: The Fellowship of the Ring*] (2004) Telecom New Zealand International Film Festivals 2004, Wellington 123

Pryor, Ian (2003) *Peter Jackson: From Prince of Splatter to Lord of the Rings*. Random House, Auckland

Pulley, B. (2004) 'Hollywood's new King Kong'. www.Forbes.com (accessed 6 June 2005)

Rae, Fiona (2006) 'Craig Parker, actor'. *New Zealand Listener*, 24 June: 12–13

Read, Ellen (2004a) 'Hollywood snaps up NZ technology'. *New Zealand Herald*, 12 March, www.nzherald.co.nz/index.cfm?ObjectID=3554245 (accessed 1 April 2004)

—— (2004b) 'Virtual Katy makes it in LA'. *New Zealand Herald*, 23 June, www.nzherald.co.nz/index.cfm?ObjectID=3574192 (accessed 1 July 2004)

Rebeiro, F. (1995) '*Heavenly Creatures*'. *Film Quarterly*, Fall, 49: 33–8

Reid, Nicholas (1994) '*Heavenly Creatures*'. *North and South*, October, 103: 152

Rendle, Steve (2003) 'Does this plot have a happy ending?' *Dominion Post*, 7 May, 8

'Return of the "Rings" merch: vid release brings slew of products' (2004) *Hollywood Reporter*, 28 April, 383.32: 13

'Ring-leader' [Cover] (2002) *Unlimited*. December 2001–January 2002

Robinson, Rebecca (1999) 'Authenticity, mimicry, industry: *The Frighteners* as cultural palimpsest'. *Illusions*, 28: 2–9

Roof, Wade Clark (1993) *A Generation of Seekers: The Spiritual Journeys of the Baby Boomers*. Harper Collins, New York

—— (2001) *Spiritual Marketplace: Baby Boomers and the Making of American Religion*. Princeton University Press, Princeton, NJ

Ross, Alex (2003) 'The ring and the rings: Wagner vs. Tolkien'. *New Yorker*, 22 and 29, December, www.newyorker.com/critics/at large/?031222crat_ atlarge (accessed 14 July 2005)

Rudell, Michael (2005) Complaint filed by writer and director of Lord of the Rings. Franklin, Weinrib, Rudell and Vassallo, P.C., New York, www. fwrv.com (accessed 10 June 2005)

Russell, Gary (2002) *The Lord of the Rings: The Art of The Fellowship of the Ring*. Houghton Mifflin, Boston

—— (2003) *The Lord of the Rings: The Art of The Two Towers*. Houghton Mifflin, Boston

—— (2004) *The Lord of the Rings: The Art of The Return of the King*. Houghton Mifflin, Boston

Ryfle, Steve (2002) '*The Lord of the Rings: The Two Towers*; interview with Philippa Boyens'. *Creative Screenwriting*, November–December: 40–2

Sage, Mariner (2001) *The Lord of the Rings: The Fellowship of the Ring Photo Guide*. Mariner Books, Boston

Sale, Roger (2000) 'Tolkien and Frodo Baggins', in Harold Bloom (ed.), *Modern Critical Views: J. R. R. Tolkien*. Chelsea House, Philadelphia, 27–63

Sampson, Desmond (2002) 'Bernard Hill: King of Rohan'. *Pavement*, December 2002–January 2003, 56: 105

Sassen, Saskia (1991) *The Global City: New York, London and Tokyo*. Princeton University Press, Princeton

—— (2002) *Global Networks, Linked Cities*. Routledge, New York and London

Schamus, James (1998) 'To the rear of the back end: the economics of independent cinema', in Steve Neale and Murray Smith (eds), *Contemporary Hollywood Cinema*. Routledge, London and New York, 91–105

Schechner, Richard (1973) *Environmental Theater*. Hawthorn Books, New York

Schembri, Jim (2004–5) 'Blockbuster overkill'. [Sydney] *Morning Herald Movie Guide*, Summer, 16–17

*Sci Fi Wire* (2003) '*King* not long enough?' 12 December, www.scifi.com/ sfw/issue347/news.html (accessed 8 July 2005)

ScoopNews (2003) 'Arise, Sir Peter', 11 December (accessed 20 December 2003)

Scott, Dick (1975) *Ask That Mountain: The Story of Parihaka*. Heinemann, Auckland

Scott, Remington (2003) 'Sparking life: notes on the performance capture sessions for *The Lord of the Rings: The Two Towers*'. *Computer Graphics*, November 37.4: 17–21

Screen Production Industry Taskforce (2003) *Taking on the World: The Report of the Screen Production Industry Taskforce*. Industry New Zealand, March, www.nzte.govt.nz/common/files/screen-taskforce-report.pdf (accessed 16 June 2005)

Serkis, Andy (2003) *Gollum: How We Made Movie Magic*. Collins, London

SGINZ (2004) 'ESP at Weta Digital, Ltd.: keeping *The Lord of the Rings* on schedule'. Silicon Graphics Inc., www.sgi.com/support/es/success/lotr.html (accessed 27 December 2004)

Shefrin, Elana (2004) '*Lord of the Rings, Star Wars*, and participatory fandom: mapping new congruencies between the internet and media entertainment culture'. *Critical Studies in Media Communication*, September, 21.3: 261–81

Shelton, Lindsay (2005) *The Selling of New Zealand Movies*. Awa Press, Wellington

Shippey, Tom (2004) 'Another road to Middle Earth: Jackson's movie trilogy', in Rose A. Zimbardo and Neil D. Isaacs (eds), *Understanding The Lord of the Rings: The Best of Tolkien Criticism*. Houghton Mifflin, Boston, 233–54

Shohat, Ella, and Robert Stam (1994) *Unthinking Eurocentrism: Multiculturalism and the Media*. Routledge, New York and London

Shore, Howard (2003) *The Lord of The Rings The Two Towers*. Warner Brothers Publications, Miami

Sibley, Brian (2001) *The Lord of the Rings' Official Movie Guide*. HarperCollins, London

—— (2002a) *The Making of the Movie Trilogy (The Lord of the Rings)*. Houghton Mifflin, Boston

—— (2002b) *The Lord of the Rings: The Making of the Movie Trilogy*. HarperCollins, London

—— (2006) *Peter Jackson: A Film-maker's Journey*. HarperCollins, Sydney

Simmons, Laurence (1996) 'A little clunky and manic (interview with Peter Jackson)'. *Midwest*, 10: 12–13, 15, 17, 19

Simpson, Paul, Helen Rodiss, and Michaela Bushell (2003) *The Rough Guide to Lord of the Rings*. Penguin, London

Simpson Grierson (2004) 'Simpson Grierson – Film and Entertainment Lawyers, broadcasting, NZ'. www.simpsongrierson.com/expertise_child.cfm?page_id=103&component_id=273&page_id=103 (accessed 27 November 2004)

Smith, Chris (2003) *The Lord of the Rings: Weapons and Warfare*. Houghton Mifflin, Boston

Smith, Jim, and J. Clive Matthews (2004) *The Lord of the Rings: The Films, The Books, The Radio Series*. Virgin Books, London

Smith, Jo (2003) 'The plasticity of ethnicity', seminar presentation, University of Auckland, 16 October

Smith, Linda Tuhiwai (1999) *Decolonizing Methodologies: Research Methods and Indigenous Peoples.* University of Otago Press, Dunedin, New Zealand

Smith, Nick (2004) 'Poll: Rings maker crowned king of Kiwi business world'. *National Business Review*, 16 April: 12

Smith, Patricia Burkhart (2000) 'Ring bearer: Patricia Burkhart Smith talks to Philippa Boyens'. *Creative Screenwriting*, 30: 4–6

Snider, Mike (2004) ' "Return of the King" extended DVD may miss some holiday shoppers'. *USA Today*, 27 September, www.usatoday.com/life/movies/news/2004-09-27-lotr-dvd_x.htm (accessed 3 July 2005)

Sorrell, Adam (2005) 'Employment law: James Bryson versus Three Foot Six'. *Onfilm* online editorial (accessed 29 March 2005)

Stallabrass, Julian (1993) 'Just gaming: allegory and economy in computer games'. *New Left Review*, 198: 83–106

States, Bert (1995) 'The actor's presence: three phenomenal modes', in Phillip B. Zarilli (ed.), *Acting Reconsidered*. Routledge, New York, 22–42

Stenger, Josh (1997) 'Consuming the planet: Planet Hollywood, stars, and the global consumer culture'. *Velvet Light Trap*, Fall, 40: 42–55

*Sunday* (2003) TVOne (New Zealand), March

Sutton-Smith, Brian (2001) *The Ambiguity of Play.* Harvard University Press, Cambridge, MA

Taylor, Apirana (2004) *Te Ata Kura: The Red-Tipped Dawn.* Canterbury University Press, Christchurch, New Zealand, 20–1

Taylor, Richard (2002) *The Lord of the Rings: Creatures (The Two Towers Movie Tie-In).* Houghton Mifflin Co., Boston

theonering.net (2000) 'Q+A with Peter Jackson from theonering.net (official site)'. www.lordoftherings.net/index_filmmakers.html (accessed 12 January 2002)

Thompson, Kristin (2003) 'Fantasy, franchises, and Frodo Baggins: *The Lord of the Rings* and modern Hollywood'. *The Velvet Light Trap*, Fall, 52: 45–63

—— (2007) *The Frodo Franchise: The Lord of the Rings and Modern Hollywood.* University of California Press, Berkeley

Thompson, Kristin, and David Bordwell (2003) *Film History: An Introduction.* 2nd edn. McGraw-Hill, Boston

Thomson, D. (2004) 'Bored of the Rings'. *Independent*, 5 March

Tipton, Stephen (1982) *Getting Saved from the Sixties: Moral Meaning in Conversion and Cultural Change.* University of California Press, Berkeley

Tizard, Judith (2002) *Lasting Effects of the LOTR Project* [Speech]. New Zealand Government, 23 April, www.beehive.govt.nz/ViewDocument.cfm?DocumentID=13610 (accessed 4 February 2005)

Tolkien, J. R. R. (1968) 'Foreword', *The Lord of the Rings*. George Allen and Unwin, London

—— (1977) *The Silmarillion*, Christopher Tolkien (ed.). George Allen and Unwin, London

Totaro, Donato (2001) 'Your mother ate my dog! Peter Jackson and gore-gag comedy'. www.horschamp.qc.ca/new_offscreen/goregag.html (accessed 15 March 2004)

Totosy de Zepetnek, Steven (2000) 'Toward a Framework of Audience Studies' http://clcwebjournal.lib.purdue.edu/library/audiencestudies.html (accessed 18 March 2005)

—— (2004) Email correspondence with Stan Jones, 8 March

Urban, G. (1989) 'The "I" of discourse', in B. Lee and G. Urban (eds), *Semiotics, Self, and Society*. Mouton de Gruyter, Berlin, 27–51

Vossen, U. (ed.) (2004) *Von Neuseeland nach Mittelerde: Die Welt des Peter Jackson*. Schüren, Marburg

Walton, Mark, and Ian Duncan (2002) *Creative Industries in New Zealand: Economic Contribution: Report to Industry New Zealand*. March. New Zealand Institute for Economic Research, Wellington, www.nzte.govt.nz/section/13608/10947.aspx (accessed 16 June 2005)

Wasko, Janet (1994) *Hollywood in the Information Age: Beyond the Silver Screen*. Polity, Cambridge

—— (2001) 'Is it a small world after all?', in Janet Wasko, Mark Phillips, and Eileen R. Meehan (eds), *Dazzled by Disney: The Global Disney Audiences Project*. Leicester University Press, London and New York, 3–28

—— (2003) *How Hollywood Works*. Sage, Thousand Oaks

Watson, Chris (1994) 'If Michel Foucault had seen Peter Jackson's *Heavenly Creatures*'. *New Zealand Journal of Media Studies*, 1.2: 2–13

Watson, Paul (2002) 'Fellowship of the script: an adaptation of *The Two Towers*'. *Screentalk*, November–December, 3.1: 40–7

'Websites honour three second non-speaking performance by mysterious elf in Fellowship' (2002) *Guardian*. http://film.guardian.co.uk/print/0,3858,4566924-110242.00.html (accessed 7 February 2005)

Webster, Frank (2002) *Theories of the Information Society*. 2nd edn. Routledge, New York and London

Wedde, Ian (2003) 'Colin McCahon: a question of faith'. *Landfall*, 206: 61–70

Welch, Dennis (1995) '*Heavenly Features* (interview)'. *New Zealand Listener*, 28 October, 31

—— (2003) 'The producer'. *New Zealand Listener*, 5 July, 20–4

Wernick, Andrew (1992) *Promotional Culture: Advertising, Ideology and Symbolic Expression*. Sage Publications, London

*West of the Moon* (2004) 'LOTR Cast and Crew Oscar Night Stage Presentation at the One Party'. *West of the Moon: A Tolkien Fan Fiction Archive*, www.west-of-the-moon.net/stagepres.htm (accessed 28 December 2004)

Whannel, G. (2002) *Media Sport Stars: Masculinities and Moralities*. Routledge, London

Wolf, Matt (2003) 'Composer reflects on epic assignments'. *The Lubbock Avalanche-Journal*, 3 January, http://lubbockonline.com/stories/010303/aro_0103030011.shtml (accessed 3 February 2004)

Woodhead, Linda, and Paul Heelas (2000) *Religion in Modern Times: An Interpretive Anthology*. Blackwell, Oxford

Wyatt, Justin (1994) *High Concept: Movies and Marketing in Hollywood*. University of Texas Press, Austin

Xoanon (2003) 'Interview with Jasmine Watson'. Theonering.net, www. theonering.net/features/newsroom/files/033002_jasmine.html (accessed 28 December 2004)

*Yahoo News* (2004) 'Amazon reports record-setting holiday sales'. 27 December, http://us.rd.yahoo.com/dailynews/afp/brand/SIG=ofqlv2/*http://www.afp.com (accessed 6 January 2005)

Yatt, John (2002) 'Wraiths and race'. *The Guardian*, 2 December, http://film. guardian.co.uk/print/0,3858,4558916-110242,00.html (accessed 5 January 2004)

Yeabsley, John, and Ian Duncan (2002) *Scoping the Lasting Effects of the Lord of the Rings. Report to the New Zealand Film Commission*. New Zealand Institute for Economic Research, Wellington and Auckland, April, www.nzier. org.nz/SITE_Default/SITE_Publications/x-files/181.pdf (accessed 16 June 2005)

Young, Robin (2003) 'Under-15s face ban from *Lord of the Rings* film'. *The Times*, 27 December, 5

## Websites

Websites for actors: www.miranda-otto.com, www.billyboyd.net, www.liv-tyler. com, www.mckellen.com, www.seanastin.com, www.compleatseanbean.com, www.theorlandobloomfiles.com, www.always.ejwsites.net, www.cateblanchett. net, www.johnrhys-davies.com

The official website of *The Lord of the Rings* trilogy: www.lordoftherings.net

The Home of the Official Peter Jackson Fan club: tbhl.theonering.net/ (includes interviews tbhl.theonering.net/peter/interviews/ and press clippings from the time of the release of *Bad Taste* tbhl.theonering.net/films/bad_ taste_articles.html)

The Film Unit: filmunit.co.nz/

Weta Digital: www.wetadigital.com/digital

Weta Workshop: www.wetafx.co.nz/workshop

The New Zealand Film Commission: www.nzfilm.co.nz

The official site for Destination New Zealand, 'New Zealand home of Middle-earth': www.newzealand.com/homeofmiddleearth/

# Index